Academic Leadership

Academic Leadership

*A Practical Guide to Chairing
the Department*

SECOND EDITION

Deryl R. Leaming

ANKER PUBLISHING COMPANY, INC.
Bolton, Massachusetts

ANKER

Academic Leadership
A Practical Guide to Chairing the Department
Second Edition

ISBN 978-1-933371-17-7

Composition by Julie Phinney
Cover design by Dutton & Sherman Design

Anker Publishing Company, Inc.
563 Main Street
P.O. Box 249
Bolton, MA 01740-0249 USA
www.ankerpub.com

Library of Congress Cataloging-in-Publication Data
Leaming, Deryl R.
Academic leadership : a practical guide to chairing the department /
    Deryl R. Leaming.—2nd ed.
    p. cm.
Includes bibliographical references and index.
ISBN-13: 978-1-933371-17-7
1. Departmental chairmen (Universities)—United States—Handbooks,
    manuals, etc. 2. Universities and colleges—United States—Depart-
    ments—Administration. 3. Educational leadership—United States.
    I. Title.

LB2341.L269 2007
378.1'11—dc22   2006025666

To

Barbara Haskell

&

Arthur L. Langvardt

*"A great part of art consists in imitation. For the whole conduct
of life is based on this: that what we admire
in others we want to do ourselves."*
—Quintilian

1516 words

Table of Contents

About the Author

Deryl R. Leaming is former professor of journalism and dean of the College of Mass Communication at Middle Tennessee State University. He earned his Ph.D. in mass communication from Syracuse University, his M.A. from the University of Nebraska, and his B.A. from Fort Hays State University. He is also a graduate of a special program at the Menninger School of Psychiatry. Dr. Leaming served for more than 20 years as a department chair and dean at several universities. He is an active member of the Society of Professional Journalists, having also served on the society's national board and as a regional director. He and his colleagues at Marshall University won the coveted First Amendment Award from the society in 1993 for their courageous support of the university's student newspaper and the principles embodied in the First Amendment. He is editor of *Managing People: A Guide for Department Chairs and Deans* (Anker, 2003); the founder, editor, and publisher of the online journal *Academic Leadership*, which he recently turned over to his undergraduate university; and the author of many journal articles. Dr. Leaming is in the process of developing two other new web sites—www.academicleadership .net and www.grammargeeks.com—both of which will be live by fall 2006.

Foreword

The roles and responsibilities of academic department chairpersons have always been a challenge because of the context in which the chairperson is expected to provide leadership. Providing leadership is complex in any organization but it is especially difficult in institutions of higher education. Faculty view themselves as independent entrepreneurs with a great deal of autonomy—with their own goals, agendas, and expectations—while upper administration is responsible for implementing institutional goals, agendas, and expectations which are influenced and sometimes directed by the expectations of state government and the governing board of the institution. Therefore, the chairperson is often caught in the middle trying to negotiate between faculty interests and institutional expectations, which can be very far apart and at times in conflict. Given this situation, a logical question is: Why would anyone want to aspire to or accept the department chair position? Individuals considering or being considered for a department chair position should ask themselves if they are really interested in assuming the multiple roles and responsibilities of the job. For those who have a strong desire to provide leadership for faculty and student development, as well as a passion for making the department stronger and more effective and efficient, the chair position offers great opportunities. So the first question an individual needs to consider is his or her own development, interests, and motivation. Is a department chair position right for you? This book provides some excellent information to help answer this question.

Many studies have documented that department chairpersons make some of the most important decisions within the institution. The department is where faculty find a home and, it is hoped, find enjoyment and satisfaction in doing what is expected and required of them: teaching, conducting research, and providing service. The department is where students take courses, are advised, make career decisions, and prepare for their futures. The department is where programs and curricula are designed, developed, and assessed, and where resources are allocated. Finally, the quality of the academic department determines the reputation of the institution.

As we enter the 21st century, the landscape of higher education is changing and the number of issues on the horizon is expanding almost exponentially. Providing leadership given the current internal and external environment presents a real challenge to even the most creative and innovative chairperson. The skills needed to prepare students to live successfully and happily in our knowledge-driven global society are new, numerous, and multifaceted. One only has to observe the higher education landscape or read the current literature on the issues of finance, student financial aid, learning outcomes, accountability, technology, changing faculty roles, emphasis on research, competition by for-profit institutions, unethical practices, external relations, fundraising, and innovation for this to become all too obvious. There is no longer a stable environment as universities are surrounded by change, by competition for students and resources, and by the transformation of the world economy from the industrial to the information and service economy. To be successful in this new world, universities have to seize opportunities, adjust and adapt, reform and develop. These changes and issues present a new and different set of challenges that chairpersons and faculty working together must address, as well as greater opportunities to become involved in this important process of change. The two central issues for any higher education institution are change and accountability.

In the second edition of *Academic Leadership: A Practical Guide to Chairing the Department*, Deryl Leaming has restructured the book into a more user-friendly resource and has reorganized the chapters around six major parts: leadership, department, legal issues, faculty, students, and looking ahead. Many new suggestions have been added to the practical advice presented in the first edition, and several new chapters speak directly to some of the changing conditions of higher education such as developing a departmental vision, managing conflict, and working with constituents. Other new issues will appear on the radar screen in the future, but for the present, this book contains an excellent set of practical advice.

Being a chairperson is one of the most challenging leadership positions in higher education, but it can also be one of the most rewarding. Think and plan your leadership journey, study and reflect on your leadership style, listen to and determine faculty expectations while also giving consideration to institutional expectations. Using these perspectives as a foundation, develop strategies to deal with everyday issues while also keeping an eye on the future. If you heed the advice and suggestions presented in this book, I predict that first you will gain satisfaction from a job well done, your faculty will be pleased and become even more productive, and your students will express appreciation for the quality of your programs. Finally, I predict you will be recognized by upper administration and find yourself climbing the administrative ladder very rapidly, if you are interested in making such a move.

Alan T. Seagren
Professor of Educational Administration and Director of the Center
    for the Study of Higher and Postsecondary Education
University of Nebraska–Lincoln

Preface

In the preface to the first edition of *Academic Leadership: A Practical Guide to Chairing the Department*, I wrote,

> Department chairpersons play a vital role in the university administration. They, more than other administrators, work closely with all who make up the university family—students, faculty, and staff members. Their duties and responsibilities are broad and vast. They must see the "big picture" while at the same time give meticulous attention to minute detail. If they provide strong leadership in their roles as department chairpersons, the university is made stronger.

My views on the role that department chairpersons perform remain unchanged.

What has changed, however, is that the responsibilities of today's chairpersons continue to expand exponentially at a time when they face mounting budget problems. Doing what must be done without adequate funding is just one of the many conundrums chairpersons encounter. Global problems demand answers, and as in the past, colleges and universities must help provide them. It's at the departmental level where research must be done, new courses taught, and students exposed to knowledge and leadership so that they can help solve society's challenges.

Today's department chairperson is a juggler who at any given time has too many pins in the air. Unfortunately, there is no prize for perfect juggling. On the other hand, dropping one of the pins is not an option—it represents failure. A successful chairperson must be nimble, skillful, and courageous. The days when chairpersons could glide along in the job without changing the curriculum, redefining the department's mission, or refusing to take risks are gone forever. Taking risks has become routine. Designing and adding new courses is a never-ending process. The leadership skills of today's department chairpersons will be tested regularly. They must delegate authority, inspire leadership, and find ways to see that all faculty are engaged and recognize the urgency of developing new knowledge.

The bottom line is that the department remains the nexus of the university. If we are to solve problems, chairpersons must pave the way. They must help find research dollars, see that faculty remain current in knowledge and skills, get faculty to work collaboratively, and encourage faculty and students to embrace and acknowledge—with confidence and wisdom—that today's warp-speed changes demand urgent responses and adjustments.

The chairperson remains responsible for the administration and promotion of all affairs pertaining to the academic well-being and morale of the department. This responsibility involves such activities as faculty counseling and guidance, student advising and counseling, curriculum planning, scheduling, maintenance of academic relevancy, and all budgetary considerations. The maximum participation in the administrative decision-making process is encouraged at the chairperson's level. Every effort should be made to foster departmental autonomy and to assure that decisions are formulated closest to the students and faculty affected.

Also unchanged since I wrote the first edition of this book is my belief that chairpersons have enormous responsibilities, and that universities still do little to orient or train new chairpersons who are often thrust into the job without any knowledge of what is expected of them. Most faculty members have no concept of a chairperson's many responsibilities, the many decisions that must be made, or how their day is spent. Most training is left up to the administrative assistant. Chairpersons learn from doing, and most are kept so busy in the first few years after their appointment that they have no time to do anything but serve as caretakers. But too much is at stake for university presidents, provosts, vice presidents of academic affairs, and deans to continue ignoring the need for educating and helping chairpersons become quintessential leaders.

The Purpose of This Book

While this book remains oriented to the practical, I have incorporated best practices and ideas from some of today's leading scholars. The text is based on the 20 years of experience I had as chairperson at four different universities, one private and the rest public. Over a 20-year period, chairpersons will face most of the problems they will ever have to deal with. They will make some mistakes along the way; I certainly did. But I learned from them and try to pass on the lessons learned in this book.

This text is written to assist chairpersons to carry out their duties and responsibilities. It offers a variety of ideas and information that should be useful to all chairpersons, especially those new to the job. The chapters provide an idea of what's expected of chairpersons and give examples of ways that specific tasks can be handled. They are as brief and as practical as possible, presenting options for effectively managing responsibility. The suggestions and ideas presented may have direct application for some departments and minimal application for others. Nonetheless, if they motivate chairpersons to analyze their own departments and develop their own approaches to solving problems or improving their departments, this book will have served its purpose.

I pass on advice presented in the first edition: If you are a recently elected chairperson and from time to time find you're not sure how best to address a specific problem or opportunity, ask for help from others—chairpersons, deans, or senior university officials. The best way to master your new administrative responsibilities is to understand their requirements and implications.

And keep in mind that your primary job continues to be that of an educator/scholar. Universities exist not simply to dole out data, give tests, award diplomas, and keep precise records. Their larger purpose is to promote the discovery, preservation, and transmission of knowledge; to help students grow intellectually; and to enhance their cultural and ethical values. Becoming a good administrator is a worthwhile goal; using the skills of efficient administration to enhance teaching is a far greater accomplishment.

Acknowledgments

There are many persons who deserve credit for helping with this book. My wife Lila was patient and understanding as she took on chores that I normally attended to, and she remained unflappable in the face of these added responsibilities. I thank her.

Those of us who encounter a handful of brilliant colleagues are indeed fortunate, and because I had this good fortune, my life changed forever after I met Wallace E. "Ed" Knight. He not only enriched my life, he also became my friend and soulmate. "WE" Knight helped to make this book more readable, and while the reader may not see his handiwork, I know that his "scratches"—as he called his editing suggestions—not only taught me much but also gave the book life. To offer a mere "thanks" seems woefully inadequate. So, in addition to my thanks, I knight him Sir Wallace E. Knight, editor par excellence.

I thank Alan B. Gould, director of the Drinko Program at Marshall University. Alan was my dean and later my vice president for academic affairs, and it was he who suggested that I write this book. I appreciate his help and encouragement.

I am indebted and grateful to individuals who read my manuscript and offered suggestions for improvement: Howard B. Altman, emeritus professor, University of Louisville; R. Ferrell Ervin, Southeast Missouri State University; Jerry Frieman, Kansas State University; Susan Kupisch, Lambuth University; and Kina Mallard, Union University.

Finally, I am particularly grateful for having the opportunity to work with Carolyn Dumore, my editor at Anker Publishing. Carolyn is more than an editor. She is a friend who gently pushed, prodded, and cheered me on. Carolyn, thanks much for all you did to help make my work pleasant and rewarding. I shall be forever grateful.

While those who helped or inspired me are due thanks, none is responsible for any mistakes. I made all those by myself.

Deryl R. Leaming
May 2006

Advice for New Chairpersons

Encourage faculty members to be open with you and invite them to help you form the kind of team needed to move the department to a higher level of excellence.

As a new department chairperson at Kansas State University, I recall reflecting on my first day in the position. The main office was quiet, and I felt at peace with myself, even though I had many questions about my new responsibilities. I recognized that I was bound to make mistakes, and then I searched my mind for things over which I had control. One came quickly to mind: I could always be honest with others. It was then that I swore that I would always try hard to be honest when interacting with faculty, staff, and students, and I knew as I made that pledge there would be many times when being direct and honest would be difficult. After all, how do you find a nice way to tell faculty members that you will not be recommending renewal of their contracts? How do you tell students that their grades are so low that they'll not be able to return to school after the current term ends?

These challenges—and many others—are exacerbated because so many faculty members are thrown into the chairperson's job without any training. They must learn on the job—just as I did. And they will make many of the same kinds of mistakes I made in my early years as a department chairperson. Most educators will tell you that mistakes are not bad because we learn from them. However, chairpersons typically are not in a position to make many mistakes. Not answering a memo, not telling your administrative assistant to post an expenditure, not keeping good notes for yourself can all cause colossal errors—the kind that can quickly lead to the undoing of any administrator.

I hope in this chapter to provide you with the kind of advice I would liked to have had that Indian summer evening many years ago, on my first day as a department chairperson.

Chairpersons do not have the luxury of making many mistakes, so one might assume the position will provide benefits that make the job attractive. Sadly, this is not always the case. Whether at the community college level or at flagship institutions, many chairpersons often are not paid particularly well, especially when the tremendous contributions they make to the institution are taken into account. Chairpersons—because of their unique position—can have profound influence on students and faculty alike, and they often contribute to the general morale of faculty members throughout the institution. They shape the curriculum, mentor new faculty, and decide who gets promoted. They allocate funds, prepare teaching schedules, and serve as spokesperson for their department. Chairpersons also must look out for the welfare of all faculty, staff, and students in their unit. Their tasks are almost limitless.

Even so, on-the-job training is about the only training a chairperson gets. Moreover, not much of it is provided after a chairperson assumes the job. Seagren, Creswell, and Wheeler (1993) point out that "training for department chairpersons can be characterized as casual to nonexistent, oriented only toward understanding administrative procedures, and situational rather than holistic or systematic" (p. xvi). Chairpersons are left on their own to acquire needed skills. Their success generally is determined on how well they adapt to the role of leader and how much support they have from faculty and their dean.

As a new department chairperson, you are going to make mistakes. If they're small mistakes, some will not even be noticed and most will likely be forgotten in a short time. On the other hand, if you make a large mistake or two, you may not be able to survive as chairperson, and even if you do survive you may have a hard time living down your blunder. Obviously, my advice is to keep your mistakes small.

How you came into the job may make a difference on the latitude you receive when mistakes are made. Whether you are appointed from within the faculty ranks or come as an outsider from another university can influence the first months of your tenure—as well as how much trust faculty members in your department and your dean may grant you. Taking this into account, I offer the following advice for the newly appointed chairperson.

- Get to know your faculty.

You should solicit their views regarding strengths and weaknesses of the department. Encourage faculty members to be open with you and invite them to help you form the kind of team needed to advance to a higher level of excellence. Assure each faculty member that his or her ideas and opinions matter. Meet promptly, and privately, with each faculty member so that you can learn as much as possible about them and discover their hopes for the department. Find out about their teaching, research, and service interests. You will be a better chairperson if you get to know something about each faculty member's personal life. Knowing how they spend their time away from the university will help you understand why they behave as they do. When you meet, let them know that it's "their" time to talk—and you are there to listen. Also, learn as much as you can about each faculty member's family. Then write a short note for your files summarizing the thoughts of each member. During the meeting, you should establish awareness that you are a good listener, which is something required of all successful chairpersons and is one of the marks of an effective leader. More on listening will be discussed in Chapter 6.

It is also a good idea to stop by faculty members' offices from time to time for informal chats. You should want to know what faculty members are thinking, and have a sense of their moods, attitudes, and goals. Ask them how their classes are going, or if you know that a faculty member is doing research, ask him or her to tell you about it. They will appreciate your concern, provided, of course, that it is genuine.

- **Set the right tone.**

One of your goals should be to nurture a work environment where each faculty member feels valued. Remind faculty that it is necessary for them to participate in the development of a shared vision and that they have some responsibility for the department's success. Encourage dialogue and help faculty members feel comfortable expressing their views no matter how much they may differ from your own. Lucas (1994) points out, "When conflict emerges, disagreements are fully aired because faculty recognize that, when different points of view are explored, the quality of decision making will be improved" (p. 45). When I look back on my time as both chairperson and dean, I feel indebted to the faculty members who disagreed with me. I am confident that they helped make me a better leader.

- **View the department as a community.**

As a chairperson, you should help faculty, staff, and students connect with and support one another. Much has been written about the coarsening of our values, the decline of moral responsibility, and the paucity of strong leadership—and to many this indicates a breakdown of community. Tannen (1998) writes, "Community is a blend of connections and authority, and we are losing both" (p. 24). She sees the "increasingly adversarial spirit of our contemporary lives" (p. 24) as being one of the principal factors for this breakdown. Experienced chairpersons have no problems identifying with her views.

- **Use all available means to communicate regularly with faculty, staff, and students.**

This helps build a collaborative environment, which in turn helps build a sense of community. It is important that in all communications we invite public discourse and do all we can to avoid polarized debates. Tannen (1998) reminds us that "in conversation we form the interpersonal ties that bind individuals together in personal relationships; in public discourse, we form similar ties on a larger scale, binding individuals into a community" (p. 25).

Effective communication can be achieved without flooding your department with memoranda. While working to assure that faculty members get the information they need, remember there are many effective ways to relay information. Holding regularly scheduled faculty meetings is one. Memoranda and email and telephone messages have their place in the communication scheme. Whatever the medium, if faculty members get information they believe is useful, and if it gets to them on time, they appreciate it. Bennett (2003) observes, "Identifying imaginative strategies for promoting greater communication is at the heart of leadership. . . . The practice of sharing information plays an important part in how academic leaders generate respect" (p. 174). Chairpersons, if they are to be effective, must have respect.

- **Avoid showing favoritism.**

No matter what you do, some faculty members will always be convinced that you favor one person over another. In part, this is because as a society we have come to mistrust leaders. As Kouzes and Posner (1995) observe, ". . . trust in our leaders and our major institutions has been steadily declining over the last few decades" (p. 163). We blame leaders when things in our lives go awry, when we don't get the raise we believe we deserve, when those other than ourselves get promoted, or when we cannot accept responsibility that "we" might be the problem. It is certainly true that some faculty members are easier to work with than others, and whenever those individuals earn praise, the chairperson is likely to be accused of showing favoritism. Even so, you cannot give favorable schedules or allocate funding on the basis of congeniality.

> Resources of all kinds are limited and are invariably outpaced by demand. Do not concentrate most of the resources on a few: all members should receive their fair share. However, make public the criteria informing the distribution of departmental funds and use them consistently: otherwise, you'll be (rightly) accused of favoritism or shiftiness. (Arslanian, 1990, p. 5)

Faculty members may perceive favoritism where none is intended, so take care to avoid even its slightest suggestion.

- **Regularly recognize faculty.**

All faculty members need a pat on the back from time to time, and you must make an effort to show support for the entire faculty. At the same time, this support must be balanced by treating people individually through consideration of their strengths. Nelson (1999) points out, ". . . the most powerful forms of positive incentives are also the easiest and least expensive to do" (p. 271). For example, sending a birthday card to a faculty member's child or his or her spouse is an easy way of letting faculty know that you care about them and their families. Writing a personal letter to acknowledge a faculty member's achievements helps build community—and costs a chairperson very little.

- **Avoid playing gotcha.**

Leaders are only human, and every now and then some unfortunately fall into the trap of exercising their power and/or knowledge by lording it over others. They correct and/or demean others or act in ways that make a faculty or staff member, or a student, feel inferior. This flies in the face of the kind of leadership by which department chairpersons should be guided. As Bennett (2003) reminds us, "Leadership means making a positive difference" (p. 170). To achieve this, we cannot allow ourselves to be negative toward others.

- **Don't back yourself into a corner when making decisions.**

This is a close cousin to playing gotcha. We do this when we make decisions that leave no room to back down without losing face. One of the things I learned in the Armed Forces Leadership Program was that we should always leave room for an out—both for ourselves and others. It is tempting—usually when we are irritated—to box others in, leaving no way to escape. We should avoid that temptation. An absolute yes or no, if awarded too soon, can be a dangerous matter indeed.

- **Be sensitive to the needs of faculty, staff, and students.**

Having worked for insensitive supervisors, I have always tried to be sensitive to the needs of others, especially those who reported to me. Am I treating them as I would want to be treated?

Is it possible to have high standards and at the same time be understanding of others? I think so, especially when faculty and staff have the right incentives. While we cannot always offer pay that meets all expectations, we can make the department a challenging, enjoyable place to work.

I've found that faculty and staff members work more effectively when they are trusted to do their work. Although some chairpersons may be determined to get their 40 hours a week from everyone, it sometimes became my job to insist that many faculty members leave work because they were putting in too many hours—often more than 60 a week.

- Plan.

I can't say enough about the importance of careful planning. You need a set of goals and a vision, and an honest assessment of the department's strengths and weaknesses. Moreover, you must determine what resources are needed to accomplish your goals.

The literature contains little discussion of long-term visions for departments. Departmental leadership cannot afford to be shortsighted, however. Discussions about the current and future stages and needs of the department ensure the projection and development of needed leadership. To achieve the department's stability and continuity of leadership requires a serious commitment and understanding that planning is more than hiring good people and maintaining the usual routines (Seagren et al., 1993).

In good times, the importance of planning will be less obvious. However, when resources are not plentiful and enrollments take a downturn, the lack of planning becomes painfully clear. Careful planning not only helps you assess needed resources, it also helps you make good use of available resources.

- Be careful when hiring, and be honest when evaluating.

A colleague once said to me that hiring was at best a crap shoot. While he may be right at times, careful checks of a potential faculty member's background can increase the odds in your favor. Check all listed references carefully; then, if possible, call some knowledgeable people who are not listed. Let's face it: Potential faculty members are not going to list people as references who are likely to have negative things to report.

Some years ago, when I was dean of liberal arts, a chairperson brought me the name of a candidate to whom he wanted to offer a job. I had interviewed the person and felt uneasy about making the candidate an offer since something didn't seem right. After one telephone call, I discovered that the individual in question had many, many problems. After several more calls and a discussion with the chairperson, we decided not to make an offer. I am convinced to this day that we saved the department and the university much grief.

It is just as important to be honest and thorough when evaluating faculty members as it is to be careful when hiring. As Drucker (1999) notes, "Performance review must be honest, exacting, and an integral part of the job" (p. 5). In my judgment, the only thing worse than making a bad hire is to renew the appointment of a bad hire. I've worked with dozens of chairpersons over the years, and I've encountered many who tended to give above-average evaluations to weak faculty members. They did so for any number of reasons, but mostly because they had not worked hard enough to document a weak evaluation. Sometimes they simply wanted to avoid a confrontation. Providing a less-than-honest evaluation is unfair both to the person involved and to your department and institution. Moreover, if you end up having to extend tenure to a weak faculty member, it is unfair to the other faculty members.

No matter how much work is involved and how difficult it is to explain to a faculty member that he or she has weaknesses, it is worth the time and anguish.

- **Encourage change and innovation and forgive failures.**
If your department is going to be dynamic, it must have faculty members who are willing to take risks and be innovative. You must encourage and be a catalyst for change. This is one of the characteristics of good leadership. In fact, if you are not planning for change, you are failing as a chairperson. Likewise, you must be patient with those who try new things but fail.

Don't be afraid of change. Departments that resist change are likely to face troubled times as we move further into the information age.

- ### Pay attention to the budget.

If allocating, accounting, and purchasing practices did not differ so much from one university to another, I could offer much help on budgeting. Because that is not the case, I can provide only a generalized budget discussion.

I caution you to pay close attention to all budget matters. Having a bright, efficient administrative assistant who is good with budgets is essential to your mental health, and even to keeping your job. I have difficulty keeping my personal checking account balanced, so I have always left budget monitoring to my administrative assistant. I have always been fortunate to have exceptional administrative assistants—ones who kept me informed, and above all, ones who understood that I tended to be conservative in fiscal matters. I would not permit spending more than has been allocated.

- ### Use your creative talents.

If you want to set yourself apart from the ordinary, you need to do more than answer the mail and see that classes are covered—be creative! For example, start some new initiatives: Create a scholastic program to interest high school students from your region and state in your discipline; create an alumni organization; publish an alumni newsletter; raise funds for faculty development; establish an annual high school career day.

Departments should be like dynamic, living organisms that grow and change continuously. Be prepared to face resistance from faculty members who are comfortable with the way things are. To some, the idea of change is repugnant; they fear it and will fight to protect their ways of doing things. In Chapter 26, I will discuss how to deal with faculty members who resist change.

- ### Be upbeat, steady, and predictable.

There will be days when it's difficult to smile, but as a chairperson you will create morale problems if you are regularly glum and moody. Faculty members should not have to ask your administrative assistant, "Is he or she in a good mood today?"

- **Learn what is expected of you.**

Before you accept any administrative position, ask for a description of it, then discuss the specific expectations of the person or people to whom you will report. It will also help to understand your supervisor's style of leadership. Is it one that you find agreeable? For example, you may find it hard to work for someone who tends to micromanage, and you sense that your supervisor-to-be is prone to do that. Should you accept the job? Is it something you can clear up before accepting the position?

You should know precisely what the expectations are before you take a job so that you don't later say, "I didn't know I was supposed to do that." You should assess your level of comfort with all the areas of responsibility and determine how much support you will receive in those areas where you might be somewhat weak. Seagren et al. (1993) recommend that chairpersons gain a clear understanding of their role and tasks when accepting or continuing in the position of chairperson.

- **Keep your hand in teaching.**

Most of you can skip this section because you have no choice about teaching; it's required. However, for those who chair large departments and are not expected to teach, I urge you to find a way to teach at least one course.

Even when I was a dean, I continued to teach; getting out of my office and into the classroom helped preserve my sanity. An added benefit is that I was forced to keep current in my discipline. Moreover, I got to know students—beyond those who came to my office to complain—and teaching helped me understand the concerns that other faculty members had.

Learning how to use your time wisely is an important consideration in this matter. If you teach a class in which you have a great depth of knowledge, you will not have to work so hard to prepare for it (though it is important to keep abreast of the literature in your field). I have always liked to set aside at least an hour before teaching a class so that I could "woodshed," as I called it. For me it meant delving deeply into the subject matter, so that I knew exactly how I would present the material and how I would engage students.

I knew that I did not have the time to teach classes involving a lot of paper grading. Accepting this is essential if you chair a large department; don't do as I did and learn the hard way. Not only will you make matters difficult for yourself, you'll shortchange students.

- **Make time to create a professional development plan for yourself.**

It is all too easy to overlook your own development after you become department chairperson. In addition to keeping your hand in teaching, you should try to find time for research. Also, you should find ways to improve your skills as chairperson. Attending workshops for chairpersons will enable you to learn more about areas for which you are responsible. Workshops for chairpersons are available from the following sources. (Additional workshops are listed in Appendix A.)

American Council on Education
One Dupont Circle NW
Washington, DC 20036–1193
www.acenet.edu

National Center for Higher Education Management Systems
3035 Center Green Drive, Suite 150
Boulder, CO 80301–2251
www.nchems.org

Academic Chairpersons Conference
Division of Continuing Education
Kansas State University
3 College Court Building
Manhattan, KS 66506–6001
www.dce.ksu.edu/academicchairpersons

College of Continuing Studies
The University of Alabama
Box 870388
Tuscaloosa, AL 35487-0388
http://continuingstudies.ua.edu

School of Continuing Education and Summer Sessions
Cornell University
Box 530, B20 Day Hall
Ithaca, NY 14853–2801
www.sce.cornell.edu

- **Consult others.**

Chairpersons have many duties and responsibilities, many of which are time consuming and complex. When you are faced with difficult decisions, consult others on campus who can be of help. Many of your fellow chairpersons across campus will have solved similar problems and will gladly offer advice.

- **Learn to say no.**

There is a human tendency to try to please everyone, but for a chairperson that is simply impossible. Some of the most ineffective chairpersons I've known were those who never learned how to say no. They somehow had the notion that they could win respect by pleasing others.

Most faculty members know that some of their requests are going to be denied. They expect it. Likewise, they expect to be treated fairly. They want fairness far more than they want you to make promises you can't fulfill—which is what happens when you don't know how to say no.

Saying no can sometimes be painful, but knowing how and when to say no pays rich dividends. You may have to struggle to find the key to success, but not being able to say no will provide a quick, sure ticket to failure. As Bennis (1997) writes, "Trying to be everything to everyone was diverting me from real leadership" (p. 13). We must learn to say no so that we can lead.

- Be somebody who cares.

Along with learning how to say no, you must also do what you can to make people more productive and content. If this isn't your approach, chances are you will not be either happy or successful as a chairperson. Let's face it: Most of your time is spent helping solve other people's problems.

Unfortunately, most chairpersons have not had training in counseling, and they feel helpless trying to work with troubled faculty. You've probably known faculty members who were so distraught that they became suicidal. Others have ruined their lives engaging in destructive behavior.

What can you do, short of going back to school to earn a degree in counseling or social work? You can read everything you can find about working with troubled associates; you can consult with trained counselors; or you can bring in trained colleagues to help. You can also care: You can listen, empathize, and use your best instincts to recommend a course of action aimed at persuading troubled faculty members to seek professional help.

Some years ago, while trying to find help for our son, who subsequently was diagnosed with Asperger's syndrome (a cousin to autism), my wife and I went to all kinds of medical practitioners in search of help. Time after time we were told that there was nothing wrong with him, though we knew otherwise. Eventually we had the good fortune to meet a specialist in Asperger's, and I shared with him our difficulties in getting help, concluding with, "The only thing I knew to do was to give him love." The physician agreed that love is a very powerful medicine.

The lesson here is that if we have distressed associates, they deserve to be helped, and while we may not have the expertise to provide professional help ourselves, we can let faculty members know that we have a genuine concern for their welfare.

- Stay in love.

In the last suggestion, I advised, "Be somebody who cares." Until recently I thought that was enough, but the more I've thought about those words, the more inadequate they sound. Somehow for me they just are not strong enough to convey what I mean. Instead of simply being about caring, I was thinking about sharing love; that is, compassion and empathy. Thus,

I searched through leadership books to see if I could find any mention of love as a component of leadership. I looked through index after index without much success, until finally I came upon something that conveys exactly how I feel. In their book *Encouraging the Heart: A Leader's Guide to Rewarding and Recognizing Others*, Kouzes and Posner (2003) tell about asking former Major General John H. Stanford how he would go about developing leaders. Here is his reply:

> When anyone asks me that question, I tell them . . . the secret
> to success is to stay in love. Staying in love gives you the fire that
> really ignites other people, to see inside other people, to have
> a greater desire to get things done than other people. A person
> who is not in love doesn't really feel the kind of excitement that
> helps . . . to get ahead and lead others to achieve. I don't know
> any other fire, any other thing in life that is more exhilarating
> and is more positive a feeling than love is. (p. 150)

- Develop written policies and procedures (and follow them).
The best way to assure that all faculty are treated fairly is to have written policies and procedures governing such things as travel funds, released-time assignments, allocation of departmental funds for equipment, supplies, faculty development, and so on.

You should be able to provide new faculty members with written policy statements that outline promotion and tenure procedures. New faculty deserve to know what is expected of them, how and when they will be evaluated, and what they must do if they are to be promoted and granted tenure. Written guidelines on these questions will go a long way to ease tensions and misunderstandings in your department.

- Keep good records.
You will find it helpful to make some kind of written record of any important meeting you call. It should include the date and time of the meeting, who was present, what it was about, what decision was reached, whether any action is to be taken, and whether follow-up is expected. Faculty

members, after all, are human. And you will be surprised at how often their memories of meetings and decisions will reflect what they wish had occurred, rather than what in fact did occur.

Likewise, it is helpful to keep good correspondence files and a record of all budget transactions. It is impossible for most of us to remember all the details of every meeting we attend and all we wrote in a letter or memorandum. You will discover how true this is the first time you have to go back a few years to refresh your memory about an important meeting.

- **Set a good example for faculty.**

If you are to be an effective leader, you must lead by example. You must present a good work ethic and demonstrate the qualities that you would like to see in faculty members and in your supervisors. It's hard, for example, to reprimand faculty for not showing up for a department-sponsored event when you fail to show up at certain events faculty members are involved in. Keep in mind that others look to you as a role model. Many will try to pattern their behavior after yours.

- **Study the art of decision-making.**

As a leader, you must learn to be decisive. There are many decisions that you can make jointly with your faculty, which is as it should be. However, there will be others that you must make alone. Unless you are willing to make decisions—no matter how difficult—you are not likely to be successful as an administrator. Moreover, you must learn how to make good decisions.

Bethel (1990) devotes a chapter of her book to the leader as a decision-maker. She writes,

> One of the most important tools you have is the ability to
> release potential and make something happen. Courageous
> decision making does that. . . . When we are indecisive we for-
> feit everyone's future and we waste time, energy, talent, money,
> and opportunity. The most effective leaders are vitally aware of
> this and would rather make a wrong decision than none at all.
> (p. 149)

Learning this skill is not easy, but the consequence of not learning how to make decisions can be your downfall as a leader. Consider what Jeff Cannon and Lieutenant Commander Jon Cannon (2003) say about this in their book *Leadership Lessons of the Navy SEALs:*

> His name was Jim, but we called him the flag. Why? Because he never made a decision. He just blew in the direction of the prevailing wind. We included him in the meetings because of his title, but none of us ever paid any attention to him, and none of us ever relied on him. Why? Because he never stood up and took the lead. If you're in charge, people need to know that you're in charge. The only way they know is by watching you make decisions. And if you don't do that, someone else will. And that person will be the leader everyone follows from then on, regardless of his or her rank or title. Are you waiting until you have all the information? You're never going to get it. Are you waiting to weigh all options? By the time you figure them all out, the first option will have changed, and you're back to the drawing board. Are you waiting for a sign? Are you waiting because you're scared? That's part of the job—it's never going to change. (p. 95)

What is important here is to see how other leaders make decisions. Typically, leaders make good decisions when

- They keep abreast of what's going on and collect information that will aid them when it's time to make a decision.
- They weigh all options as they collect information—that is, what happens if I make decision A versus B, and so on.
- They ask themselves who will be affected by their decisions and how they should deal with those affected.
- Decision-making does not paralyze them.
- They develop skills at what psychologists call thin-slicing. According to Gladwell (2005), this term "refers to the ability of our unconscious to

find patterns in situations and behavior based on very narrow slices of experience" (p. 23).

- They move forward boldly when it is time to make a decision. They don't look over their shoulders to see who is following. They have confidence. They have a winning air about them that encourages others to follow. Most especially, they have their antennae out to pick up the attitude of others—to learn about motivations, fears, prejudices, and the like.

- They put power in the hands of those who do the work, thus empowering others.

- As Kouzes and Posner (1995) point out, "Leaders actively seek out ways to increase choice and provide greater decision-making authority and responsibility for their constituents" (p. 191).

- **Employ a good administrative assistant.**

If I were to say that good administrative assistants are worth their weight in gold, it would be a cliché, but it would be true. A trusted administrative assistant is indispensable. To the general who would say "War is hell," a chairperson would answer, "Have you ever tried running a department with a weak administrative assistant?"

Summary

Let's look at leadership. Kouzes and Posner (1995) describe leadership as *"the art of mobilizing others to want to struggle for shared aspirations"* (p. 30). When they studied what people valued in their superiors, they discovered that honesty, vision, competence, and the ability to inspire were characteristics most admired. Fair-minded, supportive, broad-minded, and intelligent followed the top four. We ought not overlook the fact that managers and leaders are different. Bennis (1997) observes,

> More than anything, the difference between a leader and a manager rests on the status quo: Managers are willing to live with it, and leaders are not. Leaders are the ones with vision,

who inspire others and cause them to galvanize their efforts and achieve change. (p. 17)

Chairpersons should ask themselves whether they are "willing to stand on principle and make their voice heard" (Bennis, 1997, p. 17). Yet as Bennett (2003) reminds us, "In the academy, good management is a necessary condition for effective leadership, and vice versa" (p. 184). Indeed it is difficult to be a department chairperson unless you have good management skills. Having them gives you a chance to lead. What you do with that chance is up to you, of course.

Resources

Web Sites

Academic Leadership
www.academicleadership.org

Department Chair Online Resource Center
www.acenet.edu/resources/chairs

Books

Badaracco, J. L., Jr. (2002). *Leading quietly: An unorthodox guide to doing the right thing.* Boston, MA: Harvard Business School Press.

Bennett, J. B. (1983). *Managing the academic department.* New York, NY: American Council on Education/Macmillan.

Bennis, W. (2003). *On becoming a leader* (Rev. and expanded ed.). Cambridge, MA: Perseus.

Bennis, W., & Nanus, B. (2003). *Leaders: Strategies for taking charge.* New York, NY: HarperCollins.

Bensimon, E. M., Ward, K., & Sanders, K. (2000). *The department chair's role in developing new faculty into teachers and scholars.* Bolton, MA: Anker.

Caroselli, M. (2000). *Leadership skills for managers.* New York, NY: McGraw-Hill.

Cohen, W. A. (2000). *The new art of the leader.* Paramus, NJ: Prentice Hall.

Diamond, R. M. (Ed.). (2002). *Field guide to academic leadership.* San Francisco, CA: Jossey-Bass.

Goleman, D., Boyatzis, R., & McKee, A. (2002). *Primal leadership: Realizing the power of emotional intelligence.* Boston, MA: Harvard Business School Press.

Hecht, I. W. D., Higgerson, M. L., Gmelch, W. H., & Tucker, A. (1999). *The department chair as academic leader.* Phoenix, AZ: American Council on Education/Oryx Press.

Higgerson, M. L. (1996). *Communication skills for department chairs.* Bolton, MA: Anker.

Lyles, D. (2000). *Winning ways: Four secrets for getting great results by working well with people.* New York, NY: Berkley.

McKenna, P. J., & Maister, D. H. (2002). *First among equals: How to manage a group of professionals.* New York, NY: The Free Press.

Raelin, J. A. (2003). *Creating leaderful organizations: How to bring out leadership in everyone.* San Francisco, CA: Berrett-Koehler.

Seagren, A. T., Wheeler, D. W., Creswell, J. W., Miller, M. T., & VanHorn-Grassmeyer, K. (1994). *Academic leadership in community colleges.* Lincoln, NE: University of Nebraska Press.

Seldin, P., & Higgerson, M. L. (2002). *The administrative portfolio: A practical guide to improved administrative performance and personnel decisions.* Bolton, MA: Anker.

Wergin, J. F. (2003). *Departments that work: Building and sustaining cultures of excellence in academic programs.* Bolton, MA: Anker.

References

Arslanian, A. (1990). A few suggestions to new department chairs. In J. B. Bennett & D. J. Figuli (Eds.), *Enhancing departmental leadership: The roles of the chairperson.* New York, NY: American Council on Education/Macmillan.

Bennett, J. B. (2003). *Academic life: Hospitality, ethics, and spirituality.* Bolton, MA: Anker.

Bennis, W. (1997). *Managing people is like herding cats.* Provo, UT: Executive Excellence.

Bethel, S. M. (1990). *Making a difference: Twelve qualities that make you a leader.* New York, NY: Berkley.

Cannon, J., & Cannon, J. (2003). *Leadership lessons of the Navy SEALs: Battle-tested strategies for creating successful organizations and inspiring extraordinary results.* New York, NY: McGraw-Hill.

Drucker, P. F. (1999). My mentors' leadership lessons. In F. Hesselbein & P. M. Cohen (Eds.), *Leader to leader: Enduring insights on leadership from the Drucker Foundation's award-winning journal* (pp. 3–7). San Francisco, CA: Jossey-Bass.

Gladwell, M. (2005). *Blink: The power of thinking without thinking.* New York, NY: Little, Brown and Company.

Kouzes, J. M., & Posner, B. Z. (1995). *The leadership challenge: How to keep getting extraordinary things done in organizations.* San Francisco, CA: Jossey-Bass.

Kouzes, J. M., & Posner, B. Z. (2003). *Encouraging the heart: A leader's guide to rewarding and recognizing others.* San Francisco, CA: Jossey-Bass.

Lucas, A. F. (1994). *Strengthening departmental leadership: A team-building guide for chairs in colleges and universities.* San Francisco, CA: Jossey-Bass.

Nelson, B. (1999). Creating an energized workplace. In F. Hesselbein & P. M. Cohen (Eds.), *Leader to leader: Enduring insights on leadership from the Drucker Foundation's award-winning journal* (pp. 265–274). San Francisco, CA: Jossey-Bass.

Seagren, A. T., Creswell, J. W., & Wheeler, D. W. (1993). *The department chair: New roles, responsibilities, and challenges.* Washington, DC: The George Washington University, Graduate School of Education and Human Development.

Tannen, D. (1998). *The argument culture: Moving from debate to dialogue.* New York, NY: Random House.

2

Seven Habits of Successful Chairpersons

One of the biggest complaints I have heard against administrators is that they don't give faculty members straight answers.

Successful chairpersons come in all shapes and sizes. While there is no one formula for success suitable for all chairpersons, there are certain habits and characteristics that most successful chairpersons have in common. As someone who has been both a chairperson and a dean, I have observed these similarities over the years regardless of the size of the institution from where the chairperson hails.

It was not difficult to move from this observation to the ideas Stephen R. Covey outlines in his bestselling book about the seven habits of highly successful people. In a 1999 interview with Frances Hesselbein, he had this to say:

> Organizational effectiveness is so interwoven with the personal
> side that they're almost inseparable. Organizational behavior
> is simply the collective outcome of individual behavior. But as
> you develop cultural norms and mores inside an organization, a
> spirit of we rather than a spirit of me can begin to emerge.
> So that is the fundamental habit. (Hesselbein, 1999, p. 216)

Even casual visitors to most college campuses can quickly identify chairpersons who have created a team environment. These extraordinary individuals are able to garner the respect and the trust of their faculty so that they can forge a community where teamwork is commonly accepted and practiced. They and their departments are viewed on and off campus as somehow special. Indeed, an air of energy usually surrounds a department headed by such a person, which is evident in the behavior and attitude of the faculty and students. Pride seems to emanate from the department itself.

So what is it that these chairpersons have in common? Is it something others can acquire? I will try to answer the first question; you can answer the second.

1. Successful chairpersons have goals.

Their goals are no secret. They are well articulated, shared with the faculty, and pursued until accomplished. Having goals is not enough, however. Successful chairpersons must first earn the respect and support of faculty members in their department, as well as the trust and support of the dean. Equally important, their goals must be effectively communicated. As Shaw (1999) notes,

> Identified goals and values are all well and good, but even the clearest and most inspirational of these will die on the vine if they are not communicated effectively and often. . . .
> Leaders need not fear overstressing their goals and values. One of my teachers in elementary school stressed that repetition was the key to learning—and she said that often! Nothing I've observed in the years since has proved her wrong. (pp. 10–11)

Some years ago, when my provost and vice president for academic affairs asked deans to submit goals for the year, she said to limit them to not more than four or five. "I don't think you can focus sufficiently on too many more than that," she explained. She's right, I think. Four or five important goals are sufficient for any year. Each may have many parts, so you will accomplish more than a few things annually.

No matter how many goals you settle on, it is important that you define and develop them fully. You then must commit the department to carrying them out, and you must see that sufficient time and resources are made available to satisfy the goals. Then, you should set your sights on the one goal that you believe can be easily accomplished with the support of the faculty. Accomplishing it is a sign of success and can help galvanize support for the remaining goals. It also will enable you to recognize those faculty members who carried out the most important tasks, which in turn will help you to build the cohesive community that is necessary in today's climate of change.

2. Successful chairpersons get to know their colleagues and fellow administrators.

They know the interests of faculty members, both professional and personal. They come to know the potential of each person in the department, and they provide room for them to grow and develop—even to make mistakes.

Have you ever noticed how much harder you are willing to work for someone who seems to understand you, who inquires from time to time about your family, who remembers your favorite baseball team, and who does not get angry and hold it against you forever if you make a mistake? As chairpersons we need to be sensitive to the needs of the faculty, and we cannot do that unless we get to know them.

3. Successful chairpersons are agents of change.

Chairpersons understand that the status quo—even if comfortable—often may stunt progress or fail to meet the needs of students. We must look as far into the future as our best lights permit. What's out there? And what does it mean to students who will be in the workforce 10, 15, or 20 years from now? What are the scientific, technological, social, and economic forces that are shaping society? Are we helping our students understand these forces?

With the world changing so quickly, we must be knowledgeable about directions and tendencies. We must be avid readers and observers of new professional developments, and we must be persuasive enough to engage the faculty in this pursuit as well.

Change involves risk-taking, and the successful chairperson knows that striking out on new, bold ventures is necessary. Regrettably, some ventures will not end successfully. Nonetheless, leaders must take risks, and they must tolerate and encourage others to be bold enough to try such ventures. And they must reward those who take risks.

4. Successful chairpersons understand and appreciate teaching, research, and public service.

Although most chairpersons have heavy administrative burdens, they must try to find time to stay personally involved in these three areas. Faculty members respect chairpersons who are active in the areas in which they are evaluated. They resent administrators finding fault when the administrators themselves have not proved themselves in teaching, research, or public service.

I remember how faculty members at one school resented a dean who often rejected applications for promotion because the applicant supposedly "had not done enough research." They resented his assessment because the dean himself had never done any research. The point here is that as a chairperson you are expected to serve as a role model when it comes to fulfilling responsibilities that you expect of others.

Successful chairpersons must provide leadership for the assessment and evaluation of teaching, scholarship, and service (see Chapter 23). Also, time management is an absolute necessity for chairpersons who want to be active scholars, teachers, and public servants (see Chapter 5). Top-level administrators must recognize the heavy burdens on chairpersons if indeed they are expected to teach, do research, and provide public service. Provosts and deans must provide the time and money to allow chairpersons to stay active in these three areas if this is expected of them. It is promising to see that many colleges and universities are beginning to reevaluate the meaning of public service and research. The trickle down of the "publish or perish" mentality from large research institutions to regional public and private universities and colleges has not served students well.

5. Successful chairpersons are honest, forthright, decent people.

They make tough calls and are decisive even when the decision goes against those whom they would most like to please. Also, they make clear that they cannot respond favorably to all requests.

One of the biggest complaints I have heard against administrators is that they don't give faculty members straight answers. Too often they say what others want to hear rather than what should be said.

I've worked with many different kinds of administrators. Most were honest, but some were less than honest. And there were some I always had to play games with. When I was dean at Middle Tennessee State University, I worked for a provost who was honest and there was no game playing. Consequently, I liked my job all the more, and I always worked hard to meet her expectations. In my mind, she set the gold standard for what supervisors should be like—honest, decent, caring, supportive, and an especially capable leader no matter how it's defined. I always knew that I could count on her, and if you are fortunate enough to have such a supervisor, I hope you will do as I did—pray every night that she'd be there the next day!

6. Successful chairpersons are fair and evenhanded.

No matter how fair we are, it is difficult not to want to favor those we get along with best. Understanding this, you must contemplate carefully all your actions and words. Practice this often, as we know messages often are altered because of "noise" in the communication system. What you may have meant to say and what others understood you to say are often strikingly different. Craft your message carefully.

For your own good and for the good of the department, you must learn that everyone profits from fairness and evenhandedness. Many of the faculty members in your department will be resentful and unsupportive if there are lapses.

7. Successful chairpersons are consensus builders and good communicators.

Their leadership style is to develop ideas and persuade others to support them. They are good, and they also are good at communicating their ideas.

I've watched and evaluated many different chairpersons. Some try to lead without first trying to build consensus, and I have seen these fail, even when they had good ideas. Faculty members need to be involved in the department and its changes. Failure to involve generally means that new ideas are not going to be accepted. Successful chairpersons understand this and work carefully to keep faculty members informed and supportive. Successful leaders are good listeners. As Lucas (1994) reminds us, "Active listening demonstrates respect for the speaker, because it conveys that the listener is interested in the speaker and thinks that what he or she feels is important" (p. 176). This essential part of the communication process often is overlooked.

While there undoubtedly are other character traits that successful chairpersons have in common, those described here seem to stand out above all others. If you have these qualities, you are likely to succeed. Faculty members will give you their support, and you will find that your dean and provost will provide support as well. Most of all, you will achieve credibility.

Of course, when you are successful the job is more enjoyable. Others notice and praise your work, and, above all, your students are the big winners. They are studying in a stronger, more vital department, and people who are happy with their jobs are teaching them.

At the beginning of this chapter, I raised two questions: What do successful chairpersons have in common? Can these traits be acquired? I said I would try to answer the first question and leave the second to you. However, I can't resist trying to answer the second as well. I strongly believe that successful habits can be acquired. With hard work and practice, we can all learn to develop goals, get to know people who make up the department, and become agents of change. Likewise, we can develop an understanding of and appreciation for teaching, research, and public service. Furthermore, we can be honest and fair, and we can work to be consensus builders. In short, we all have a chance to be successful if we acquire these habits.

Leadership scholars point out there are leaders in all walks of life, yet many go unnoticed. If you look around your department, you will undoubtedly see faculty members assuming leadership roles as they chair committees, oversee the work of student projects, supervise field experience, and so on. Successful chairpersons encourage this sort of leadership from their faculty members, and they find ways to evoke it. Moreover, they reward those whose leadership makes a positive difference for the department. There is no mystery surrounding the issue; it is a reassuring, settled matter. As Kouzes and Posner (1999) advise, we must encourage the heart. They quote from a Kepner-Tregoe study revealing that

> Only about 40 percent of North American workers say they receive any recognition for a job well done, and about the same percentage report they never get recognized for outstanding individual performance. . . . We can do a lot more. We must do a lot more. (p. 4)

I encourage all chairpersons to be open and honest and to work diligently to understand faculty and staff members as well as students in their department. I can't say enough about the many demands chairpersons have on their time and how far the spirit of openness goes toward creating the kind of trust and credibility chairpersons must have to become successful. You need to be candid, but avoid being defensive. Chairpersons should have the hide of a pachyderm—they are likely to be criticized often and praised too little. Leaders understand this and accept it as one price for making a difference.

What Unsuccessful Chairpersons Do

Just as there are habits of successful chairpersons, there are habits of those who do not succeed. Let's examine some of these.

- **They try to control others.**

I've seen many chairpersons fail because they would not allow faculty members to participate fully in departmental governance. Such chairpersons seem insecure and untrusting. Often their manners are harsh. And just as often they bark out commands and expect others to obey without questioning.

- **They are devoid of ideas.**

Some chairpersons tend to accept what is and move along in their jobs on cruise control. Successful leaders are laden with ideas; indeed, they have so many ideas that they sometimes are prone to establish new approaches and new ways of looking at things faster than others can comprehend their ideas—but they are smart enough to know when to pull back.

- **They are out of their element.**

Some chairpersons are unable to develop leadership skills. I can't tell you how many faculty members over the years have said to me, "Dr. Soandso belongs in the classroom. I don't know why he wants to be a chairperson. He just can't handle the job." While I have no answer to the question, I believe it resides in another: Do they understand themselves?

- **They are humorless.**

Here is a true story: One chairperson went into his night class on an April 1, and immediately students began leaving. Soon only the chairperson was left. Mystified, he then went out into the hallway—where the students met him with a loud chorus of "April Fool." He ordered them back into the classroom and told them—with a red, angry face—that he was going to lower their grades for the semester unless he got a written apology from each of them. I don't think I have to add anything more about the need for leaders to have a sense of humor.

- **They don't know how to meet people.**

Some chairpersons seem unable to connect with those outside their own world. Chairpersons don't have to have the gift of gab, but they need some conversational skills. At the very least, they must be comfortable when around any of their constituents.

- **They buckle under pressure and abandon their principles.**

Chairpersons often feel pressure, but the successful ones know their own values and guiding principles. They don't let go of them even if pressured. I would have to ask this question of any chairperson: Would you be willing to give up your job if your supervisor asked you to do something you know was wrong? Once when I was a dean, the counsel for the president suggested to me that I should lie under oath in a civil case in order to protect the university. I told him that I would not do that and, when I did testify, I told how I was pressured to lie. Obviously, I made no friends in the president's office. I soon accepted another job. Sometimes we have to stand up to those who would have us abandon our principles.

- **They fail to hold faculty to high standards.**

Some chairpersons cannot tell faculty things they may not want to hear. I remember asking one faculty member what his chairperson thought on a certain subject. His response was, "It depends on who he last spoke to." These words spoke volumes about the chairperson: He told faculty members exactly what they wanted to hear. Leaders must do better than that.

Resources

Bennis, W. (2003). *On becoming a leader* (Rev. and expanded ed.). Cambridge, MA: Perseus.

Chödrön, P. (2001). *The places that scare you: A guide to fearlessness in difficult times*. Boston, MA: Shambhala.

Eble, K. E. (1992). *The art of administration: A guide for academic administrators*. San Francisco, CA: Jossey-Bass.

Lucas, A. F., & Associates. (2000). *Leading academic change: Essential roles for department chairs*. San Francisco, CA: Jossey-Bass.

O'Toole, J. (1996). *Leading change: The argument for values-based leadership*. San Francisco, CA: Jossey-Bass.

References

Covey, S. R. (1999). *The habits of effective organizations*. In F. Hesselbein & P. M. Cohen (Eds.), *Leader to leader: Enduring insights on leadership from the Drucker Foundation's award-winning journal* (pp. 215–226). San Francisco, CA: Jossey-Bass.

Hesselbein, F. (1999). Introduction. In F. Hesselbein & P. M. Cohen (Eds.), *Leader to leader: Enduring insights on leadership from the Drucker Foundation's award-winning journal.* San Francisco, CA: Jossey-Bass.

Kouzes, J. M., & Posner, B. Z. (2003). *Encouraging the heart: A leader's guide to rewarding and recognizing others.* San Francisco, CA: Jossey-Bass.

Lucas, A. F. (1994). *Strengthening departmental leadership: A team-building guide for chairs in colleges and universities.* San Francisco, CA: Jossey-Bass.

Shaw, K. A. (1999). *The successful president: Buzzwords on leadership.* Phoenix, AZ: American Council on Education/Oryx Press.

3

Providing Leadership

You have the opportunity to provide a wonderful gift to people—by encouraging them and helping them believe in themselves.

As a chairperson, you are expected to be a leader. You have many opportunities to demonstrate leadership skills as you develop plans, set budget priorities, encourage faculty development, update the curriculum, recruit faculty members, foster higher standards of teaching, resolve conflicts, serve on committees, or deal with other responsibilities.

Yet it is probable that most of you came into your positions with little training in management or leadership, and that you never had given much time to any study of leadership. Consequently, you have had to depend on your instincts and the application of practical knowledge. You may have emulated the leadership skills of people you have worked for or have known.

Each of us can make a difference in the lives of others if we are committed to becoming a leader and trying to do the right thing. Still, developing your own leadership style is a formidable task. One way of establishing leadership capabilities is to make a list of the good and bad qualities of leaders you have known. This exercise can provide a picture of the kind of leader you aspire to become—as well as a list of traits to avoid.

Studies show that leadership often defies simple description. As Burns (1978) notes, "Leadership is one of the most observed and least understood phenomena on earth" (p. 2). For the purposes of this chapter, let's define leadership as the ability to motivate others to take certain courses of action, to persuade others that prescribed tasks must be done on time and in a particular way, and to gain and retain the respect of others, especially those with whom one works or associates.

31

One way to understand leadership is to consider leadership theories. When applied to higher education, the more general theories of leadership tend to emphasize behavior traits (Dill & Fullagar, 1987). "Successful academic leaders, in addition to their professional credibility, display certain characteristics, such as vigor, decisiveness, and a willingness to take chances" (Seagren, Creswell, & Wheeler, 1993, p. 20). According to Seagren et al. (1993), cognitive resource theory

> Is particularly relevant to higher education institutions. Cognitive theory emphasizes the need to understand the relationship between the leader's qualities and experience and the group's. For a high ability group, a nondirective leader is predicted to be more effective than a directive or autocratic leader. (p. 18)

Leadership Qualities

One leadership theory is supported by research in terms of behavior traits—that leaders possess certain common qualities (Yukl, 1989). While Luthans (1992) shows that the existence of certain traits is likely to increase a leader's effectiveness, by no means is strong leadership certain. With that caveat, the following qualities can help you provide departmental leadership.

- **Do not covet the job.**

You should not covet your job as chairperson. This does not mean that you should not want to be a chairperson. Instead, the word *covet* relates to greed and avariciousness, and to situations where a person is willing to bend principles or ignore the truth to hang on to a job. Thus, those who covet a job are unlikely to be as strong as those who are secure in their positions. If you are worried about protecting your job, you seldom make forceful or independent judgments.

Too many administrators will listen to a recommendation or idea and then say, "I agree with you, but . . ." What they do not explain, of course, is that "if I support your recommendation, I may be putting my job in jeopardy, or, at the very least, I might incur the wrath of my boss."

Strong leaders look at the merits of whatever recommendations or ideas come before them. They analyze each of them carefully. They may consult with others before giving their support, but they do not reject an idea simply because it may not please those to whom they report. If an idea has merit, and if it suggests the right course of action, you should back it. Fear of losing your position can paralyze you and make you ineffective. You will be less fearful when making decisions if you do not covet your job. And you will become a stronger, more respected administrator.

- Have a sense of humor.

Strong leaders have a good sense of humor. Those who are deadly serious about everything almost always fail at inspiring others. This does not suggest, of course, that a chairperson must possess a bag of tricks or a joke for every occasion. However, there are times when those working on a project become weary or too serious. A well-timed humorous aside, even a bad pun, can help put everyone at ease or put the task in proper perspective. More than likely the matter does not have life-and-death consequences. The world will not stop if the chairperson's task force does not reach an immediate decision or complete a routine assignment. You shouldn't be afraid to laugh or smile when someone utters a comic aside. At times you may even make light of yourself. You will gain respect if you do, and others will enjoy working with you.

In addition to having a sense of humor, chairpersons also need to possess a sense of modesty and humility. University administrators I have known who lack these qualities have been miserable people. Indeed, most were unable to keep their jobs for sustained periods of time.

- Have vision.

The best chairpersons have vision. They also are able to articulate it and convince others to share their vision (Cameron & Ulrich, 1986; Maxcy, 1991). Strong leaders know what the department should become, what it should stand for, and how it can get there. They see the big picture and are able to assess the strengths and weaknesses of the department. They can provide a blueprint for getting resources and the wherewithal to bring about needed changes. Moreover, such chairpersons tend to be passionate about seeing their department move to a higher level of excellence. They present their ideas clearly and engage others in their passion; they know how to build consensus and encourage productive dialogue; they provide encouragement and allow risk-taking; and they value each faculty member and his or her ideas. As Kouzes and Posner (2003) posit, "Teaching a vision—and confirming that the vision is shared—is a process of engaging constituents in conversation about their lives, about their own hopes and dreams" (p. 43). The point here is that if we come to understand others—and provided we understand ourselves—then we earn trust and in turn let faculty members know that we trust them. All chairpersons must value shared trust. When this takes place, your vision becomes inclusive.

Chairpersons with vision stay current in their disciplines, attend and participate in professional conferences, and are regular readers of professional journals and publications that address higher education issues. Ideas fascinate and invigorate strong chairpersons. Those with vision look for opportunities to share and implement their ideas. They are men and women creatively obsessed.

- **Stay focused.**

There is no question that departmental goals are difficult to achieve unless the chairperson is able to give thorough attention to the details of any plans that have been developed. Even after chairpersons establish goals, some fail to develop the necessary plans to see them realized, or fail to include faculty in the development process. This can lead to disinterest, distrust, and serious morale problems. Moreover, chairpersons must focus on clear standards, and when possible allow faculty members to establish their own goals. If chairpersons have done what they should in establishing values and goals, their jobs become easier. Start by working with faculty members to establish goals, values, and plans. When these are agreed upon, you should assign responsibility for each activity. There should be a timetable that gives due dates and a method for assessing accomplishments. The chairperson should make the plans public, showing who is responsible for each task. Notices need to go out regularly to remind faculty members of due dates.

A word of caution: Be aware of having too many goals; in other words, spreading oneself too thin. Even the best-organized chairperson will have trouble juggling many different tasks that are tied to action plans.

- ### Delegate responsibility.

Strong chairpersons have little difficulty with the delegation of departmental duties. They also delegate appropriate authority to those who have earned their trust. By delegating, they are sharing power. This also helps chairpersons to teach their vision to others.

To delegate effectively, the chairperson needs to know the strengths and weaknesses of each faculty member. If something needs to be done, the chairperson must determine who has the talent and motivation to complete the job in a satisfactory manner.

Whenever you delegate responsibilities, you need to provide appropriate support and resources. Faculty members will become demoralized if you assign them tasks without the right tools.

Delegating responsibility is difficult for many, but it is an essential characteristic of effective leadership. By delegating, and then seeing that tasks are completed, chairpersons have many opportunities to recognize the efforts of faculty members. A personal note of appreciation can encourage even the most cynical.

- ### Know yourself.

To be effective, you must know your own strengths and weaknesses. Knowing yourself helps give you confidence. If you know your weaknesses, you can generally get the support you need from those whose strengths match your weaknesses. Indeed, you can turn over to others the projects that demand skills you don't have, then concentrate your attention where your own talents are strongest.

- ### Do not fear to make mistakes.

No matter how well you understand your duties and goals, you will make mistakes. If you worry unduly about this, however, your performance will suffer. All good leaders recognize the possibility of mistakes, but they are confident enough to know that their accomplishments will far outweigh their errors.

One of the characteristics successful academic leaders display is a willingness to take chances (Seagren et al., 1993). However, Kouzes and Posner (2003) provide an important cautionary note: "Challenging the process is essential to innovation and progressive change. Seizing the initiative and taking risks are necessary for learning and continuous improvement. But take this to extremes and you can create needless turmoil, confusion, and paranoia" (p. 99). I suggest that while taking chances is a characteristic of leadership, we should strive to communicate our ideas clearly and develop community and teamwork so that taking chances will provide willing followers—those who can even embrace your ideas as their own. Without followers, there can be no leaders.

- Be self-confident.

Strong leaders are confident as demonstrated in their speech and by their demeanor. Everything about them communicates self-assurance, yet they manage this without offending colleagues or being considered cocky or egocentric. Self-confidence based on accumulated knowledge and preparation can do much to inspire others to support the agenda of any good chairperson. It promotes trust and respect, both requisite for effective leadership.

Just as important is to help faculty members develop self-confidence. Over years of working with faculty members, I recognized that many of those labeled as "troubled" actually had low self-esteem. If faculty members lack self-confidence, they tend to avoid taking on tough challenges, and so are often seen as shirkers. You have the opportunity provide a wonderful gift to such people—by helping them believe in themselves. Leaders must help others gain self-confidence. You can do much to liberate others, and when you do, you will see that a higher level of performance is often the outcome.

We also need to remember that formal authority as a source of power has eroded, and by giving power to others, we make them feel stronger. They have more confidence, and likely will be more willing to support your actions.

- Be decisive.

Strong chairpersons can make difficult decisions because they trust their own judgments sufficiently. They don't postpone decisions that demand immediate action. Faculty members probably complain more about indecisiveness than any other administrative weakness. Indecisiveness undermines trust and respect. Thus, decisiveness is a behavior worth cultivating.

At times, though, decisiveness can erode a chairperson's popularity. Difficult decisions are bound to generate some disagreement. If a decision is unpopular with some faculty members, the chairperson may be faulted for the decision and any problems it may subsequently generate.

You, of course, must do what you believe is right, even at the risk of unpopularity. In the long run, if you are willing to make decisions, even unpopular ones, you will earn the respect of your colleagues. Most understand that you cannot please all faculty members all the time.

- Accept blame for failure and share credit for success.

Leaders accept blame when things go wrong; they are not finger pointers. Instead, they regroup and establish corrective plans. They go forward.

Just as important, strong leaders see no benefit in being alone in the spotlight when success wins praise and recognition from others. They know they could not have achieved their goals without help. They are quick to acknowledge those who have contributed—even in the smallest way—to the success. In the process they gain respect from their colleagues and inspire them to work even harder the next time tasks are assigned.

- Embrace change.

Change can be exciting, even intoxicating. It motivates leaders. Yet change without direction, or simply for its own sake, creates uncertainty and engenders little enthusiasm. You should consider change carefully, and you need some assurance that it will produce positive results.

Whenever you plan significant changes, you should discuss your ideas with all faculty members, especially those who tend to cherish the status quo. They need to understand that the changes are not going to destroy their daily lives.

The effective chairperson recognizes that change is a necessary component of growth and improvement, yet it does not come without generating anxiety. If appropriate care is taken to involve all faculty members in planning, the chances of success are increased considerably and the road to change is smoother.

- **Be sensitive and caring.**

Not all faculty members think alike. Recognizing that professional and personal philosophies separate faculty members, and that these differences surface when issues are confronted, you should allow differing views to be expressed without fear of retribution. Moreover, you need to carefully consider those different views. You might find reasons to modify your ideas when the suggestions of others clearly have merit. Any good chairperson knows he or she does not have all the answers. Kouzes and Posner (2003) write that

> Sensitivity to others is no trivial skill; rather, it is a truly precious human ability. But it isn't complex: it requires receptiveness to other people and a willingness to listen. It means being delicately aware of attitudes and feelings of others and the nuances of their communication. (p. 44)

I cannot emphasize enough the importance of listening. Giving your undivided attention to another person shows your respect for that person, and it allows you to get an idea of that person's needs and aspirations.

There are occasions when even the most reliable, even-tempered faculty members have a bad day. You must know when to tolerate behavior that at other times would not be acceptable. If you show sensitivity in these moments, faculty members are likely to see the chairperson as someone they can willingly work with.

As noted in Chapter 1, you should get to know something about the families of faculty members. Extend congratulations when they are due, and be there to console a faculty member when he or she suffers a personal or family setback. A well-timed note, a card of congratulation or condolence, or a bouquet of flowers can go a long way toward showing that you care about the well-being of faculty members and their families.

- ## Possess strong communication skills.

No matter how brilliant your plans are, you are not likely to succeed unless you can clearly communicate goals and expectations. Even if you are an honest, dedicated, and skilled leader, you will have difficulty getting others to follow your cause if you fail to make clear what it is you stand for and the hopes you have for the department.

Strong writing and speaking skills are essential to leadership. These qualities often separate those who succeed from those who fail. Having wonderful ideas isn't enough. Unless you have the power to persuade others and cause them to buy into your ideas, you stand alone. On the other hand, if you can persuasively communicate ideas and provide important insights and details, even the most skeptical faculty member will likely give the plan a chance.

Chapter 6 will explore this subject in more depth, but I do want to add here that face-to-face communication is preferable to virtually every other kind of communication.

- ## Provide ideas and be flexible.

Whenever you deal with problems, you should develop possible solutions. It is a weak leader who calls a meeting and introduces a problem without offering ways of dealing with it. By the same token, invite others to present possible solutions. You should remain open-minded as you listen to them. Rejecting ideas without fair consideration marks you as inflexible and does nothing to encourage others to provide ideas. What faculty members hear is, "I already know what I plan to do."

- ## Have a good work ethic.

You must set a good example by making effective use of time. The chairperson who comes to work late, wastes time in the office, and leaves early speaks volumes to his or her staff. This kind of behavior indicates a lack of commitment. It encourages others to be uncommitted and uncaring. If you expect others to give time and effort to produce excellence, you must serve as a role model. But you should not feel guilty when not working on academic matters since you should be involved in the world around you. As Kouzes and Posner (2003) note, "The very best leaders have numerous pursuits and interests—arts, literature, science, technology, entertainment, sports, politics, law, religion, friends, and family" (p. 101). The same statement applies to good faculty and staff members.

- **Be honest and fair.**

Being honest and forthright is not always easy. It is not pleasant to have to tell a faculty member that he or she is a weak teacher or that assigned duties are not being handled properly. Still, it must be done. If you learn how to evaluate faculty members fairly, honestly, and forthrightly, and if you are honest and fair in your dealings with others, you will have taken an essential step toward becoming the leader every department deserves.

Chairpersons who are not honest and fair in their dealings with others are bound to fail. If faculty members are suspicious of your motives and see you acting unfairly, trust and respect vanish.

- **Know when to spend your social and political capital.**

"There's a time and place for everything" is a truism of real pertinence when it comes to knowing when to spend your social and political capital. You need to decide whether the gain is worth the price you must pay. Most of us have limits on our social and political clout, and when it's spent, it's not easily replenished. Is the issue you are facing serious enough to compel you to tangle with your dean? Is the matter simply an irritation or are principles at stake? Good leaders know that just as there are times to stand up and fight, there also are times to swallow one's pride and let something pass.

It is generally believed that leadership traits are not innate, but are acquired. This view gives all of us hope. We can become leaders if we are willing to work at it. Trachtenberg (1992) summed it up this way: "Good leadership depends on the ability to tolerate anxiety, loneliness, and the threat of unpopularity" (p. 38).

Some suggest that a better way to view leadership is to revise our way of thinking about it. In their discussion of cultural and symbolic theories of leadership, Bensimon, Neumann, and Birnbaum (1989) assert that these theories suggest that the role of a leader may be more modest—less heroic—than is usually portrayed in education publications. The diffusion of authority and power in academe, not to mention the absence of clear and measurable outcomes, puts additional constraints on higher education leaders. Realistic managers will be less concerned with bold leadership and more concerned with making small improvements.

Kouzes and Posner (2003) make a powerful point when they write, "Leadership is not an affair of the head. Leadership is, after all, an affair of the heart" (p. 114). But what they write before that statement is, to me at least, even more powerful:

> Of all the things that sustain a leader over time, love is the most lasting. It's hard to imagine leaders on any college campus getting up day after day, and putting in the long hours and hard work it takes to get extraordinary things done, without having their hearts in it. This may just be the best-kept secret of successful leaders: If you love what you're doing, you will never have to work. Stay in love with leading, stay in love with the people who do the work, with the students, faculty, staff, and alumni that are transformed because of their time at your institution, with the scholarship, ideas, programs, and applications that emerge through and because of what you and so many others contribute. (p. 114)

Personality Assessment Instruments

Another way to understand leadership is through an examination of leadership styles. Because you may have behavioral qualities that show up in several different models, the purpose is not to pin a label on you, but rather to help you see where your strengths and weaknesses lie. Remember, too, that you need to reinvent yourself from time to time (Bennis, 2003).

The following are some inventories and instruments that can assist you to become more self-aware. I caution you, however, that even the best ones can only assist. The real work—the painful work, if you will—is up to you.

Implicit Association Test (IAT)

This is an interesting and profound way to look at the role that our unconscious associations play in our beliefs and behavior. As Gladwell (2005) writes, "One of the reasons that the IAT has become so popular in recent years as a research tool is that the effects it is measuring are not subtle" (p. 81). An electronic version of IAT is available at www.implicit.harvard .edu, and I strongly encourage all leaders to complete it. It may lead to some unsettling thoughts, but you need to remember that the IAT is much more than just an abstract measure of our attitudes. As Gladwell notes, "It's also a powerful predictor of how we act in certain kinds of spontaneous situations" (p. 85).

Minnesota Multiphasic Personality Inventory 2 (MMPI 2)

Originally designed to speed diagnosis and psychiatric treatment, its new scale (the MMPI 2) has uses that can benefit all of us. There are, for example, scales that show over-controlled hostility, anxiety, ego strength, repression, and so on. American psychologists have consistently ranked the MMPI 2 as one of the top two psychological instruments of all such instruments in use. It is one of the most researched tests as well, with more than 500 articles, books, and chapters published about it. It has both strengths and weaknesses, but used properly it is an invaluable tool. See www.psychpage.com/objective/mmpi2_overview.htm for more information about the MMPI 2.

Myers-Briggs Type Indicator (MBTI)

Consulting Psychologists Press, Inc. (CPPI) owns the MBTI, and terms it the most widely used personality inventory in history. My guess is that you have taken it more than once. CCPI offers a variety of instruments to be used in conjunction with MBTI, such as the Fundamental Interpersonal

Relations Orientation-Behavior, or FIRO-B, which can help you better understand your leadership style. For more information about the products offered by CPPI, visit www.mbti.com.

Thomas-Kilmann Conflict Mode Instrument (TKI)

The TKI provides a way to learn how different conflict-handling styles affect personal and group dynamics and how to select the most appropriate style for a given situation. TKI is a 30-item, self-scoring assessment. The owners claim that it's a key tool for managers, team leaders, and human resource experts to safely open a productive dialogue about conflict. The TKI toolkit includes an interpretive report, a workshop facilitator's guide and participant's booklet, a collection of card games, and a video that demonstrates how to use the different conflict-handling styles to effectively deal with clashes between coworkers, communication breakdowns, and power struggles. More information is available at www.cpp.com/products/tki/index.asp.

360-Degree Instruments

These are designed to help you learn how others perceive you. Diamond and Spuches (2002) point out that "research on the use and value of 360-degree feedback is increasing." (p. 83). However, they note that if not used well, or overused, this approach has the potential of interfering with teamwork and producing stress. Further, if the information gathered is not used, it may even be viewed as counterproductive and a waste of time. Visit www.shl.com/SHL/es/Products/Access_Competencies/360/to learn more.

Leadership Styles

The Internet is a good source for learning about the many instruments and inventories that will help you identify your leadership style. Leadership style refers to examining the manner and approach of providing direction, implementing plans, and motivating others. Several leadership styles are mentioned in current literature. While they go by different names, the three most common follow.

Authoritarian or Autocratic

Chairpersons who tell faculty members what should be done and how they should do it without getting advice from them display this style of leadership. While this is not a style I recommend, don't dismiss it as some do because they see it as yelling, using demeaning language, and leading by threats and abuse of power. Leaders who do that are being abusive and unprofessional, they are not leading. However, there may be times when this style of leadership is appropriate.

Participatory

The chairperson includes faculty members in the decision-making process (determining what to do and how to do it). However, as chairperson, you retain the final decision-making authority. This style is used most often: It shows faculty members that you respect them, and in turn, you earn their trust.

Laissez-Faire

In this style, the chairperson allows faculty members to make decisions. However, the chairperson is still responsible for the decisions. This is used when faculty members are able to analyze the situation and determine what needs to be done and how to do it. As a chairperson, you can use this style when you must delegate authority. Indeed, some refer to this leadership style as delegative.

We know that leadership styles cannot be fully explained by behavioral models. The situation in which the group is operating also determines the style of leadership adopted. Several models exist which attempt to understand the relationship between style and situation, four of which are described here.

Fiedler's Contingency Model

Fiedler's model assumes that group performance depends on the following:

- Leadership style, described in terms of task motivation and relationship motivation

- Situational favorableness, determined by three factors:
  1) The degree to which a leader is accepted and supported by the group members
  2) Task structure: The extent to which the task is structured and defined, with clear goals and procedures
  3) Position power: The ability of a leader to control subordinates through reward and punishment

High levels of these three factors give the most favorable situation, low levels, the least favorable. Relationship-motivated leaders are most effective in moderately favorable situations. Task-motivated leaders are most effective at either end of the scale. Fiedler suggests that it may be easier for some leaders to change the situation to achieve effectiveness, rather than change their leadership style.

Theory of Leadership

Bass's (1990a, 1990b) theory of leadership states that there are three basic ways to explain how people become leaders. The first two explain the leadership development for a small number of people. These theories are:

- *Trait theory.* Some personality traits may lead people naturally into leadership roles.
- *Great events theory.* A crisis or important event may cause a person to rise to the occasion, which brings out extraordinary leadership qualities in an ordinary person.
- *Transformational leadership theory.* People can choose to become leaders and can learn leadership skills. It is the most widely accepted theory today and the premise on which this book is based.

Hersey-Blanchard Situational Theory

This theory suggests that leadership style should be matched to the maturity of the subordinates. Maturity is assessed in relation to a specific task and has two parts:

- *Psychological maturity*. Self-confidence and the ability and readiness to accept responsibility.
- *Job maturity*. Relevant skills and technical knowledge.

As the subordinate maturity increases, leadership should be more relationship motivated than task motivated. Leadership can consist of delegating to subordinates, participating with subordinates, selling ideas to subordinates, and telling subordinates what to do.

Path-Goal Theory

While the Path-Goal Theory has a contingency perspective, it is different from Fiedler's Contingent Theory in its focus. The Path-Goal Theory focuses on the situation and leader behavior rather than leader personality traits. It is closely related to the Expectancy Theory of Motivation, according to which the effort a person is willing to put forth is influenced by two factors—expectancy and valence. Expectancy is the degree to which a person expects that his or her behavior will lead to certain outcomes. Valence is how attractive these outcomes are to that person.

Those who support this theory believe that a leader can change a subordinate's expectancy by clarifying the paths between the subordinate's action and the outcome, which is the goal the employee wants to achieve. Whether a leader's behavior can do so effectively also depends on situational factors.

Vroom-Yetton Leadership Model

This model suggests the selection of a leadership style for making a decision. There are five decision-making styles:

- *Autocratic 1*. The problem is solved using information already available.
- *Autocratic 2*. Additional information is obtained from the group before the leader makes a decision.
- *Consultative 1*. The leader discusses the problem with subordinates individually, before making a decision.
- *Consultative 2*. The problem is discussed with the group before deciding.
- *Group 2*. The group decides on a problem, with the leader simply acting as chairperson.

The style is chosen by the consideration of seven questions, which form a decision tree. For more information on this model, see Vroom and Yetton (1973).

Each of these four theories has limited validity, though they are still widely used. Table 3.1 provides a useful way to look at different styles of leadership and motivation.

Table 3.1 Motivation and Leadership Styles

Leadership Style	Motivation Type	Motivation Is Based On	Personality Type	Efficiency
▪ Limited supervision ▪ Worker with decision-making responsibility	▪ Self-motivated ▪ Team motivated	Creativity	▪ Leader of ideas or people ▪ Independent ▪ Achiever ▪ Thrives on change	High
Mixed styles	▪ Goal motivated ▪ Reward motivated ▪ Recognition motivated	▪ Opportunity ▪ Materialism ▪ Social status	Personality type and efficiency depend on leader's skill and/or the work environment he's created	
High level of supervision Command and control	▪ Peer motivated ▪ Authority motivated ▪ Threat, fear motivated	▪ To be like others ▪ Follows policy ▪ Reacts to force	▪ Status quo ▪ Dependency ▪ Resist change	Low

Note. From www.motivation-tools.com. Used with permission of Robert Webb.

No matter how we choose to think about leadership—even if we are content to forgo thoughts of bold leadership in favor of making small improvements—decisions must be made. And you must call on your best leadership skills to make them. The qualities of leadership discussed in this chapter provide a framework on which to build. Undoubtedly there are other qualities that mark leadership. If you are willing to assess your strengths and weaknesses realistically, you can take advantage of those that are strong, then work to correct your deficiencies.

Resources

Web Sites

Advancing Women in Business and Careers
www.advancingwomen.com

Business.com
www.business.com

Business Know-How
http://businessknowhow.com

Leader to Leader Institute
www.pfdf.org

Leadership Styles
www.nwlink.com/~donclark/leader/leadstl.html

Motivation in the Workplace
www.motivation-tools.com/workplace/index.htm

Secrets of Success
www.secretsofsuccess.com/leadership

University of California Leadership Institute
www.ucop.edu/ucli/resources_books.html

Books

Bennis, W. G., & Thomas, R. J. (2002). *Geeks and geezers: How era, values, and defining moments shape leaders.* Boston, MA: Harvard Business School Press.

Bryant, P. T. (2005). *Confessions of an habitual administrator: An academic survival manual.* Bolton, MA: Anker.

Buckingham, M., & Coffman, C. (1999). *First, break all the rules: What the world's greatest managers do differently*. New York, NY: Simon & Schuster.

Gmelch, W. H., & Miskin, V. (2004). *Chairing an academic department*. Madison, WI: Atwood.

Johnson, M. J., Hanna, D. E., & Olcott, D., Jr. (Eds.). (2003). *Bridging the gap: Leadership, technology, and organizational change for university deans and chairpersons*. Madison, WI: Atwood.

Kouzes, J. M., & Posner, B. Z. (1999). *The leadership challenge planner: An action guide to achieving your personal best*. San Francisco, CA: Jossey-Bass.

References

Badaracco, J. L., Jr. (2002). *Leading quietly: An unorthodox guide to doing the right thing*. Boston, MA: Harvard Business School Press.

Bass, B. M. (1990a). *Bass and Stogdill's handbook of leadership: Theory, research, and managerial applications* (3rd ed.). New York, NY: The Free Press.

Bass, B. M. (1990b, Winter). From transactional to transformational leadership: Learning to share the vision. *Organizational Dynamics, 18*(3), 19–31.

Bennis, W. (2003). *On becoming a leader* (Rev. and expanded ed.). Cambridge, MA: Perseus.

Bensimon, E. M., Neumann, A., & Birnbaum, R. (1989). *Making sense of administrative leadership: The "L" word in higher education*. San Francisco, CA: Jossey-Bass.

Burns, J. M. (1978). *Leadership*. New York, NY: Harper & Row.

Cameron, K. S., & Ulrich, D. O. (1986). Transformational leadership in colleges and universities. In J. C. Smart (Ed.), *Higher education: Handbook of theory and research, Volume II* (pp. 1–42). New York, NY: Agathon Press.

Diamond, R. M., & Spuches, C. M. (2002). Building on style for more effective relationships and results. In R. M. Diamond (Ed.), *A field guide to academic leadership* (pp. 75–86). San Francisco, CA: Jossey-Bass.

Dill, D. D., & Fullagar, P. K. (1987). Theories of leadership and administrative style. In M. W. Peterson & L. A. Mets (Eds.), *Key resources on higher education governance, management, and leadership: A guide to the literature* (pp. 390–411). San Francisco, CA: Jossey-Bass.

Gladwell, M. (2005). *Blink: The power of thinking without thinking.* New York, NY: Little, Brown and Company.

Kouzes, J. M., & Posner, B. Z. (2003). *The Jossey-Bass academic administrator's guide to exemplary leadership.* San Francisco, CA: Jossey-Bass.

Luthans, F. (1992). *Organizational behavior* (6th ed.). New York, NY: McGraw-Hill.

Maxcy, S. J. (1991). *Educational leadership: A critical pragmatic perspective.* New York, NY: Bergin & Garvey.

McKenna, P. J., & Maister, D. H. (2002). *First among equals: How to manage a group of professionals.* New York, NY: The Free Press.

Seagren, A. T., Creswell, J. W., & Wheeler, D. W. (1993). *The department chair: New roles, responsibilities, and challenges.* Washington, DC: The George Washington University, Graduate School of Education and Human Development.

Trachtenberg, S. J. (1988). The apprenticeship approach to leadership. In J. L. Fisher & M. W. Tack (Eds.), *New directions on teaching and learning: No. 61. Leaders on leadership: The college presidency* (pp. 37–41). San Francisco, CA: Jossey-Bass.

Vroom, V. H., & Yetton, P. W. (1973). *Leadership and decision-making.* Pittsburgh, PA: University of Pittsburgh Press.

Yukl, G. A. (1989). *Leadership in organizations* (2nd ed.). Englewood Cliffs, NJ: Prentice Hall.

4

Duties and Responsibilities
of Chairpersons

*Leaders do what they say they will do. Their actions are consistent
with their words.*

As a department chairperson, you have a wide variety of duties and
responsibilities. On any given day you may be teaching a class, preparing
annual reports, putting together next semester's schedule, counseling a
faculty member, conducting a faculty meeting, or developing a plan for
obtaining outside funding. While the time you must give to managing
your department depends partly on the size and nature of the department,
the responsibilities are nonetheless time consuming.

The roles and expectations of chairpersons vary from institution to
institution and often are not well defined. We can even see different interpretations of what a chairperson is and what he or she is responsible for
from department to department on the same campus. One explanation
for this is that most universities have no written job description for department chairpersons. This permits chairpersons themselves to define their
role in accordance with

- Their own comfort level
- Wishes of the faculty in the department
- How their predecessors defined the job
- How some of the campus's more seasoned chairpersons interpret their
  roles
- How their dean defines the position
- A combination of all the above

Chairpersons have a long list of responsibilities, and in order to accomplish them they assume different roles. Tucker (1993) lists 28 roles that chairpersons assume at one time or another. No matter how long the list, it remains clear that the chairperson's role is "ambiguous, unclear in authority, and difficult to classify as faculty or administrator" (Seagren, Creswell, & Wheeler, 1993, p. iii).

Those who have served as chairpersons know that to be "first among equals" means managing conflict resolution, building community and teamwork, mentoring faculty, overseeing curricular changes, providing support for faculty, creating a vision that faculty can embrace, continuing one's own scholarship, encouraging faculty to engage in public service and scholarship, serving as a role model, defining faculty needs, managing the budget—and the list goes on.

If we conclude that chairpersons in the past had demanding, critical jobs, then it seems fair to say that today's chairperson is burdened in ways not imagined by his or her predecessors. Today's department chairperson must deal with ever-increasing demands for public accountability at a time when resources are declining. Thus, the chairperson of today must be an astute manager. Seagren et al. (1993) point out that the importance of the chairperson as manager is expected to increase with fewer resources. However, managing is not enough. Exceptional leadership skills are required if we are going to meet the challenges we can expect in the decades ahead. Department chairpersons will have to provide the way for their faculties to discover new models of teaching and learning, and for helping faculty members to learn new skills. If universities are to change as profoundly as many people believe they must, then the role of a chairperson as a leader becomes even more critical.

What are some of the important roles, responsibilities, and challenges that you will assume as a chairperson?

Most importantly, you must serve as the spokesperson for the interests and the welfare of the entire department. Your role is one of communicator and facilitator. You must learn to recognize the strengths and weaknesses of the department and its faculty, and seek to improve strengths and correct weaknesses. You must assist and counsel faculty members with a sense of fairness, open-mindedness, and concern. As spokesperson for the interests and the welfare of the entire department, you have a responsibility to see that your department gets its fair share of resources and that members are not shortchanged when salary increases, promotions, sabbaticals, faculty development grants, and other benefits are made available.

If you are aggressive in fulfilling this role, you may at times cause some chairpersons to resent or envy you. This is certainly true if you succeed in securing a large share of university resources. Still, you need to be fairly aggressive in your role as spokesperson for the interests and the welfare of your department. It's your job, and if other chairpersons are equally aggressive, all things tend to balance out in a way that should not be seen as a lack of collegiality. Note that I said *fairly* aggressive: You must learn how to be persistent without being unpleasant. Learning how to be aggressive and still be liked and respected calls for a certain amount of finesse and the fine-tuning of your interpersonal skills.

Orchestrating Change and Planning for the Future

Strong interpersonal skills are needed to bring about change. The time has passed when chairpersons could serve simply as caretakers; they must now be agents of change. Indeed, those who study change believe that in the past, departments—even universities—were often rewarded for not taking risks. They feel, as well, that the modern department or university that does not take risks will suffer, and some may even perish.

As the leader of the department, you will be expected to keep the department current and to light the way for the future, a responsibility that will challenge all your leadership skills. You will find some faculty members who will resist even the slightest change. All too often these are senior members who wield a lot of influence. Another problem is the need to identify what the future holds, even though in today's fast-paced world it is difficult enough to say confidently where we are at present.

Here are some suggestions for assessing how the future may affect your department.

- Keep up with what's happening in your discipline by reading books and journal articles and attending conferences.
- Read what some of the best futurists are writing. There are hundreds of web sites that deal with futurism. I can attest to one thing: Some of what is written about higher education is eye-opening.
- Stay in touch with those outside the university who employ your graduates. When I served as chairperson and dean, I regularly conducted focus groups comprised of regional leaders to learn about changes they expected and how they might affect disciplines within the department or college under my responsibility. I always took an associate with me who would take extensive notes so that we could analyze and share the information with all faculty members.
- Stay in touch with your alumni to learn as much as you can about what they learned—and didn't learn—in school that they regularly use on their job.

Preparing a Mission Statement

One important responsibility you have as a department chairperson is that of planning, and an essential first step in that process is developing a mission statement and assessing core values. Not enough is written about the necessity of an intelligently conceived and well-written mission statement. This statement should clearly explain a department's reason for being. It should answer the questions "Where are we going?" and "How are we going to get there?" A mission statement shows where you intend to go by indicating your core values.

A good leader can lead without a mission statement, but he or she can lead even better with one that is pertinent and clear. During the troubled times of the *Saturday Evening Post*—the late 1950s and early 1960s—the editor Robert Fuoss explained that he saw editing the *Post* as something like leading troops into battle without knowing why we're at war. He proclaimed, "We had no reason for existence" (personal communication,

December 20, 1968). Some departments appear to be groping for direction just as did the *Post* under Fuoss. As a department chairperson you can remedy this situation by working with faculty members to develop a mission statement to assess the department's core values. Although it is not important that your statement be a sophisticated document, it should be in line with the mission of your university, straightforward, and easy to understand. Once your dean has approved it, you must communicate its message at every available opportunity, for example, in your alumni newsletter and in letters to potential donors.

Not long ago I visited a school where the mission statement was printed on a large banner that students and faculty had signed to show their support for it. It gave force to what the department was trying to achieve, and it appeared to bolster morale as well.

Long-Range Planning

It is crucial that your efforts to achieve needed change include long-range planning. Here are some key questions to address.

- What are enrollment projections for the next five years? Given departmental resources, should we expand or curtail our efforts to recruit? Should we limit enrollment?
- What resources are needed to meet anticipated changes? Will these resources be available? If university funding is inadequate, can outside funding be obtained?
- Are our current facilities adequate to meet changing needs?
- What kind of faculty additions will we need in the next decade? Is the makeup of the current faculty appropriate?
- What will the educational needs of students be in coming years? What curricular changes should be made?
- What are the department's equipment needs in the coming years?
- Are new instructional methods necessary?
- If the department has an accrediting agency, are new standards anticipated? If so, how can they be met?
- Do planned changes fit with the institution's mission?

- Are planned changes of such magnitude that they require approval by the academic planning committee and other university bodies before implementation?

Questions of this nature should be a part of any long-range planning. One does not have to be a futurist to respond to them, although precise answers may not be easily found. Indeed, it might be necessary to involve the institution's research center to get information to frame well-reasoned answers. Obviously, if you have kept abreast of your discipline and are current with the broader issues of higher education, you will find it easier to answer these questions and plan ahead. It might be prudent to appoint a departmental planning committee and charge its members with developing plans about where the department is going and how it should get there.

Much has been written about academic strategic planning. While the concept is fairly simple, to most chairpersons the idea is fuzzy. For the department, the concept is related to how the department achieves its mission and the resources it will need to carry out that mission. Unless you have some control over the allocation of resources, strategic planning can become a waste of time. Consequently, the process should not be a lengthy one with a lot of information gathering. The reason for this is simple: Strategic planning should be driven by ideas, not by data and paper. The process should result in common understandings, shared expectations, and a shared sense of direction. Thus, if you write a plan, it should be about how to implement these understandings of the department's direction. Note that a strategic planning document is always incomplete, always in need of revision.

Obtaining and Allocating Funds

You are responsible for obtaining funds and determining how the funds are allocated and spent. You must determine the cost of operating your department to carry out its mission. In this light, you also must be aware of changes in your department's mission and anticipate costs associated with any changes. As discussed in Chapter 17, you must understand your university's budget process and know how your department funding level is determined. You also need to understand how to plan a budget and develop priorities for spending.

A growing number of chairpersons are expected to engage in fundraising as more and more public universities turn to the private sector to supplement their budgets. Chapter 17 provides information to help your efforts as a fundraiser.

You should consult with all department faculty members to determine funding needs. You must assume responsibility for providing equipment and supplies needed for instruction and academic activities. Moreover, you must bear responsibility for seeing that each faculty member has sufficient funds to fulfill his or her research and service responsibilities.

Caring for the Curriculum

Managing the curriculum is another important responsibility. You should evaluate the curriculum regularly to see how well all courses support the overall educational objectives (see Chapter 15). You need to stay current with changes within your discipline and those of your department if more than one discipline is represented, maintain professional contacts, and keep abreast of literature—including those that affect higher education in general. As a corollary, you need to see that assessment programs are in place to determine whether students are getting what they should from the educational programs of the department (see Chapter 27). Likewise, you should ensure that all faculty members remain aware of current advances and practices in their fields.

Supporting Research and Development Activities

Encouraging faculty members to become involved in research and faculty development is another of your important responsibilities. This is especially challenging when faculty appear to have no real interest in pursuing such activities. They always can provide reasons (note I did not say excuses) for not doing research. Heavy teaching responsibilities can be a legitimate reason for limited research activity. Moreover, if faculty members spend a lot of time advising students and working with them out of class, if they sponsor student organizations and serve on committees, and if they are active in the community, they may not have appreciable time for research.

Some faculty seem to get involved in research despite obstacles, however. For this they deserve appreciation and should be encouraged to apply for faculty development grants offered by the university, research grants through the graduate school, or the option to work with the staff of the research and development center to seek other grants.

It is important for you to set a tone that emphasizes the importance of research and faculty development. Faculty meetings should include discussion of what might be done to support these efforts through rearrangement of teaching, advising, and activity sponsorship assignments. Indeed, it might be possible to give faculty members released time on some kind of rotation basis. If this can be arranged, accountability must follow; those who are given released time must show that they are using it on worthwhile projects.

Bland, Weber-Main, Lund, and Finstad (2005) make an important point about how research enriches teaching.

> For decades, the creation of knowledge through research has been an integral, valued part of postsecondary education. Faculty in all disciplines are eager to put their hypotheses to the test, to answer some of society's most pressing questions, and to try out their most inspired, creative ideas. For many faculty, this stimulating process of inquiry and discovery is precisely what drew them to their profession. It is also what informs, enriches, and keeps current their teaching. In short, it helps satisfy and sustain them over their long careers as academicians. (p. xii)

Working With Students

While much of what has been said up to this point has focused on faculty-related matters, the importance of your relationships with and responsibilities to students should not be overlooked. Certainly it is necessary to get to know students and to work closely with them. You need to know how students feel about their coursework, faculty, department-sponsored activities, and the department in general. Students can be especially helpful on many matters. They can help plan and implement student recruitment efforts, for example, and help evaluate the effectiveness of student advising. Moreover, most are eager to contribute. If you do not take advantage of student participation in department affairs, you are missing a promising opportunity.

One method of involving students is to create a student advisory committee that can be assigned a number of important tasks: Members can assist with administering student evaluations of the department; individuals can serve on faculty search committees; some can meet with candidates for faculty positions. The committee can also serve as a link between department faculty members and the general student body. Students who have complaints or concerns can be invited to bring them before the student advisory committee; some will share such matters with other students when they are reluctant to discuss them with the chairperson or faculty members.

There are many ways to form a student advisory committee. One example is found in the journalism programs that I have directed. There the presidents and vice presidents of each of the three professional student groups—the Society of Professional Journalists, the Advertising Club, and the Public Relations Student Society of America—along with an elected graduate student, comprised the Journalism Student Advisory Council.

Mentoring Faculty and Serving as a Role Model

The first-time college teacher should not be left alone to devise his or her approach to teaching. Some department chairpersons are guilty of doing little more than providing new faculty members with old course syllabi, telling them what courses they will teach, and pointing them in the direction of the classroom. You should do whatever you can to make new faculty members feel welcome; you also might assign a veteran faculty member to mentor a first-time college teacher. In this role, the veteran professor would meet regularly with the newcomer to discuss teaching methods, grading, handling absences, or any number of other problems or concerns. This dialogue should help orient new faculty members and ease any apprehensions.

You should serve as a role model for young teachers, making clear that they can come to you with questions or for advice. There undoubtedly will be times when they need to talk to someone about a problem when their assigned mentor is unavailable. New faculty should also learn from the chairperson what is expected of them for promotion and tenure. For example, what level of research is expected, or how much time they should devote to office hours. Finally, they also need to be told something of the history of the department, what its traditions and goals are, and how it fits into the structure of the college and university.

When I served as dean, I held a monthly meeting for all new faculty members, including those who were in their second year. Faculty members and administrators were invited to talk about the university's history and its cultural values, service possibilities, research grant availability, and a host of other matters—tenure and promotion issues, performance evaluations, on-campus recreation availability, and so on. I also emphasized the need for faculty to devote time to their families and not feel they always had to be working. This is important. After all, when faculty members are not teaching, they need to be preparing for their classes, reading, giving time to students, providing service, engaging in research, writing grant proposals—the list goes on and on. Chairpersons should help young faculty members see that there is a need to spend time with family, to exercise, and not feel guilty when they are involved in pleasurable pursuits outside of work. There are those outside the academy who believe that faculty members don't earn their salaries. During my long association with faculty members at several different universities, I found that by and large faculty members are hardworking and fiercely dedicated to students, service, and scholarship. All administrators—including chairpersons—need to help the public understand the time faculty give to their jobs and the important role they play in helping students have a better life.

Making the Department a Pleasant Workplace

Promoting faculty morale is another of your responsibilities (see Chapter 11). You need to let faculty members know when they have done a job well. It does not take much time to write a short letter showing appreciation for a job well done. Likewise, a note or a card sent to a faculty member who is ill or dealing with personal adversity means a lot.

You should make a habit of meeting regularly with faculty members to ask how they are doing, find out what they need, and what concerns they have. Faculty generally like to talk about their work, and it boosts their morale when the chairperson asks occasionally, "Tell me how your classes are going."

Morale can become a problem if you fail to respond quickly and fairly to faculty conflicts. Honest differences of professional opinion always exist, and when differing viewpoints are expressed with civility they can be healthy. Debate causes faculty members to think and respond to ideas. Yet when faculty see these differences as personal attacks, conflict results. You often can deal effectively with such problems by getting the involved faculty members together to talk and to see if differences can be resolved. Participants must understand the importance of avoiding personalization of professional differences, of course. Moreover, chairpersons should encourage dialogue rather than debate (Tannen, 1998).

The department can be a pleasant place if you work to foster a feeling of participatory membership. Reference to "the history family," "the journalism family," or "the marketing family" can be an outward sign of an attitude that fosters togetherness—if it is really meant. Sponsoring department activities that bring faculty, staff, and students together also can be meaningful. For example, many departments regularly sponsor picnics, holiday parties, and an end-of-year awards banquet. Each activity does much to bring faculty, staff, and students together; students develop warm feelings toward the department and members of the faculty and staff, and most become supportive alumni. Symbolic team building is something chairpersons generally don't do enough of because, as one outstanding chairperson said to me recently, we fear that "our efforts will be ridiculed by jaded academics or will be viewed as too transparent." These techniques work, however.

As we can see, departmental chairpersons have many responsibilities. Often these are ill defined and murky. Many of the specific duties required of them—such as faculty evaluations, budgets, purchasing, and faculty recruitment—are dealt with at length elsewhere in this book.

Signs of a Troubled Department

Over the years, I've observed that unhealthy departments have tended to be chaired by individuals who simply were drifting. Goals generally had not been clearly communicated, and faculty members often worked to enhance their professional portfolios at the expense of departmental objectives. A culture of community and teamwork was missing, and instead faculty bickering and fighting were common.

I have also observed department chairs who were not willing to assess faculty fairly and honestly. The resources of the department went to those who surrounded and vocally supported the chairperson. Dialogue was discouraged—especially if it concerned ways to improve the department. The chairperson tended to be feared. He or she wanted to control faculty members and chose to do so by refusing to share information. Trust in such a chairperson is noticeably absent, and it fuels gossip. Indeed, the department is filled with rumor. Unfortunately, students often are caught up in this. As a dean, I saw a department split into many factions because of bickering among faculty. Students felt forced to take sides. It's bad enough when disputes create tension among faculty members, but when students become involved, someone needs to step up and provide leadership.

The weakest chairpersons I've known do not have a strong inner voice, which may be the reason they seem to be drifting. I have asked some to tell me whom they had patterned their leadership behavior after, only to get a quizzical look—one that said, "What are you talking about?" They are not able to inspire others because they don't seem to understand the very nature of inspiration. They don't reveal their character—thus, don't have a chance to earn trust. Most of these weak chairpersons are unable to identify with the plight of others; they don't have empathy. Many are defensive and will not tolerate anyone who questions them. Finally, weak chairpersons have not done the hard work needed to gain self-knowledge.

We have examined many of the critical skills chairpersons need, as well as some of their duties and responsibilities. The following provides a summary of the duties and responsibilities of departmental chairpersons.

Roles and Responsibilities of Department Chairpersons

Department chairpersons serve as the chief administrative officer of the department, and are responsible for representing the department to the university administration, to the dean of the college, and to the department's faculty and students. The position of the department chairperson is integral to the university's central mission: the education of its students.

To Faculty

Department chairpersons report directly to their academic dean and are responsible for

- Establishing and implementing procedures within university guidelines for the recruitment of new faculty
- Counseling and guiding faculty; encouraging outstanding teaching, research, and other professional activities; organizing faculty meetings and departmental committees to further the business of the department
- Enforcing faculty responsibilities
- Promoting faculty development, including encouraging faculty members to attend professional conferences, join professional organizations, travel, and so on
- Protecting faculty rights, including recommendations on personnel matters such as leaves of absence, sabbatical leaves, research grants, and the like

- Periodic appraisal for recommending reappointment, tenure, promotion, and salary adjustments
- Fostering productive, interpersonal, professional relationships among department faculty

To Students

- Ensuring that proper curricular and career advice is available to all students majoring and/or taking courses in the department
- Monitoring student-department scholarships and prizes, and, within university procedures, responding to student grievances and grade appeals
- Coordinating the active recruitment of undergraduate and graduate students

To Curriculum and Programs

- Establishing department mission statements and objectives within those of the university and periodically reviewing the department's progress in achieving them
- Establishing department policies in cooperation with faculty related to curriculum content and changes, instructional standards, evaluation methods, textbooks, and course syllabi
- Planning and presenting course schedules
- Appointing faculty members to cocurricular responsibilities and recommending released time to the dean

To Budget and Instructional Resources

- Reporting to the dean for fiscal management of departmental accounts
- Managing departmental facilities and instructional resources
- Recommending faculty and staff salaries to the dean within the limits imposed by the respective salary schedules
- Preparing, presenting, receiving, and administering the departmental budgets, which include the following:
  - Annual operating and capital equipment budget
  - Library appropriation

- ◆ Allocating the resources of the department so that institutional, research, administrative, and travel needs can be met equitably
  - ◆ Fostering extramural support for and helping staff members apply for such assistance, which may come from federal and private agencies; business, industry, and professional groups; alumni and friends
- Handling responsibility for departmental liaison with university offices dealing with particular fiscal activities such as the dean's office (for budgets, travel, and extramural funding) and business offices (for activities relevant to purchasing, personnel, and accounting)
- Planning for long-range financing for special programs and activities
- Writing and reviewing funding proposals in cooperation with the department faculty and the appropriate academic support areas; administration and evaluation of the proposal and/or projects as the department's chief administrator
- Ensuring that all budgetary operations conform to institutional and governing board guidelines and policies

To External Relations

- Conveying university and college policies, procedures, and actions to the department
- Representing the department in the college and university and with off-campus organizations
- Presenting departmental policies, procedures, and actions to the students

To Office Management

- Administering departmental facilities; hiring, supervising, and evaluating department staff; and establishing the department's office procedures

To Personal Professional Performance

- Providing professional leadership and example in the department
- Maintaining and demonstrating competence in teaching, research, and professional activities including participation in professional

associations and community service in accordance with university-mandated standards

Miscellaneous

- Carrying out other duties as assigned by the dean

You have an important role to play in the college and university. If you perform it well, you will contribute significantly to smooth operations. You can make a difference in the lives of students, faculty, and staff members. And while the financial rewards admittedly are not what they should be, your service and dedication are generally valued. Your effective efforts and talent do not go unnoticed; few would dispute one person's observation that an institution can run for a long time with an inept chief executive, but not long at all with inept department leaders.

Resources

Albright, M., & Carr, C. (1997). *101 biggest mistakes managers make and how to avoid them.* Paramus, NJ: Prentice Hall.

Badaracco, J. L., Jr. (2002). *Leading quietly: An unorthodox guide to doing the right thing.* Boston, MA: Harvard Business School Press.

Bensimon, E. M., Ward, K., & Sanders, K. (2000). *The department chair's role in developing new faculty into teachers and scholars.* Bolton, MA: Anker.

Caroselli, M. (2000). *Leadership skills for managers.* New York, NY: McGraw-Hill.

Jenkins, W. A., & Oliver, R. W. (1997). *The eagle and the monk: Seven principles of successful change.* Norwalk, CT: Gates & Bridges.

Kouzes, J. M., & Posner, B. Z. (2003). *The Jossey-Bass academic administrator's guide to exemplary leadership.* San Francisco, CA: Jossey-Bass.

Seldin, P., & Higgerson, M. L. (2002). *The administrative portfolio: A practical guide to improved administrative performance and personnel decisions.* Bolton, MA: Anker.

Sherman, V. C. (1987). *From losers to winners: How to manage problem employees... and what to do if you can't* (Rev. ed.). New York, NY: American Management Association.

Thornton, P. B. (2001). *Be the leader: Make the difference.* Irvine, CA: Griffin.

References

Bland, C. J., Weber-Main, A. M., Lund, S. M., & Finstad, D. A. (2005). *The research-productive department: Strategies from departments that excel.* Bolton, MA: Anker.

Seagren, A. T., Creswell, J. W., & Wheeler, D. W. (1993). *The department chair: New roles, responsibilities, and challenges.* Washington, DC: The George Washington University, Graduate School of Education and Human Development.

Tannen, D. (1998). *The argument culture: Moving from debate to dialogue.* New York, NY: Random House.

Tucker, A. (1993). *Chairing the academic department: Leadership among peers.* Phoenix, AZ: American Council on Education/Oryx Press.

5

Timesaving Tips for Effective Chairpersons

We quickly discover how many of the tools that should make our lives easier can make them more complicated and require more of our time, not less.

In their book *First Among Equals*, McKenna and Maister (2002) provide a long list of activities that leaders must supervise, and it quickly becomes apparent that each is a time consumer. Indeed, it is often impossible to find the time to do them all, which means that we must be selective while managing our time efficiently, and most importantly, managing ourselves wisely.

At the outset, let me confess that I've found few secrets to saving time. We know there are many tools at our disposal, especially now that we live in an electronic age. However, we quickly discover that many of the tools that should make our lives easier can make them more complicated and sometimes even require more of our time, not less. When I was a dean, I would go to work early, but I vowed never to read any email messages before 9:30; I knew there would be literally hundreds of them and I did not want to be distracted from working with faculty. When the time came to read them, I was especially selective in the emails I opened and those I chose to answer. Spending hours answering email messages was not how I defined my role since I felt there were many more imperative matters to handle.

Spending time with faculty is especially important for chairpersons. It costs time, but it's time that must be made. I like the words of Deepak Chopra (1994):

> We have stopped for a moment to encounter each other, to meet, to love, to share. It is a precious moment, but it is transient. It is

a little parenthesis in eternity. If we share with caring, lightheart-edness, and love, we will create abundance and joy for each other. And then the moment will have been worthwhile. (p. 111)

As a chairperson, you must make your moments worthwhile.

There is no short answer to the question "How do I do everything that I feel I must?" I recall the words of Ben Bissell, a psychologist and consultant, when he reminded me that whenever a faculty member asks for five minutes and I don't have that much time to give, I should be honest and say some-thing like, "Don, I am working on an important report. Therefore, I only have about two minutes, but they are all yours." Hunsaker and Alessandra (1980) seem to reinforce this in their book *The Art of Managing People*.

Because our use of time is such an expressive language, being aware of its meanings can facilitate our communications. This is especially true for managers because of the tendencies of subor-dinates to watch intensely for nonverbal feedback. Being accu-rate and openly stating reasons for our use of time can go a long way in avoiding misunderstandings and building more trusting and productive relationships. (p. 200)

No one but you can manage your time, and the classic rules of time management do not work for everyone. It is interesting how impatient we have become with speed, or the lack thereof. I am used to my computer giving me information in a nanosecond, and when it takes longer I become frustrated. Remember that a nanosecond is one billionth of a second, and many computers today perform operations in one trillionth of a second. Think about this for a minute—or perhaps a nanosecond: We are so con-sumed with speed that many of us cannot relax. There is something wrong when that applies to you—or me.

To be effective, you must be well organized and use your time wisely. Although I have read books and been to conferences and workshops designed to help me save time and to become better organized, only a few of the ideas presented could be incorporated into my way of doing things.

Finally, I sat down and tried to determine what I could do, considering my own personality, to use time more wisely. A number of ideas occurred to me, and I now use them effectively enough to feel comfortable passing them on to you. If they don't work for you, you might come up with your own list—as I did. Moreover, you will discover as I did that computers and other timesaving devices won't change your bad habits, although they can add efficiency to your normal routine.

- **Make a to-do list every day, and follow it.**

Perhaps your memory is better than mine, but I find myself forgetting to do something unless it's written down. I am satisfied with merely typing "Things To Do" at the top of a page and then listing those things that I need to get done.

- **Establish goals.**

If you set both short- and long-term goals, you almost always will have something to do. After your desk is cleared and you've finished with the projects on your to-do list, you can set out to fulfill your goals. Establishing goals will help give your life direction.

- **Handle all paper as few times as possible.**

Once is ideal. Until I adopted this as a part of my behavior, I tended to keep stacks of paper that I went through several times a day. When I opened mail, I immediately took care of those that required very little of me. I put into an "Action" folder those messages that required more time.

Hemphill (1997) has developed a paper management system that I found workable. She says that every item should be put ". . . into one of seven places: 1) 'To Sort' Tray, 2) Wastebasket, 3) Calendar, 4) 'To Do' List, 5) Rolodex/Phone Book, 6) Action File, 7) Reference File" (p. 26).

- **Keep a log of how you use your time.**

By logging, you can see where the time has gone and how it was spent. By studying how your time was used over a period of a few weeks, you can find ways to manage your time better. Table 5.1 is one example of a work log. (See Cook, 1999, for another example of a work log as well as ideas on tracking the use of your time, particularly pages 24–29.)

Table 5.2. Work Log

Date	Name	Task	Interruptions	Phone Calls	Due	Completed

- Keep your desk organized.

Most who work in the field of time management advocate that well-organized desks help save and manage time (e.g., Cook, 1999).

- Delegate responsibility.

I felt that I had to do everything. I suspect it was my own insecurity that caused me to be that way, but I had to learn to give work to others. Make yourself turn some chores loose. Give up some of the minor projects even if you can't bring yourself to delegate others. You will soon find that you have associates who can be trusted to do things well and on time. The importance of delegating responsibility should not be minimized.

- Train your support staff to help you save time.

A very simple example of this is to insist that those answering the telephone for you get callers' telephone numbers so that you can call them back. It was not unusual for me to have a half dozen or more calls to return when I had been out of the office for an hour. If I had to look up every number before returning the calls, I would be wasting my time.

I am sure there are many other such ways to save time. Your support staff should understand that time is important, and they should do all they can to help you save it.

- Buy and use timesaving devices.

There are many new tools that help us use time more effectively. The computer is one. The pocket tape recorder is another. I carried one in my book bag, which I used to take papers back and forth from home to office. When I was in the car I talked into the tape recorder—to remind myself of something that needed to be done, preserve ideas, or dictate a memorandum.

Although some of these devices are quite sophisticated, most are user-friendly. For example, the Memo Manager is a digital voice recorder with a four-page graphic LCD screen that visually displays every message for easy retrieval. Then, of course, many light but powerful laptop computers are available. You must match your personality and work habits with the devices, however; otherwise they become nothing more than expensive gadgets that take up space.

- **Develop a tickler system.**

Devise a way to systematically remind yourself of something that you need to do. My system is very simple. It requires 31 index guides (one for each day of the month), an index file box, and some cards. If you have a project that must be completed by January 15, for example, fill out an index card with that information on it and place the card behind the index guide number 15. Each day you or your administrative assistant will need to check the card behind the index guide for that day. With good input, there is no reason for you to ever miss a deadline.

- **Use pocket or desk organizers.**

Many of my colleagues use organizers such as Day-Timer, Day Runner, At-A-Glance, or Filofax. There are also handheld organizers such as the PalmOne Zire 72, which includes a camera, color screen, and Word- and Excel-compatible files, among other features. Another popular handheld device is the BlackBerry, available in many models. The company describes it as a phone, an inbox, an HTML browser, and an organizer.

- **Use available software programs.**

There are many on the market. For example, Now Up-to-Date & Contact is a personal organizer that maintains your schedule, reminds you of upcoming events, manages your to-do list, and keeps associates up to date. Its on-screen reminders tell you in advance of important appointments or deadlines.

Other software programs are available that have nothing to do with planning and organizing but may still save you time. For example, if you must evaluate faculty and/or staff members on a regular basis, Employee Appraiser assists effectively.

- **Learn to be straightforward with others.**

At first glance, this reminder may seem inappropriate for this chapter, but I feel that it is apt. Playing games with others is time consuming.

I used to work with an administrator who would always resist any request, but then would always give in. One had to argue with him for 15 minutes when making a proposal. It was a game with him—but it was my time that was being wasted. (Of course he also was wasting his time, but it would have been a waste of time for me to worry about that!) For more descriptive information on games, see Berne (1996) and Hunsaker and Alessandra (1980), especially pages 84–89.

- **Learn to say no.**

If you are asked to do something that does not contribute to your goals, you need to learn how to decline. Chairpersons have many demands on their time. To be an effective leader, you must learn to say no when asked to take on assignments or attend events. We must be very protective of the time we have. Giving time to others is noble, but it can rob us of the time needed to do our jobs.

- **Learn speed reading.**

If you are a slow reader, you know how handicapped you are. One of the most helpful courses I ever took as an undergraduate was a speed-reading and vocabulary development course. Because I read quite fast, I was able to get through a lot of paperwork in a relatively short time. If you have the opportunity to enroll in a speed-reading course, do it; it will not be a waste of money or time.

- **Multitask.**

Commuting time can be used productively if you dictate memoranda or listen to educational or self-improvement tapes. I would often have lunch at my desk and read while I ate. It was relaxing and refreshing. The term *multitasking* has been with us for some time, and some people are better at it than others. Only you can assess your ability to multitask.

- **Get rid of unnecessary interruptions.**

In my last position as dean, it did not take me long to learn that I was spending 20 to 30 minutes a day on an activity that could be delegated, so I transferred responsibility for it to a colleague. He appreciated my trust in him; I valued the extra time it gave me each day. Whenever you have interruptions, ask "Was that interruption necessary?" Then find what you can do to get rid of those that are unnecessary.

This leads to the question of an open-door policy. If you follow such a policy, you will certainly have interruptions, and they can be time consuming. Frankly, I liked having an open door, and I was willing to spend extra hours on the job to pay for it. However, when there were many deadlines to meet, I would often close my door. Faculty members and others learned that most of the time they could see me, but that on occasion I didn't have time unless it was about something especially important. In that case, they got on my calendar.

- **Determine what activities are a good use of your time.**

We should allow ourselves time to do certain things without feeling guilty. For example, is time spent with faculty, staff, or students a waste of time? Is playing racquetball a waste of time? Only you can answer those questions. I believe that spending time with faculty, staff, or students and playing racquetball are all good uses of my time. If you agree, then in order to accommodate these activities, you must be willing to put in longer days if necessary. Prioritize your work, which will allow you to focus more efficiently on what you must get done.

- **Don't try to be a perfectionist.**

Learn to let go. The notion that everything must be perfect slows you down. This has always been difficult for me. I want things done "just right," and there were times when I mistakenly believed that I was the only person who could accomplish this. Foolish me!

- Get out of your office.

It's beneficial to take a break and to get away now and then from the stack of work on your desk. Take a walk across campus, visit with faculty members, or find other ways to relax. You often return to your work refreshed and with more vitality.

No matter how much you read about time management, I urge you to inventory your life and work habits and to develop your own techniques for saving time and becoming better organized. Try some of the tips I've provided. They may prove useful.

Resources

Web Sites
California Polytechnic State University, Student Academic Services
(Although aimed at the needs of students, these tips are useful to all of us.)
www.sas.calpoly.edu/asc/ssl/time.mgt.tips.html

Cornerstone Word Company
www.cornerstoneword.com/edgepage/timetip/timetip.htm

Day-Timer
www.daytimer.com/Time-Management-Resources/home/
4E8AD599A24C40EEBB8F66CE0A3B4A0F/False

Evolt.org
http://lists.evolt.org/archive/Week-of-Mon-20030915/148718.html

FranklinCovey
http://franklincovey.palmgear.com/index.cfm?fuseaction=software
.category&catid=539&PartnerREF=&siteid=104

Microsoft
(Although this generally promotes Microsoft Office, it includes some valuable timesaving tips.)
www.microsoft.com/AtWork/getworkdone/timesaving.mspx

Books

Bliss, E. (1984). *Getting things done: Timesaving strategies that make the most of your day.* New York, NY: Bantam.

Mayer, J. J. (1999). *Time management for dummies* (2nd ed.). New York, NY: Hungry Minds.

Ormiston, M. J. (2004). *Conquering infoclutter: Timesaving technology solutions for teachers.* Thousand Oaks, CA: Corwin.

Silver, S. (2000). *Organized to be the best! Simplify and improve how you work.* Los Angeles, CA: Adams-Hall.

References

Berne, E. (1996). *Games people play: The basic handbook of transactional analysis.* New York, NY: Ballantine.

Chopra, D. (1994). *The seven spiritual laws of success: A practical guide to the fulfillment of your dreams.* San Rafael, CA: Amber-Allen.

Cook, M. (1999). *Time management: Get more done with less stress by efficiently managing your time.* Holbrook: MA: Adams Media.

Hemphill, B. (1997). *Taming the paper tiger at work.* Washington, DC: Kiplinger.

Hunsaker, P. L., & Alessandra, A. J. (1980). *The art of managing people: Person-to-person skills, guidelines, and techniques every manager needs to guide, direct, and motivate the team.* New York, NY: Simon & Schuster.

McKenna, P. J., & Maister, D. H. (2002). *First among equals: How to manage a group of professionals.* New York, NY: The Free Press.

6

Communicating

Charismatic people who know how to use words can mesmerize others and lead them to do noble or ignoble deeds.

It is essential that you understand the power of language—its richness, elasticity, flavor, symbolism, rhythm, and many other qualities that give it fullness and beauty. Charismatic people who know how to use words can mesmerize others and lead them to do noble or ignoble deeds. Great leaders—as well as evil ones—have used language to persuade others into action. When we think of the former, several past presidents come to mind—Franklin D. Roosevelt, John F. Kennedy, Ronald Reagan, and William J. Clinton. Billy Graham, who delivered sermons to millions of people all around the world, masterfully used the power of the language to inspire and encourage hope. Adolph Hitler, on the other hand, used the power of language for evil purposes like few others have, the consequences of which are still visible.

The primary purpose of this chapter is to show how communication can improve your effectiveness as a chairperson. If you communicate effectively, you will be able to motivate faculty members better and help them to gain a sense of connection to you and what you're trying to achieve. Moreover, good communication will help faculty members feel included so they will care about what they do. It will also enable you to preserve and honor faculty members through acknowledgment of worth.

Faculty members want leaders who will impart information on all matters that affect them. They want leaders who can communicate their needs to university officials and other publics. Indeed, most position announcements for chairpersons list among the desired qualifications the ability to communicate effectively.

What does it mean to be an effective communicator? Foremost, it means providing various publics with information about department operations. It means telling how funds are allocated and spent, which requires being open and candid. It also means communicating about policy changes and providing anything else needed to facilitate the carrying out of individual responsibilities. In addition, you also have responsibility for communicating with students of your department, alumni, and the general public.

Communicating With Faculty

Faculty Meetings

Schedule faculty meetings on a regular basis, at least one a month. Special meetings can be called as needed. Prepare and distribute in advance a formal agenda so that faculty members know what to expect. Also let them know how to get items on the agenda.

It is your job to chair the faculty meeting, and you should follow these basic guidelines.

- Make certain the meeting starts on time.
- Allocate appropriate time for the discussion of all items.
- Bring the discussion to a halt when all sides of an issue have been discussed adequately.
- Make certain that issues that can be resolved are resolved.
- Suggest how certain issues can be handled.
- Bring the meeting to a close when all business has been transacted.
- Provide the faculty with written, minimal meeting procedures that guarantee each person's right to speak on all deliberative issues and allow for orderly, timely decision-making.

Chapter 16 discusses how to conduct successful meetings.

Memoranda

You will need to communicate some matters to the faculty between faculty meetings. A short memo can accomplish this if a written message is important. While I dislike contributing to the never-ending stack of memoranda, from time to time putting things in writing is necessary. If you don't write, you will find that some faculty members will overlook a deadline or assignment. All important matters of agreement between one person and another should be written. Written communication reduces the chances of misunderstanding.

Email

Email is an effective way to communicate with faculty and other administrators. It also can be used to communicate with alumni and fellow professionals around the country. It has many advantages: communicating instantaneously at a relatively low cost and freeing up clerical personnel for duties other than typing, for example. It does, however, have drawbacks unless certain guidelines are followed.

Limit email messages to close-by colleagues. If we are not careful, email can greatly reduce the contact we have with our colleagues, and professional interaction is healthy for many reasons. There is a tendency to send a quick email to a colleague in order to save time, when a face-to-face meeting or telephone call might be more appropriate. Words—no matter how colorful or how well crafted—are often sterile when they appear on a screen or a written page, especially when compared to spoken words. The nonverbal language we introduce in face-to-face meetings helps us communicate. Body language and voice intonation can add much to what we are trying to communicate.

Email messages ought not to be used for reprimands. It would be extremely insensitive to send an email reprimanding a faculty or staff member. If you are unhappy with the performance of an individual you supervise, you owe it to that person to meet face-to-face to discuss the matter. Indeed, sensitive information of any kind should be delivered in person.

E-snooping is for real. Remember that everything you write using your computer can be traced back to you, including email messages. I have known of instances where administrators and faculty members have had their email messages read by staff members in information technology centers. My suggestion: If the message you write would be embarrassing if aired publicly, then don't write or send it. Also, keep your email messages limited to work-related matters; you should never go wrong if you follow this advice.

Hard copies are essential for certain kinds of communication. Use letterhead stationery when writing letters of thanks or congratulations to faculty and staff. They are more personal, and copies go in their personnel files. Likewise, write more short personal notes to try to make up for the impersonal email communications. As hard as we might try, an email message is not particularly personal.

I am personally taken with the Internet and how it can improve communication, but it is not a panacea. It won't solve all our problems. If your campus is not wired—which I have a hard time believing is possible in these times—or if not all your faculty members use the Internet—which I can believe—then this means of communication cannot be fully exploited.

Face-to-Face Meetings

Face-to-face meetings with faculty members are needed occasionally. Indeed, they can help build positive relationships and are generally the most effective method of communication. Set aside time to spend with individual faculty members even if there is no important business to discuss. Such meetings can do much to improve faculty morale and give faculty members a sense that you care about them as individuals.

While face-to-face meetings often do not result in concrete progress toward achieving goals, their importance should not be underestimated. They are especially helpful in encouraging dialogue. You can ask questions, seek clarification, and thus show respect for your colleague's point of view. Of course, you should do this in public meetings as well. Additionally, you should show your willingness at every opportunity to consider another person's point of view, which helps to keep communication open, regardless of the setting. Listen intently—this means putting yourself in that person's shoes and being empathetic.

Voicemail Messages

Telephone systems at many universities provide a convenient way to pass information to your faculty. Systems such as Audix have the advantages of cutting paperwork and getting information to faculty members instantly. Keep a file copy of your Audix messages so that you have a record for future reference.

Systems such as Audix enable you to send messages to one person or several hundred, and they can be sent immediately or at a specified time. Also, you can relay to others any messages you receive.

Formal Publications

Some departments publish formal newsletters two to three times each semester. With the technology now available, producing professional-looking newsletters is a fairly easy task. (See Appendix B for newsletter sources.) Newsletters should be distributed to campus leaders as well as to members of the faculty.

The late Harold C. Shaver, director of the W. Page Pitt School of Journalism and Mass Communications at Marshall University, published the Monday Morning Memo each week for the faculty and staff in his department. It was such an efficient way of providing information that I adopted his idea and developed an email version of his Monday Morning Memo that went to all faculty members in the College of Mass Communication at Middle Tennessee State University when I served as dean. (See Appendixes C and D for sample Monday Morning Memos.) I received positive feedback, including a comment from one faculty member who said that it was a unifying force for the college. I don't know whether that's true, but it did provide a convenient way for me to disseminate information to faculty members in the college.

Remember that communication is a two-way process—it is just as important to hear what faculty members say and think as it is to inform them. Faculty members need opportunities to respond about departmental and personal matters. They can provide valuable input, and they resent not having opportunities to give their ideas on policy matters. I have heard more complaints about having too few departmental faculty meetings than about too many.

Communicating With Alumni

An alumni newsletter is a valuable way to keep alumni informed about department activities as well as a good way to let them know what their former classmates are doing. One of the most popular sections of any alumni newsletter is news about the alumni accomplishments.

Letters also can be sent to alumni, both globally to all alumni of your department or selectively as the case requires. There are times when a newsletter will not be as personal as desired. A call for donations to a scholarship fund, for example, is likely to get more response if individual letters are sent out.

There also are times when communication with alumni needs to be even more personal. A telephone call or a private meeting may be necessary.

Communicating With Students

Pamphlets, brochures, catalogs, calendars, and flyers are all used to get information to students. (A word of caution: Written documents provide terms of a contract unless a disclaimer in each piece notes that there is no contract implied in the publication.)

When you need to get information to students on short notice, posted flyers and announcements by faculty members in classes probably are the most effective method.

If you publish student information that pertains to graduation requirements or policies affecting their scheduling of courses, make certain that the same information is provided to all faculty members who have the responsibility for student advising.

Bulletin boards that are maintained with care also can do much to provide students with information. Bulletin boards need attention, however. Those that are multilayered and full of outdated announcements are useless.

Middle Tennessee State University has an unusually nice mass communication building, and when I was a dean there, we purchased an electronic board that scrolled messages. We used it regularly to let students know about upcoming events. It was positioned on a balcony overlooking the first floor so that students could read the messages soon after they walked into the building.

Communicating With the General Public

Find out what newsworthy events or activities your faculty and students are involved in, then provide that information to your office of university relations so that news releases can be prepared. Appointing a faculty or staff member who is responsible for gathering information and sending it to the office of university relations is worth considering.

Here are some other steps you can take to improve efforts to reach the general public through the news media.

- Encourage your faculty to think and look for potential news stories within the department.
- Give your university relations office a list of trade publications that are potential news outlets for activities of your department.
- Get to know those who work in the university relations office, and invite one of its professionals to attend a faculty meeting to discuss ways that that office can help get stories placed.
- Encourage your faculty to cooperate with the university relations office staff and news reporters and to be available to provide assistance when asked.

Working With the News Media

Some people in higher education seem to be naturals at working with the news media, while others find it unsatisfying and unrewarding. With a little study and effort, however, most can learn how to work effectively with news media personnel. Learning how reporters and editors work will help you do a better job. Understanding some basic principles of news writing and news gathering can help get your message to the public.

Several years ago a chairperson said to me, "I don't understand what's happening, but every time I write a story and give it to the newspaper, the most important part of the story is missing when it's printed." During the course of our conversation, it became clear that he was "burying" what he thought was the most important part of the story. I suggested he put the most important elements of the story at the very beginning. His response was, "Gee, I hadn't thought of that." News reporters and news editors always have that on their minds.

Think visually. Editors like to use good, strong pictures with stories. You can help them by suggesting picture ideas or making pictures available if you have them.

Don't duck reporters. Although you prefer that only good news from your department gets into print, that is not always realistic to expect. You need to be available to answer a reporter's questions even if you don't like the subject. Be honest and forthright.

Do not allow yourself to be caught off guard. If we respond to questions when we are caught off guard, we risk giving unthoughtful—or even stupid—answers. When a reporter calls to talk to you, ask what he or she wants to talk about. It the subject is controversial, say that you will call right back. This will give you time to decide how to respond most effectively. You may even want to write out some answers before you return the reporter's call. Whatever you do, however, don't fail to return the call promptly.

Be concise with any answers to questions. Don't say anything that you would not want to see in print or hear on radio or television. Even though I have had experience as a reporter myself, I learned the hard way that "off the record" is not always respected by all reporters. I remember being disappointed when I viewed a television story for which I was interviewed because the real point I wanted to make was omitted. I had been invited to give the keynote speech at a conference with much public appeal, and when I was interviewed by local television I was too talkative for my own good. As a young, inexperienced academic, I assumed that the television station would run the entire interview, but it didn't happen that way, of course, and the sole point I would have liked aired was edited out. I should have spoken only to that point.

You probably know that print reporters are not likely to let you see the story they write before it appears. However, that doesn't mean that you have to give up all control after you've been interviewed for a story. If you don't know the reporter, be very cautious, and say things like, "I am not sure that I am making myself clear. Would you mind reading that back to me?"

Here are additional practical suggestions for dealing with reporters.

- Make sure you get the name of the reporter and his or her publication.
- Don't hesitate to refer the reporter to someone else if you are asked questions that are out of your area of expertise.
- Be cautious about answering hypothetical questions.
- Watch out for silence. A good reporter knows that most of us are uncomfortable with silence, and sometimes can get people to talk too much by asking a question and then keeping silent.
- Be cautious about being drawn into controversy. You will need to be alert to reporters' questions designed to get a comment from you regarding some ongoing campus feud, for example.

Communicating With Your Dean

It is necessary that you keep your dean informed about important departmental matters. Obviously, you can use all the forms of communication that you use with your faculty, but I strongly recommend that you have face-to-face talks with your dean on a fairly regular basis. Determining how often that should be is up to you, unless of course your dean specifies how often you need to meet with him or her. In addition, it is important to provide progress reports to your dean—at the end of the academic year, for example. John McDaniel, dean of the College of Liberal Arts at Middle Tennessee State University, puts together a progress report for his provost and others (see Appendix E). It is a good summary of what the faculty members in his college accomplished during the academic year.

If you publish a departmental newsletter, make certain that your dean and other university administrators are on the mailing list. Above all else, don't fail to sit down with your dean from time to time to discuss what's happening in your department, and to let him or her know your concerns.

The Role of Communication in Improving Morale

Studies of faculty morale show that many faculty members lack confidence in the leadership of the institution, and that can cause major morale issues. The same studies show, however, that faculty members have the most confidence in their chairpersons.

> These findings suggest that faculty feel more trust for those they know better and presumably communicate with more frequently. This finding may serve to alert senior administrators to the need for increased communication and interaction with all members of the campus community. (Johnsrud, 1996, p. 118)

Increasing the level and quality of communication is a forceful way to improve faculty morale. Another important finding is that "relations existing between the chair and faculty members and within the department as a whole are crucial to the morale of faculty" (Johnsrud, 1996, p. 120).

> One of the primary roles of the department chair should be to build and nurture a positive collegial climate in the department for all faculty. To accomplish this objective, the selection of chairs should be monitored carefully and ongoing training instituted.
>
> Training should include attention to issues of professional work climate, professional development and academic support, evaluation, sexual harassment, and affirmative action. Department chairs should also be trained to recognize and confront inappropriate conduct. Chairs are in key positions to recognize and eliminate discrimination at the department level. (Johnsrud, 1996, p. 120)

Certainly you need to have strong communication skills to be an effective chairperson, and improving interpersonal, supervisory, and public communication skills is a lifelong concern. The successful chairperson participates regularly in communication workshops designed to improve his or her interpersonal, supervisory, and presentational communication skills. Rewards follow those who do.

Effective communication is essential for all who hold leadership positions. Good leaders find ways to reach their students, faculty, alumni, and the general public. They use many tools to get messages out, and they listen to what others say.

Resources

Web Sites
Air War College
www.au.af.mil/au/awc/awcgate/awc-comm.htm

CEO/Senior Executive Reward, Performance, and Benefits
www.ceoforum.com.au/200211_remuneration.cfm

Change Management Learning Center
www.change-management.com/

Development Resource Guide
http://web.mit.edu/ist/competency/tldev/communication-skills.html

Seven Principles of Good Communication
www.rcmp-learning.org/docs/ecdd0065.htm

Books
Elgin, S. D. (1997). *How to disagree without being disagreeable: Getting your point across with the gentle art of verbal self-defense.* New York, NY: John Wiley & Sons.

Harkins, P. (1999). *Powerful conversations: How high impact leaders communicate.* New York, NY: McGraw-Hill.

Heyman, R. (1994). *Why didn't you say that in the first place? How to be understood at work.* San Francisco, CA: Jossey-Bass.

Higgerson, M. L. (1996). *Communication skills for department chairs.* Bolton, MA: Anker.

Higgerson, M. L., & Joyce, T. A. (2007). *Effective leadership communication: A guide for department chairs and deans for managing difficult situations and people.* Bolton, MA: Anker.

Munter, M. (2005). *Guide to managerial communication: Effective business writing and speaking* (7th ed.). Upper Saddle River, NJ: Prentice Hall.

References

Johnsrud, L. K. (1996). *Maintaining morale: A guide to assessing the morale of midlevel administrators and faculty.* Washington, DC: College and University Personnel Association.

7

Developing a Departmental Vision

If we are going to help shape tomorrow, then we need discussion, dialogue, and even dissent.

As you read about leadership and management, you will see that not all scholars agree that leaders should provide or create a vision. For example, McKenna and Maister (2002) say this about the "vision thing":

> Many management texts, and many of our clients, suggest
> that one key contribution of a leader is to provide or create a
> "vision." We are skeptics here, not on any theoretical grounds,
> but simply because as longtime consultants we have seen many
> professional environments, and have rarely met managers or
> leaders who have pulled off this approach. (p. 8)

Bennis (2000), however, writes that "while leaders come in every size, shape and disposition—short, tall, neat, sloppy, young, old, male and female—every leader I talked with shared at least one characteristic: a concern with a guiding purpose, and an overarching vision" (p. 6). Bennis makes this comment after writing that he had spent 10 years talking with hundreds of leaders, including many of our country's high-profile leaders.

So what do we make of this disagreement? Personally, I agree with both views—at least to a point—mostly because McKenna and Maister (2002) summarize their beliefs about the "vision thing" by writing, "The key point is that the central goal of either approach is to get people enthused, excited, energized. Unless you have a very special skill, then we suggest you focus on what excites each of your people, not (just) on what excites you" (p. 9). And I agree with Bennis (2000) when he writes about the need to have a concern with a guiding purpose and an overarching vision. As chairperson, you need to know where you want your department to be in the next 5 or 10 years—or even farther if it's possible. To begin, I suggest you may want to look at a shorter period—perhaps two to three years—and if you make good progress and achieve the goals you and your faculty have agreed upon, you'll have reason to celebrate and recognize those who have championed the way. You need, of course, to get your faculty members "enthused, excited, energized" as McKenna and Maister suggest.

In my judgment, Kouzes and Posner (2003) wrap up nicely any differences there may be regarding the "vision thing."

> Leaders have a desire to make something happen, to change the way things are, to create something that no one else has ever created before. In some ways, leaders live their lives backward. They see pictures in their mind's eye of what the results will look like even before they've started the project, much as an architect draws a blueprint or an engineer builds a model. Their clear image of the future pulls them forward. Yet visions seen only by leaders are insufficient to create an organized movement or a significant change. A person with no constituents is not a leader, and people will not follow until they accept a vision as their own. Therefore, leaders must inspire a shared vision. (p. 5)

As a chairperson, you should have in your mind's eye where you want to see the department in the next several years, but then you must share your ideas with faculty members and do what you can to persuade them that this "vision" is also theirs. You want faculty members to share ownership in the department's future. Each individual should realize that so much is at stake that no one can afford to opt out of the process of making the department relevant for students who will be graduating not just this year but many years ahead. Creating a vision can motivate most faculty members, especially when they take ownership of it. Even some faculty members who have seemed apathetic in the past are often challenged and renewed. Kouzes and Posner (1999, p. 19) provide excellent guidelines for inspiring a shared vision.

- Determine what you want.
- Act on your intuition.
- Test your assumptions.
- Become a futurist.
- Develop your interpersonal competence.
- Breathe life into your vision.
- Speak positively.
- Speak from the heart.
- Make the intangible tangible.
- Listen, listen, listen.

To accomplish this task, faculty must consider many questions, such as the following:

- How does each course in our curriculum relate to our objectives and mission statement? To our values? To the university's mission?
- Do we have the resources to meet the challenges that lie ahead?
- Have we done all we can to involve all our stakeholders?
- Is our upper-level administration supportive?
- How does our vision of the future "fit" the faculty we now have?
- Will we need to hire new faculty members, retrain present faculty members, or do both? If so, what will the cost be?

These are just a sampling of important questions to be considered as your department plans for the future. There are many more, and these will be discussed more specifically in Chapter 10 on managing change.

Developing a departmental vision statement necessarily involves change, which must be understood by all faculty members. Even the word *change* will likely cause some people to wince. As Kouzes and Posner (2003) write,

When faced with new challenges people live with a high degree of ambiguity. Change and the accompanying uncertainty throw off customary equilibrium. Yet it's these fluctuations, disturbances, and imbalances that are the primary sources of creativity. Leaders must embrace innovation as they navigate their departments, programs, and institutions through what are becoming the permanent white waters surrounding higher education. (p. 54)

Before discussing how to develop a departmental vision, let me recommend that you read John Bennett's (2003) book *Academic Life: Hospitality, Ethics, and Spirituality*. Bennett has written a particularly profound leadership book for academics in which he posits this idea: "Hospitable leaders push, cajole, arouse—and listen" (p. 185). I emphasize this here because I believe that *listening* may well be the most important thing you can do to involve faculty members so that they will respond.

Now, let's turn to strategies for developing a vision for your department and what you might do to get your faculty members to embrace it. I suggest you follow these steps.

1. Write down your thoughts about what you believe your department should look like in 5 years. Do the same thing for 10 years. Do it again for 15 and 20 years into the future if you can. Put it in outline form if you wish. The point is to begin thinking about the future. For example, do you see enrollment growth? Enrollment decline? How do patterns that you see correspond to the overall enrollment expectations for your university? How is the economy likely to impact your university and thus your college? Do you need to hire new faculty, purchase new equipment, and so on?

2. After you have completed step one, look for the common threads that characterize your department for each period of time. For example, suppose you outlined the need for curricular changes for 5, 10, or 20 years out. Now, try refining this to indicate what kind of curricular changes you think should be made. Ask yourself at this point whether there are faculty members—especially senior faculty—who would agree with you. Make

extensive notes outlining these changes, including resources needed to bring about the kinds of changes in the curriculum you envision.

3. Once you've completed these two tasks, it is time to draft a vision statement.

4. If you do not already have a planning committee, I suggest you appoint one. Then, in a meeting with the members, ask that they think about the vision statement draft and add their own ideas, plus any they can solicit from other members of the faculty.

5. After the planning committee has completed its task, you need to finalize the vision statement, which should include as many faculty ideas as practical. Once you have a statement that you believe is worth sharing, meet next with your dean. Get his or her reactions. Can she support your ideas? Can he make needed resources available? Does your dean believe the statement should be modified in any way? Is a rewrite or clarification necessary?

6. Once you and the dean agree upon a final draft, it's time to present the statement to your faculty as a whole. I believe we might presume that many of your faculty by this time would have a fairly good understanding of the statement itself, including most of the ideas you would be presenting. Here you need to call on all your leadership skills. Listen carefully to what each faculty member has to say. This is a good time to let everyone know that they and their ideas are valued.

There are many other ways of doing this, of course. You might want to have a faculty retreat, for example. For a good way to go about doing this, I suggest you read Ann Lucas's (1994) excellent book *Strengthening Departmental Leadership: A Team-Building Guide for Chairs in Colleges and Universities*. Especially helpful are the questions she proposes that chairs can use to stimulate their thinking.

What would this department look like if it were functioning better?

What dysfunctional behavior would disappear and what positive behaviors would take its place? What would these behaviors look like, sound like, feel like? (For example, I would not feel tense before a departmental meeting.)

You're looking at this department two years down the road, two good years. What do you see? (p. 57)

Once you have created an agreed-upon vision, you need to assign priorities to each point. You and your faculty members then need to develop action plans and designate who will be responsible for each goal. Also—and this is important—there should be discussion and agreement on how the department should measure success for each of its goals.

I have found developing a departmental vision to be an exhilarating experience. When done with energy and talent, it can do much to shape the future of your department. And faculty members—it's hoped all of them—can take pride in achieving goals, even if the goals represent only small steps forward. Moreover, you will have the opportunity to recognize faculty members for their contributions. It is possible that the department will become more vital and faculty members will take more pride in it. The outcomes will correspond to the energy given to the vision's development. More importantly, however, outcomes are likely to reflect to an even higher degree your communication skills and how you were able to involve faculty members.

This process gives you an opportunity to use—and test—virtually all your leadership skills. Perseverance, listening, integrity, risk-taking and other qualities will be necessary. With leadership skills—and perhaps some luck—you can help to make your department even stronger.

Resources

Web Sites

Basics of Developing Mission, Vision, and Values Statements
www.managementhelp.org/plan_dec/str_plan/stmnts.htm

Building a Collective Vision
www.ncrel.org/sdrs/areas/issues/educatrs/leadrshp/le100.htm

VanCity—Developing a Vision
www.vancity.com/MyBusiness/PlanningandAdvice/NonProfit/Vision/

Vision, Mission, and Values
www.brefigroup.co.uk/facilitation/vision.html

Books

Abrashoff, D. M. (2002). *It's your ship: Management techniques from the best damn ship in the navy.* New York, NY: Warner Books.

Bennis, W. (2003). *On becoming a leader* (Rev. and expanded ed.). Cambridge, MA: Perseus.

Bethel, S. M. (1990). *Making a difference: Twelve qualities that make you a leader.* New York, NY: Berkley.

Bland, C. J., Weber-Main, A. M., Lund, S. M., & Finstad, D. A. (2005). *The research-productive department: Strategies from departments that excel.* Bolton, MA: Anker.

Hesselbein, F., & Cohen, P. M. (Eds.). (1999). *Leader to leader: Enduring insights on leadership from the Drucker Foundation's award-winning journal.* San Francisco, CA: Jossey-Bass.

Hesselbein, F., Goldsmith, M., & Somerville, I. (Eds.). (2001). *Leading beyond the walls: How high-performing organizations collaborate for shared success.* San Francisco, CA: Jossey-Bass.

References

Bennett, J. B. (2003). *Academic life: Hospitality, ethics, and spirituality.* Bolton, MA: Anker.

Bennis, W. (2000). *Managing the dream: Reflections on leadership and change.* New York, NY: Perseus.

Kouzes, J. M., & Posner, B. Z. (1999). *The leadership challenge planner: An action guide to achieving your personal best.* San Francisco, CA: Jossey-Bass.

Kouzes, J. M., & Posner, B. Z. (2003). *The Jossey-Bass academic administrator's guide to exemplary leadership.* San Francisco, CA: Jossey-Bass.

Lucas, A. F. (1994). *Strengthening departmental leadership: A team-building guide for chairs in colleges and universities.* San Francisco, CA: Jossey-Bass.

McKenna, P. J., & Maister, D. H. (2002). *First among equals: How to manage a group of professionals.* New York, NY: The Free Press.

8

Improving Your Department

Resistance to change will vary from faculty to faculty, but in large part resistance grows out of the department's culture.

Making a difference in the quality of your department is within your grasp. You can bring about improvement by utilizing leadership skills and creating a spirit of teamwork and community. There are many things that should be considered, however, before undertaking the task of improving your department.

First, it is assumed that you are not new to the university or college where you serve as chairperson. Can it also be assumed that you have a full understanding of your department's culture? Your answer may be problematic at best. No matter how you answer, I hope that you will dig deep to try to understand your department in ways probably not done previously. What are its core values? Its history? What unites—or divides—faculty members? In your department, just as in other organizations, there are informal and formal rules and procedures that guide the way faculty members function. In time these rules and procedures become accepted practices that are seldom questioned: They are "the way things are done." This is what is meant by the term *departmental culture*. To understand more about the subject, you might want to read *Organization Culture and Leadership* by Edgar Schein (2004), who defines culture as

> A pattern of shared basic assumptions that was learned by a
> group as it solved its problems of external adaptation and inter-
> nal integration, that has worked well enough to be considered

valid and, therefore, to be taught to new members as the correct way to perceive, think, and feel in relation to those problems. (p. 17)

Note that Schein writes "that was learned by a group." This is important because your group—or department, if you will—will not be like other groups or departments on your campus. It will have its own culture.

As chairperson, you will soon see that much of what and how things are done in your department can be traced back to its culture. For example, when I was a dean at Middle Tennessee State University, it was common for faculty members in one of the college's departments to work on Saturdays. When I went to my office on Saturday, I regularly saw the same faculty members from this particular department toiling away. It was almost as if it were a ritual—which is not that much of a stretch when we think about culture and the normative values of a group.

So, if you are going to involve faculty members in a plan to improve your department, then you must know and understand the department's existing culture. Improvement no doubt will mean change. And as has already been pointed out, change will almost assuredly be met with resistance. This will vary from faculty to faculty, but in a large part resistance grows out of the department's culture. I like what Lucas writes (1994):

> Departmental chairs have a significant role to play in motivating faculty because they can either perpetuate the existing climate or confront it and its positive and negative norms. A challenging task for the chair is to help faculty identify departmental norms and to ask whether these norms work to the good or the detriment of the department. (pp. 51–52)

Before you set out to develop an improvement plan, you should ask yourself if you know each of your faculty members well enough to get them to buy into it. Do they trust you? And do you value each of them, and are you willing to consider each of their points of view? You also need to determine the cost of improving the department according to your ideas and whether your dean will support your efforts.

Let's presume that you have already developed a mission and vision statement for your department. What specific things should you do next to create a step-by-step plan for your department—presuming that faculty members agree that the department needs to be improved? More than once I have seen complacent faculty members shrug off the need for *any* improvement. A department in one of the colleges where I once served as dean needed to fill the chairperson's position. When I met with the faculty members, I mentioned that I saw a need for someone who could take the department to another level of excellence. I was stunned by the reaction I received. At least five faculty members immediately bristled. One said, "We are the best department of our kind in the country. Do you really mean it when you say you expect us to get better? How could we?" As it turned out, this was the sentiment of the entire faculty—about 20 in all. I was faced with silent but deadly stares when I asked, "Cannot each of us seek to improve who we are and cannot the department work collectively to improve what it is?" In the end the department insisted on appointing one of its own members who they knew would maintain the status quo.

Let's presume that faculty members agree that improvements are needed. In that case, the following plan should be useful.

A Step-by-Step Plan for Departmental Improvement

1.   Make a short list of your department's essential responsibilities. For example, I would put teaching students at the top of my list. After faculty members have agreed on the essentials, decide how to measure how well those responsibilities are currently being met.

2.   Prepare a detailed action plan.
You and your faculty members should be able to prioritize what must be done to bring about improvements. For example, suppose it's determined that faculty need to spend more time advising students. How high a priority is this? Once priority is determined, faculty must identify the steps in

the advising process, answering many questions before the plan is operative. For example: What do we mean by "more time"?

I expect that you already have conducted surveys of alumni and some of the principal employers of your recent graduates. If not, find someone on your campus skilled at developing surveys. Make use of his or her talents to help you construct surveys, which will yield useful data for plans for improving your department. Data from those who hire your recent graduates are also particularly useful. At Middle Tennessee State University, we had a large program associated with the recording industry, so my assistant and I had about a dozen luncheon meetings with groups in the field who worked in nearby Nashville. In all, we probably met with about 60 individuals. We asked each group the same questions: Were our students performing, and what we could do to improve the quality of instruction and advising? We likewise followed the same pattern to assess the other major programs in the college. Sharing the information we gathered was particularly useful for chairs and others who saw a need for change, but I would be less than honest if I did not add that the data failed to persuade those faculty members who fought change. In Chapter 10, I present some strategies for dealing with change, including some of the best practices for encouraging faculty members to promote performance improvement via change.

3.   Set aside time for discussion of the action plan.

Do faculty members agree not only on what should be done, but also on how the plans should be carried out? Do they agree on the assessment methods? Do you see any resistance? Are there others on campus who could help? For example, do we need someone to help analyze the data we gather? In these meetings, pay careful attention to body language, not just to the words being spoken.

Use your best leadership skills. Any good counseling psychologist will tell you to let silence work for you. Most of us are uncomfortable with silence, and for that reason, we start talking. Allow *your* silence to generate faculty discussion. Say things like, "That sounds like a reasonable idea. Tell me more about it." Relax. Be confident. Be humble. Respect and value the opinions of each faculty member. Do not get caught up in your position and the power attached to it. Any success you have results from a team effort. You cannot improve your department alone.

4. Having agreed upon an action plan, assign responsibilities and deadlines.

Give faculty members the chance to volunteer for assignments, and even suggest ones they might like to work on. I think it's more likely that each assignment will get done according to your expectations if you permit faculty members to choose their own tasks as well as colleagues with whom they prefer to work.

5. Set aside time for regular meetings with faculty groups.

These could be either a task force or selected faculty members who are working on similar projects. Here you need to assess progress and give encouragement. It goes without saying that faculty members must be provided with the resources they need in order to fulfill their assignments.

6. Measure as you go.

You do not have to wait until all projects are completed before beginning to assess progress.

7. Monitor carefully for any group slowdown.

There will be times when some faculty members start dragging their feet. Those who balk at change can sometimes hide behind the group. Unless the leader is willing to deal with these faculty members, it will become your job as chairperson to intervene.

Sometimes meeting with the group can move things along. There may be occasions where you will need to meet face-to-face with individuals to encourage them and to listen to their concerns. You may discover that they have legitimate problems working with others in the group, and there may be things that you can do to help. Indeed, your intervention may prove to be crucial.

8.   Determine assessment methods.

See Allen (2004) for more information on this topic. She reminds us that assessment is "not rocket science" (p. 156). She also makes this important point:

> Assessment programs are likely to fail if faculty and adminis-
> trators forget the purpose of their efforts. Assessment studies
> examine student learning in the entire program; they should
> not focus on individual students or faculty. The purpose is not
> to assign blame, but rather to identify program strengths, areas
> of concern, and solutions that faculty are willing to implement.
> (p. 157)

Work with faculty members to make assessment an ongoing process. It needs to be embedded in the department's culture. Appoint faculty members to mentor all faculty newcomers so that they too will accept regular assessment as a part of their responsibility.

9.   Reinforce the purpose of the agreed-upon plan.

There are many opportunities for you to recognize and reward those making progress toward completion of their tasks—and also to remind all faculty members what goals *they* and *you* share—and have agreed upon. From time to time, remind faculty members how both they and students benefit from the changes they are making. This is a critical component of your overall strategy.

10. Remind faculty to be patient with change.

You are likely to have faculty members who are impatient. They see something that they believe should be accomplished, and getting it done tomorrow is not good enough. We all need to slow down occasionally. In fact, it's a good idea to step back from a task from time to time. If you are able to do this at the right time, you will earn appreciation and trust—and you also are likely to get a higher level of achievement from each faculty member. When we share power and decision-making, we liberate others.

11. Keep your eye on your mission.

How does your department's mission align itself with that of the university? Do your course offerings help the department and the university accomplish their separate missions? What do you do to support the research agenda of faculty members in your department? What systems are in place to help improve teaching performance? How is service valued and measured?

12. Encourage comity.

We all know faculty often enjoy debate. At times, however, some seem to enjoy putting each other down and making those who question their ideas look or feel foolish. This is a part of what Tannen (1998) calls the argument culture: "The increasingly adversarial spirit of our contemporary lives is fundamentally related to a phenomenon that has been much remarked upon in recent years: the breakdown of a sense of community" (p. 24). We have seen it operate. Tannen recognizes that intellectuals have responsibility to explore potential weaknesses in the argument of others, and writes,

> But when opposition becomes the overwhelming avenue of inquiry—a formula that requires another side to be found or a criticism to be voiced; when the lust for opposition privileges extreme views and obscures complexity; when our eagerness to find weaknesses blinds us to strengths; when the atmosphere of animosity precludes respect and poisons our relations with one another; then the argument culture is doing more damage than good. (p. 25)

I have watched this happen, as I'm sure others have. As chairperson, you need to provide strong leadership that discourages personal attack and encourages dialogue rather than debate. You need to engage and connect with faculty members in your department to build a sense of community. Encourage all faculty members to help you create a healthy department where the important work they do occurs in a place where happiness and joy are the norm—part of the department's culture.

This step-by-step plan is nothing more than a set of guidelines designed to provoke your thinking so that a plan emerges which you and your faculty can agree upon. Such a plan allows for the changes needed so that students in the coming years will gain skills and knowledge. Making a difference in the quality of your department is within your grasp.

Resources

Web Sites

Academic Reviews of Graduate Programs
www.indiana.edu/~grdschl/programReviews.php

Improving Academic Program Review
http://education.berkeley.edu/accreditation/ee_essays_4.html#casestudies

Strategies for Improving Academic Advisement
www.uncfsu.edu/plret/chairsmeetsummary.htm

Books

Corson, D. (Ed.). (1995). *Discourse and power in educational organizations*. Cresskill, NJ: Hampton.

Fox, M. A., & Hackerman, N. (Eds.). (2003). *Evaluating and improving undergraduate teaching in science, technology, engineering, and mathematics*. Washington, DC: National Academies Press.

McKenna, P. J., & Maister, D. H. (2002). *First among equals: How to manage a group of professionals*. New York, NY: The Free Press.

References

Allen, M. J. (2004). *Assessing academic programs in higher education*. Bolton, MA: Anker.

Lucas, A. F. (1994). *Strengthening departmental leadership: A team-building guide for chairs in colleges and universities.* San Francisco, CA: Jossey-Bass.

Schein, E. H. (2004). *Organization culture and leadership* (3rd ed.). San Francisco, CA: Jossey-Bass.

Tannen, D. (1998). *The argument culture: Moving from debate to dialogue.* New York, NY: Random House.

9

Developing Outcome Assessment Programs

Chairpersons must be up to the demanding work that it takes to improve the educational processes in their departments.

In a time of rapid change, understanding the entire campus and how each unit contributes to student learning is essential. Colleges and universities can no longer afford the complacency exhibited by many institutions in the past. As the cost of a college education increases, we should expect that politicians, parents, governing boards, and others will continue to insist on accountability—for us to show what we've added to a student's education. Indeed, society is telling those in higher education to educate *all* students to a much higher level. In this climate, chairing a department today is decidedly more difficult than it was when I served as chairperson. I don't remember hearing anything about assessing learning outcomes until after I became a dean. However, I should point out that at the time, I—along with other chairpersons—was assessing what our students had learned, although it was not nearly as formal or as thorough as are assessments today. Today's chairperson must be a strong leader who is especially well informed; anything less is simply unacceptable. So, it's important for all chairpersons to learn as much as they can about outcome assessment programs because it is one of the tools needed to make informed judgments.

Fortunately, student assessment is a topic of much discussion, and there are many books and online sources about it. Several scholars cite assessment as a chief concern in the academy. One of them is Bruce Kimball (1997), who lists assessment as one of seven areas of widespread interest in contemporary higher education. Other issues he lists include multiculturalism, general education, the common good and citizenship, K–16 continuities, teaching as inquiry, and values and service.

In explaining what assessment can do for the department, it is good to remind faculty members that you will be able to adopt better and more specific program outcomes, gain support from the administration for their program initiatives, and learn about their collective teaching effectiveness. Once faculty members see that these benefits are achievable, they will likely take more interest in working to refine and improve the program.

As you and your faculty discuss developing outcome assessment programs, it is advisable to consult those who have expertise in the field. In other words, don't try to reinvent the wheel. For example, Allen (2004, p. 10) notes six basic steps for developing assessment programs.

1) Develop learning objectives.
2) Check for alignment between the curriculum and the objectives.
3) Develop an assessment plan.
4) Collect assessment data.
5) Use results to improve the program.
6) Routinely examine the assessment process and correct, as needed.

If an outcome assessment program is to succeed, effective communication, as well as strong leadership and support, is required. You must be positive when convincing faculty members to get involved in the process. Assessment has many academically beneficial results, and time and effort spent to develop and administer the program will not be wasted. Thus, as you approach assessment, you need to make certain that all faculty members know its meaning, purpose, and uses. Be prepared to answer faculty questions about its need. Of course, in some instances such questions are moot because many governing boards require outcome assessment programs.

Developing Desired Educational Outcomes

One of the first steps in developing an assessment program is to specify desired educational outcomes. These include the knowledge, skills, values, attitudes, and behaviors that graduates are expected to possess as a result of having earned a degree, and they should be developed in consultation with faculty members.

In many instances, these goals are already outlined elsewhere—in your catalog or in promotional material. If you've been through accreditation, there is likely to be a statement on file to help you get started.

After identifying educational outcomes, you must then select assessment methods. For the purposes of illustration, let's identify several educational outcome targets and then select assessment methods for each. Let's assume your department is business administration.

The Associate to Advance Collegiate Schools of Business (AACSB) has broad curriculum-related outcomes as a part of its accreditation standards. The Atlanta Board of Regents (1992) published a manual that included this statement regarding educational outcomes:

> Students graduating from the School of Business Administration will be prepared for imaginative and responsible citizenship and leadership roles in business and society—domestic and worldwide. All business graduates will demonstrate competency in a common body of knowledge including the following areas:
>
> 1) A background of the concepts, processes, and institutions in the production and marketing of goods and/or services and the financing of the business enterprise or other forms of organization
> 2) A background of the economic and legal environment as it pertains to profit and/or nonprofit organizations along with ethical considerations and social and political influences as they affect organizations
> 3) A basic understanding of the concepts and applications of accounting, quantitative methods, and management information systems including computer applications
> 4) A study of organization theory, behavior, and interpersonal (oral and written) communications
> 5) A study of administrative processes under conditions of uncertainty including integrated analysis and policy determination at the overall management level

6) Students must also demonstrate competence within their specific major area of study. (pp. 3.39–3.40)

Developing and Administering Assessment Methods

You should encourage faculty members to use a variety of methods to assess students on the learning objectives of each course. These may include but are not limited to the following: hands-on demonstrations, capstone courses or projects, care plans, classroom assessments, departmental exit exams, direct and indirect assessment, group and individual presentations, in-house designed tests, internships, journals, licensing exams, portfolios, pre-test/post-test, research papers, rubrics, simulations, standardized tests, teamwork, and writing synthesis.

Measuring learning outcomes can be done in many ways. You may want to see what other schools in your area are doing, and explore what standardized tests are available to assist with the measurement. In addition to not relying on any one assessment method, I encourage you to seek advice from someone on campus who is a specialist in testing and measurement to help assure that your evaluation methods are valid and reliable.

Here are some general assessment methods for your department to consider.

Capstone Course and/or Experiences

This is a widely used method. Essentially it covers the range of major area subject matter. Coursework, tests, and projects are designed to elicit demonstrations of student proficiency in knowledge and skills. It provides a good opportunity for assessing student competence attained through major area coursework. Some examples are exhibitions or performances, theses, dissertations, presentations, and oral defenses.

Entrance and Exit Examinations

By administering both of these examinations, a determination of so-called value added can be made. Entrance examinations are obviously not intended to measure achievement at your institution, but they are essential for establishing the baseline of academic competency from which your accomplishments can be judged.

Survey of Employers

One valuable way of assessing what students learned from a program of study is to survey those who have employed your students. Faculty members should analyze the results to determine strengths and weaknesses of the program.

Portfolio Review

Students can be required to assemble portfolios that contain examples of their work—papers they've written, projects completed, and so on. Students should be told of this requirement at the beginning of their studies, and they should be reminded from time to time of the necessity of keeping their work and preparing a portfolio. Some schools collect portfolios and file them in the name of each student major in the program. Student portfolios have gained increasing acceptance as a means of evaluating both general knowledge and learning in the major field of study. For more information on the use and development of portfolios of student work, see *Assessing Student Learning: A Common Sense Guide* by Linda Suskie (2004). In a chapter of her book devoted to "Assembling Assessment Information Into Portfolios" she makes an important point:

> Portfolios may be the most exciting, the most misunderstood,
> and the most challenging assessment tool that we have. They
> can be extremely valuable learning opportunities and assessment
> tools, but they can also take a tremendous amount of time to
> manage and evaluate. (p. 185)

Student Reflections

They provide students with an excellent way to get direct evidence of personal values and responsibility, and an ability to understand and manage themselves and their commitments.

Survey of Alumni

Graduates of your program should be surveyed on a regular basis—perhaps every five years—to determine their satisfaction with their studies in your department. Also, you can ask them to evaluate the strengths and weaknesses of the program itself. Figure 9.1 (pp. 112–113) is an example of such a survey that you may want to use once every five years (see also Appendix F). The purpose of such a survey is to determine how graduates feel they are using their training and how each course has contributed to the overall education of those who have earned degrees from the department.

Internships/Field Experience Ratings

Supervisors usually evaluate a student's performance when he or she completes an internship or some other kind of field experience. These evaluations provide direct evidence of student learning.

Focus Groups

This is a relatively easy way to determine satisfaction with student learning. These may be held at any time (as opposed to the exit interviews, which are done, of course, when students are about to graduate).

Exit Interviews

Many schools rely on exit interviews to assess programs. Graduating students are asked a series of questions regarding the overall quality of education provided. (See Appendix G for a sample student exit interview.)

Honors, Scholarships, and Awards

These provide good indirect evidence of student learning. Keep track of any your students and alumni receive.

Licensure Examinations

Various disciplines have used licensure examinations for some time, and they are among the best end-of-program assessment procedures.

In addition to these methods, we could add student grades, assignment grades, admission rates into graduate programs and graduation rates

Figure 9.1 Alumni Survey

City University
Department of History

Please help us measure how well the Department of History is meeting its objectives. Complete the survey and return it in the enclosed postage-paid envelope. Your assistance will be very much appreciated. Thank you.

Name _____

Address _____

Occupation _____

Year of graduation from City University _____

Evaluation of Courses Offered by the Department

Rank each of the following courses according to their value to you. For example, if you took Ancient History and found it to be the course most helpful to you, give it a ranking of 1. If you found the History of Medicine to be the least helpful of the 10 history courses you took at City University, rank it 10.

__The Great Civilizations to 1300
__The World and the Rise of the West
__History of Medicine
__English History to 1642
__Ancient History
__War in Modern Times
__Women in the United States
__Latin America: Discovery of Independence
__American Social, Cultural, and Intellectual History, 1607 to Present
__History of Black America to 1885
__European History, 1492–1815
__American History to 1877
__American Labor Party
__China and the Western World, 1500–1900
__Religion in America

__The 20th-Century World
__History of Modern Science
__The American Military Experience
__English History Since 1642
__European History, Medieval
__The Rise and Fall of Nazi Germany
__India and Southeast Asia: Modern
__Latin America: Independence to the Present
__American Social, Cultural, and Intellectual History, 1865 to Present
__History of Black America Since 1885
__Modern Europe Since 1815
__American History Since 1877
__American Legal History
__American Business History
__China and the 20th Century
__Methodology

Figure 9.1 Alumni Survey (*continued*)

How would you rate the quality of each of the following in your academic program of study? 1 = Poor, 4 = Excellent.

	Poor	Fair	Good	Excellent
1. Overall quality of faculty	1	2	3	4
2. Availability of my advisor	1	2	3	4
3. Willingness of my advisor to help	1	2	3	4
4. Fairness of grading in my courses	1	2	3	4
5. Quality of instruction in my courses	1	2	3	4
6. Opportunities for interaction with faculty	1	2	3	4
7. Intellectual climate of the department	1	2	3	4

If you participated in any of the activities listed below, please evaluate them by circling the appropriate number.

History Honorary

Outstanding Experience 5 4 3 2 1   No Value

National History Day

Outstanding Experience 5 4 3 2 1   No Value

Moffat Lectures

Outstanding Experience 5 4 3 2 1   No Value

In the space below, please provide a frank evaluation of the value you attach to the education you received in the Department of History.

We appreciate the time you took to complete this questionnaire, and we hope you will return it without delay. Thank you.

from those programs, placement rates into appropriate career positions, and admission rates into four-year institutions for graduates of two-year programs. Do not rely on just one of these methods; multiple methods should be used to assess each learning outcome. Faculty members need to know that there are other ways of assessing learning outcomes. A good faculty discussion should produce ideas beyond those mentioned in this chapter. The benefit of having faculty members talk about different approaches should be evident: If they develop their own approaches as a group, more are likely to buy into the concept and view the program as their own. Regardless of the methods used, they must provide ways to diagnose program weaknesses and strengths so that faculty members can target specific ways to improve the program's quality.

Assessment is not a panacea. It won't solve many of your problems, but it has tremendous value in its own right. If it assists in strengthening the department, everyone wins, and all will feel a sense of accomplishment. Finally, while many departments have not yet put together assessment programs, the time will come soon when most—if not all—will have mandates to do so. As resources become tighter, legislators and governing bodies will insist on more accountability. The strong department that can objectively demonstrate its strengths is likely to be at the top of the list of those departments receiving funds.

Nine Principles of Good Practice for Assessing Student Learning

Here are nine principles of good practice for assessing student learning as developed under the auspices of the former American Association for Higher Education's Assessment Forum (Astin et al., 1991):

1. The assessment of student learning begins with educational values.
2. Assessment is most effective when it reflects an understanding of learning as multidimensional, integrated, and revealed in performance over time.
3. Assessment works best when the programs it seeks to improve have clear, explicitly stated purposes.

4. Assessment requires attention to outcomes but also and equally to the experiences that lead to those outcomes.
5. Assessment works best when it is ongoing, not episodic.
6. Assessment fosters wider improvement when representatives from across the educational community are involved.
7. Assessment makes a difference when it begins with issues of use and illuminates questions that people care about.
8. Assessment is most likely to lead to improvement when it is part of a larger set of conditions that promote change.
9. Through assessment, educators meet responsibilities to students and to the public.

Resources

Web Sites
Internet Resources for Higher Education Outcomes Assessment
www2.acs.ncsu.edu/UPA/assmt/resource.htm

Mesa Community College Office of Research and Planning
www.mc.maricopa.edu/organizations/employee/orp/assessment/FAQ.html

Outcomes Assessment
http://gradstudies.csusb.edu/outcome/time_line.html

Student Outcomes Assessment at NTID
www.ntid.rit.edu/ntiddean/soa/pages/started.html

University of Wisconsin–Madison Assessment Manual
www.provost.wisc.edu/assessment/manual/

Books
Allen, M. J. (2006). *Assessing general education programs*. Bolton, MA: Anker.
Blanchard, R. O., & Christ, W. G. (1992). *Media education and the liberal arts: A blueprint for the new professionalism*. Mahwah, NJ: Lawrence Erlbaum Associates.

DeZure, D. (Ed.). (2000). *Learning from change: Landmarks in teaching and learning in higher education from* Change *magazine 1969–1999.* Sterling, VA: Stylus.

Hashway, R. M. (1998). *Assessment and evaluation of developmental learning: Qualitative individual assessment and evaluation models.* Westport, CT: Praeger.

Maki, P. L. (2004). *Assessing for learning: Building a sustainable commitment across the institution.* Sterling, VA: Stylus.

Palomba, C. A., & Banta, T. W. (Eds.). (2001). *Assessing student competence in accredited disciplines: Pioneering approaches to assessment in higher education.* Sterling, VA: Stylus.

Serban, A. M., & Friedlander, J. (Eds.). (2004). *New directions for community colleges: No. 124. Developing and implementing assessment of student learning outcomes.* San Francisco, CA: Jossey-Bass.

Willingham, W. W., & Cole, N. S. (1997). *Gender and fair assessment.* Mahwah, NJ: Lawrence Erlbaum Associates.

References

Allen, M. J. (2004). *Assessing academic programs in higher education.* Bolton, MA: Anker.

Astin, A. W., Banta, T. W., Cross, K. P., El-Khaswas, E., Ewell, P. T., Hutchings, P., et al. (1991). *Nine principles of good practice for assessing student learning.* Washington, DC: American Association for Higher Education.

Atlanta Board of Regents, Office of Research and Planning. (1992). *A resource manual for the university system of Georgia.* Atlanta, GA: Author.

Kimball, B. A. (1997). Naming pragmatic liberal education. In R. Orrill (Ed.), *Education and democracy: Re-imagining liberal learning in America* (pp. 45–67). New York, NY: The College Board.

Suskie, L. (2004). *Assessing student learning: A common sense guide.* Bolton, MA: Anker.

10

Managing Change

If we are going to prepare students for tomorrow's challenges, our departments must become dynamic, ever-changing units.

Change can be a seductive, exhilarating activity for those who like it, but it can produce a great deal of anxiety for those who don't. This is the difficulty confronting you as chairperson. One of your important roles is to effect change. The turbulent society that we live in demands it. If we are going to prepare students for tomorrow's challenges, our departments must become dynamic, ever-changing units. Faculty members must recognize that change is inevitable and that the quality of instruction and the relevance of the entire curriculum must undergo continuing scrutiny.

Indeed, all educators must recognize the increasing emphasis on accountability. Academic leaders must encourage faculty members to recognize the ever-changing cultural climate. The academy must recognize that our responsibility goes beyond simply seeing that students have an overall liberal education, even though this remains a basic foundation. We must help align student interests with their capabilities and identify fields of study that will enable them to get a job upon earning a degree. Parents demand this, and as the cost of tuition, fees, and books continues to rise, faculty members will be judged on this basis as never before.

So what does this mean? In a nutshell, it means that chairpersons have much work ahead of them. It means that your role is even more demanding. It also means that you must speak out about faculty workloads and respond to external critics by effectively explaining how the academy works. Above all else, you must be a change agent. This book could be devoted entirely to the subject of change, but this discussion will focus on issues especially important to chairpersons. I hope to give the reader a sense of the urgency of change and explain that maintaining the status quo is not a choice.

Let me illustrate. In his 2005 book *China, Inc.: How the Rise of the Next Superpower Challenges America and the World*, Ted Fishman analyzes the stunning growth of the world's most populous nation, the threats and opportunities the juggernaut poses, and the importance of education. He writes that one of the most critical realizations for any community is overcoming the illusion that American children are the best educated. He insists that by any kind of global standard, we are slipping.

What Fishman has to say should motivate all chairpersons to help tomorrow's graduates obtain an education comparable to, or even greater than, those in other countries. Clearly the task is challenging and will require that chairpersons surround themselves with the most capable faculty members available. We cannot be concerned about who gets the credit. Further, we must remember that leadership without change is not leadership at all. As Kouzes and Posner (2003) point out, "You can't manage yourself, the department, the institution to a better tomorrow without change" (p. 50).

Reasons for Resisting Change

Why do people resist change? Diamond (2002, p. 476) lists the following reasons:

- Too much change already
- Lack of community; territoriality among units
- Lack of trust, respect, and openness
- Lack of will, inertia, fear of the unknown
- Less risk in maintaining the status quo
- Vested interest in maintaining the status quo
- Lack of money, time, equipment

Here is an example. I joined a department as its chairperson, succeeding a man who had held the position for 44 years. He was a legend who was worshipped by many friends and acquaintances. His renown didn't bother me, but one young faculty member thought that having this man's picture displayed prominently in our offices was a put-down to me. He took it upon himself to rearrange things; one night he moved the picture to a room across the hall without getting anyone's approval.

When I arrived the next morning, the department was in chaos. Every faculty member and administrative assistant had taken a stand. They were crying and angry. They were arguing bitterly with the man who had moved the picture. I ordered the picture returned to its original place and had a frank talk with the faculty member. I explained that it was not up to him to make such changes and that I was in no way offended by honors given the founder of the department.

Of course, there are times when tradition must be thrown out in favor of a new way of doing something, but we cannot ignore people's reactions to the loss of a tradition. Bolman and Deal (1997) write about what they call the rites of mourning.

> From a symbolic perspective, ritual is the essential companion to significant change. A military change-of-command ceremony is formally scripted. A wake is held for the outgoing commander, and the torch is passed publicly to the new commander in full ceremony. After a period of time, the old commander's likeness or name is displayed in a picture or on a plaque. (p. 330)

The point of these transition rituals is that it gives employees an opportunity to bid farewell to the past so that they can get on with the present.

The Changes Ahead

There seems to be little to dispute the idea that universities must change, and those of us in higher education can expect to confront turbulent times. Among the changes we can anticipate developing in our workplace, in addition to changing faculty demographics, Diamond (2002, pp. 484–485) notes the following:

- As state and federal aid per student diminishes and the number of students being served increases, large state institutions will behave more and more like the private schools, with greater selectivity and an increased emphasis on fundraising.
- Institutions will become more sensitive to student needs and demands, with administrations becoming more proactive in determining departmental programs and institutional agendas.
- Relying heavily on technology, state institutions will expand their efforts to establish satellite units to serve students in remote locations.
- Certificate and other nondegree programs will increase in number.
- The home base of faculty at many campuses will shift from traditional disciplinary-based departments to programs.
- Individual accountability, including faculty and unit rewards and recognition, will be more closely aligned with priorities and missions.
- Academic affairs and student affairs programs will increasingly work together and blend their efforts.

It seems clear that if departments—or colleges and universities, for that matter—are to survive, they must change. Further, it will not be the kind of change we've experienced in the past. Instead, it must be dramatic, and the academic department will be its fulcrum. The decisions and actions you take in the coming years will make a difference in how well your department is positioned to foster transformation. The decisions will likely determine whether your department will be able to take advantage of transformation activities 5 and 10 years in the future.

Here are some things you can do to move your department forward.

- Use the Internet for undergraduate education.
- Provide faculty members with released time to study changes that are taking place. You must raise everyone's knowledge base.

- Encourage strategic thinking.
- Accept the idea that a missed opportunity can be as lethal as a mistake.
- Recognize that the current educational model is insufficient to meet the needs of learners in the 21st century.
- Exercise true leadership in shaping the debate and helping the campus build a new set of shared values regarding learning in the information age.
- Encourage and support innovation in learning.
- Encourage risk-taking behavior.
- Model the way.
- Be confident and bold, but always humble.
- Work hard to understand faculty members in your department and treat each one with respect, giving special attention to those who fight and struggle with change.

Thus, you must do all you can to counsel and inform those who resist change. Today there is no choice but to change, and it is helpful if you understand the causes underlying a faculty member's resistance to it.

I have worked with faculty members who thrive on producing change, and such people usually embrace new ideas without fear. Those who deal positively with change are constantly on the lookout for something they believe needs changing; they are energized by initiating change. I also have worked with faculty members who will go to extreme lengths to get out of the way of change; they will not accept the idea of change.

Faculty members react to change differently, but with practice, they can get better at it. Cheldelin (2000) suggests that chairpersons provide the following information to faculty:

> ... there is greater likelihood of support if the essential ingredients of successful change are provided: a thorough understanding of the implications of the change and a careful alignment of the change and the values held by department members. Chairs will receive support if faculty believe that the benefits of the change initiative are worthwhile, and if they know what impact

the change will have on their lives, including their workload, relationships, and stress level. (p. 60)

You will face resistance nearly every time you try to make a change, no matter how insignificant it is. Unfortunately, this resistance generally is not minimized even when plans are carefully thought out and presented. But the department that resists change risks its future; maintaining the status quo in higher education is not an option.

Not only is change inevitable, it often is massive. If we recognize and accept the proposition that we must change, then we have an opportunity to manage it. Faculty members must understand that change is society's only constant.

Strategies for Dealing With Faculty Resistance to Change

Ease in Change

Select plans that require the least drastic change in order to solve a problem. A physician doesn't perform major surgery to alleviate a mild headache. Likewise, before you set out to change something, you should determine what, why, and how it should be changed. If minor changes will produce the desired results, you ought to make only minor alterations.

Make the change temporary, initially. Announce that the proposed change is being presented on a trial basis, and that it will become permanent only if it succeeds.

Consider the Timing

There are times when hiring a new person to implement change is easier than gaining cooperation from those who are opposed to any kind of change. Obviously this is not always possible, so you may have to postpone change until a foot-dragging faculty member retires.

I've actually had the experience of waiting for a certain person to retire. Most faculty members in a department wanted to move their program to another department, and nearly everyone agreed it would be a smart move. However, one long-time, influential faculty member opposed the move and began lobbying and calling in past favors to convince her colleagues to join her in resisting the move. As it happened, she was retiring at the end of the academic year, so I simply put the matter on the shelf until she had retired. Then we made the move with no opposition, a change that benefited virtually all involved. Certainly, everyone was happy with it.

Plan Carefully

Before implementing any kind of change, plan carefully to avoid possible chaos and disruption. When change is not carefully planned, it can produce upheaval, which in turn causes stress. Because adapting to change of any kind requires psychic energy and is therefore tiring, it is important to reduce other draining variables that are caused by poor planning.

Communicate

As mentioned throughout this book, good communication is key to the success of a department chairperson. When change is the subject, it takes on even greater importance. Part of your plan for change should be your communication strategy.

Choose your words carefully when announcing change. It perhaps seems a bit obtuse, but sometimes we can get support for change by not talking about it as change. Instead, we can talk about faculty development or self-renewal, which are code words for change. As Robert Eaker, former dean of the College of Education at Middle Tennessee State University, said (with tongue in cheek), "I am all in favor of improvement, it's just the change I'm against."

Let the faculty know what's happening. Regular communication prior to the introduction of a change helps alleviate anxiety. Moreover, you need to continue communicating during and after the change. Faculty members want to be informed, and their imaginations sometimes run wild when they don't hear from you. This is especially true of those who oppose change.

Present options. Rather than announcing that specific changes will be implemented, it is often effective to tell faculty members that changes must be made, and then list optional plans that would correct a certain problem. They can then help choose which option would be best.

Be open and honest. Faculty members should know exactly what the change will mean. Explain it and then urge them to be equally forthright with you.

Explain the consequences of not changing something. If the curriculum is outdated and competing schools have updated theirs, most faculty members will see the need for making changes. If enrollment drops off significantly, the reasons for this must be examined and changes devised. If faculty members know that funding will fall off sharply because the department is producing fewer student credit hours, they usually understand that change is in order.

Anticipate Opposition

There are people who simply cannot be convinced that any kind of change should be made. They will do whatever they can to sabotage efforts, especially when the change affects them. You must recognize this and learn to work around such individuals. One way is to get enough support to make the change and then implement it, which means those who are balking will have to accept it. Of course, don't expect this to be done willingly. You may have to have a straightforward talk with faculty members who defy change, but do talk it over. Don't avoid discussions simply because they might be unpleasant.

Meet individually with those who are likely to oppose change. Learn what fears and concerns they have. Sometimes fears are imagined and due to lack of information. Meeting and explaining what the change involves and the necessity for it may help to alleviate concerns. A faculty member's first reaction to change is to contemplate how it will affect him or her in terms of salary, work assignment, or promotion. You should let faculty members know that their jobs, or the status of their jobs, are not in jeopardy (when, of course, that's true).

Try convincing recalcitrant faculty members that they're movers and shakers. I've occasionally gone to faculty members whom I knew to be fearful of change and persuaded them that they were the movers and shakers of the department who could convince others that changes were needed. I would meet individually with them and say something like, "I know good ideas excite you just as they do me. I think we need to make some departmental changes to accommodate some ideas. Let me explain." I then proceeded to lay out plans and concluded by saying, "Can you help me convince our colleagues that we must make this change? I really need your help."

You would be surprised how often this approach works.

Send resisting faculty members to workshops or conferences. Sometimes those who oppose change can be brought around if they learn something about the program to be implemented. Suppose, for example, you know you will be expected to develop and administer an outcomes assessment program. If you know your faculty well enough, you can identify who may oppose the program. Then research whether there are any workshops or conferences on the topic to which you can send one or more of the opposing department members. Obviously, if funds are limited, you would be well advised to spend money on the one who is likely to be the most vocally opposed to the change. After the conference, ask faculty to tell what they learned about assessment programs. Have them talk about how to get them started, how to identify learning outcomes, and how to develop methods for measuring them.

Treat the faculty member's concern with dignity. If you put down or ridicule the faculty member because of his or her concerns, you will deepen the resistance. Try to understand how and why resisting faculty members feel as they do.

Use peer pressure. Occasionally, peers can pressure obstinate faculty members into accepting change. This is especially true when they have close friends who favor the change. If that is the case, it is wise to talk with those who support the change and ask that they talk with those who are likely to be against it.

Use outside consultants to recommend change. Occasionally, I have invited outside consultants to campus to help convince the faculty that certain changes were needed. In each case, I knew the consultant and knew what would be recommended. The consultants had exceptional credentials, and the resisting faculty members found that they couldn't get very far arguing with experts. With their arguments shredded, they acquiesced.

Demonstrate Leadership

Introducing and implementing change requires the strongest leadership skills. It is not a task for the weak of heart, but the rewards of active leadership are tremendous.

Be decisive, and create an atmosphere of entrepreneurship. In his book *Lincoln on Leadership*, Phillips (1992) writes, "Genuine leaders, such as Abraham Lincoln, are not only instruments *of* change, they are catalysts *for* change" (p. 137). He points out that Lincoln quickly took charge and

> Effected the change needed by being extraordinarily decisive and creating an atmosphere of entrepreneurship that fostered innovative techniques. In doing so, he not only got things moving, he also gained commitment from a wide array of individuals who were excited at the prospects of seeing their ideas implemented. He adopted a "more than one way to skin a cat" attitude and would not be consumed with methodology.... Lincoln's obsessive quest for results tended to create a climate for risk taking and innovation. Inevitably there were failures, but Lincoln had great tolerance for failure because he knew that if his generals were not making mistakes they were not moving. (p. 137)

In his annual message to Congress in 1862, Lincoln said, "Still the question recurs 'can we do better?' The dogmas of the quiet past are inadequate to the stormy present. The occasion is piled high with difficulty, and we must rise with the occasion. As our case is new, *so we must think anew and act anew.*"

A study of other great world leaders would undoubtedly reveal that each were, or are, both instruments *of* change and catalysts *for* change.

Get faculty members involved. Create a task force to study and recommend a course of action. If most members of the task force are faculty members who support change, they normally prevail even when others oppose a recommended change. Faculty members who are involved in studying the need for change generally will lend their support to seeing that the change works. They have a stake in the new program or activity.

Apply a range of leadership strategies. James MacGregor Burns (1978) notes that

A number of strategies have been developed to overcome resistance to change: coercive strategies, normative strategies (achieving compliance by invoking values that have been internalized), utilitarian strategies (control over allocation and deprivation of rewards and punishment), empirical-rational strategies (rational justification for change), power-coercive strategies (application of moral, economic, and political resources to achieve change), and reeducative strategies (exerting influence through feeling and thought). (p. 417)

He points out that a common thread running through all the strategies is their difficulty, which is something we've already emphasized. You must bring about change, no matter how difficult the job becomes.

We must remind ourselves from time to time that not all change is good. Certainly deterioration can be a mark of change. In some instances catastrophes are required to produce change. Some companies have gone bankrupt before being convinced that changes were necessary. Likewise, "explosive force is often required to bring about substantial changes in individual beliefs, attitudes, customs or procedures once they have become hardened" (Gardner, 1981, p. 44). You must provide the leadership that produces change before it's too late.

Persuading others to support change will be a continuing challenge. It will require your talents—and a good store of patience. Despite problems that come with making changes, you must accept this challenge. Use the brightest faculty members you have to assist in planning for change. See what other universities are doing and how any related change has worked for them.

On the positive side, change often brings about a new vitality; it can energize even the foot-dragging faculty members. You will feel good when you see once-reluctant professors speaking proudly about what *we* are now doing. Let them feel good; don't say "I told you so." Then when you must make further changes, you can remind them of past successes.

A final word on change: Take the time to lay the proper foundations and ensure that certain conditions prevail. Qualters and Breslow (2002, p. 28) cite the following strategies as necessary for change:

- Leaders need to have and sustain a vision.
- Define change in terms of the discipline's culture.
- Reinforce the message through a variety of media.
- If appropriate, use external validation and drivers.
- Realize that faculty, staff, and students are each at a different stage of recognizing and accepting change.
- Make all faculty accountable and tie change into rewards.
- Involve students in change.
- Highlight the department's success throughout the university and beyond.

Change can create a mood of excitement in the department. It can give new life to a dull environment. Moreover, with the right kind of leadership, change can set a department on a new course toward excellence. Students for years to come will be the beneficiaries.

Resources

Web Sites
Change Management 101: A Primer
http://home.att.net/~nickols/change.htm

Change Management Learning Center
www.change-management.com

Directing and Managing Change
www.solbaram.org/articles/directing.html

Managing Change in Organizations
www.mapnp.org/library/org_chng/chng_mng/chng_mng.htm

Thirteen Tips to Managing Change
www.ncrel.org/sdrs/areas/issues/educatrs/leadrshp/le5spark.htm

Books

Bennis, W., Spreitzer, G. M., & Cummings, T. G. (Eds.). (2001). *The future of leadership: Today's top leadership thinkers speak to tomorrow's leaders.* San Francisco, CA: Jossey-Bass.

Jenkins, W. A., & Oliver, R. W. (1997). *The eagle and the monk: Seven principles of successful change.* Norwalk, CT: Gates & Bridges.

Kotter, J. P., & Cohen, D. S. (2002). *The heart of change: Real-life stories of how people change their organizations.* Boston, MA: Harvard Business School Press.

Lees, N. D. (2006). *Chairing academic departments: Traditional and emerging expectations.* Bolton, MA: Anker.

References

Bolman, L. G., & Deal, T. E. (1997). *Reframing organizations: Artistry, choice, and leadership* (2nd ed.). San Francisco, CA: Jossey-Bass.

Burns, J. M. (1978). *Leadership.* New York, NY: Harper & Row.

Cheldelin, S. I. (2000). Handling resistance to change. In. A. F. Lucas & Associates, *Leading academic change: Essential roles for department chairs* (pp. 55–73). San Francisco, CA: Jossey-Bass.

Diamond, R. M. (2002). Some final observations. In R. M. Diamond (Ed.), *Field guide to academic leadership* (pp. 471–490). San Francisco, CA: Jossey-Bass.

Fishman, T. C. (2005). *China, Inc.: How the rise of the next superpower challenges America and the world.* New York, NY: Scribner.

Gardner, J. W. (1981). *Self-renewal: The individual and the innovative society.* New York, NY: W. W. Norton.

Kouzes, J. M., & Posner, B. Z. (2003). *The Jossey-Bass academic administrator's guide to exemplary leadership.* San Francisco, CA: Jossey-Bass.

Phillips, D. T. (1992). *Lincoln on leadership: Executive strategies for tough times.* New York, NY: Warner.

Qualters, D., & Breslow, L. (2002, Spring). Planned departmental change. *The Department Chair, 12*(4), 26, 28.

11

Building and Maintaining Morale

Capable chairpersons know they must regularly get a sense of the department's climate and deal with morale issues.

Dispirited faculty members can make life miserable for their colleagues, department chairperson, even students, and low faculty morale can be infectious. However, building and maintaining morale is something that chairpersons seldom deal with systematically or formally, or even consider to be a major responsibility. Capable chairpersons know they must regularly get a sense of the department's climate and deal with morale issues no matter how vague and complex they may be. They know better than to turn their backs on any simmering issues.

Mary Lou Higgerson (1996) tells us,

> The department chair has direct influence over how faculty and staff perceive external conditions. The department chair can minimize the destructive effect of campus conditions and other external forces upon department morale. Chairs can influence how faculty and staff perceive external events and forces. Even adverse conditions can be presented in a manner that encourages the department faculty to believe that they have choice and ultimately some control over their fate. It is one thing to communicate fiscal crisis as though all hope is lost and the department has no control over its future. It is another thing to present a fiscal crisis as a time for rethinking the department mission in order to guarantee a strong future. As the key inter-

preters of campus conditions, department chairs determine their influence on the department climate. (p. 42)

The unhappy faculty member can do much harm to the spirit of the department, especially when chairpersons don't take action. And far too many administrators believe that it takes money to deal with all morale problems, and that if they don't have money, there is nothing they can do about morale. But this thinking ignores low-cost and no-cost responses to faculty morale problems. This chapter examines ways to assess faculty morale and presents some ways to deal with it.

Before defining morale, let's examine some of the many wants and needs of faculty members. After all, if we can appropriately address faculty wants and needs, we're likely not to have to worry so much about low morale. Lynn Little (2003) identifies the following faculty wants and needs:

> They want the chair's attention when they need it, and to be left alone when they don't need it. They want the chair to go to bat for them with the dean, with other faculty members in their own department, with other faculty members in other departments, and with the system at large to help them get what they need to accomplish their professional goals. They want pay raises and promotions on a regular basis, despite institutional shortfalls in funding . . .
>
> Faculty members want upgrades to computer hardware and software, teaching assignments and schedules that will accommodate their busy lives, and an office with a window. They want the chair to point the way, and to show them how to do the things they don't know how to do, but not to "show them up" in showing them how to do those things. They want to be kept informed of what is going on around the school but not to be overburdened with administrative duties or other service work. They want to be recognized for their teaching ability, envied for

their scholarship, appreciated for their service work, loved by their students, and admired by their chair and dean. They want to be able to balance their professional needs with their personal needs, to be given time off when they ask for it, and to be brought up-to-date when they return. (p. 36)

Answering these wants and needs provides a big challenge for any chairperson, and those who can satisfy all of them are likely to be individuals who can catch speeding bullets with their teeth!

What do we mean when we talk about morale? One of the few scholars to deal extensively with the subject is Linda Johnsrud (1996), who defines morale as "the level of well-being that an individual or group is experiencing in reference to their worklife" (p. 1). Johnsrud (pp. 4–5) makes several important assumptions relative to the meaning of morale and our attempts to assess and deal with it.

- The factors that administrative staff and faculty perceive as having an effect on morale can be measured.
- Morale exists in individuals and groups.
- Morale matters. This is based on the evidence that demonstrates that morale affects performance.

Causes of Low Morale

The causes of low morale are virtually unlimited. Moreover, they may have to do with factors beyond your control, such as personal or family problems. Some of the causes most cited that are strictly work related follow.

Salary and Related Matters

Given the reduced level of support for higher education in the U.S. in recent years, salary increases seldom exceed increases in the cost of living. Faculty members are understandably concerned about this. Johnsrud (1996) states that "salaries that are perceived as being unfair lead to long-term dissatisfaction and can have a great effect on the faculty members' morale and effectiveness" (p. 31). Salary by itself is not the only issue. Fringe and retirement benefits matter, too. Faculty members also expect support for professional development.

Leadership

Many faculty members do not have good feelings about their university's leadership. Johnsrud (1996) says that "the confidence the faculty have in their leaders decreases with the distance the leaders are from the faculty (i.e., they have the most confidence in their chairs, less in their deans, even less in vice presidents and presidents, etc.)" (p. 34).

Collegial Relations in the Department

This refers to the kind of relations faculty members have with their chairperson. It also represents how well faculty members feel that they fit into the department intellectually and socially. Faculty members who are difficult to get along with and who are themselves unhappy can create low morale for a whole department.

Professional Worklife

Teaching, advising, and committee responsibilities all affect how faculty members assess their professional worklife. Moreover, the kind of support they receive—whether clerical or technical—affects this. Even the parking situation can make a difference in a faculty member's professional attitude.

Faculty Governance

Faculty members want and expect to have some input at both the department level and the college and university levels. They want some say about budgets and personnel matters. They also expect clear protection of their academic freedom. I've found that faculty members would rather deal with the unvarnished truth than be left in the dark. As a dean I worked with chairpersons who would not share budget information, and I saw the frustration of faculty members who did not understand why certain budget allocations were made. As might be expected, morale in these departments was low.

Reward and Evaluation System

Faculty members look for rewards when their productivity in teaching and research increases. They also want clearly stated promotion and tenure expectations. Faculty members who are not praised for doing a good job or who think that tenure guidelines are ambiguous are unlikely to have high morale.

Quality of Students

Students at all levels who have ability and a strong work ethic make a difference in the way faculty members feel about their professional worklife.

Support Service

A good library provides support for faculty members, as do the offices of research, faculty development, and computing. Even duplicating/printing facilities make a difference in the way faculty members assess their morale.

The erosion of working conditions and the public's dissatisfaction with higher education also affect the morale equation. As we know, the public is demanding greater accountability, complaining about faculty workloads, and questioning the tenure system. Many believe that faculty members are arrogant, out of touch, and undeserving of higher salaries or additional support. Moreover, many of those outside the academy—often including elected representatives—believe that we are not doing a good job of educating students.

In recent years, tenure has come under attack, the relevance of our research has been questioned, and our expanding programs and increased tuition have been criticized. Many states have developed policies intended to reduce program duplication at public institutions. Now some legislators who have offered supported in the past are listening to their constituents. Unfortunately, many constituents are angry taxpayers who insist that taxes be lowered. Moreover, legislators have found that cutting higher education funding and diverting money to such things as building prisons, improving roads, and fighting drug problems causes little public outcry.

Whether justified or not, many nonacademics—including a fair number of legislators—believe that higher education wastes taxpayers' dollars. Those same people perceive that college faculty lack a work ethic (in other words, they have soft jobs) and are overpaid, given the hours we are perceived to work. Kerlin and Dunlap (1993) found that

> Retrenchment activities in higher education learning institutions in the U.S. have seriously undermined the morale of faculty members. There has been a notable deterioration in both education quality and faculty morale as a result of austerity measures initiated by administrative officials of educational institutions. Retrenchment and reorganization measures have also increased the incidence of occupation-related stress and overall job dissatisfaction among faculty members.

Improving Faculty Morale

The following are some steps that you can take to improve morale in your department.

- **Communicate, communicate, communicate.**
Faculty members want to know what's going on; they want to feel they are a part of things. They should know how money is allocated to the department and how it is spent. Keeping faculty members in the dark regarding budget matters contributes to low morale whereas having regular faculty meetings and communicating in other ways on a regular basis helps to build morale.

- **Let faculty know they are appreciated.**
You must be alert for the accomplishments of faculty so that you can congratulate them and tell them how much their efforts are appreciated. If a faculty member does an especially good job of supervising a project or chairing a committee, tell that individual how much the effort is appreciated and congratulate them on a job well done.

- **Involve faculty in the governance of the department.**
All major policy decisions made at the departmental level should have faculty input. For example, if the department is expected to have a merit

salary plan, faculty members should help to develop one. Likewise, departmental promotion and tenure guidelines should grow out of faculty committee work. Indeed, the more ways in which you can involve faculty in the major affairs of the department, the better off both you—and faculty morale—will be.

Budget decisions should be made public, and faculty members in your department should be asked for input regarding academic program priorities and how funds should be spent. Most faculty members are aware that difficult choices have to be made, but they resent not being included in the decision-making process.

- **Establish a positive tone of cooperation.**

If all faculty members work to cooperate with each other, department morale will be enhanced. As chairperson, you should let faculty know that cooperation is expected. When a faculty member is ill or must be away from campus, do other faculty members willingly cover his or her classes? Are they willing to share equipment?

- **Address the issue of high starting salaries.**

Today, salary increases are often small and mandated, which leaves little flexibility regarding salary increases. However, when you hire new faculty members, there is often some latitude regarding starting pay. I believe that you should stretch this to the limit by providing the best beginning salary possible. If you do this, however, you will want the support of current faculty. If you independently create inequities, you will do much to create morale problems.

- **Don't permit small amounts of money for merit raises to divide your faculty.**

I don't know whether you've been faced with this or not, but I was several times—and on more than one campus. A small salary increase has been approved, and you are asked whether you want to provide across-the-board salary increases or to provide merit increases. If the amount is small and you have a choice, I believe you ought to favor across-the-board increases. Merit increases may not be worth the tensions they cause when the dollars add up to less than cost-of-living increases.

- **Establish clear policies and distribute them widely.**

Faculty members have every right to be upset and dissatisfied with their professional status when policies are unclear and shifting. Whether these policies have to do with promotion and tenure or travel funds, faculty members need to know the ground rules. Moreover, it is especially important that you are consistent with policy application and interpretation.

- **Treat all faculty fairly and without favoritism.**

There always will be the temptation to reward some faculty members and punish others. This, of course, is permissible providing we reward and punish within acceptable and known policies. We shouldn't be governed by ad hoc policies.

- **Look for opportunities to provide faculty with consulting.**

In your position as chairperson, you are often asked to recommend faculty for consulting. By recommending faculty on the basis of their competence—rather than on how you feel about them personally—and by spreading these opportunities around, you can help boost faculty morale.

- **Work to develop positive relations with community members.**

If you can develop a special tie to the local community, this relationship will enrich the lives of individual faculty members.

- **Treat all faculty as professionals and with respect.**

You will have a positive influence on faculty morale if you treat all faculty members with respect and as professionals. Faculty members need to be told precisely what is expected of them and then left alone to do their jobs so long as they are fulfilling expectations. No one likes to have another person looking over his or her shoulder, and if appropriate leadership is provided, most faculty members will not need excessive supervision. Generally, faculty members will work better and be more productive if treated as professionals.

- Spread the work around.

While it is tempting to assign work to those you know will do the job well and on time, doing so penalizes the good workers and rewards the slackers. Moreover, it can create an unhealthy work environment and lead to low morale. Make certain that all faculty members know that you expect them to do their fair share of departmental work.

- Avoid the unilateral contract.

Partin (1991) asserts that the unilateral contract can be one of the most insidious causes of low faculty morale. A unilateral contract is "an unwritten, unspoken agreement between two parties—only one of whom is aware of its existence" (Partin, 1991, p. 1). Most chairpersons have had to deal with this problem at one time or another. We've all had faculty members who will take on almost any assignment in the department. They are on virtually all department committees, they teach those night classes that must be covered, and they work hard at recruiting students. But they are not doing research or publishing, those things that they must do to get promoted. When they are not promoted, they want to know why you have not lived up to your end of the bargain.

We must make certain that faculty members do those things that will increase their chances of getting promotions and tenure and that they do not spend an inordinate amount of time on other assignments. Those who are not making appropriate progress toward promotion and tenure need to be counseled.

- Work to create a supportive culture.

A chairperson who listens to faculty members and discusses their concerns without judging goes far to create a supportive culture. Other supportive actions include finding funds for faculty travel, covering for faculty when they are ill, or taking an interest in their research projects.

Make a habit of meeting regularly with faculty members to see how they are, to find out what they need, or to listen to their concerns. Faculty members like to talk about their work, and it boosts morale for the chairperson to say occasionally, "Tell me how your classes are going."

Do what you can to provide an environment and structure that adequately satisfies the human needs of your faculty and encourages new ideas, risk-taking, and creativity. An exciting, reinforcing environment encourages faculty members to engage in professional activities and seek new challenges.

- **Tolerate differences.**

A university ought to be a place where ideas are challenged. Faculty members should be encouraged to voice their disagreement with ideas advanced by other department faculty members. They should be reminded that debate is invigorating and healthy, and that while professional differences of opinion are to be expected, the differences should not be carried over into their personal lives.

Factors That Produce High Morale

Rice and Austin (1988) found four key features that produced high morale at 10 liberal arts colleges. They discovered, first of all, that the colleges where high morale exists had distinctive organizational cultures that are carefully nurtured. They also found those colleges have strong, participatory leadership that provides direction and purpose while conveying to faculty the empowering conviction that the college is theirs. Third, all of the colleges where high morale exists have a firm sense of organizational momentum. They were colleges "on the move." Finally, the faculty members at the 10 colleges have an unusually compelling identification with the institution that incorporates and extends the other three characteristics contributing to high morale.

Rice and Austin (1988, p. 58) list the following characteristics of high-morale colleges:

- High involvement of faculty in decision-making
- Environment that supports faculty and their work
- Collaborative environment
- Risk-taking encouraged

- New ideas likely to be tried
- Anticipatory long-range planning
- High proportion of faculty attended liberal arts colleges
- Narrow gap between perceived and desired involvement in decision-making
- Individual career orientations likely to be accommodated by the organization
- Administrators and faculty have similar views about the academic workplace.

Morale can be a problem if you fail to respond quickly and fairly to faculty conflicts. Honest differences of professional opinion always exist, and when differing viewpoints are expressed with civility, they can be healthy. Debate—devoid of personal attack—causes faculty members to think and respond to ideas. You often can deal effectively with such problems by getting the involved faculty members together to see if differences can be resolved.

Chairpersons need to model the way: "Titles are granted, but it's your behavior that wins you respect" (Kouzes & Posner, 2003, p. 4). Chairpersons need to be upbeat and cheerful. If they give the slightest hint of low morale, they can soon expect faculty members in their department to exhibit disgruntled behavior associated with problems of low morale. Successful chairpersons won't let that happen.

Resources

Web Sites
Boost Employee Morale
www.sideroad.com/Management/boost_employee_morale.html

Boosting Employee Morale
www.agmrc.org/agmrc/business/gettingstarted/boosting
employeemorale.htm

Fun and the Bottom Line: Using Humor to Retain Employees
http://humanresources.about.com/library/weekly/uc030302a.htm

Practical Leadership Concepts
www.ruralhealthresources.com/EMSreview/Practical_Leadership_
Concepts.htm

Books

Beyerlein, M. M., Freedman, S., McGee, C., & Moran, L. (2003). *Beyond teams: Building the collaborative organization.* San Francisco, CA: Jossey-Bass.

Boverie, P. E., & Kroth, M. (2001). *Transforming work: The five keys to achieving trust, commitment, and passion in the workplace.* New York, NY: Perseus.

Bruce, A. (2003). *Building a high morale workplace.* New York, NY: McGraw-Hill.

Ford, L. (2002). *FAST52: Building an exceptional workplace environment.* Rome, NY: Ardan Press.

Payne, V. (2001). *The team-building workshop: A trainer's guide.* New York, NY: American Management Association.

Topchik, G. S. (2001). *Managing workplace negativity.* New York, NY: American Management Association.

Whitaker, T., Whitaker, B., & Lumpa, D. (2000). *Motivating and inspiring teachers: The educational leader's guide for building staff morale.* Larchmont, NY: Eye on Education.

References

Higgerson, M. L. (1996). *Communication skills for department chairs.* Bolton, MA: Anker.

Johnsrud, L. K. (1996). *Maintaining morale: A guide to assessing the morale of midlevel administrators and faculty.* Washington, DC: College and University Personnel Association.

Kerlin, S. P., & Dunlap, D. M. (1993, May/June). For richer, for poorer: Faculty morale in periods of austerity and retrenchment. *Journal of Higher Education, 64*(3), 348–377.

Kouzes, J. M., & Posner, B. Z. (2003). *The Jossey-Bass academic administrator's guide to exemplary leadership.* San Francisco, CA: Jossey-Bass.

Little, L. M. (2003). Establishing a positive leadership approach. In D. R. Leaming (Ed.), *Managing people: A guide for department chairs and deans* (pp. 29–41). Bolton, MA: Anker.

Partin, B. L. (1991, Fall). The unilateral contract: A faculty morale nightmare. *The Department Chair, 2*(2), 1, 20.

Rice, R. E., & Austin, A. E. (1988, March/April). High faculty morale: What exemplary colleges do right. *Change, 20*(2), 51–58.

12

Managing Conflict

When dealing with matters that tend to be emotional, the chair-person must be particularly cognizant of any dysfunctional conflict, and he or she must deal with it swiftly.

As chairperson, you must provide a healthy and positive workplace. Unless there is good chemistry between faculty members and you and your values, you will not likely be able to provide the leadership needed to establish a first-rate department. How does a healthy department differ from one that is fractious? How can you go about creating a community in which people and ideas are valued?

Much has been written about conflict management, yet most chairpersons are poorly prepared to settle disputes. In his book *Work and Peace in Academe*, James Coffman (2005) speaks about the importance of conflict management.

> Of greatest importance is the role of the department chair in creating an environment that allows for productive conflict, raw debate, and reasoned discourse, but mitigates unproductive conflict and disputes. She can do this through the allocation of work, the annual goal setting and evaluation and reward process, and also by adding the right personal touch day to day. For this to work well, the head must know the strengths, weaknesses, and aspirations of every member of her faculty. She must optimize individual strengths and minimize individual weaknesses in the setting of goals and allocation of effort. . . . Only

an able head or chair that has a passion for the job and wants to serve in that way can do this well. A mediocre, unimaginative leader cannot, and a personnel committee cannot. (p. 77)

What Coffman describes are essential leadership characteristics—most, if not all, are advocated elsewhere in this book—and he underscores the importance of strong leadership.

Chairpersons will face many sticky situations that will challenge even those whose leadership skills are exceptional. Nonetheless, there are those on campus who can be of great assistance, such as the dean and the affirmative action office. Additionally, Coffman (2005) suggests that an ombudsperson, a mediator, multicultural affairs, attorneys, trusted intermediaries, and staff might also be called upon in matters involving dispute resolution.

This chapter will explore what chairpersons can do to create a friendly but respectful departmental environment where intolerance of any kind is unwelcome.

The following are tips that can help prevent conflicts from occurring.

- Model tolerance.

Modeling the way is a recurring theme in most books on leadership. Kouzes and Posner (2003) note, ". . . it's your behavior that wins you respect" (p. 4). While modeling the way is an ongoing process for any chairperson, there must be constancy when it comes to modeling behavior in the chairperson's attempt to create a warm, friendly, tolerant department. Giving even the briefest comfort to intolerance can destroy your campaign for tolerance—a slip of the tongue, a double-entendre, the hint of a smile at a racist joke. Failure to signal disapproval toward intolerant behavior can deal a deadly blow to creating a warm, friendly, tolerant department.

- Share information.

When chairpersons keep faculty members informed, they buoy morale. When attitudes are positive and faculty and staff members are smiling, the department's ambience takes on a warmth. It's a place that feels good.

- Invite individuals to speak about racism, feminism, and homophobic behavior.

Some faculty members may resist by voicing objections such as "I am tired of talking about thus and so," but revisiting these issues from time to time can be a needed boost. The effects of a first (or perhaps even a second or third) inoculation against intolerance can wear off in time. Practicing tolerance is made easier when we talk openly about some of the issues that cause it.

- Recognize your tipping point.

In *Primal Leadership: Realizing the Power of Emotional Intelligence*, Daniel Goleman, Richard Boyatzis, and Annie McKee (2002) provide their definition of the tipping point as "the level at which a relatively small improvement or increase in frequency of competence will tip someone into outstanding performance" (p. 146). Knowing your tipping point enables the chairperson to fortify skills necessary to create a more productive department where intolerance ceases to be an issue.

- Reward appropriate behavior.

Department chairpersons should be alert to ways for complimenting and rewarding performance. When a chairperson sees a faculty member go out of the way to display tolerance, the chairperson should make a point of praising or otherwise showing appreciation for the contribution the faculty member is making to helping establish a warm, friendly, tolerant department. Most chairpersons routinely do this whenever a faculty member publishes a paper or receives recognition for service. Why not do the same when faculty display unusual qualities of tolerance?

- Exploit the perception that the department is a family.

Using this positive communication strategy builds teamwork and faculty bonding. By regularly referring to the "chemistry family," the "history family," or the "social work family," for example, faculty members will recognize the need to work collectively to accomplish departmental goals. However, we need to do more than talk the talk. A picnic and softball game as a faculty and student back-to-school get-together in the fall, a Halloween party, or a Christmas or holiday dinner prepared by students and faculty help the chairperson walk the talk. Each gives support to the perception of family.

- **Consider the feelings, values, and behavior of all faculty.**
In his book *Creating Leaderful Organizations*, Joseph Raelin (2003) writes,

> Not only do people sometimes not do what they're told, especially if they determine that it is not in their best interest, but they may also be affected by others who have their own agendas. Change-making, then, has to consider the feelings, values, and behaviors of people in addition to the physical processes that operate on the system in question. (p. 172)

Ignoring feelings, values, and behavior—and not knowing your faculty members—creates a leadership vacuum. Exposing an individual's values without any appreciation and respect for their feelings, values, and behavior can create resentment and hard feelings. The truly "leaderful" chairperson can avert such problems.

- **Understand the different levels of conflict.**
One of a chairperson's primary responsibilities is to manage conflict. As Ann Lucas (1994) correctly notes,

> Conflict can energize a group and assist its members in coming to a thoughtful, comprehensive decision characterized by ownership and commitment. However, chairs must manage conflict effectively, so that it does not become dysfunctional, and they must recognize the many levels of conflict. In an academic department, conflict may occur between colleagues or factions, creating a fragmented department; between faculty member and student; between faculty members and the dean; and between the chair and the dean. (p. 28)

When dealing with matters that tend to be emotional, as many of the issues discussed in this chapter do, the chairperson must be particularly cognizant of any dysfunctional conflict, and he or she must deal with it swiftly.

Resources

Web Sites
Conflict Management in Groups
www.managementhelp.org/grp_skll/grp_cnfl/grp_cnfl.htm

Conflict Management Skills
www.cnr.berkeley.edu/ucce50/ag-labor/7labor/13.htm

International Association for Conflict Management
www.iacm-conflict.org/

Why Mediation and Conflict Resolution Services Matter for Faculty
www.campus-adr.org/Faculty_Club/rationales_faculty.html

Books
Higgerson, M. L., & Joyce, T. A. (2007). *Effective leadership communication: A guide for department chairs and deans for managing difficult situations and people.* Bolton, MA: Anker.

Morrill, C. (1995). *The executive way: Conflict management in corporations.* Chicago, IL: University of Chicago Press.

Withers, B. (2002). *The conflict management skills workshop: A trainer's guide.* New York, NY: American Management Association.

References

Coffman, J. R. (2005). *Work and peace in academe: Leveraging, time, money, and intellectual energy through managing conflict.* Bolton, MA: Anker.

Goleman, D., Boyatzis, R., & McKee, A. (2002). *Primal leadership: Realizing the power of emotional intelligence.* Boston, MA: Harvard Business School Press.

Kouzes, J. M., & Posner, B. Z. (2003). *The Jossey-Bass academic administrator's guide to exemplary leadership.* San Francisco, CA: Jossey-Bass.

Lucas, A. F. (1994). *Strengthening departmental leadership: A team-building guide for chairs in colleges and universities.* San Francisco, CA: Jossey-Bass.

Raelin, J. A. (2003). *Creating leaderful organizations: How to bring out leadership in everyone.* San Francisco, CA: Berrett-Koehler.

13

Working With Constituents

Chairpersons must widen their circles of influence as they reach out to various constituents.

Working with constituents is a basic responsibility for all chairpersons, and the successful ones know how to leverage their influence so that all constituents come to share the department's goals, mission, vision, and values. These leaders understand the importance of collaboration, networking, and relationships. Furthermore, they understand what Stephen Covey (1989) teaches in his book *The Seven Habits of Highly Effective People* about our circles of influence.

Covey points out that we have circles of concern, which can include concerns about "our health, our children, problems at work, the national debt, nuclear war" (p. 81). He then shows that within each circle, there is what he calls a "Circle of Influence." Covey writes, "Proactive people focus their efforts in the Circle of Influence. They work on things they can do something about. The nature of their energy is positive, enlarging and magnifying, causing their Circle of Influence to increase" (p. 83). On the other hand, people who are reactive give their attention to areas over which they have no control. Thus, they blame, accuse, and feel victimized. "The negative energy," Covey writes, "generated by that focus, combined with neglect in areas they could do something about, causes their Circle of Influence to shrink" (p. 83).

Chairpersons must widen their circles of influence as they reach out to their constituents. Let's begin this discussion of working with constituents by examining useful ways of establishing connections with alumni. Too often our former students feel that we no longer care about them.

This is especially true for those who seldom return to campus, but even graduates who live nearby can feel this way unless we give them reasons to be part of our "family." Here's an example of what happened when I was director of the School of Journalism at Marshall University, an approach that worked for me and something you may want to consider.

It occurred to me that few alumni made any kind of contact with members of the department, except in isolated ways. As a subscriber to the local newspaper, I was impressed with the writing, editing, and photography of some staff members who were our graduates, and I encouraged faculty members to invite alumni to their classes to talk about their work. One of the local newspaper staff writers was especially gifted. Who better to invite into a class of young journalists to talk about writing? He became a regular visitor to campus, and I'll never forget what he said: "You know, before you became head of journalism, I never felt wanted or valued as an alumnus."

I began to see a need for the School of Journalism to bond with our former students and to recognize them for their achievements. It struck me as something we could do even with limited resources. Thus, I decided to develop an alumni association and a "wall of fame."

When I arrived on campus, I began working with faculty members to assess the quality of the department with the clear intention of raising standards across the board. In the recent past, the journalism program had begun to slip as interim chairpersons and appointees failed to recognize or address weaknesses. In a meeting with the publisher of the local newspaper, one of the many newspapers owned by Gannett, he told me that if I could convince him that the Marshall journalism program was turning around he would see to it that we got a Gannett grant.

Working with faculty members, we addressed all issues of quality and continuous improvement, including raising standards so students would receive a rigorous education—not just in journalism but in the liberal arts, business, and sciences as well. For example, knowing that journalists must have a good understanding of government at all levels, we required a number of political science courses. Economics and history courses were required as well. Our faculty agreed that all graduates must demonstrate high levels of writing, editing, and reporting skills.

Slowly, we made progress, and received money to fund a Gannett Chair. Then, for the first time, we received national accreditation through the Association of Education in Journalism and Mass Communication. We were one of the first small programs that broke through what had become a "Good Ole Boy" network, paving the way for other smaller journalism programs. We then worked through a tough political process to be elevated to school level, and named the school after its longtime leader, W. Page Pitt.

Creating an Alumni Association

Recognizing a need to develop an association for our graduates came easily. To get it started, I contacted some who lived within a day's drive of campus and invited them to become a member of an organizing team. We met several times to develop bylaws and other organizational specifics so that we could elect officers and get the organization up and running. The Marshall Alumni Association assisted and recognized our organization. However, getting names of those who had earned degrees in journalism was not easy. I developed a simple database, gathering names from old yearbooks and the archives of our daily campus newspaper. In some instances I had to rely on the memory of graduates I knew. We created a newsletter and encouraged those whose names we already had to supply names and addresses of journalism friends from their time at Marshall. We also offered a job search program in which we mailed information about journalism openings to those who signed up for the service. In time, we built up a solid database of alumni. The alumni association helped to raise funds, recruit students, and foster good relations with numerous media outlets. In Chapter 17 I will describe some of the especially successful fundraising efforts supported by the alumni association.

Creating a Wall of Fame

I created a wall of fame at Marshall and also at Middle Tennessee State University. At Marshall, everything was handled by the alumni association, with the selection of individuals to be recognized following specific guidelines established by the association with my participation. At Middle Tennessee, which when I retired was the second largest program of its kind in the country, we broadened the concept. In addition to the alumni we recognized yearly, we chose a "friend" of the College of Mass Communication whose picture with a short biography was placed on the wall alongside our distinguished alumni. Moreover, we created a great deal more fanfare for the induction ceremony. At Middle Tennessee, our building had a wide first-floor corridor where live trees had been planted. The interior walls on this level were brick, and we found an ideal spot to mount the impressive wall of fame logo. At our inaugural initiation, we set up what we thought would be enough chairs for all in attendance. That was the only thing that went wrong: We had an overflow crowd, which actually enhanced our celebration.

We had decided our wall of fame would be done with class, and we developed the support of friends on and off campus to make this happen. I remember that after our first initiation, the provost told me she had never witnessed a nicer or more moving ceremony at the university. It was planned that way!

Working With Professionals Outside the University

The wall of fame efforts led naturally to further achievements. Getting to know our distinguished alumni brought myself and others into contact with numerous high-profile professionals. I also made a point to belong to those organizations that were meaningful to our graduates. I became a regional director and a national board member for the Society of Professional Journalists, and I belonged to the Academy of Television Arts and Sciences and helped select Emmy Award winners.

Networking with key professionals broadens our awareness of what students need to become successful upon graduation. Also, it makes collaborations that benefit students and faculty possible. If we enable faculty members to work closely in professional settings outside the university, they gain a wider perspective of the marketplace and make connections that will be helpful in placing students for internships or entry-level jobs.

I recognize the difficulties certain departments in liberal arts might face in similar undertakings. Still, this can be done if chairpersons are creative and open to finding those special individuals who can help define new and interesting boundaries of study.

Any successful chairperson—as with all leaders—knows he or she does not have all the answers and is constantly energized by ideas and learning. No longer can any of us in higher education be complacent, and chairpersons have a special responsibility to facilitate the efforts of all faculty members. And these collaborative efforts must, if we are serious about helping our students shape a better tomorrow, reach beyond the campus.

On-Campus Networking

Just as we need to reach out to those off campus, we must not isolate ourselves on campus. It becomes all too easy to get caught up in our work and neglect interacting with others from whom we can learn. Here is where your dean can help. If he or she holds regular meetings with chairpersons, suggest that guests from across campus be invited to explain their roles and responsibilities. Chairpersons then can take the new information back to their faculties. Let me give an example.

As dean of the College of Liberal Arts at Marshall University, I once asked the director of a program for handicapped students to speak at one of our regular meetings. She later wrote to our president about her visit:

> Dr. Leaming is also the only dean who has asked me to speak to his college about the legal rights of handicapped students. We met for two hours, and I felt that the exchange that followed was healthy and informative. It was apparent to those who were present that the Dean was very supportive of qualified handicapped students.

What my colleague wrote was flattering, but that's not the point. Every chairperson in the college took the information to their departments, and some even followed up with invitations for her to speak to their faculty members. We all benefited. You could do the same thing for the person in charge of student affairs, the individual who guides affirmative action, the professor heading up African-American history month, and so on.

Learning how to do one's job comes in many forms. I learned by talking to other chairpersons, interacting with staff members in the advising center, and talking to the person in charge of book orders. Most of all I learned about leadership from those who modeled the way for me. President James Walker and Provost Barbara Haskew were two such people at Middle Tennessee State University, just as President Dale Nitzschke and Provost Alan Gould were at Marshall. Also, I learned much from my fellow deans. John McDaniel, dean of the College of Liberal Arts at Middle Tennessee, is one who comes quickly to mind. I can't tell you how many times I turned to him for advice when I first became dean there. Further, I learned by observing how he did his job. The point here is that departmental academic leaders must reach out to others on campus.

Becoming involved with others can lead to productive collaboration as well. Years ago when I was college dean, I felt the need to provide some kind of workshop for those who wanted to improve their teaching. I contacted leaders in the College of Education and asked for their help. Together, we sponsored a highly effective series of panels, lectures, and seminars on what we could do to improve teaching skills. I sat in on the sessions and picked up many ideas that I took to my own classes. Even as a dean, I always tried to teach one course a semester. It not only kept me in touch with students, but I believe it gave me credibility regarding my concerns for faculty members. We ought not to forget that we can—and should—reach out to students just as we reach out to other constituents.

Accept the Challenge of Networking

In addition to working with off-campus professionals, chairpersons need to scan the landscape for those important community and regional—perhaps even statewide—leaders who can provide assistance to their departments. As director of the School of Journalism at Marshall, I had then Governor Jay Rockefeller speak to a large class of journalism students. I stayed in touch with U.S. House leaders both at Marshall and at Middle Tennessee. They helped bring money and recognition to programs for which I had responsibility.

Seeing the Big Picture

Good leadership is at the heart of effective relationships with constituents. Chairpersons must constantly come up with ideas, gain the trust of others, and persuade faculty members that risk-taking is necessary to become a stronger department. Effective chairpersons will be those who find new pathways and discover what others have overlooked. They will challenge the status quo and demand quality. Successful chairpersons will work well with constituents, and they will empower faculty members to develop skillful ways of doing the same. Futurists predict that in coming decades we will meet global challenges that cannot even be imagined today. No longer can any chairperson be content with the insular attitudes that permeated so many colleges and universities until recently. The future is here.

Recognizing the various constituencies of the department and working with them to enhance student learning is essential. Successful, idea-generating chairpersons will seek to connect and network with those who can help light the pathway. Such chairpersons are passionate in their efforts to do this. A recent study conducted by Executive Development Associates found that 70% of the 100 companies polled indicated having moderate to major leadership shortages, which will affect the companies' growth (Antonucci, 2005). Effective chairpersons will work hard to see that students become leaders, so that these statistics become a thing of the past.

Resources

Web Sites
Bridging the Digital Divide
www.soros.org/initiatives/information/articles_publications/articles/
bridging_20000615

Consortium for North American Higher Education Collaboration
www.conahec.org/conahec/index.jsp

Executive Development Associates
http://edanetworks.com

Leadership Development
www.leadervalues.com/Content/detail.asp?ContentDetailID=258

National Leadership Area in Re-engineering Schools: Key Issues
www.nwrel.org/scpd/reengineering/keyissues/leadership.shtml

Working with the Power Constituents in Communities
www.oznet.ksu.edu/library/agec2/mf2225.pdf

Books

Bennis, W. (2000). *Managing the dream: Reflections on leadership and change.* New York, NY: Perseus.

Bennis, W. (2003). *On becoming a leader* (Rev. and expanded ed.). Cambridge, MA: Perseus.

Langseth, M., & Plater, W. M. (Eds.). (2004). *Public work and the academy: An academic administrator's guide to civic engagement and service-learning.* Bolton, MA: Anker.

References

Antonucci, E. (2005). *The leadership benchstrength challenge: Building integrated talent management systems.* San Francisco, CA: Executive Development Associates.

Covey, S. R. (1989). *The seven habits of highly effective people: Powerful lessons in personal change.* New York, NY: Simon & Schuster.

14

Working With Your Dean

*Having a positive working relationship with your dean is good for
your department and is worth the effort.*

It should go without saying that you and your dean generally want
the same thing: a positive working relationship. Your dean wants your
department to run smoothly, stay within budget, and provide students
a good, solid education. Moreover, your dean wants and expects you
to provide the kind of leadership that will enable your faculty to work
together in harmony.

Most deans do not want to micromanage departments in their colleges—they don't have time for that. Your dean expects you to take charge,
to be the leader, to be a strong advocate for faculty and the department,
and to be collegial as well. Deans I've known see effective chairpersons as
indispensable to their own success. If you are an outstanding chairperson,
the dean feels better and looks better—to those at the next administrative
level. Both dean and chairperson should recognize the value of helping
and supporting one another. Most deans have served as chairpersons, so
they can identify with many of the issues unique to the position, such as
evaluating faculty members. Most deans also know the difficulty of coping
with skimpy budgets.

As with any relationship, both chairpersons and deans must try to
understand each other. This requires work. Even so, veteran deans and
chairpersons know that there will be times when their views on important matters will clash. They also know that their differences must not
adversely affect their personal or professional relationship. The experienced

chairperson knows that talking with his or her dean regularly and airing any differences helps to build a stronger relationship. Imagine what could happen if the chairperson and dean didn't talk—even the smallest problem, if left unattended, could cause the relationship to deteriorate. Trying to understand each other and strengthen the relationship serves the interests not only of ourselves, but of faculty and students as well.

What John Bennett (2003) writes about leadership is instructive.

> As teacher, the hospitable leader extends the educational conversation by distributing, not sequestering, information. He or she includes others in institutional decision-making . . .
>
> Hospitable leadership does not mean one is unable to be decisive and make quiet decisions when necessary. But it does require ongoing attention to others—understanding their perspectives from their points of view. Informed by these viewpoints, hospitable leadership relies upon persuasion rather than command. It requires the energy and flexibility to recognize and even encourage changing coalitions. Issues change, often quite rapidly, and authority and power change as well. (p. 180)

Chairpersons who model hospitable leadership will develop a positive relationship with their dean, the results of which benefit both the chairperson and the department's faculty and students.

Effective chairpersons communicate regularly with their dean and demonstrate that their department is engaged. Your dean should be familiar with your goals and know the extent to which you are advocating higher aspirations in your department. In *Departments That Work*, Wergin (2003) defines engaged departments as those that

> . . . ask very basic questions about themselves—"What are we trying to do? Why are we trying to do it? Why are we doing it that way? How do we know it works?" In essence, these departments have created a climate for reflection . . . (p. 33)

Discussing your program with your dean will make clear the ideas you hope to implement and what resources will be needed, including additional faculty and financial support. A careful reading of Wergin's book provides an overview of activities deans should pay special attention to. Far more important, however, is the knowledge that will be gained by understanding "excellence" as Wergin describes it.

> The quality of an institution is marked, more than anything else, by the quality of its departments and its academic programs. Departments aren't mere organizational units charged with carrying out the purpose of the institution; rather, they are semi-autonomous organizations themselves, and their vitality is what makes institutions tick. Without program quality, what happens in the rest of the institution makes little difference. (p. 131)

My purpose for dwelling on this theme is that issues and activities related to excellence are vitally important matters your dean should know about, and your discussions with him or her can have a powerful influence on how your dean evaluates you and your department.

Chairpersons need to work effectively with deans and other high-level administrators. Daniel Wheeler (2002) makes a good point about differences in management or personality styles.

> Explore with the dean or supervising higher-level administrator how that person prefers to be informed and what he or she wants to be informed about. If you have different styles, it will be important to acknowledge that and make sure you agree on goals even if you have different ways of getting there. (p. 458)

Here are some ideas that may help you to build a stronger relationship with your dean.

- **Keep your dean informed.**

Your dean needs to know what's going on. A dean does not like to be taken by surprise—he or she does not take kindly to being blindsided. Sometimes it is little things that make a difference in how the dean regards your leadership. If you must be out of town, let your dean know how to get in touch with you. Years ago, when I served as director of the W. Page Pitt School of Journalism at Marshall University, each August I would take my family to a South Carolina beach for a weeklong vacation. My dean knew how to reach me, and I cannot remember one vacation when he did not call to discuss my budget needs. Not only did I let him know how to reach me, but I also made certain that I had my budget facts available.

- **Keep the lines of communication open.**

Your dean should know your goals and objectives, and you should send her or him a copy of whatever plans you develop. Let your dean know of any potential problems. Likewise, if faculty members in your department do something that merits commendation, let your dean know. Often it's the little things that chairpersons do that foster goodwill. An even more positive byproduct is the elevation of faculty morale.

- **Take responsibility for your decisions.**

Not every decision you make will produce the desired results. Just as you are willing to accept praise for good decisions, you must be willing to admit when you are wrong. You don't like to hear excuses from faculty members in your department, and your dean doesn't want to hear excuses from you. Good deans know that if you are going to be creative and innovative, you are going to make mistakes from time to time.

- **Meet deadlines.**

Deans establish deadlines for a reason; often the information you submit must in turn go into the dean's report to the vice president for academic affairs. If you are late, it may well cause your dean to be late.

- Stay within your budget.

As mentioned earlier, deans expect their chairpersons to keep track of their funds and not overspend. Most deans will keep a small amount of money in reserve for emergencies, but they don't like to use the funds in behalf of poor managers. If you have budget trouble, get some help from the financial affairs office and set up a system to manage it.

- Know university policy—and follow it.

One of the first things you should do upon being appointed is to study the university's policy manual carefully. Generally your administrative assistant will know university policies thoroughly, but what if he or she retires or takes another job?

- Try solving departmental problems yourself before going to your dean for help.

The dean will help when asked, but will not appreciate your turning to him or her every time a problem comes up. Do what you can to deal with the problem. If you cannot solve it, then go to your dean.

- Be open with your faculty and share information with them.

Over the years, I've been puzzled that many faculty members never seemed to get information that I asked chairpersons to share with them. On occasion, chairpersons would be so insecure that they hid information as a way of controlling their faculty. Information often is power.

I am a strong proponent of sharing all budget information with chairpersons, and I expect them to share budget information with their faculties. I have not always been able to convince some chairpersons that they should do this. Yet the strong, secure chairpersons have always complied.

- Be a strong advocate for your faculty and department, but be collegial.

Deans expect you to be an advocate, but they do not want you to be so narrow in your advocacy that you are willing to hurt other departments in the process.

I do believe that you must be a strong departmental advocate, of course. The exceptional chairperson will know exactly when to stop; however, chairpersons can present vigorous, robust arguments in support of positions that may be different from the one their dean takes. They should be able to push hard to persuade the dean. However, once the matter has been resolved, it is wrong for a chairperson to continue trying to get his or her way with the dean.

- **Be honest and forthright.**

Just as you should be honest and forthright with faculty, you must likewise be honest and forthright with your dean.

- **Be understanding of your dean and his or her role.**

The dean's job is not the same as a chairperson's. He or she must deal with several different departments. Most deans do all they can to be fair. There may be times when it appears that the dean is not being fair to you. When this happens, discuss the matter and try to see things from the dean's point of view. Just as you must at times make decisions that are not popular with your entire faculty, the dean will have to make some decisions that not all chairpersons like.

- **Don't talk behind your dean's back.**

Don't criticize your dean. You would be surprised how fast news travels and how many times the dean learns precisely what you have said. Your dean must be able to trust you. If he or she cannot, you probably will not remain in your position very long.

- **Consult with your dean before making difficult, far-reaching decisions.**

When you must make decisions that you know will dismay some of your faculty let your dean know what you're doing. When decisions will make a difference in the lives of many faculty, staff, or students, you owe a full explanation to your dean—as well as to them.

- Don't make problems for your dean.

Your dean has enough problems already. Often you can avoid creating problems simply by keeping the dean informed. He or she will step in to settle things when your problems get too big, but it's wisest not to let them get to that point.

- Talk candidly with your dean from time to time.

These chats can be therapeutic. Chairpersons have a tough job, and there are times when a pep talk or reassurance helps. At other times a good discussion on educational philosophy is useful. These help us to keep our focus.

- Convey to your faculty a sense of partnership with your dean.

What you say to your faculty about college policy, and how you say it, often can reveal much about your relationship with your dean. If you have the opportunity to present your side of an issue, you should support whatever decision is finally reached. Don't routinely tell your faculty that you argued for a position but the dean overruled you; if you do, your faculty will lack confidence in the college's leadership. Instead, indicate that there was much discussion—and the decision was not arbitrary.

- Work to become an effective spokesperson
  for your department.

Your dean—and the faculty members in your department—expect this. You must have a lot of information about the department. Use every opportunity to promote the department and its faculty, staff, and students.

A suggestion: Keep a list of potential news stories. Encourage your faculty to share expertise when the media seek a local perspective about a news event. If, for example, you have an expert on Iran in your department, you should introduce him or her to local media to provide views about that part of the world.

One idea you might consider is publishing a booklet to introduce your faculty to the news media. Give background on each member of your faculty and provide information relative to his or her expertise. (Check this with your university relations department, of course.)

Your dean shares in the responsibility for creating positive working relations. Deans should provide support for and encourage development of chairpersons, and serve as their teachers and mentors.

> No dean can have a completely open-door policy, but it should be as close to that arrangement as possible for the chairs. This means listening to their concerns and following through on commitments promptly and conscientiously. It means giving undivided attention when they visit or call, and it means taking the initiative in staying in touch, not waiting for the next problem to develop before talking to them again. (Bright & Richards, 2001, p. 93)

Having a positive working relationship with your dean and with other administrators across campus is good for your department and is worth the effort. Regular talks can develop better understanding. An effective relationship is not just to your advantage; it's to your dean's advantage, too.

If your performance evaluations suggest that you are lacking some interpersonal skills, review the points in this chapter to see if there are areas where you could improve. Also, it would probably be to your benefit to ask your dean what you might do to improve your interpersonal skills. Of course, if you ask that question, don't resent any criticism. Take it as you should, and see what you can do to correct any problems.

Resources

Web Sites

Creating and Sustaining Positive Organizational Relationships
www.bus.ualberta.ca/hos/news/print/POR_and_Culture_FINAL_
VERSION_SEP20_05.pdf

Positive Employee Relationships
www.hr.duke.edu/train/relationships.htm

Books

Gryskiewicz, S. S. (1999). *Positive turbulence: Developing climates for creativity, innovation, and renewal.* San Francisco, CA: Jossey-Bass.

Lees, N. D. (2006). *Chairing academic departments: Traditional and emerging expectations.* Bolton, MA: Anker.

References

Bennett, J. B. (2003). *Academic life: Hospitality, ethics, and spirituality.* Bolton, MA: Anker.

Bright, D. F., & Richards, M. P. (2001). *The academic deanship: Individual careers and institutional roles.* San Francisco, CA: Jossey-Bass.

Wergin, J. F. (2003). *Departments that work: Building and sustaining cultures of excellence in academic programs.* Bolton, MA: Anker.

Wheeler, D. W. (2002). Chairs as institutional leaders. In R. M. Diamond (Ed.), *A field guide to academic leadership* (pp. 451–468). San Francisco, CA: Jossey-Bass.

15

Dealing With Curriculum Matters

*Managing the curriculum and adding new courses produces its
share of problems, but if you are the kind of chairperson who
invites change, you will find these tasks fulfilling.*

Today's chairperson faces internal and external pressures to overhaul the
curriculum, and abundant evidence suggests these pressures will not abate
anytime soon. The effective chairperson will regularly challenge faculty
members with probing questions about what students need to know. He
or she will create an environment that fosters risk-taking and encourages
faculty members to challenge the curriculum's status quo. According to
Ferren and Mussell (2000),

> In addition to those factors that are unique to disciplines,
> external considerations also raise curricular issues that test the
> leadership skills of department chairs. Revision of general edu-
> cation requirements, changes in student interest or demand,
> evolution of institutional values, change in administration,
> shifts in employment opportunities, or new legislative mandates
> or accreditation standards can require faculty to rethink their
> assumptions about the curriculum. (pp. 247–248)

However, not all faculty members are enthusiastic about making
changes in course offerings. Some are reluctant to give up courses they've
taught for any period of time, even when presented with convincing evidence that a course should be dropped or radically changed. Chairpersons
must make it clear that faculty members do not "own" the courses they

teach. We've all know faculty members who not only refer to a course as theirs, but also will battle anyone who would dare suggest that the course be modified—or dropped from the curriculum. I recall when a faculty member in a department I chaired took a sabbatical and returned complaining that those who had covered his schedule during his absence had changed "his" courses.

The successful chairperson must carefully monitor all curricular matters. As Ann Lucas (1994) points out,

> One of the chair's key administrative tasks is to initiate a periodic review of the curriculum. This typically involves updating courses, eliminating overlap, ensuring that the curriculum is consonant with the goals of the department, and frequently, resolving territorial issues among faculty. (p. 31)

Allowing the curriculum to become stale or permitting faculty members to "own" their courses does a disservice to students. Chairpersons must find ways to engage faculty members in an ongoing process of evaluating the curriculum—course by course.

Ways to Evaluate the Curriculum

Most chairpersons recognize the need to frequently examine the course offerings in their departments. Faculty members who participate regularly in faculty development generally will push their chairperson to add new courses or to update existing ones.

Conduct a Course Audit

One of the best techniques for examining the curriculum is to use course audits. They enable you and your faculty to examine each course and to justify its existence. After a course has been taught for years—especially when it has been taught by a number of different faculty members—it often becomes, over time, a different course. Minor modifications are desirable and should be encouraged; however, when changes alter basic objectives or change the course into something that does not resemble the course description, an evaluation is needed. One approach is to conduct periodic course audits.

Faculty members should be told the purpose of course audits and given a schedule showing when their courses will be audited. To conduct an audit, you can use the following guidelines.

1. Faculty members should submit course outlines for each course to be audited.
2. Faculty members should obtain and submit outlines of similar courses taught at recognized (and agreed-upon) universities.
3. A meeting is scheduled at which faculty members will present their courses to the chairperson and two other faculty members. Course outlines should be reviewed in advance by those who will hear the presentations.
4. The purpose of the presentation is to allow faculty members to explain:
   - The objectives of the course
   - How the objectives are being met
   - What kind of assignments are given to students
   - How student grades are determined
   - What textbooks are used as well as how they are used
   - Any unusual teaching techniques employed
   - The grade distribution for the last three times the course has been taught
   - What special assignments are given to graduate students if the course is double-numbered
   - What variance exists from the original course description
5. Faculty members should be challenged to defend their teaching methods, assignments, and grading.
6. Those hearing the presentation should take notes and prepare evaluations. These will be summarized by the chairperson and then given to the faculty member whose course is being audited.
7. If substantial changes are recommended, another meeting between the faculty member and those making the recommendations should be set up to discuss the evaluations.

8. The faculty member whose course is being audited should prepare a report indicating what, if any, changes he or she wants to make.

It is not likely that all courses in the department can be audited during a single academic year. It is probably best to plan on completing audits for all course offerings over a two- or three-year period. Although they take time, properly done audits cause faculty members to analyze and reevaluate their teaching—and the effectiveness of their courses.

You also should examine other university catalogs regularly to see what is offered and where. Likewise, you should talk to other chairpersons at conferences about what courses they offer. Ask especially if they are offering anything new.

Sponsor a Retreat

A successful retreat requires careful planning. First, you must decide how much time you need. Is it possible to take care of the issues in a half day, a full day, or a weekend? For curriculum matters, a full day is likely sufficient. Other important considerations include:

1. Where will the retreat be held and what will it cost? These often are interrelated. Typically we think of retreats as being off campus, but there is no reason why you cannot have one on campus, unless there is no space available. My preference is for having them off campus, but this usually means having to rent space. Occasionally, there may be corporate friends, including banks, who will allow you to use a conference or board room. Obviously, if you have the money in your budget to rent space, your options are expanded.

2. What are other costs, and who will pay them? Some arrangements will need to be made for lunch and beverages during morning and afternoon breaks. If the department does not have funds for food and refreshments, faculty will have to be asked to share the costs; most will not mind doing this. But, this determination should be made in advance, and faculty members consulted if they are expected to share the cost.

3. A formal agenda should be prepared—you cannot announce simply that curriculum is the retreat agenda and anything goes. Here is a sample agenda:

- Discussion of disposition of courses that have not been taught in the last five years. Why are they not being taught? Should we continue to keep them on the books? Why or why not?
- Do we have courses whose titles are no longer adequate or accurate? Are there suggested changes in any course titles to be considered?
- Do we have course descriptions that are no longer adequate or accurate? Are there suggested changes in course descriptions to be considered? Should we assign a faculty member or members to rewrite course descriptions?
- Are there new courses we should consider?
- For those courses that have prerequisites, do we need to reconsider whether the stated prerequisites are appropriate? Should any changes be made or considered?
- Is the core curriculum adequate and appropriate?
- Are the nonmajor requirements adequate and appropriate?
- Do we have courses that do not seem to be meeting student needs?
- Are our assessment activities adequate for measuring effectiveness?
- What are we doing to ensure content consistency for courses where multiple sections are regularly offered?
- Are we using the best textbooks available in all our courses?

You could also change the questions into statements if you prefer, and there are several other important matters that you might add to this agenda, such as:

- Who is going to serve as moderator?
- Do we need to make copies of any materials to pass out during the retreat?
- Should we assign someone to take notes and write a report?

Meet in Small Groups

Sometimes, meeting in small groups to discuss curriculum matters makes more sense than a retreat for the entire faculty. There are times when small groups can be more productive than large ones. If that is the case with your faculty, this may be the better approach for you. Certainly if you have a large faculty, you may wish to begin by having small group meetings and then taking ideas that come out of them to the larger group for a final decision.

Develop Minicourses

Minicourses offer a way to try out a course idea and see if it has the potential to be offered regularly. Minicourses, as I define them, are courses that do not run the entire length of the term. For example, in a 15-week semester you might offer three minicourses of five weeks each. One of the values of this concept is that minicourses allow you to offer courses for one hour of credit—and certain courses should not receive any more credit than that, especially until they are fully developed.

Special topics courses at some universities permit you to achieve some of the same results. Either a minicourse or a special topics course can generally be added without going through the bureaucratic maze required for adding a new course. Faculty members—and even students—often come up with solid ideas for these kinds of courses. Several years ago while analyzing survey data from our alumni, we discovered that many of our graduates were telling us that we needed a course in graphic design. We tried it as a special topics course before taking it to the department, college, and university committees to get it approved as a regular course. This allowed us to begin offering the course immediately and to work through the problems of refining it before seeking approval as a regular part of our curriculum. The biggest advantage was that we were able to serve students immediately rather than having to wait a year or two.

We must be responsive to student needs. Universities cannot afford to be slow in responding to curricular changes, yet we are not currently geared up to act quickly. One suggestion is to have an assistant vice president for academic affairs serve as a curriculum ombudsperson. His or her duties would include examining course proposals and allowing them to be introduced pending some kind of up or down vote by a curriculum committee. It could be higher education's answer to fast-tracking.

Invite Reviews

A review of the curriculum by someone who is not in the department can provide a fresh, objective perspective. Reviews can be conducted by a number of different individuals.

By outsiders. You can invite notable educators or professionals in your field to examine your course offerings. It is generally a good policy to have others look at what we are doing; often we are too close to make objective judgments about our own programs. One of the values of accreditation is that outsiders examine your department on a regular and comprehensive basis. Even if you don't have an accreditation body, you can achieve—at least in part—essentially the same evaluation process by having others do a thorough examination of your curriculum.

If you ask outsiders to examine your curriculum, you need to provide them with specific instructions so that you and they agree on what you are asking to be done. Here is an example of what you might ask for:

1. Do you see any gaps in our course offerings? In other words, are there legitimate areas that we are not currently addressing?
2. Do you see too much overlapping of what we offer?
3. Do the prerequisites seem appropriate?
4. Are the course descriptions adequate? Do you believe they provide enough information about what is covered in the courses?
5. Do you believe our core is sufficient? If not, what should be added or changed?
6. Do you believe our nonmajor requirements support the kind of education we are attempting to provide? Would you recommend changes?

By your planning committee. The planning committee is concerned about the future, and few things could be more pertinent to the future than the courses we offer. The committee should do a systematic study of what similar departments at other universities across the country are offering and what recent alumni think about course offerings. Also, we should consult those who hire our students to learn if they have found that our students are adequately educated.

Introducing New Courses
and Changing Existing Ones

Chairpersons need to understand and appreciate what is involved in designing a course. Robert Diamond (2002) notes, "Over the next decades we can expect to see increasing emphasis on course and curriculum design" (p. 145). He points out that new demands for improved academic programs, greater student retention, and other outside forces all contribute to "an increased concern about what is taught and how" (p. 145).

Universities have policies and procedures for adding and/or changing courses. The forms to be filled out are all quite similar. The first step after completing the appropriate forms is to take the proposed course addition or change before the department's curriculum committee. After this committee has signed off on the proposal, the next step usually is to take it "on up the line" for approval. Generally, this means that the proposal goes before a college curriculum committee, university curriculum committee, and the vice president for academic affairs. Generally, your college dean will sign off on it before it goes to the university curriculum committee, although this varies from campus to campus.

Some things committee members and you must think about seriously before giving approval to new courses are:

- Whom do we have to teach the course?
- Do we have the required resources? For example, if special equipment is necessary, is it available, or do we have funds to purchase it?
- Will proposing the course create problems with any other department on campus? If so, can we solve it by getting permission from the affected department(s)? Because a problem may be created is not enough reason for not considering adding a course. On the other hand, we must develop a strategy for solving the problem to everyone's satisfaction.
- Does the course duplicate anything we are already doing?
- Do the library holdings support such a course? If not, can they be purchased?

- How will the course fit into our curriculum? Will it be required? Will there be prerequisites?
- How will adding the course affect enrollment?
- Are there special space considerations?
- How many students do we anticipate taking the course each term?
- Will we need to offer more than one section of the course?
- How often should the course be offered?
- How does offering the course fit into our overall mission?
- What is the course's educational value?

If your department is going to be on the cutting edge, you must introduce and change courses fairly regularly—especially in fields where knowledge is fluid and rapidly mined. We need faculty members who can recognize the need for changing and adding courses. We need teachers who are willing to take on new teaching assignments.

Faculty members should be provided with some incentives for designing new courses and making the preparations for teaching them. To do this, giving released time and providing some travel funds is often required. Remember to consider this extra effort as well when you evaluate faculty members or award merit salary increases.

Eliminating Courses

Deciding when to eliminate a course appears to be a relatively simple matter. It is not. Some universities allow departments to place a course they no longer teach into an inactive bank so it can be reintroduced should the department decide later to offer it. Others require courses that have not been offered for a given period of time (three or five years, for example) to be dropped from the catalog. Should the department wish to offer the course at a later date, it must submit a proposal for a new course.

I do not favor keeping untaught courses in the catalog. It is misleading to potential students who use the course catalog to help make a decision about attending your university and majoring in your department.

Here are some questions to ask when you confront issues about eliminating a course.

- Is the course offered regularly? If not, when was the last time it was offered?
- What were the enrollments during the last six times it was offered?
- Do we have faculty qualified to teach it? Interested in teaching it?
- What is its educational value?
- How does offering the course affect enrollment in other classes?
- What factors favor keeping the course?
- What factors favor eliminating it?
- Is this course taught at most other universities?

Assigning Courses

Making teaching assignments is easy in some respects and difficult in others. For example, if you have a course that only one person is qualified to teach, your decision is obvious. What gets complicated is assigning to one faculty member a course that everyone in the department wants to teach. You assign the best teacher to the course, and then develop some kind of rotation plan out of fairness to all involved.

Then there are questions about who teaches when. Some faculty members don't mind teaching evening courses, others don't mind early morning courses. But often, you have to assign a faculty member to times he or she dislikes. Once again, a rotation plan can help resolve this issue.

Setting the schedule can be participatory. I would develop a draft schedule and then ask each faculty member to examine and discuss it with me. If I could accommodate all concerns, I did. If not, I had an opportunity to explain why.

It is important to be fair to all faculty members—and you must also be fair to students. If you have some faculty members who for some reason cannot teach large courses, it is a tremendous disservice to assign them large classes. Trying to match the right faculty member to the right course (by size, content, level, etc.) is never easy, but is a task that comes with the job of department chairperson.

Part-Time Faculty

If you can find qualified persons, you should consider hiring part-time faculty members. However, in certain specialized areas it is next to impossible to find qualified individuals off campus.

Possible disadvantages of hiring part-time faculty members. Often this is a way to save money; we usually pay so little it's embarrassing. Too many universities resort to this practice simply because of the economy, and students end up the losers.

Another problem associated with hiring part-time faculty members is that they may have other jobs, so time only permits them to come in just before a class and depart right after it. This leaves student advising to full-time faculty members who may resent the extra responsibility and feel that it is unfair. John Bennett (2003) makes a strong case against the excessive dependence on adjunct or part-time professors.

> . . . the liabilities of turning over significant (and growing) chunks of the curriculum to adjuncts are worrisome. Although there are few studies of the teaching effectiveness of part-time faculty, other critical issues are clear. Part-time faculty are less available to students for advising—a situation aggravated by little office space for meeting students. In addition, part-time faculty are rarely available to each other or to full-time colleagues for discussion of pedagogical issues. Teaching initiatives and progress reports cannot be pursued in systematic fashion. As a result there is no ordered information that can be used collectively to improve teaching. (pp. 18–19)

Possible advantages. There are advantages to hiring part-time faculty, aside from saving money. They often bring a wealth of professional experience into the classroom, along with new ideas and enthusiasm. In certain disciplines this can be a particular advantage, and accrediting agencies recognize what professionals can add to the classroom.

As Wallin (2005) notes, part-time or adjunct faculty members have "become an integral part of the community college landscape" (p. 4), who are here to stay. She also points out that part-time faculty members are often neglected by busy department chairpersons: "A major issue for many community colleges across the nation is providing part-time faculty with appropriate support and pedagogical assistance" (p. 4). If you do hire part-timers, remember that you have a responsibility to them. You must look after their welfare just as you do that of your full-time faculty, and you must realize that they will have a different set of concerns. You need to assist by providing each with a mentor, and you should visit their classes from time to time. Examine their syllabi and look carefully at their student evaluations so that you can get a feel for how they are doing, and where they could use help.

Interdisciplinary Courses

Well-conceived and well-taught interdisciplinary courses offer a lot to students, and they can be enjoyable and challenging to teach. Talk to some of your colleagues at conventions to see what, if any, courses they teach as interdisciplinary.

Managing the curriculum and adding new courses presents its share of problems, but if you are the kind of chairperson who invites change, you will find these tasks fulfilling. Moreover, you will share in the critical responsibility of seeing that students get solid courses that are up to date, relevant, and taught as described in your university's catalog.

Resources

Web Sites
Distance Education Clearinghouse
www.uwex.edu/disted/home.html

The "Public Curriculum" of Colleges and Universities
www.greaterexpectations.org/briefing_papers/PublicCurriculum.html

Teaching Tips
http://honolulu.hawaii.edu/intranet/committees/FacDevCom/
guidebk/teachtip/teachtip.htm

Books

Astin, A. W., & Astin, H. S. (2001). *Leadership reconsidered: Engaging higher education in social change.* Battle Creek, MI: Kellogg Foundation.

Diamond, R. M. (1998). *Designing and assessing courses and curricula: A practical guide.* San Francisco, CA: Jossey-Bass.

Mentkowski, M., & Associates. (2000). *Learning that lasts: Integrating learning, development, and performance in college and beyond.* San Francisco, CA: Jossey-Bass.

Mestenhauser, J. A., & Ellingboe, B. (1998). *Reforming the higher education curriculum: Internationalizing the campus.* Phoenix, AZ: American Council on Education/Oryx Press.

References

Bennett, J. B. (2003). *Academic life: Hospitality, ethics, and spirituality.* Bolton, MA: Anker.

Diamond, R. M. (2002). Curricula and courses: Administrative issues. In R. M. Diamond (Ed.), *Field guide to academic leadership* (pp. 135–156). San Francisco, CA: Jossey-Bass.

Ferren, A. S., & Mussell, K. (2000). *Leading curriculum renewal.* In A. F. Lucas & Associates, *Leading academic change: Essential roles for department chairs* (pp. 246–274). San Francisco, CA: Jossey-Bass.

Lucas, A. F. (1994). *Strengthening departmental leadership: A team-building guide for chairs in colleges and universities.* San Francisco, CA: Jossey-Bass.

Wallin, D. L. (Ed.). (2005). Valuing and motivating part-time faculty. In D. L. Wallin (Ed.), *Adjunct faculty in community colleges: An academic administrator's guide to recruiting, supporting, and retaining great teachers* (pp. 3–14). Bolton, MA: Anker.

16

Conducting Effective Meetings

I have seen many leaders get bogged down in minutiae, exploring paths where no light shines, where nothing gets accomplished, and where ultimately all participants are left in the dark.

Anyone who has been appointed to the position of department chairperson has sat through innumerable meetings, many of which may have seemed like a waste of time. I can't count the number of meetings I've left wondering what purpose was served. It's a feeling shared by thousands of faculty members and administrators, many of whom are undoubtedly attending another poorly planned, boring meeting as you read this. (See Appendix H for a humorous perspective on meetings.)

We can do better. Department chairpersons, as with all leaders, must understand when and why they should call a meeting—or just as important, when not to call one. Well-run meetings are essential. They provide invaluable feedback, opportunities to lay out planned scenarios, and a forum in which to share information and power and to learn from others. They enable leaders to seek and attain consensus. Finally, effective meetings give chairpersons the opportunity to let others shine so that extraordinary things can happen.

According to North (2003),

Academic institutions, more than any other type of organization, should be on the forefront of being really proficient at encouraging, monitoring, and using group discussion on issues. Our meetings should be wonders to behold.

> All too often we take meetings for granted, assuming that no special efforts or skills are necessary for a group to sit together, talk, and make decisions. However, like parenting or teaching, participating in a meeting, especially a department meeting, is a complex human interaction with multiple goals, histories, and personalities, with an intricate subtext and high stakes attached to success or failure. (p. 74)

This chapter will examine aspects of meetings that differentiate the good from the bad. We'll draw on what some authorities say about making meetings effective. Moreover, I present some of my own experiences—both good and bad—in the hope of providing useful information. You'll likely not find what it takes to make your meetings "wonders to behold," but I hope you will find ideas that will be useful in crafting productive meetings—the kind where faculty members work together for the common good.

Basic Considerations

The most fundamental consideration to structuring your meetings and keeping them moving is to know what you hope to accomplish.

- Don't call unnecessary meetings. I have known department chairpersons who meet for the purpose of meeting. We must be more considerate of faculty members' time—meetings are costly in terms of labor.
- Always start on time; this respects those who arrive on time and reminds those who are late that the scheduling is serious. Far too many meeting conveners violate this seemingly simple consideration.
- Don't give short shrift to building an agenda. What do you hope to accomplish? Can it be done in the time allocated? Will those in attendance have time to discuss all items? Where will the meeting be held? Is the meeting room adequate and does its design facilitate discussion? We know, for example, that the usual classroom tends to inhibit discussion. It is too formal. As North (2003) reminds us, "Space is a powerful symbolic tool, which can be used to increase departmental cohesion

and to make department meetings more pleasant" (p. 73). Also, the chairperson should always invite faculty members to submit agenda items. Obviously, this must be done well in advance.

- Distribute your agenda in advance of the meeting. Doing this allows those attending to consider issues ahead of time, collect data, and discuss matters with others.
- Indicate intended action for each agenda item. Will there be a vote? Will an agenda matter be referred to a committee?
- Review the agenda at the beginning of each meeting, giving participants a chance to assure they understand all proposed major topics.
- Designate someone to record what transpires during the meeting. I often used my administrative assistant to handle this, in part because she knew shorthand. She also would type and circulate minutes of the meeting.
- Model the kind of energy and enthusiasm you expect from participants.
- Remember your role as a leader. Before you ask how certain problems might be resolved, you may want to place suggestions on the table and then invite discussion. Be aware, however, that you must make it clear that dissent and criticism will not be tolerated. Faculty who introduce a possible solution to a problem and then attack those who have differing views is unacceptable. Issues may be attacked, but impugning another's character is out of order. In short, chairpersons must be able to manage conflict and help others abandon egos in pursuit of a goal. During meetings it is thus important to encourage dialogue and diminish the notion that there are only two sides to an issue. Problem solving at the departmental level must involve all faculty members—from the elder statesperson to newest hire.
- Keep the momentum going. The skillful chairperson will know when to nudge, when to prod, when to close discussion, how to monitor time, and how to keep the meeting moving. He or she will understand that communication is more than just talking.
- Take time to evaluate a meeting's effectiveness. Many chairpersons are amazed at how often faculty members complain that a meeting is a

complete waste of time—but they say so only after the meeting. Get their feedback during the meeting. If you see a meeting bogging down, you might want to suspend discussion and conduct a satisfaction check, which means having each participant indicate how he or she thinks the meeting is going. From this, faculty members may see a need to bring about consensus and to make the entire meeting worthwhile.

Chairpersons must understand that in the final analysis they will be judged not so much on adherence to rules, fairness, impartiality, or how wise they appear to be, but on how much actually gets accomplished. This, of course, does not excuse the chairperson who is unfair or who turns a blind eye to rules. Chairpersons must have strong communication skills, know how to listen, and when to end discussion. I have seen many leaders get bogged down in minutiae, exploring paths where no light shines, where nothing gets accomplished, and where ultimately all participants are left in the dark.

The Big Picture

When successfully managed, meetings can be powerful tools for uniting faculty members and fostering a cohesiveness that can help any department chairperson give voice to those who feel disenfranchised, left behind, or otherwise disengaged. Skillful chairpersons will use meetings to paint vivid pictures of what might be. They will listen intently and they will use every opportunity to achieve credibility and gain trust. These chairpersons will not only become confident in the way they conduct meetings and nudge faculty members toward consensus, they will master the art of leading, whether in large meetings or in one-on-one informal chats.

As Eble (1978) writes in *The Art of Administration,*

> There are skills those who preside over meetings must develop
> in themselves: clarifying motions and seeing that they are
> understood by all; keeping track of those wanting to be recog-
> nized and being fair in giving recognition; holding individuals
> to the question but not stifling discussion; sensing when debate

has moved to a consensus or has reached a division that further discussion is not likely to resolve; keeping the group aware of time but not oppressed by it; and intervening to sharpen issues, to clarify, to abbreviate debate, to move to another item on the agenda. (p. 32)

In *Primal Leadership: Realizing the Power of Emotional Intelligence*, Goleman, Boyatzis, and McKee (2002) discuss various leadership styles. They mention that visionary, coaching, affiliative, and democratic styles "create the kind of resonance that boosts performance, while two others—pacesetting and commanding—although useful in some very specific situations, should be used with caution . . ." (p. 53). In their discussion of the democratic style, they write that they believe leaders with a strong vision can make use of this style to gather ideas both about implementing and executing a vision. However, they also discuss the drawbacks of the democratic style.

One result when a leader overrelies on this approach is exasperating, endless meetings in which ideas are mulled over, consensus remains elusive, and the only visible outcome is to schedule more meetings. A leader who puts off crucial decisions, hoping to thrash out a consensual strategy, risks dithering. The cost can be confusion, with resulting delays or escalating conflicts. (p. 68)

The point these authors make is worth our consideration. Any department chairperson will be well served to understand the emotional intelligence abilities needed for the various leadership styles. As Goleman et al. (2002) point out, empathy plays a role in democratic leadership, especially when the group is strongly diverse: "Without the ability to attune to a wide range of people, a leader will be prone to miscues" (p. 69).

We have all seen how ideas are mulled over in "exasperating, endless meetings" where consensus indeed seems elusive. The departmental leader's toolkit should include each of the styles mentioned by Goleman et al. Knowing when and how to use any of these styles is a key skill.

Misuse of Meetings by Some Faculty

Strong chairpersons know how to handle faculty members who become bullies during faculty meetings. However, faculty who are intent on undermining the chairperson often become masterful schemers. I especially recall one such faculty member. No one was nicer to me in person. Yet he regularly gossiped about me to other department members, and he used his position as a senior faculty member to threaten untenured faculty and enlist them in his cause, which was to seek and destroy any and all efforts to bring about change. He was good at staying just beneath the radar, intimidating faculty members who embraced change and creating general unrest.

This faculty member learned and taught the masterful art of "committeeing things to death." Any experienced chairperson has seen this happen. The one example that remains vivid in my mind was a university-wide proposal to reduce the credit hours needed for graduation from 132 hours to 124. When it came time for the matter to be discussed by the faculty members of this individual's department, he made certain that it was referred to a committee where nothing would happen. Week after week the committee members met, but never were able to reach a recommendation. This dragged on until the term was over. The effort of the university to address a serious concern languished because of one faculty member's deviousness. The proposal, to my knowledge, was never revisited.

It's not enough for department chairpersons to know how to conduct successful meetings. They must also possess the skills required to bring resolution to matters where foot-dragging members hold power.

However, there are still other ways that recalcitrant faculty members can sabotage the efforts of others. They can carefully disguise their own views and persuade others to do their bidding. They become skillful at using or misusing whatever procedures—whether Roberts' Rules of Order or more informal rules—are adopted.

Chairpersons with strong leadership skills know that they must model the way. They must be open, have confidence, be humble, know themselves and their faculty members, and have high standards. Once faculty members trust their chairperson, it becomes difficult for saboteurs to succeed. When the department begins to move forward and when faculty members are duly rewarded for taking risks and making good things happen, then meetings can be a place where civility reigns, even though they may never become those "wonders to behold" that North (2003) envisions.

Strategies for Dealing With Meeting Saboteurs

Successful chairpersons must be bold in dealing with those who would misuse meetings. Those who attempt to hijack meetings need to be dealt with directly. Chairpersons must not allow such faculty members to intimidate others, and need to deal forthrightly with what Bennett (2003) describes as insistent individualism.

> The most conspicuous academic insistent individualists develop skills in self-promotion and self-protection. They construct self-referential frameworks that associate increase in personal standing with self-sufficiency and independence. They use verbal agility and knowledge to manipulate and control. They select few compatriots, distancing and excluding others. They invest in careerism, regardless of a more fulfilling selfhood for students, colleagues, or themselves. In a variety of ways, insistent individualists cultivate personal identity through using others. (p. 6)

Indeed, such individuals are on every campus. Here are some practical ways for dealing with faculty members intent on using meetings for their own agendas.

- Stop them in their tracks at their first attempt to misuse any meeting. Be straightforward by saying something like, "We're not going there today. You and I can talk later about this."
- Deal individually with insistent individualists. You must tell them as forcefully as you can that this kind of behavior will not be tolerated.

Most know exactly what they are doing and they presume that others—including and perhaps most significantly the chairperson—will not confront them.

- Make it clear to all that any faculty member bent on promoting themselves at the expense of the department's common good will be dealt out of any decision-making. A part of leadership is modifying behavior. While it is especially difficult, chairpersons should be precise when talking about expected behaviors.

- Chairpersons must recognize dysfunctional faculty members and learn how to deal with them. Chapter 26 specifically discusses this issue.

Resources

Web Sites
Conducting Meetings
www.cnr.berkeley.edu/ucce50/ag-labor/7labor/11.htm

Conducting a Productive Meeting
www.sideroad.com/Meetings/productive_meeting.html

Tips and Incentives for Conducting Productive Meetings
www.elementkjournals.com/premier/showArticle.asp?aid=10120

Books
Caroselli, M. (2000). *Leadership skills for managers.* New York, NY: McGraw-Hill.

Lucas, A. F. (1994). *Strengthening departmental leadership: A team-building guide for chairs in colleges and universities.* San Francisco, CA: Jossey-Bass.

McKenna, P. J., & Maister, D. H. (2002). *First among equals: How to manage a group of professionals.* New York, NY: The Free Press.

Thornton, P. B. (2001). *Be the leader: Make the difference.* Irvine, CA: Griffin.

References

Bennett, J. B. (2003). *Academic life: Hospitality, ethics, and spirituality.* Bolton, MA: Anker.

Eble, K. E. (1978). *The art of administration: A guide for academic administrators.* San Francisco, CA: Jossey-Bass.

Goleman, D., Boyatzis, R., & McKee, A. (2002). *Primal leadership: Realizing the power of emotional intelligence.* Boston, MA: Harvard Business School Press.

North, J. D. (2003). Using meetings to create cohesion. In D. R. Leaming (Ed.), *Managing people: A guide for department chairs and deans* (pp. 65–75). Bolton, MA: Anker.

17

Budget and Financial Management

As chairperson, you should study the fiscal context of higher education and recognize the increased competition for funds.

Today's financial picture for higher education is bleak. Financial constraints and managing limited budgets are challenging, and these problems likely will become even more time consuming. According to Jones (2003),

> After almost a decade of good economic conditions and strong revenue growth, most states entered fiscal year 2003 facing sharply reduced revenues, and are now struggling to constrain expenditures. Unfortunately, this situation is unlikely to change any time soon, according to projections developed for the National Center for Higher Education Management Systems by Donald Boyd of the Rockefeller Institute on Government. Even if states experience normal economic growth over the next eight years, all but a handful of states will find it impossible, given their existing tax policies, to continue funding their current level of public services. (p. 1)

The study focused on what is likely to happen in the eight years following the report. It further indicated that state and local tax revenues are unlikely to grow as fast as state economies because:

- Economic growth is projected to be more balanced than in the late 1990s, which generated extraordinary surges in capital gains income.

- Increases in sales tax revenues are projected to slow significantly due to (a) continued shifts in consumption from goods to lightly taxed services and (b) the inability to collect sales taxes on Internet-related transactions.
- State revenue dependence on excise taxes is growing, and growth in these revenues lags behind overall economic growth. (pp. 2–3)

Department chairpersons in the years ahead must be more attuned to budgets and financial management than ever before, not only to see their programs improve, but in some instances survive. As chairperson, you should study the fiscal context of higher education and recognize the increased competition for funds. This chapter will consider different budget approaches, what a chairperson can do to maximize dollars received, how to develop contacts and links to outside funding sources, and some strategies for fundraising.

As noted, managing the department's money consumes much of a chairperson's time, and most likely will consume even more time in the future. Financial decisions are difficult. Even as faculty members want and deserve more funds to support their professional activities, the costs of goods and services continue to increase at a rate much higher than funding. "Between 1990 and 1993 public spending on higher education in the United States declined by $7.76 billion (including budget cuts and inflationary losses)" (Munitz, 1995, p. 9). Zumeta (2005) gives more encouraging news.

Public colleges saw the first signs of relief in mid-2004, after a long period of deep budget cuts and painful tuition increases. FY 2005 budgets, though tight, were less draconian than the three budgets that followed the recession of 2000–01. Perhaps colleges and universities could stop "playing defense" and resume progress towards providing quality postsecondary education to more citizens. (p. 27)

Monitoring the budget—that is, knowing at any given time how much money the department has and how much it owes—has always been an important chair function. But today, the chairperson must manage department resources with precision. For example, wise and careful equipment purchase decisions are necessary when equipment needs are far greater than funding.

Allocation of Funds

After funds are allocated to public universities, they are parceled out. The provost or vice president for academic affairs gets money for the university's academic sector. In turn, this money is apportioned to the various colleges and other campus units that report to him or her (admissions, registrar, library, etc.). The provost will use some kind of formula for distributing these funds. It may be a sophisticated formula that takes into account many different pieces of information (student credit hours produced, number of majors, value of equipment inventory, etc.). On the other hand, the formula may be one that is quite simple. For example, it may be based on what each college has received in the past. If that is the case, you may want to lobby for a change because such formulas generally fail to take into account many changes, thus penalizing growing, progressive programs.

At some universities, the provost will allocate funds to all spending units. At others, the deans will allocate funds to departments that report to them. Once again, each dean will use some formula, and it likewise can be sophisticated or simplistic. Figure 17.1 presents a typical funding formula.

Analyzing this formula, one can see that 10% of the total allocation is earmarked to support the college office. The department base is 4.99%, which means that 4.99% of the total allocation is set aside for academic departments. In this particular college there are 14 departments, so 1/14 of the amount is set aside for each. Let's use a hypothetical example for distributing funds for the category "faculty."

If you look at faculty in the current expense section, you will see the figure 17.92%. For illustration, let's assume that the total allocation for the

Figure 17.1 College Funding Formula

Current Expense
  College Office....................................10%
  Special Needs 25%
  Department Base 4.99%
  Student Credit Hours
        (.125% basic) (.875% other) 26.69%
  Major Programs 4.55%
    Majors 10.85%
    Faculty......................................17.92%

Equipment: Formula Based on Department Size
  $4,433   Large Departments (16 or more faculty members)
  $2,980   Medium Departments (5–15 faculty members)
  $965   Small Departments (1–4 faculty members)

Travel: Based on projected recruitment needs for the year. A certain percentage is held by the college with the balance divided by the number of faculty members and distributed to departments.

college is $200,000. To find what amount the category "faculty" receives, first determine what 17.92% of $200,000 is—$35,840. If $35,840 is divided by the total number (117) of faculty members in the college, we will then know how much to distribute to the various departments for each of their faculty members: $306.32. Thus, a department with eight faculty members would receive $306.32 x 8, or $2,450.56. This amount would be added to money allocated to that department from other parts of the formula.

Allocating Department Funds

At many universities, funds allocated to departments are designated as "current expense" and "equipment." Travel funds may or may not be merged into the "current expense" category. If they are merged, you will have the flexibility to increase or decrease travel funding depending on the needs of the faculty. If, for example, in a given year faculty members, for whatever reason, do not plan to travel as much as in other years, you may decide to increase the current expense and/or equipment budget and decrease the travel allocation.

You should be precisely aware of your equipment needs. As you put together your department's annual budget, ask each faculty member to provide a list of equipment needs. The list should be specific as to price, specifications, justification for purchase, recommended vendors, and so on. After all faculty members have turned in their equipment recommendations, you should develop a master list that establishes purchase priorities. This will enable you to make prompt decisions on how to spend the equipment allocation.

In order to develop budget plans, you should also consult faculty members to see if extraordinary supplies will be needed for the upcoming year. These costs are paid for out of the "current expense" and "equipment" funding line items, which must be stretched to cover all supplies, including paper, pens, note pads, calendars, paper clips, staples, duplicating fluids, and the like; telephone expenses; postage; faculty travel; and honoraria.

Purchasing Supplies, Equipment, and Services

Public universities generally vest purchasing authority in a director of purchasing and his or her staff. At many universities, purchases made by other individuals are unauthorized and will not be approved retroactively. Individuals may be held personally liable for purchases they make. This is true regardless of the source of funds.

You are charged with initiating all requisitions. The dean of the college typically is required to sign a requisition after you have prepared it. When a requisition reaches the purchasing office, a purchase order number is assigned, and accounting verifies that the department has sufficient funds to pay for the goods or services. The requisition is then competitively bid or approved by a procurement officer and mailed to the vendor. A copy of the requisition is then sent back to the department.

At most universities, if the purchases are below a certain dollar value, competitive bids are not required unless deemed appropriate by purchasing or the department. Purchases over the designated amount require competitive bids that are handled by the purchasing department based on specifications provided by the department. After bids are received by purchasing, orders generally are awarded to the lowest responsible bidder who meets the specifications.

One caution here to chairpersons new to the job: At most universities it is a violation of university policy to obligate the university for amounts exceeding a certain designated amount (e.g., $500 at many institutions). Don't try to get around this by permitting a vendor to talk you into purchasing something for $1,996.00, let's say, and billing your institution $499 at four separate times so that you can immediately get what you want. If you must have a costly item in a hurry, ask your purchasing office for help.

Many schools have established alternative purchasing methods through which a department can obtain nearly all goods and services in advance of the department's needs. You should remember that at many institutions payment will not be made for after-the-fact purchases.

Routine Orders

If the cost of a purchase is under the established dollar amount, and bids are not required, submit a requisition, and an order will be mailed to the vendor. At some universities, requisitions are bid orally by the purchasing office or the department. If the purchase is over the specified dollar amount, written bid requests go out with a deadline for their return. Generally, it takes about 18 days to confirm bids and mail an order to the successful vendor.

Contracts

Most departments can purchase many commonly used items from state and university blanket contracts. The advantage is convenience for the department and the knowledge that requisitions do not have to be bid. Carpeting, furniture, chemicals, laboratory supplies, computers, and copiers are a few of the items usually available in this manner.

Agreements

These special orders allow the department to contract for such things as technical and professional services, engage consultants or lecturers, or pay accreditation services. Generally, they are noncompetitive. The advantage for the department is that the vendor simply submits an invoice as services are rendered. Individual purchase orders are not required after the agreement has been approved.

Office Supplies

These may often be obtained from your campus bookstore, an intra-university voucher form, or from other office suppliers.

Completing Purchase Orders

Preparing a purchase order or an intra-university departmental transfer voucher is relatively easy. Look at past purchase orders to assist you, or call someone in the purchasing office for help. Once the purchase order or voucher is filled out, you will need to sign the form and forward it to your dean's office. After the dean approves and signs the purchase order, it is sent directly to purchasing. Purchasing in turn sends the order to the vendor and returns a copy to the department. The department may check the status of an order with the vendor. However, changes to the order may not be made unless they are coordinated with purchasing.

Budgeting Approaches

Budgeting and purchasing practices vary from university to university, so it is difficult to provide advice that is not general. If you are new in your job as chairperson, it is wise to talk to personnel in the budget and purchasing office, consult with veteran chairpersons on campus, and listen to your administrative assistant. Something that does not vary, however, is the need to involve faculty in the budgeting process. Share a copy of the total departmental budget at the beginning of the fiscal year, and then provide updates at least every quarter. Get faculty input when sending through your funding and budget requests by having faculty members submit their projected financial needs for the coming year. Not only should your efficiency in allocation improve with faculty input, but overall faculty morale should be increased as well.

Be an advocate for adequate funding for your department. Your "goal is at minimum to maintain the department's current resource base, and at best to acquire as many additional resources as possible" (Meisinger, 1994, p. 50). Your faculty will think you are not an effective chairperson if you request fewer resources than are currently available. And they will be especially pleased with your leadership if you are successful in getting increased funding for your department.

> Advocates often ask for more resources than they really need because they know that the cutters will reduce budgets regardless of the amounts requested. The cutters will reduce budget requests, knowing that the requests are padded and that by cutting the budgets there is little danger of injuring programs. This behavior demonstrates the built-in pressure for expansion that characterizes the budget process. (Meisinger, 1994, p. 51)

Universities have different approaches to budgeting, and understanding these will be helpful. The essentials of these approaches are described briefly here, though keep in mind that they are not mutually exclusive.

Incremental Budgeting

Lindblom (1959) described this approach as the science of muddling through. Barr (2002) writes, "An incremental approach to budgeting is based on the assumption that both needs and costs vary only a small amount from year to year" (p. 37). With this approach, departments and other spending units will have their budgets increased or decreased depending on that amount of money. For example, if the state allocates fewer dollars to the university, your department will likely have its budget reduced incrementally. Whatever allocation model has been used for funding your department will not be altered from year to year when this budgeting model is used. Barr (2002) observes that incremental budgeting models minimize conflict within the organization because the university's units are all treated the same way.

Planning, Programming, and Budgeting Systems

This approach calls for examining the costs and benefits of programs and activities and links planning to the allocation of resources. A program budget will provide information about the costs and benefits of its activities. It calls for sophisticated—and often expensive—information gathering and detailed analyses of policy alternatives.

Zero-Base Budgeting

This approach focuses on examining all programs and activities during each budget cycle. It assumes no budget leftovers from previous years, and so each year's budget is begun from a base of zero.

Performance Budgeting

This approach focuses on measures of program performance. It attempts to improve efficiency and improve outcomes. In recent years, some states have mandated some funding through this approach, though often it is an add-on feature rather than an integral part of budgeting. When it is used, specific outcomes are generally defined both in qualitative and quantitative terms.

Formula Budgeting

This approach focuses on some type of distribution that attempts to achieve a "fair share." Quantitative measures are established and funds are allocated based on those measures, as seen in the formula presented earlier in Figure 17.1. Formula budgeting is the budget model most states use to allocate money to state-appropriated institutions of higher education.

Responsibility-Center Budgeting

This approach—sometimes called cost-center budgeting—focuses primary responsibility on colleges and schools for the management of resources, which become revenue and cost centers. Your department is expected to count on revenue tuition dollars, research funds, gifts, and so on, and to include salaries and expenses for operating as costs. It also will likely be assessed for its share of indirect costs for operating and maintaining the university.

Clearly there are strengths and weaknesses to each of these approaches. Some are especially bothersome if they seem to focus too much attention on the bottom line at the expense of academic performance. Most institutions rarely use a pure form of the models; colleges and universities instead adapt budgeting to their unique circumstances.

Budget Issues for the Chairperson

Some colleges and universities use the centralized method for developing budgets, and many believe that this approach discourages sound management within the system's units. As Barr (2002) observes, "There are few if any incentives for a unit to employ cost-saving measures because there is little reward for doing so" (p. 45). She goes on to assert that morale is generally lower where this approach is used, and further suggests that ". . . a great deal of time and energy is expended in finding methods to get around the system and manipulate resources" (p. 45).

A unit-based approach, on the other hand, allows unit managers to have some input in decision-making. Each campus unit generates a budget request reflecting the needs of the unit, but this, too, has its weakness. Barr (2002) notes, "Unit-based budgeting approaches have two weaknesses. First, such approaches encourage a myopic view of fiscal matters. The driving force is the unit rather than addressing larger institutional issues. Second, it may encourage unrealistic expectations" (p. 45).

Universities where I have worked have used a combination of these two models. Either as a dean or a department chairperson, I received general guidelines and was expected to develop revenue and expense requests. As Barr (2002) points out,

Although the unit may not always receive everything that is requested, greater understanding is achieved regarding the reasons for eventual budget decisions. A shared approach increases the ability of faculty and staff involved in the budget process to understand what factors influence decisions. (p. 46)

That certainly has been my experience.

Barr's book is essential for new budget managers, particularly regarding pitfalls in budget management. Here are the questions she asks.

1. Do you fall into the trap of overestimating revenue? What assumptions underlie your revenue figures? Can you explain them to decision makers?

2. Does your budget address long-term and chronic issues facing the unit, or are you still trying to ignore them?

3. Is there someone or some office in the institution that can assist you in addressing a long-term or chronic problem?

4. What are the hidden costs associated with each project or program within your unit? Can you identify those costs, and are they accounted for in the budget plan?

5. If you are administering a time-limited grant or contract, what plans are in place for the end of the grant?

6. What are the multiyear consequences of the budget decisions made within your unit? Are those consequences defensible?

7. What are the implications of your budget decisions beyond your specific unit?

8. Have you made the fatal error of assuming the good times will continue unabated? Have you established reserve funds for equipment, repair and renovation, or contingencies? (p. 87)

These are all useful questions. So much of what we do as chairpersons consists of learning on the job. Since they can never have too much knowledge, experienced chairpersons attend workshops, read, and learn from others as well. It is especially important to use every available opportunity to learn and grow. Understanding as much as you can about budget matters will enhance your standing on campus and enable you to have a greater opportunity for helping your department realize its goals.

Fundraising

Raising funds to supplement the money your college or university allocates to your department can augment the department's mission and make big dreams come true. However, fundraising—as with counseling low-achieving faculty members or preparing detailed budgets—is something likely not learned in advance of one's appointment as chairperson. The remainder of this chapter presents some basic strategies for fundraising.

Fundraising Strategies

If you are able to raise private funds to support the mission of your department, the quality of instruction can be enhanced greatly. Likewise, your reputation as an administrator is likely to be viewed more favorably. Despite these incentives, few chairpersons engage in ongoing efforts to raise private funds. There are reasons for this, of course. First, almost none of us has any formal training in fundraising, as I've already suggested. We don't know how to go about it, and we feel uncomfortable asking for money. Second, it is a time-consuming effort, and we find ourselves putting it off to attack more pressing matters, especially those for which we are better trained or suited.

Educators can be more successful fundraisers, especially if they keep in mind several basic concepts.

- Show how giving money to your department is a good investment.

Many of us assume that the best way to raise money is to demonstrate that we have a great need for it. But most of those who give money are tired of hearing organizations plead poverty. Instead, they want to know what the department can do to meet the needs of others. Donors want to invest their money, not merely give it away, and they expect a return on their

investment. You need to show how a gift will be used and what benefits it
will produce.

- **Get to know potential donors.**

You are not likely to be successful when potential donors know next to
nothing about you and your department. Listen carefully to what they say
and find out what they want—then make your approach accordingly.

- **Develop a strategic plan.**

Design a plan for the department's future. What does future enrollment
look like? If growth is expected, how will you handle it? If the number of
students is expected to decline, what action will follow? How will curriculum offerings change in the years ahead? What new equipment will be
needed? These and other questions need to be carefully thought through
and spelled out so that you can share the information with those you are
asking to support your program. If you can provide a quick summary of a
plan as well as detailed information about what it will take to fulfill your
vision, raising private funds will be easier.

- **Remember that academic enterprise and fundraising are linked.**

The quality of classroom instruction is a factor in alumni giving. Weak
programs are not likely to get much support, and strong alumni giving
encourages private donations.

Alumni interviews show overwhelmingly that the faculty is the key
determinant in motivating graduates to provide financial support. When
we earned our first degree, many of us left with the feeling that we owed a
debt to the college. It was closeness with faculty that fostered such a feeling. Indeed, many of us still keep in contact with former teachers and former students.

Here's a personal illustration of how others think about quality before
giving. When I became chair of a weak, troubled department several years
ago, I was expected to turn it around. I remember very well meeting with
a community leader who said he would help the department financially if
I would improve the quality of instruction, raise standards for students,

and get rid of some weak faculty members. I had already planned to do all these things anyway, and the community leader was true to his word. A few years later he came to me and asked how he could help. In the end, he endowed a distinguished chair. Interestingly, other giving also picked up. Our student scholarship fund grew exponentially over a five-year period.

- **Ask your alumni for support.**

Before doing this, however, be sure to establish some kind of ongoing communication with your alumni. Your pleas for financial support will be largely ignored if you go to your alumni without first having some kind of regular communication with them. You will be surprised how interested and responsive many will be once you tell them about department activities and provide information on how they might invest in the department.

The easiest way to develop communication is to publish a regular alumni newsletter. A better way of developing a personal dialogue is to form a departmental alumni association. Your campus alumni director should be glad to help with this. To get started, identify some local alumni who were active as students and who have maintained contacts with faculty members. Ask them to serve on a committee to get an alumni association started.

In the department I cited earlier, we established an alumni association whose members became active and supportive and helped us raise funds. Indeed, through its own activities the association was able to raise between $15,000 and $20,000 each year. The effort that went into founding the association was richly rewarded.

- **Build bridges with the outside community.**

It helps you get to know potential donors—individuals, foundations, and corporations. It means telling the outside community your vision for the department and becoming known in the community. It also means attracting the attention of alumni and others who can make a difference in your department by supporting it financially. Building bridges to the community requires interpersonal skills. It helps if you are excited about your department and know virtually everything about it. Know your faculty and students.

- Sponsor special fundraising events.

The nature of your program may determine the kind of special fundraising events you can sponsor. "Roasting" one of your distinguished alumni has fundraising possibilities. Years ago, a department I chaired worked with our alumni association to sponsor a roast. We were fortunate to have among our alumni a widely known entertainer whom we asked to serve as master of ceremonies. He agreed. Thus, we had Soupy Sales at the top of our ticket, which gave us a huge boost when it came to promoting the event. We sold corporate table and individual tickets and raised $20,000 that was used to fund student scholarships.

- Set aside some time for fundraising.

One of the biggest obstacles is finding time to do fundraising. Most chairpersons I know—particularly those with large and complex departments—have more to do than they can get done even without fundraising. The best approach: Delegate, then support the person or team you've named to the job. One thing that can be discouraging, especially for the fundraising beginner, is that even if you devote a lot of time to fundraising, your efforts will not necessarily be successful. Even professional fundraisers have learned to accept rejection as an ever-present possibility.

- Get some training in fundraising.

Most chairpersons are not trained as fundraisers: They don't know where to start, they are embarrassed to "beg," and they are quickly hurt by rejection. If you've not had any training, you can begin by reading books on the subject, getting advice from development officers at your school, and attending some workshops. Any training generally will pay off.

- Listen to your faculty for names of prospective givers.

Most departments have some faculty members who have been around a long time and who are well connected in the community. They know who has money and who is likely to give. They know the individuals who have some ties to your department or those who could become friends. Get them to help devise a strategy for cultivating these connections.

Obviously, there are others that you should seek out to help identify prospective donors. Take advantage of anyone who is willing to help.

- **Evaluate a gift carefully before accepting it.**

You don't want to appear to be ungrateful, of course, but you need to know the terms of any gift. Will it be costly to administer? Could its "strings" cause problems?

Some years ago, one of my predecessors accepted a fairly small gift to be used for student scholarships. After I had become chairperson, we were given a large oil painting of the person honored by the gift, and were asked by the family to display it in the department. We happily complied. Then we started getting family complaints because we were not getting widespread publicity whenever we awarded the scholarships. (The scholarships had not been large ones at the time of the gift, and because of inflation they were insignificant when compared with most of the scholarships we awarded.) We tried to explain to the family that we were grateful, and we did the best we could to get publicity. Our explanation was unsatisfactory, and the family removed the gift and gave it to another department on campus. It was one of those gifts that probably should never have been accepted. The donors should have been steered to the development office.

- **Consider the appropriateness of a gift.**

Would you, for example, accept money to endow a chair in the name of someone with a particularly troubling reputation? The person giving the money probably is going to expect publicity. You know, of course, that the publicity will come at great expense if the person is widely mistrusted or disliked.

- **Use the gift in the way it was intended.**

You have a special responsibility to keep your word to those who are generous and kind enough to give to your department. If the money is earmarked for faculty development, you have an obligation to use it solely for that purpose. Whoever follows you as chairperson must know that promises were made and that they must be kept. You will need to keep good records of the gift and its terms.

- **Use your public relations office to help with the publicity whenever you get a gift.**

Unless the donor wishes to be anonymous, he or she will expect some kind of announcement to be made about the gift. The bigger the gift, the more publicity is expected. Your university's public relations staff will know what to do to get publicity that will please the donor.

- **Always thank the donor, no matter the size of the contribution.**

A well-composed letter of thanks is sufficient in many instances. A plaque or a certificate can clearly demonstrate appreciation. Whatever you do, it is important that you let the donor know how much you appreciate his or her generosity.

- **Coordinate your fundraising activities with your dean and the development office.**

It is essential that those charged with the primary task of raising funds at your university—the development office personnel—know and approve of what you are doing. Unless all fundraising is well coordinated, it can become chaotic and unsuccessful. If, for example, development office personnel are working closely with a potential donor on a large gift, they will not want you approaching that person as well. Moreover, if your dean and development office know what your plans are, they can give you some assistance.

- **Develop a case statement that summarizes the fundraising program to be implemented.**

Here you must spell out and document your needs. Tell who will benefit, how the gift can be made, and what the benefits of giving are. Explain in some detail why a potential donor should give to your department rather than to others. Tell why your department exists and share its mission statement.

Engineers Without Borders (EWB) (2005) provides these useful ideas as the six core philosophies of fundraising.

1. People want to support the cause.
2. Know what EWB [or your organization] is about.
3. Know your funder.
4. Take the time to do it right.
5. Be creative.
6. Don't just raise money, build relationships.

These are all excellent ideas to factor into your overall scheme of fundraising.

Remember, fundraising is not about us or even about our college or university. We are trying to motivate people to give in order to help students and the world around them. I especially like suggestions four and six above. Note that taking time to do it "right" means that we should carefully proofread every document that potential donors will see, remembering that we create impressions of what kind of organization we are. We also should personalize letters, which means staying away from form letters. In suggestion six, raising money must be about building for the long term. It is vital that we keep in touch with those who give to us even when we are not asking for money.

Resources

Web Sites
Association of Fundraising Professionals
www.afpnet.org/index.cfm

Fundraising Tips and Plans to Maximize Your Fundraising Opportunity
www.profitpotentials.com/FundraisingTips.cfm

Grantsmanship Techniques: Academic Fundraising Web Resources
www.lib.msu.edu/harris23/grants/4acfrais.htm

Books

Byrson, J. M. (2004). *Strategic planning for public and non-profit organiza-tions: A guide to strengthening and sustaining organizational achieve-ment* (3rd ed.). San Francisco, CA: Jossey-Bass.

Maddox, D. (1999). *Budgeting for not-for-profit organizations.* New York, NY: John Wiley & Sons.

Yeager, J. L., Nelson, G. M., Potter, E. A., Weidman, J. C., & Zullo, T. G. (Eds.). (2001). *ASHE reader on finance in higher education* (2nd ed.). Boston, MA: Pearson.

References

Barr, M. J. (2002). *The Jossey-Bass academic administrator's guide to budgets and financial management.* San Francisco, CA: Jossey-Bass.

Engineers Without Borders. (2005). *Six core philosophies of fundraising.* Retrieved July 16, 2006, from www.ewb.ca/mainsite/pages/resources/toolbox/05-Fundraising.pdf

Jones, D. (2003, February). State shortfalls projected throughout the decade: Higher ed budgets likely to feel continued squeeze. *Policy Alert,* 1–4.

Lindblom, C. E. (1959, Spring). The science of muddling through. *Public Administration Review, 19*(2), 79–88.

Meisinger, R. J., Jr. (1994). *College and university budgeting: An introduc-tion for faculty and academic administrators.* Washington, DC: National Association of College and University Business Officers.

Munitz, B. (1995, Fall). Wanted: New leadership in higher education. *Planning for Higher Education, 24*(1), 9–16.

Zumeta, W. (2005). Higher education's fiscal fortunes: Some light in the tunnel at last. *Almanac of Higher Education,* 27–38.

18

Avoiding Legal Problems

One protection is to develop a sensitivity to legal concerns, so that a figurative red flag goes up each time you must make certain kinds of decisions.

To say that we live in a litigious age has become a cliché. Yet this portmanteau phrase is particularly meaningful to veteran leaders in higher education. Face it: You'll likely need legal counsel at some time during your tenure as department chairperson.

Much of what we do in our jobs today is subject to examination and questioning by others. As chairperson, you make decisions every day that have the potential of being challenged in a court of law. What can you do to avoid legal problems? One protection is to develop a sensitivity to legal concerns, so that a figurative red flag goes up each time you must make certain kinds of decisions. It warns you to be particularly cautious and to take into account the consequences of your actions.

The following questions and answers should help you develop sensitivity to matters that have legal ramifications. These are real questions, taken from real life.

1. Is it possible to dismiss a faculty member who routinely refuses to follow my instructions?

Yes, though it might not be easy. A faculty member who refuses to obey orders is guilty of insubordination, which is cause for dismissal. Insubordination should relate to a repeated refusal to obey reasonable institutional rules or administrative directives. Before you make a charge of insubordination, you should warn the offending faculty member, in writing, that his or her behavior is inappropriate and must be corrected. If, subsequently, the behavior does not change, you have reason to proceed with the insubordination charge. Before taking that step, however, be sure to discuss the matter with your dean and the university's legal counsel.

2. I have been told to keep a paper trail on faculty who regularly present problems. What is a paper trail, and is this good advice?

A paper trail is a written record of specific events related to the problems under consideration. For purposes of illustration, let's assume that faculty member John Doe refuses to attend departmental faculty meetings. You call Professor Doe into your office to discuss the matter. After he leaves your office, you should make notes to tell what transpired during the meeting, especially including the following:

- Date and time of the meeting
- Reason for the meeting
- The main points discussed
- Any agreements reached
- Any instructions or orders given
- Any unresolved points of disagreement

It is a good idea to follow up the meeting with a note to Professor Doe outlining the results of the meeting. If Professor Doe fails to attend the next departmental faculty meeting, file a copy of the minutes that show he was absent. Send him a written memorandum in which you note his absence and your disappointment and disapproval.

In brief, you should keep a written record of any discussion that pertains to the problem. This "trail" will prove critical to your case should you decide to go forward with a charge of insubordination.

3. During an interview with a finalist for a teaching position, it seemed that the candidate was withholding information. How much checking on his past should I do, and is it permissible

to call references he has not listed? In doing a background check, are there precautions I should take?

You are obligated to see that a thorough reference check has been conducted for all candidates you invite to campus as finalists for a position. Indeed, you may face legal problems if you don't. The failure to adequately check references can cause the university to be sued for negligently hiring someone inappropriate for the job where he or she can injure or otherwise endanger others.

There are other points to consider as well. It is easier to do a thorough reference check and make a decision not to hire someone than it is to recommend against reappointment or tenure of someone who should never have been hired in the first place. In order to get an accurate picture of a candidate, you must expand your reference checking beyond the list of references the candidate provided. The number of calls you need to make depends on what you learn from your initial calls. If you don't get answers to your questions, or if you get contradictory responses, keep seeking until you get a thorough profile of the candidate.

You should write down the responses you get to questions during reference checks. Also, it is important to remember that questions you must avoid in candidate interviews must be avoided in reference checks as well. For example, just as you would not ask a candidate his or her age, you cannot ask for that information during a reference check. Questions must pertain to matters directly related to job performance. You should treat all reference checks as confidential and provide the information only to those individuals who have a role in the hiring process.

4. What are my responsibilities if I receive reports that a faculty member in my department is engaging in sexual harassment? What action should I take, if any?

Sexual harassment is against federal and state laws, and universities generally have policies that forbid it. As a university administrator, you have the responsibility to inform those in your unit of the policy and to see that it is enforced. Thus, it is your responsibility to investigate carefully any reports you receive regarding sexual harassment. They must not be ignored. On the other hand, you cannot take any specific action until someone complains about a particular individual.

What you can and should do is remind all faculty and staff members in your department on a regular basis that the university has a policy that forbids sexual harassment. Circulate the printed policy dealing with sexual harassment, and let everyone know that you take the matter seriously and that it will not be tolerated. You may want to invite a spokesperson from affirmative action to a faculty meeting once a year to discuss the matter. As many lawyers have pointed out, to avoid damages—personal and monetary—the best course is thorough understanding, planning, and education.

If a student complains to you that she or he has been sexually harassed, you should make arrangements for the student to see someone in affirmative action. You also should advise the student to:

- Tell the harasser to stop, making clear that the behavior is unacceptable.
- Keep a written record detailing the offensive behavior—a description of the behavior, where it happened, and when.
- Avoid being alone with the harasser.
- Wear a small, hidden tape recorder that can be activated in the event the offending behavior continues. Before you take such action, however, you need to know whether or not your state law prohibits surreptitious taping.
- Report to you immediately if the offending behavior continues.

Sexual harassment has far-reaching implications. If you take the steps just outlined to familiarize those in your department with your university's policy on sexual harassment and its importance, you will have taken a positive step toward minimizing problems.

5. Can I legally remove a student from a class if he or she causes disturbances in the classroom?

A faculty member faced with this problem should be advised to contact the university officer responsible for student affairs. At most universities, this person has been given the authority by the university president to remove a student from a class. At one such university, the authority is covered under an emergency action policy which states,

> Emergency action is a special category that may be used by the
> president or his/her designee when, on special occasions, he has
> the authority to impose the sanction, inter alia, of suspension to
> a student or group of students from school or from a residence
> hall who act or refuse to act, the result of which conduct is to
> interfere with the rights of others and which conduct is non-
> peaceful or is disruptive or which conduct constitutes a danger
> to health, safety, or property of others or his/herself provided
> that a hearing is held within 72 hours of the decision.

6. What precautions should I take when providing information about a former employee?

You should have no concern about this if you give accurate information that is related to job performance. Avoid questions about age, physical or mental disabilities, previous discrimination complaints, or periods of unemployment.

There is a growing tendency to give only dates of employment and nothing more. Society is poorly served if we feel constrained from sharing proper information. I encourage you to be helpful—and legally safe—by providing references that are accurate and limited to job performance. Thus, you can comment on a former employee's punctuality, attendance, classroom effectiveness, and so on.

In *Olsson v. Indiana University Board of Trustees* (1991), a university instructor was asked to write a letter of recommendation for a student seeking a teaching position. The faculty member did not believe the student was adequately prepared to teach and said so on the recommendation sheet. The principal who interviewed the student for the job revealed the recommendation. The student did not get the job, and subsequently sued the instructor, claiming defamation. The state's court of appeals supported the school, ruling that the student could not collect damages because:

- The instructor had shown no "malice or reckless disregard" for the truth.
- The instructor had not written the letter in "bad faith." The letter had been seen only by the person it was intended for; the instructor was a supervisor of students, so evaluation was her responsibility.
- Others submitted negative evaluations of the student.

This ruling is still being cited when settling similar disputes today.

7. The college has mandatory advising. Suppose during the course of an advising session a faculty member—the student's advisor—pays little attention to the courses the student has selected. Suppose further that by taking these courses and not taking others, the student will have to spend an extra semester in school. What are the legal ramifications?

Bad advice can end up in court—and advisement questions do make it to court quite often. If the information provided a student is in fact wrong, the legal system may decide responsibility and assess damages. Courts often apply contract theory in the situation. They find that an agreement was made, and each party is bound to uphold its side of the bargain. Thus, faculty members who sign registration sheets indicating approval of a schedule need to examine carefully what they are signing. Signing off as an advisor is serious business and should be approached as such.

It is important to maintain regular training and updating sessions for all faculty advisors, as well as have in place some systematic means for spot checking student folders to see that advisors are maintaining adequate records for each advisee.

8. If I know that a faculty member in my department has a drinking problem, what should I do? Am I legally responsible for any harm he or she may do while drinking on the job? What should I do if I suspect that a faculty member has a drinking problem but I have nothing to support my suspicions?

If you have reason to believe that a faculty member has a drinking problem and you do nothing about it, you may find yourself in a position of having to explain why you did nothing. You may indeed bear some legal responsibility for not taking action.

What should you do? Investigate; attempt to determine if the problem exists. You can learn how to go about this by contacting professionals skilled in counseling alcoholics. They also can help you learn how to approach the individual to see that he or she gets help. Keep a written record of any action you take.

Individuals with drinking problems often are skilled at deceiving others. You may come away from an early meeting with an alcoholic convinced that there is no problem whatever. See Chapter 26 for a more complete discussion on how to deal with this problem.

9. Are faculty protected by the First Amendment in any public criticisms they make of the university, or of their department chairperson, or of faculty colleagues?

Until the 1950s, courts generally took the position that public employees agreed to suspend their rights to criticize their institutions in exchange for employment. When matters pertaining to loyalty oaths and organizational affiliations came up in the 1950s and 1960s, courts extended the constitutional free speech protections granted others to public employees, including college instructors.

Early court cases ruled that faculty members have the right to criticize their employers when they are commenting on matters of public concern. Since then the courts have been kept busy with employer-employee free speech disputes. Defining what "matters of public concern" includes has proved to be difficult. In *Connick v. Myers* (1983), for example, the court defined matters of public concern as those "relating to any matter of political, social, or other concern in the community."

Legal experts point out that courts have tended to give considerable weight to employers' decisions on employee free speech. They have done so because they believe employers must be able to maintain some control over employee conduct. Toma and Palm (1999) write that "the decision of the U.S. Supreme Court in *Connick v. Myers* (1983) could represent an emerging view according greater weight to the need of public employers to maintain discipline and harmony in the workplace (Olivas 1993)" (p. 63).

Faculty members do have the right to criticize, provided they speak out on public concerns. But courts have upheld the right of universities to dismiss faculty members in instances where the faculty members' criticisms have been viewed as personal in nature. Toma and Palm (1999) state, "As a general rule, institutions can avoid judicial invalidation of their actions in academic freedom cases if strong and dispositive grounds exist for an action independent of matters involving academic freedom" (p. 63).

10. **Can you insist that faculty and staff get permission before speaking with reporters?**

It depends. Most colleges and universities would not want to impose such a restriction. Some institutions provide their faculty and staff members with guidelines similar to the following from the University of Northern Colorado (2006): "You are not required to have any permission before speaking with the media, but we are available to help you decide whether to participate and to prepare for a positive outcome." An approach such as this one will help to ensure positive media relations.

11. **A faculty member in my department wants to copy a chapter from a book to distribute to students in his class. Is this legally permissible?**

To answer this question, we need to examine carefully the agreement on guidelines for classroom copying shown in Table 18.1. This document demonstrates a purposeful sheltering of educational copying to a greater degree than we would find in other fair-use situations.

12. **Suppose I learn that a faculty member in my department is having an affair with a student who is in his or her class. What, if anything, should I do? Is this any of my business (or the university's)?**

The faculty member's behavior in this instance is inappropriate, and you should say something to him or her. You are likely to be told by the faculty

Table 18.1 Agreement on Guidelines for Classroom Copying in Not-for-Profit Educational Institutions

With Respect to Books and Periodicals

The purpose of the following guidelines is to state the minimum standards of educational fair use under Section 107 of H.R. 2223. The parties agree that the conditions determining the extent of permissible copying for educational purposes may change in the future; that certain types of copying permitted under these guidelines may not be permissible in the future; and conversely, that in the future other types of copying not permitted under these guidelines may be permissible under revised guidelines.

Moreover, the following statement of guidelines is not intended to limit the types of copying permitted under the standards of fair use under judicial decision and which are stated in Section 107 of the Copyright Revision Bill. There may be instances in which copying which does not fall within the guidelines stated below may nonetheless be permitted under the criteria of fair use.

I.   Single copying for teachers
     A single copy may be made of any of the following by or for a teacher at his or her individual request for his or her scholarly research or use in teaching or preparation to teach a class:
     A.   A chapter from a book;
     B.   An article from a periodical or newspaper;
     C.   A short story, short essay, or short poem, whether or not from a collective work; and
     D.   A chart, graph, diagram, drawing, cartoon, or picture from a book, periodical, or newspaper.

II. Multiple copies for classroom use
     Multiple copies (not to exceed in any event more than one copy per pupil in a course) may be made by or for the teacher giving the course for classroom use or discussion provided that:
     A.   The copying meets the tests of brevity and spontaneity as defined below;
     B.   Meets the cumulative effect test as defined below; and
     C.   Each copy includes a notice of copyright.

Table 18.1 (*continued*)

Definitions
Brevity
(i) Poetry: (a) A complete poem if less than 250 words and if printed on not more than two pages or, (b) from a longer poem, an excerpt of not more than 250 words.

(ii) Prose: (a) Either a complete article, story, or essay of less than 2,500 words, or (b) an excerpt from any prose work of not more than 1,000 words or 10% of the work, whichever is less, but in any event a minimum of 500 words. (Each of the numerical limits stated in "I" and "ii" above may be expanded to permit the completion of an unfinished line of a poem or of an unfinished prose paragraph.)

(iii) Illustration: One chart, graph, diagram, drawing, cartoon, or picture per book or per periodical issue.

(iv) "Special" works: Certain works in poetry, prose, or in "poetic prose" which often combine language with illustrations and which are intended sometimes for children and at other times for a more general audience fall short of 2,500 words in their entirety. Paragraph "ii" above notwithstanding such "special works" may not be reproduced in their entirety; however, an excerpt comprising not more than two of the published pages of such special work and containing not more than 10% of the words found in the text thereof, may be reproduced.

Spontaneity

(i) The copying is at the instance and inspiration of the individual teacher.

(ii) The inspiration and decision to use the work and the moment of its use for maximum teaching effectiveness are so close in time that it would be unreasonable to expect a timely reply to a request for permission.

Cumulative effect
(i) The copying of the material is for only one course in the school in which the copies are made.

(ii) Not more than one short poem, article, story, essay, or two excerpts may be copied from the same author, nor more than three from the same collective work or periodical volume during one class term.

(iii) There shall not be more than nine instances of such multiple copying for one course during one class term. [The limitations stated in "ii" and "iii" above shall not apply to current news periodicals and newspapers and current news sections of other periodicals.]

Table 18.1 (*continued*)

> III. Prohibitions as to I and II above
> Notwithstanding any of the above, the following shall be prohibited:
> - A. Copying shall not be used to create or to replace or substitute for anthologies, compilations, or collective works. Such replacement or substitution may occur whether copies of various works or excerpts therefrom are accumulated or reproduced and used separately.
> - B. There shall be no copying of or from works intended to be "consumable" in the course of study or of teaching. These include workbooks, exercises, standardized tests, and test booklets and answer sheets and like consumable material.
> - C. Copying shall not:
>   - a) substitute for the purchase of books, publishers' reprints, or periodicals;
>   - b) be directed by higher authority; and
>   - c) be repeated with respect to the same item by the same teacher from term to term.
> - D. No charge shall be made to the student beyond the actual cost of the photocopying.

Agreed March 19, 1976.
Ad Hoc Committee on Copyright Law Revision:
        By Sheldon Elliott Steinbach
Author-Publisher Group:
Authors League of America:
        By Irwin Karp, *Counsel*
Association of American Publishers, Inc.:
        By Alexander C. Hoffman, *Chairman, Copyright Committee*

member that both the student and the faculty member are of legal age and what they do in their private lives is of no concern to you or the university. However, it is not that simple. There is a matter of conflict of interest and professional ethics to be considered. Both provide reasons for a faculty member not to be sexually involved with a student in his or her class.

13. What should I do if I think the university is going to be sued?

Advise your academic dean and the university's chief legal counsel of the situation. The latter will advise you on what you should do, if anything. He or she also will look after the university's interest by deciding what course of action the university must take to defend itself against a lawsuit.

14. What are my responsibilities if I receive reports or otherwise have reason to believe that a faculty member in my department is using department equipment, supplies, or facilities for nonuniversity-related or nonuniversity-sanctioned activities?

It is against the law for any state employee to use state equipment, supplies, or facilities for nonofficial business. Faculty members need to be reminded of this from time to time. Certainly, all new faculty members need to be informed.

If you have any reason to believe that a faculty member is using equipment, facilities, or supplies for nonuniversity-related purposes, you need to investigate and put a stop to the practice if you discover it is indeed contrary to policy or law. If you believe that a serious problem exists, talk to your academic dean and the university's chief legal counsel. Even if you believe the problem is not serious, you should keep a written record on the matter.

15. A professor in my department routinely ignores the regulation requiring all faculty to provide their students with a course syllabus. What recourse, if any, do the students have in such a case?

Most universities have a policy that deals with course syllabi. A typical one says,

> During the first two weeks of semester classes (three days of summer term), the instructor must provide each student with a copy of the course requirements which includes the following items: 1) attendance policy, 2) grading policy, 3) approximate due dates for major projects and exams, and 4) a description of general course content.

Obviously, the faculty member who fails to provide students with a course syllabus is violating university policy. Students should be advised to take up the matter with the department chairperson. If the problem is not corrected, the academic dean should be consulted.

16. Suppose a faculty member is conducting a field trip off campus. He is driving a university vehicle, and several students are with him. An accident occurs, and occupants of the car are injured. An investigation shows that the faculty member was negligent. What are the legal ramifications?

States carry insurance for their vehicles and employees. The insurance covers the student passengers riding in the university automobile. The insurance would generally cover any legal costs arising out of the accident, although some states may have the discretion on whether the involved faculty member will be represented by the state.

17. Do I have the right to insist that a faculty member cut back the hours given to a second job if I determine that the teacher is not getting university work done?

The university has a right to require disclosure of outside employment and place limits on it. Consider the case of *Cook County College Teachers Union v. Board of Trustees* (1985). The school limited outside employment by full-time faculty members and required them to complete extensive disclosure forms and report all outside income and benefits. One faculty member challenged the school. A state court ruled in favor of the school and supported the principle that schools could limit outside activities that interfered or conflicted with campus employment.

18. Can the university restrict what an instructor says in class, or does a faculty member's right to free speech and academic freedom override the university's authority?

Academic freedom can be a controversial topic, particularly as it concerns religion in the classroom. "Courts hesitate to intervene in matters of religious doctrine. If a college claims that a professor fails to meet its religious standards, and the professor disagrees, a court typically defers to the college" (McMurtrie, 2002, p. A12). It is important that universities have clear policies explaining the expectations, limitations, and restrictions of academic freedom.

19. What legal problems can arise from evaluating faculty and staff?

The performance evaluation can give rise to charges of defamation, illegal discrimination, negligence, invasion, and breach of contract.

To avoid legal problems, be fair and honest, and document everything in writing. Be careful to avoid evaluating anything that does not track the essential functions of the job. In other words, you should be cautious not to evaluate a faculty member's performance on factors that are not job related.

Rely as much as possible on objective criteria and avoid those that are subjective. Don't say, for example, that "I receive lots of complaints from students about Professor Jones's teaching." Instead, say, "This semester 14 students complained to me about Professor Jones's teaching."

Also, you should make certain that faculty members know what is expected of them. For example, courts are likely to support complaints when a faculty member can show that he or she was not told the specific requirements relating to publication until tenure was denied.

Whatever you do, be extremely careful to maintain confidentiality throughout the evaluation process. You may discuss the evaluations only with those who have a need to know. This means you are permitted to discuss a faculty member's evaluation only with those up the chain of command or those serving on review committees.

20. Can you ask a woman about pregnancy, childbearing, or childcare during a job interview?

Questions about pregnancy, childbearing plans, childcare arrangements, or birth control are prohibited. When conducting an interview, you should ask only those questions that will provide information about the individual's ability to do the job. To do otherwise may put you at risk for legal action.

21. Can you search a professor's office?

It depends. A faculty member is entitled to a degree of privacy in a campus office, but there are circumstances where you may search a professor's office without his or her permission. Before you do this, however, you should make certain that your dean and the university's legal counsel agree to this course of action. Moreover, you would be well advised to think long and hard before searching an office.

In *O'Connor v. Ortega* (1987), the Supreme Court ruled that while public employees may have legitimate expectations of privacy in their offices, administrators have a competing need for "supervision, control, and the efficient operation of the workplace." It left open the possibility that a work-related search could be legally justified. The suit was brought after the Napa State Hospital placed a staff psychiatrist on administrative leave over alleged misconduct. Administrators were concerned about the status of state property and in turn searched his office, seizing certain items. Ortega sued, claiming the search, which was conducted without a warrant—violated his Fourth Amendment rights. In making its decision, the Supreme Court considered the reasonableness of both the inception and the scope of the intrusion. Further, according to Kaplin and Lee (1995),

> The Court concluded that public employees may have reason-
> able expectations of privacy in their offices, desks, and files;
> these expectations may, in certain circumstances, be protected
> by the Fourth Amendment. A plurality of judges, however,
> agreed that an employer's warrantless search of such prop-
> erty will nevertheless be permissible if it is done for "nonin-
> vestigatory, work-related purposes" or for "investigations of
> work-related misconduct," and if it meets "the standard of rea-
> sonableness under all circumstances. (pp. 305–306)

This is an area in which universities would be well advised to develop policies and procedures. Santa Rosa Junior College in California apparently had no such policy when it was determined to find out who had written a flyer and five anonymous letters disparaging its president (Leatherman,

1997). The college hired a private investigator and a handwriting expert who delved into personnel files of 10 faculty and staff members, entered 13 faculty offices, and tapped into 50 computers in an effort to find the responsible person. A tenured professor was identified as the offender and was fired. That professor in turn sued, claiming defamation and a violation of her right to free speech.

Santa Rosa's lawyer relied on *Connick v. Myers* (1983) in developing legal strategy to defend against the faculty member's accusation that it violated her free speech rights.

22. A tenure-track faculty member in the third year of his probationary period requests a two-month unpaid leave to help his wife take care of their newborn twins or to take care of a seriously ill parent. Must you grant his request?

The Family and Medical Leave Act of 1993 requires you to grant the leave, provided certain conditions are satisfied. It requires covered employers to provide up to 12 weeks of unpaid, job-protected leave to "eligible" employees for certain family and medical reasons.

- Eligibility requirements:
  1. The employee must have worked for a covered employer for at least one year, and for 1,250 hours over the previous 12 months.
  2. There must be at least 50 employees within 75 miles.
- Reasons for taking leave:
  1. To care for the employee's child after birth, or placement for adoption or foster care;
  2. To care for the employee's spouse, son or daughter, or parent, who has a serious health condition;
  3. For a serious health condition that makes the employee unable to perform the employee's job.

23. What recourse does the department have if it is denied program accreditation?

The traditional judicial deference to decisions in higher education applies in the context of accreditation, as Toma and Palm (1999) observe. They also note, "The program or institution usually has the right to appeal any adverse decision" (p. 121). Antitrust law and constitutional standards have generally failed when used to challenge negative decisions. On the other hand, common law does apply to accrediting agencies. "Accrediting agencies must act fairly and follow their own rules" (Toma & Palm, p. 122).

24. What are the major legal issues I will most likely encounter as chairperson?

In our increasingly litigious society, chairpersons can become involved in legal disputes with faculty and staff and even parents. Goldenberg (2006) identifies promotion and tenure cases, other performance-based action (e.g., hiring, salary, reassignments, etc.), and harassment charges as the most common legal challenges for chairpersons. Legal problems of any kind can be worrisome, particularly for chairpersons with little experience with these matters. Goldenberg (pp. 308–309) recommends that chairpersons adopt the following strategies when dealing with legal issues.

1) Become familiar with department, college, and university guidelines on promotion and tenure.
2) As soon as a situation seems likely to generate conflict, start keeping notes, realizing that anything written on paper or in email can become part of a court record.
3) Understand what your obligations are in dealing with rumors, complaints, confidentiality, and privacy.
4) Try not to take legal challenges personally.
5) Understand that lawyers nearly always want to settle if they can do so with little expense.
6) Cases that proceed to the deposition stage take time; prepare to give the time that is needed.

25. What is the best way to avoid legal problems?

The best thing you can do to avoid legal problems is to be familiar with the university's policies and to carry them out. Beyond that, you must think about the consequences of your decisions. If they are negative, you should act carefully and seek advice from your dean, academic vice president, and university attorney. If you believe your actions may result in a lawsuit, ask for a consultation to discuss the matter with the university's legal counsel. Chu (2006, pp. 85–86) also offers this advice:

- *The best means of avoiding legal problems is to ensure that they do not occur in the first place.* Resolve issues when they are small so that they do not become larger problems.
- *Be crystal clear in communications* with department members and superiors and be able to provide evidence that you made every effort to communicate clearly.
- *Know the legal rights and responsibilities of those in your department,* as well as the protections and rights that you have as a representative of the institution.
- *Consult with the best chairs on campus* to get multiple perspectives on difficult issues so that actions may be taken from an informed basis.

Resources

Web Sites

Department Chair Online Resource Center
www.acenet.edu/resources/chairs/index.cfm?section=4

Hiring and Promotion
www.aaup.org/Legal/info%20outlines/leghire.htm

Legal Information Institute
www.law.cornell.edu/

Legal Watch
www.aaup.org/publications/Academe/2002/02nd/02ndLW.htm

Books

Black, D. R. (1997). *Maintaining perspective: A decade of collegiate legal challenges.* Madison, WI: Magna.

Olivas, M. A. (2006). *The law and higher education: Cases and materials on colleges in court* (3rd ed.). Durham, NC: Carolina Academic Press.

Poskanzer, S. G. (2002). *Higher education law: The faculty.* Baltimore, MD: Johns Hopkins University Press.

Weeks, K. M. (1999). *Managing departments: Chairpersons and the law.* Nashville, TN: College Legal Information, Inc.

References

Chu, D. (2006). *The department chair primer: Leading and managing academic departments.* Bolton, MA: Anker.

Connick v. Myers, 461 U.S. 138 (1983).

Cook County College Teachers Union v. Board of Trustees, 481 N.E.2d 40 (Ill. App. 1985).

Goldenberg, E. (2006, April). Surviving legal headaches as department chair. *PS: Political Science & Politics, 39*(2), 308–309.

Kaplin, W. A., & Lee, B. A. (1995). *The law of higher education* (3rd ed.). San Francisco, CA: Jossey-Bass.

Leatherman, C. (1997, June 6). Search of faculty offices and computer files riles college. *The Chronicle of Higher Education*, p. A11.

McMurtrie, B. (2002, May 24). Do professors lose academic freedom by signing statements of faith? *The Chronicle of Higher Education*, p. A12.

O'Connor v. Ortega, 480 U.S. 709 (1987).

Olsson v. Indiana University Board of Trustees, 571 N.E.2d 585, 587 (Ind. App. 1991).

Toma, J. D., & Palm, R. L. (1999). *The academic administrator and the law: What every dean and department chair needs to know* (ASHE-ERIC Higher Education Report, 26[5]). Washington, DC: The George Washington University, Graduate School of Education and Human Development.

University of Northern Colorado. (2006). *Working with the media.* Retrieved July 24, 2006, from the University of Northern Colorado, Communications and Media Relations web site: www.unco.edu/mediarelations/sub_training.shtml

19

Understanding Sexual Harassment and the Americans with Disabilities Act

Sexual harassment and the Americans with Disabilities Act are serious and significant concerns for all chairpersons. The successful chairperson will understand college and university policy related to these matters and become actively engaged in dealing with them.

Chairpersons not only must be familiar with the law regarding tolerance issues, they must go beyond the law to protect the rights and concerns of faculty members. Moreover, all faculty and staff members must be informed that sexual harassment, racism, gender inequality, or intolerance toward those who are disabled or otherwise different from the majority of the faculty cannot and will not be accepted. As chairperson, you must know and stay up to date with laws and regulations that protect faculty members, and likewise you must also know the relevant policies developed by your university or college on matters affecting faculty members.

This chapter will explore sexual harassment issues and the Americans with Disabilities Act. We will examine what chairpersons can do to establish an atmosphere of professionalism where everyone is treated with trust and respect.

Dealing With Sexual Harassment

As chairperson, you must be fully informed about your university's policy on sexual harassment, as you have the duty to see that it is enforced. It is your responsibility to see that all faculty and staff members in your department are familiar with the policy. They need to know that you take the matter seriously and will not tolerate sexual discrimination or harassment in any form. Turning a blind eye to offensive behavior constitutes bad judgment, if not malfeasance.

Sexual harassment is a form of sex discrimination prohibited by Title VII of the Civil Rights Act of 1964 and by Title IX of the Education Amendments of 1972. Moreover, it is prohibited in both employment and public accommodation contexts by laws in most, if not all, states. It is defined as unwelcome behavior of a sexual nature or with sexual overtones. Sexual harassment takes two legal forms:

1. *Quid pro quo.* This form of sexual harassment is a "this for that" demand for sexual favors in exchange for some job benefit.
2. *Hostile environment.* This refers to conditions or behaviors that interfere with the individual's job performance or that create an intimidating or offensive work environment. Employers are liable for this form of sexual harassment when they know, or should know, about the harassment and fail to take prompt and reasonable remedial action.

Within these two general categories many behaviors or conditions can constitute sexual harassment.

Behavior That May Constitute Sexual Harassment

A wide range of conduct can be considered sexual harassment, and men as well as women can be victims. Title VII forbids any harassment in which one, some, or all the employees of one sex suffer significantly unfavorable treatment on the job because of their gender. Federal courts have identified some of the following examples of sexual harassment.

Unwelcome sexual advances. A coworker repeatedly asked a female employee for dates and wrote love letters to her after she rejected his overtures. An employee who is repeatedly propositioned by a supervisor or coworker trying to establish an intimate relationship can sue the employer for sexual harassment. Some specific examples of unwelcome advances may be:

- Any form of subtle pressure for sexual activity
- Physical actions such as unnecessary physical brushes or touches, obscene or suggestive gestures, leering or ogling, physical aggression such as pinching or patting
- Verbal comments such as disparaging sexual remarks, humor and jokes about sex or male/female relationships, sexual innuendoes, or remarks about a person's clothing, body, or sexual activities

Coercion. A female employee was repeatedly asked by her boss to "do something nice," with the understanding that a favor would be bestowed or a reprisal made. In another case, two male employees were forced to engage in sexual activity with the boss's female secretary with the threat that they would be fired if they refused.

Favoritism. When employees who submit to sexual favors are rewarded while others who refuse are denied promotions or benefits, the employer may be liable for hostile environment sexual harassment.

Indirect harassment. An employee who witnesses sexual harassment can sue the employer. For example, a nurse complained that a doctor grabbed and fondled other nurses in her presence, causing an offensive sexually hostile environment.

Offensive physical environment. Graffiti and displays of nude or pornographic pictures can be sexual harassment for which the employer is liable.

Sexual harassment is defined under the law as

Harassment in which the faculty member covertly or overtly uses the power inherent in the status of a professor to threaten, coerce, or intimidate a student to accept sexual advances or risk reprisal in terms of a grade, a recommendation, or even a job.

Even with the definition and examples of sexual harassment provided, many disagreements still exist as to what constitutes sexual harassment. The point made by Black and Gilson (1988) is still pertinent today.

> The law, whether legislative or judge-made, cannot fully define sexual harassment. It can provide a framework for examining claims, but it cannot produce a comprehensive list of do's and don'ts. Evaluation of any given campus circumstance involving claims of harassment depends partly on established standards, partly on a "reasonable person" test. That is, would a reasonable person find the alleged behavior offensive? Common sense, along with the legal framework, determines the standards from which campuses should draw their policies and actions. (p. 70)

There are often many unanswered questions in sexual harassment allegations. When does an innocent flirtation become sexual harassment? How serious is one incident? How do you determine culpability? Once you do, what do you do about it? Because the personal and professional lives of individuals are involved, great care and thought must be given to handling the situation.

Chairpersons need to take advantage of training opportunities offered by their own universities or colleges, as most now have ongoing programs involving not just sexual harassment, but other civil rights issues regulated by the U.S. Equal Employment Opportunity Commission (EEOC). Furthermore, the EEOC offers many free publications and even some no-cost training programs on matters within its jurisdiction.

According to the EEOC (2005),

> Most agencies have a strongly-worded policy statement denouncing sexual harassment and threatening swift and severe action against employees who engage in such conduct; however, 51% of the agencies (20), and 85% of one agency's sub-components (50), have policies that cover only sexual

harassment. . . . . [H]arassment may occur on any basis covered by EEO statutes, including race, color, religion, sex (sexual or non-sexual), national origin, age, disability, and reprisal. Even though non-sexual harassment is the issue most frequently raised in EEO complaints, many agencies' policies fail to mention, and therefore presumably fail to cover, non-sexual harassment . . . Assuming that such policies "informally" cover non-sexual harassment, employees may not believe they have such recourse unless specific coverage is mentioned in the policy.

Early on, the EEOC acknowledged that sexual harassment often is in the eye of the beholder. Friendliness and thoughtless or innocent remarks can be misread. For example, the commission's 1988 compliance manual stated, "a single incident or isolated incidents of offensive sexual conduct or remarks generally does not create an abusive environment unless the conduct is quite severe." The commission quotes the U.S. Supreme Court: "The mere utterance of an ethnic or social [or sexual] epithet that engenders offensive feelings in an employee would not affect the conditions of employment to a sufficiently significant degree to violate Title VII."

Keeping up with legal issues surrounding sexual harassment is time consuming and often confusing for people without legal training. Nonetheless, chairpersons—with the help of the information offered by most colleges and universities—can deal with sexual harassment legal issues, especially if they seek clarification and direction from their institution's legal affairs officer.

Be aware that sexual harassment law, as with law in general, is dynamic. For example, until a recent ruling by the California Supreme Court, it was unclear whether state law supervisors who have affairs with subordinates can create a work climate that constitutes sexual harassment for the "uninvolved" employees. In *Miller v. Department of Corrections* (2005), former employees at the Valley State Prison for Women in Chowchilla, California, complained about then-warden Lewis Kuykendall, who was sexually involved with at least three women employees at the same time. Two other female employees, Edna Miller and Frances Mackey, sued the state's department of corrections, arguing that they were denied promotions and opportunities because of the warden's favoritism toward his lovers. The court ruled against the women, finding that they "were not themselves subjected to sexual advances and were not treated any differently than male employees."

However, on July 18, 2005, the California Supreme Court unanimously reversed the lower court in interpreting the state's anti-discrimination law. Tracking the language of EEOC guidance, the court reasoned that while an isolated incident of favoritism would not ordinarily establish harassment, when that favoritism is so widespread "the demeaning message is conveyed to female employees that they are viewed by management as 'sexual playthings' or that the way required for women to get ahead in the workplace is by engaging in sexual conduct."

Some courts have embraced, to at least some extent, the "untargeted victim" theory under federal and state laws. Other courts have rejected the proposition that others may suffer sexual harassment by the consensual affairs of others in the workplace. At least one court has considered the untargeted victim theory in the academic setting. In *Wilson v. Delta State University* (2005), William Wilson, director of the university's audio-visual center, sued for retaliation under Title VII after his position was eliminated and his contract not renewed. According to Wilson, his position was terminated because he reported to the university's president that his supervisor, Dr. Michelle Roberts, was unqualified for her position, and that she had received the appointment only because she was having an affair with an administrator at the university. Wilson argued that when he divulged the affair to the president, he was engaged in protected activity. The federal appellate court rejected the untargeted victim theory: "When an employer discriminated in favor of a paramour, such an action is not sex-based discrimination, as the favoritism, while unfair, disadvantages both sexes alike for reasons other than gender." In so doing, the court established that discrimination in favor of a paramour was not "an unlawful employment practice," and thus, Wilson's revelation about the affair could not have been a protected activity. Accordingly, the court concluded that the district court had properly granted the university's motion for judgment as a matter of law.

According to the American Association of University Professors (2005), "A 'small minority' of employment policies requires disclosure of office relationships . . . and some companies require written acknowledgements by the parties that the affair is consensual, to avoid subsequent claims of quid pro quo harassment." It is unclear if and how the Miller decision may influence institutional policies at colleges and universities. Many institutions already have consensual relationship policies in place. Most do not absolutely prohibit such relationships, but rather discourage them, requiring disclosure and withdrawal of the professor from any supervisory role over the student.

Most universities have a sexual harassment policy and procedures for dealing with complaints. You are obligated to deal with any such complaints that come to your attention; failure to do so can result in disciplinary action against you.

University policies generally state something to the effect that at the discretion of the president, corrective and/or disciplinary actions, ranging from a warning up to and including termination, will be taken against any academic or administrative supervisor who failed to take corrective action when there is probable cause to believe that he or she knew, or should have known, that one of the persons protected by this policy was or had been subjected to sexual harassment by one of his or her guests, employees, or contractors.

On most campuses, the affirmative action office handles sexual harassment complaints. Employees who feel they have been sexually harassed should contact their immediate supervisor; students should contact their academic dean for counseling and other appropriate action. If the complainant feels this is not appropriate, he or she should contact a member of the equal opportunity grievance panel or the affirmative action office.

Handling Sexual Harassment Complaints

It has been my experience that many students who voice complaints are reluctant to file formal charges, yet they want someone in authority to be aware of the situation. Some may complain to a faculty member they trust, or they might bring their complaint to the chairperson, expecting you to see that the offensive behavior stops. In counseling a student or faculty member who complains to you, these guidelines should be observed.

- Listen carefully and sympathetically without being judgmental.
- Advise the complainant never to be alone with the person he or she claims is doing the harassing.
- Tell the complainant that he or she should let the person doing the harassing know that the behavior is not appreciated and that it must stop. The complainant should say, for example, "Stop it. I don't like what you are doing. It makes me very uncomfortable," or "I have no wish to see you socially," or "Please stop making sexual remarks or jokes around me." These and similar statements clearly indicate that the behavior is unwelcome. Pushing away an offensive person, showing annoyance through facial expressions or other such nonverbal behaviors can also show that the advances are unwelcome. However, in unequal power situations, nonverbal behavior of this kind may be inadequate. A more direct verbal response might be called for.
- Advise the complainant to keep a journal documenting the time, place, and date, and a description of each incident. List the names of any witnesses.
- Suggest that the complainant write a private letter to the person doing the harassing. The letter should state the facts, describe how the complainant feels about the harasser's action, and indicate the complainant's expectations. A copy of this letter should be kept by the complainant.
- Suggest that the complaining person keep a small, hidden tape recorder on his or her person that can be activated if the harasser's actions continue, provided surreptitious recording is not prohibited by law in your state. If you have any questions regarding this, you should contact your campus legal affairs office.
- Suggest that the complainant talk to fellow students or coworkers to find out if others have been harassed by the same person, and try to determine if they will support the complainant if he or she decides to take action.

You should keep a record of the meeting and advise the affirmative action officer of the situation. Also, you should talk to the person accused of sexual harassment to advise him or her that a complaint has been filed, emphasizing the seriousness of the matter. Even if no formal complaint is made, you must advise him or her to avoid any behavior that could be construed in any way as sexual harassment. If the accused person is a faculty member, you need to remind him or her to review a copy of the university's sexual harassment policy statement, which should be distributed to all faculty and staff at the beginning of each academic year. Finally, you should keep notes of this meeting as well, specifying when it was held and exactly what was said. This course of action is grounded in the legal protections you need in your role as chairperson. To prevent being held liable for the acts of other people, you need to investigate claims of sexual harassment thoroughly. Section 1604.11c of the EEOC Guidelines on Sexual Harassment say:

> An employer . . . is responsible for its acts and those of its agents and supervisory employees with respect to sexual harassment regardless of whether the specific acts complained of were authorized or even forbidden by the employer and regardless of whether the employer knew or should have known of their occurrence.

If the complainant chooses not to file formal charges, and if the matter described seems of relatively minor consequence, all that is needed to prevent employer liability for sexual harassment is for you to take prompt action to end the harassment.

Preventing Sexual Harassment

The best way to deal with sexual harassment is to do everything possible to prevent it. As indicated earlier, you should establish a tone for the department that does not tolerate misconduct of any kind. If you shrug off complaints, a suggestion that you will turn a blind eye to this type of behavior has been clearly given. On the other hand, if you discuss the matter in

Table 19.1 Tips to Help Faculty Members Avoid Sexual Harassment Complaints

Faculty should • Not meet behind closed doors with students or colleagues • Avoid making sexual remarks of any kind • Keep their hands off students and colleagues • Make certain that all encounters with colleagues and students are professional in every aspect • Avoid double-entendre • Go out of their way to avoid any behavior that might be misconstrued as attention of a sexual nature

faculty meetings, handle complaints seriously and expeditiously, and make it clear that sexual harassment will not be tolerated, you will have taken the first step toward preventing this type of behavior.

While men and women alike can be victims of sexual harassment, generally the matter involves a man harassing a woman. Table 19.1 provides some tips for faculty on avoiding situations in which sexual harassment complaints could arise.

You can help educate your faculty and staff members if you are knowledgeable about the many issues related to sexual harassment. There are numerous colleges and universities that have resources available to help faculty, staff, and students understand sexual harassment issues. For example, Hughes and Sandler's 1986 publication still offers relevant guidance for today's students. Table 19.2 presents their recommendations for discouraging sexual harassment.

Sexual harassment must be a genuine concern for every chairperson and educator. Ignoring it in the hope that it will go away is irresponsible. If we believe that sexual harassment won't or can't happen, we are hiding from reality. Studies show that 20% to 30% of all female college students experience some form of sexual harassment. Two percent of all female students experience direct threats or bribes for sexual favors. While this does not sound like a great number, it in fact translates to hundreds of students at even mid-size universities. In addition to the personal anguish it causes,

Table 19.2 Ways Students Can Discourage Sexual Harassment

1) If possible, keep the door open when you visit your professor or advisor. When the door of a small office is closed the atmosphere sometimes becomes "cozy" rather than professional. If you feel uncomfortable when the door is closed, you can always say, for example, "Excuse me, but I'd prefer to have the door open" without going into any long explanations.

2) Dress neutrally in class and when visiting professors or advisors. Clothing does not cause sexual harassment. However, some men may perceive low-cut tops or skimpy shorts as a sexual invitation even though that is not what it means to the woman wearing such clothes. It might also encourage some men to think of women physically instead of intellectually.

3) Avoid any kind of flirtatious behavior with professors. Remember, too, that it is always possible for some men to misinterpret friendly behavior as an indication of sexual interest. Professors are no exception. You are generally better off to keep conversations businesslike, rather than personal, especially when you are first getting to know your professor.

4) Beware of threats of retaliatory law suits. There have been instances in which women who brought formal accusations of sexual harassment against someone were subsequently threatened with a libel suit by the harasser. (In all instances the suits were later dropped.) Our goal always is to protect those who might be harassed. There are additional reasons to be especially attentive to this problem, however; not the least of these is the legal costs that can grow out of charges of sexual harassment. Moreover, problems of sexual harassment are time-consuming, and they tend to become divisive. The matter of evidence—since sexual harassment often involves surreptitious actions—is troubling and complex. Innocent parties can be hurt, and the pain does not go away quickly.

Taking an active position against sexual harassment will do much to insure a positive, professional climate in your department. Only in such a climate can all individuals give all their efforts to what matters most—education.

Note. From Hughes and Sandler (1986). Reprinted with permission by the National Association for Women in Education.

sexual harassment has an adverse effect on the learning and working climate. That alone is reason enough to require us to deal with the problem.

The Americans with Disabilities Act (ADA)

When the Americans with Disabilities Act (ADA) was passed in 1990, its intended purpose was to help level the playing field for Americans living with disabilities. According to Bonnage (2002),

> The key component in defining a person with a disability was that the individual must be "substantially limited" in one or more "major life activities." While this may be apparent in individuals who are blind, deaf or who use a wheelchair, determinations about other limiting disabilities are not as easy to make. As a result there is a large body of case law around the question of "who is disabled," about "reasonable accommodations," (i.e., flextime, flexplace, etc.) as well as about "essential" and "non-essential" job tasks.

Since the passage of ADA, a number of Supreme Court rulings have narrowed its scope. In *Board of Trustees of the University of Alabama v. Garrett* (2001), the court determined that state employees cannot sue the state for monetary damages under Title I (Employment) of the ADA because the 11th Amendment ensures state sovereignty. Because Congress did not specifically state in the law that the ADA would override states' rights, an individual cannot sue a state for damages over failures to adhere to ADA. Some states have enacted legislation that allows legal action to be brought against the state, but in most instances only for remedy and not damages.

Other Supreme Court cases have centered on "who is disabled." In one case, two pilots filed a suit against an airline for failure to provide "reasonable accommodations" when the pilots were deemed not to have the requisite eyesight without glasses to pass the qualifications test, though with glasses they could. The court ruled that since the corrective lenses allowed the individuals to have essentially normal vision, they were not "substantially limited" in the "major life activity" of seeing, and therefore were not disabled in the sense of the law. This ruling, along with similar ones, further narrowed the scope of ADA.

Even before ADA, colleges and universities that received federal funds had been required to make their programs, services, and facilities accessible to disabled individuals after the passage of the Rehabilitation Act of 1973. Section 504 of that act states,

> No otherwise qualified handicapped individual in the United
> States . . . shall, solely by reason of his handicap, be excluded
> from the participation in, be denied the benefits of, or be sub-
> jected to discrimination under any program or activity receiving
> Federal financial assistance.

The Americans with Disabilities Act has become law, reinforcing the mandate of Section 504, expanding it to all institutions of higher education, regardless of whether they receive federal financial assistance.

This section examines how ADA affects your role as the chief administrator of an academic unit, with particular emphasis on the implications of ADA on hiring faculty and staff members and on the academic programs within your department. It will also present what faculty members must know about the law when they work with students covered by ADA. It is no longer merely an act of compassion to help disabled students; the law requires us to assist them.

Who ADA Protects

It is important to know who is protected by the ADA. According to the law, every person is covered who either has, used to have, or is treated as having a physical or mental disability. The law protects any person with a "physical or mental impairment" that "substantially limits one or more major life activity." This definition includes people:

- With mobility impairments, such as those who suffer from paralysis or use wheelchairs, crutches, or walkers.

- Who have lost one or more limbs.
- Who are blind or have vision impairments.
- Who are deaf or hearing impaired.
- Who have mental or psychological disorders, including mental retardation, emotional and mental illness, and learning disabilities.
- Those with any number of different psychological disorders, including depression and post-traumatic stress syndrome.
- With cosmetic disfigurements, such as burn victims.
- With serious contagious and non-contagious diseases, including AIDS, AIDS-related complex, epilepsy, cancer, and tuberculosis.
- Who have suffered from drug addiction in the past (people currently using illegal drugs are not protected).
- Suffering from alcoholism (but they can be required to conform to the same standards as others).
- With learning disabilities if the learning disability "substantially limits one or more" of the major life activities of the student. The ADA specifies that the ability to learn is a major life activity. Each student's disability must be viewed as unique and handled on a case-by-case basis.

The following conditions are not covered:
- Eye color, hair color, height, weight (except in unusual circumstances where obesity is the result of a medical condition)
- Hearing loss, arthritis, and Alzheimer's disease associated with advanced age
- Temporary impairments or illnesses
- Minor impairments that do not limit a major life activity
- Pregnancy

Further, it is important to recognize that if you consider a person to be disabled, the ADA protects him or her even if that person does not meet the statutory definition. This would include, for example, an individual who has an impairment that the employer erroneously perceives is substantially limiting, or an individual with an impairment that is only substantially limiting because of the attitudes of others (e.g., an employer that discriminates against a burn victim because of potentially negative reactions of others, or an individual with no impairment who is erroneously regarded as having an impairment). The inclusion of coverage for persons regarded as disabled means that if an employer rejects an applicant because he or she has a physical or mental condition, that action may be enough to bring the person within the definition of disability.

Implications of ADA in Hiring and Supervising

You cannot discriminate in hiring, review, promotion, demotion, discharge, or other aspects of employment against any applicant or employee with a disability, on the basis of the person's disability, if the person is qualified and able to perform the "essential functions" of the job with "reasonable accommodations."

The rules against discrimination require providing all disabled employees with equal or equivalent access to all benefits of the employment, in an integrated setting, that would be available to a similarly situated employee, unless doing so would be an "undue hardship." This could include the use of cafeterias, employee lounges, company cars, drinking fountains, and bathrooms. Employers can discriminate if there is a "substantial probability" that a person's disability would pose a "significant risk" to the health and safety of others. This decision cannot be based on assumptions, stereotypes, or past experience.

Employers cannot refuse to hire someone simply because it might cause workers' compensation or health insurance rates to increase, and in most cases cannot refuse to provide at least some insurance to disabled employees if insurance is provided to other employees.

Employers may set minimum qualifications for applicants or employees where the qualifications have a legitimate relationship to the job in question and the qualifications relate to essential functions of the job.

If you have any questions regarding the effects of ADA on hiring or supervising faculty and staff, you should contact your university's ADA compliance office, a position required by law.

Implications of ADA on Academic Programs

The ADA does not seek to change your fundamental methods of ensuring a sound education and successful completion of an academic program. Instead, it is designed to ensure that students with disabilities have equal access to your academic programs and can successfully complete their studies. For this reason, your university must clearly identify the essential requirements of the educational program. The ADA does not require educational institutions to "take any action that would result in a fundamental alteration in the nature of a service, program, or activity, or in undue financial and administrative burdens."

Although the ADA strongly emphasizes physical access, there is an equally important aspect of nondiscrimination for academic access. People with disabilities must meet the same criteria of admission as the nondisabled. However, once they have decided to pursue a certain study, students with disabilities are entitled, under both Section 504 and the ADA, to reasonable accommodations, placement in the most integrated setting feasible, and enjoyment of all campus activities to the extent appropriate. It is important to remember that just because a student claims a disability, it does not follow that he or she is disabled and that you must therefore make accommodations for them. Those with learning disabilities, for example, must be able to document that they qualify to be covered under ADA. If faculty members have any doubt regarding a student's claim, they ought to contact the office of disabled services. Indeed, it is probably not wise to make accommodations for students claiming to have learning disabilities until the appropriate campus official verifies their condition. Faculty members rarely have the expertise to be able to make a determination on the matter, and it is better left to those who are experienced in making such evaluations.

The following are some of the accommodations you may need to make for students covered under ADA.

- Providing more time to take tests.
- Providing special equipment. For example, if a student with a disability is taking a course requiring the use of a computer, you may have

to provide adaptive equipment to overcome a barrier. If the student is blind, you may have to equip the computer with a Braille keyboard and a voice response system.

- Giving different kinds of assignments. For example, if you require an oral presentation, you may have to substitute another kind of assignment for the student with a speech impairment.

- Modifying academic requirements. An example of this might be providing an alternative to replace the required foreign language requirement for students who are hearing impaired or who have auditory processing problems. Some schools will permit students to take American Sign Language in the place of a foreign language.

- Providing special services. Students with auditory processing problems may need help with note taking in those courses where concise and accurate note taking is required. Some universities use student volunteers or work-study students as in-class interpreters. If you do this, however, you must ensure that these students are qualified sign language interpreters.

- Providing additional instruction time. A student who is learning disabled may need more instructional time than other students. Again, student volunteers or work-study students may be able to provide this service.

- Modifying class attendance requirement. While establishing a maximum number of classes that can be missed before a student receives a failing or lowered grade is reasonable for the majority of the students in a class, it may not be for some individuals with disabilities. Some students may require bed rest or hospitalization during a semester, and others may be unable to use normal transportation routes in inclement weather.

- Giving information in class syllabi regarding what services are available on campus for those students who are disabled. Furthermore, it would be a good idea to list the campus disability issues coordinator and ask that students with disabilities make contact with that individual. Here is a sample statement:

> If you have a disability that may require assistance or accommodation, or questions related to any accommodations for testing,

note takers, readers, and so on, please speak with me as soon as possible. Students may also contact the office of disabled services (telephone number) with questions about such services.

One of your responsibilities is to see that students covered under ADA are provided the appropriate accommodations in accordance with the Americans with Disabilities Act. Faculty members need to know what the law requires of them; ignorance of the law does not excuse them. Having worked with a large number of faculty members over the years, I have found some faculty to be inflexible and unwilling to make special accommodations to assist disabled students until I have convinced them that the law requires them to make certain arrangements. I suggest you devote one faculty meeting each year to review that portion of ADA that pertains to classroom teaching. This would also provide an opportunity to discuss appropriate ways of communicating with certain disabled students. For example, a person in a wheelchair should be spoken to at eye level. Always speak directly to a visually impaired person and not to any companion. A hearing-impaired student should be asked in writing what method of communication works best. When addressing a hearing-impaired student, speak clearly and look directly at the person, not at an interpreter. If the person lip reads, speak in a normal, unexaggerated manner, and use short sentences. You are likely to be asked to repeat yourself. Be patient. Good lighting is important, and you should make sure that there are no physical barriers between you and the person with whom you are speaking.

We should also become sensitive to the appropriate language to use when referring to those with disabilities. Table 19.3 provides some examples.

Likewise, the words in Table 19.4 should be avoided because of their negative connotations.

Learning Disabled Students

We quickly recognize those students and faculty who are physically disabled, but it is much harder to identify those who have learning disabilities. Moreover, the tendency is to have less sympathy and understanding

Table 19.3 Appropriate Language When Referring to Those With Disabilities

Avoid Saying	Preferred Usage
Handicapped	Person with a disability
Blind person	Person who is blind
Deaf person	Person who is deaf
Mute	Person without speech
Retard, feebleminded	Person with mental retardation
Birth defect	Congenital disability
Confined to a wheelchair	Person who uses a wheelchair
Crazy, insane	Mental/emotional disability

Table 19.4 Words to Avoid

Abnormal	Lame
Afflicted	Maimed
Confined	Palsied
Crippled	Retard
Defective	Stricken
Deformed	Sufferer
Imbecile	Victim
Invalid	Withered

for those with learning disabilities, believing that many are just using the disability as an excuse.

What is meant by learning disabled? Stupka and Eddy (1995, p. 6) offer the following definitions:

- A learning disability is a permanent disorder that affects the way in which individuals with normal or above-average intelligence take in, retain, and express information. Like a fuzzy TV picture, incoming or outgoing information may become scrambled as it travels between the eye, ear, or skin, and the brain.

- Commonly recognized in learning disabled adults are problems in one or more of the following areas: reading comprehension, spelling, written expression, math computation, and problem solving.
- Less frequent are problems in organizational skills, time management, and social skills. Many learning disabled adults may also have language-based and/or perceptual problems.
- Often inconsistent. It may present problems on Mondays, but not on Tuesdays. It may cause problems throughout grade school but disappear during high school and resurface again in college. It may manifest itself in one specific academic area, such as math.
- Frustrating. Persons with learning disabilities often deal not only with functional limitations, but also with the frustration of having to prove that their invisible disabilities may be as handicapping as paraplegia.
- A learning difference. A learning difference is not a form of mental retardation or emotional disorder.

Disabled students can grow and learn, and with your help they have a chance to become productive citizens who feel good about themselves. Once you have seen them go on to jobs where they are valued employees, you and your faculty—like the disabled student—will feel good about the role you played in providing ADA-covered students with a chance to get a quality education.

Sexual harassment and the Americans with Disabilities Act are serious and significant concerns for all chairpersons. The successful chairperson will understand college and university policy related to these matters and become actively engaged in dealing with them.

Resources

Web Sites
ADA Accessibility Guidelines
www.access-board.gov/adaag/html/adaag.htm

Americans with Disabilities Act of 1990, Titles I and V
www.eeoc.gov/policy/ada.html

Facts About Sexual Harassment
http://www.eeoc.gov/facts/fs-sex.html

Information and Technical Assistance on the Americans with Disabilities Act
www.usdoj.gov/crt/ada/adahom1.htm

National Organization for Women and Sexual Harassment
www.now.org/issues/harass/

Questions and Answers About Sexual Harassment
www.lawguru.com/faq/16.html

Books

Bingham, C., & Gansler, L. L. (2002). *Class action: The story of Lois Jenson and the landmark case that changed sexual harassment law.* New York, NY: Doubleday.

Dobrich, W., Dranoff, S., & Maatman, G. L., Jr. (2002). *The manager's guide to preventing a hostile work environment: How to avoid legal and financial risks by protecting your workplace from harassment based on sex, race, disability, religion, or age.* New York, NY: McGraw-Hill.

Jones, N. (2003). *The Americans with Disabilities Act: Overview, regulations and interpretations.* New York, NY: Novinka Books.

Mezey, S. G. (2005). *Disabling interpretations: The Americans with Disabilities Act in federal court.* Pittsburgh, PA: University of Pittsburgh Press.

Orlov, D., & Roumell, M. T. (2005). *What every manager needs to know about sexual harassment.* New York, NY: American Management Association.

References

American Association of University Professors. (2005). *Sexual harassment in higher education: Current issues and trends.* Retrieved July 15, 2006, from www.aaup.org/Legal/info%20outlines/05sexharass.htm

Black, D. R., & Gilson, M. (1988). *Perspectives and principles: A college administrator's guide to staying out of court.* Madison, WI: Magna.

Board of Trustees of the University of Alabama v. Garrett (99–1240) 531 U.S. 356 (2001).

Bonnage, J. (2002). Update—Americans with Disabilities Act. *Collective Bargaining Reporter, 1.* Retrieved July 14, 2006, from www.afscme.org/wrkplace/cbr102_4.htm

Equal Employment Opportunity Commission. (2005). *EEO programs must have an effective anti-harassment program.* Retrieved July 15, 2006, from www.eeoc.gov/federal/harass/index.html

Hughes, J. O., & Sandler, B. R. (1986). *In case of sexual harassment: A guide for women students.* Washington, DC: Association of American Colleges.

Miller v. Department of Corrections, 36 Cal. 4th 446 (2005).

Stupka, E., & Eddy, B. (1995, December). Learning disabled student strategies. *Recruitment & Retention in Higher Education, 9*(12), 6.

Toma, J. D., & Palm, R. L. (1999). *The academic administrator and the law: What every dean and department chair needs to know* (ASHE-ERIC Higher Education Report, 26[5]). Washington, DC: The George Washington University, Graduate School of Education and Human Development.

Wilson v. Delta State University, 143 Fed.Appx. 611 (5th Cir. 2005).

20

Recruiting and Hiring Faculty

Recruiting and hiring wisely can change the culture of your depart-
ment more than almost anything else you do as chairperson.

There is nothing routine about recruiting and hiring faculty members. The process is time consuming, costly, at times frustrating, and fraught with legal and ethical issues. When it results in the hire of a highly qualified individual, you are rightfully exultant. However, if a mistake in hiring occurs, as occasionally happens, you face months or even years of tribulation.

To achieve positive results, you must give your undivided attention when hiring faculty members and not overlook even the smallest detail of the process. The following describes one of the many issues that needs your full attention.

> In addition to hiring the right person, good recruiting must include professional treatment of all applicants. It is important that even those who do not make the cut as semifinalists or who are invited for a campus visit but not offered a position, speak highly of their experience with your institution, college, and department. They, their peers, and their graduate students may seek positions at your institution in years ahead, so treat them well as part of an efficient, effective, and ethical search. (Perlman & McCann, 2003, p. 157)

In a first-person article titled "The Price of Indifference" that appeared in a 2005 issue of *The Chronicle of Higher Education*, Henry

Raymond (a pseudonym, we learn) recounts his experience when he interviewed for a teaching position. He notes that the search committee seemed interested in his research and he concluded that his day was "one of those rare occasions when everything just seems to fall in place. Nevertheless, as I walked away from the campus, I knew I'd never accept the job, if it were offered" (p. C1).

He explained that search committee members, while kind and attentive, poorly represented their department. They were neither flexible nor flattering about their institution. His subsequent meeting with the dean was even worse. By the end of the day, he thought he had not masked his disappointment well.

> So it was a complete surprise when . . . the chairman of the committee called to offer me the job. Granted, I wasn't going to take it. But the chairman even managed to botch the final sell.
>
> Here are the terms of the offer, he told me. "This isn't a negotiation." Take it or leave it. (p. C1)

Hopefully, Raymond's story is not representative of what we do in hiring. While Raymond's interview may have been ethical, it certainly was not efficient or effective. What can a chairperson do to see that the processes of recruiting and hiring will be smooth? This chapter explores practical ideas that can facilitate the process. Further, the guidelines presented should help chairpersons identify candidates who are well qualified and a good fit for their institutions. A reminder: Newly appointed chairpersons should discuss recruitment and hiring procedures with their dean and others experienced with their institution's recruitment and hiring practices. (See Appendixes I, J, and K for sample procedures.)

Be Aggressive in Recruiting Faculty

Recruiting and hiring wisely can change the culture of your department more than almost anything else you do as chairperson. If, for example, you are unsatisfied with the quality or quantity of research by your current faculty, you should try to hire people who have strong research records.

> Recruiting a new member of the faculty is much more than simply adding a new colleague to share teaching and service responsibilities. It is also an opportunity to bring about desired changes by recruiting colleagues with particular areas of expertise that the department needs. Vacancies also provide an opportunity to achieve greater diversity in the composition of the faculty. To take advantage of the search process as a strategic opportunity, chairs have to take into account the composition of the search committee, the content of the position announcement, and the organization of the interview so as to attract the kind of candidate the department needs. (Bensimon, Ward, & Sanders, 2000, p. 5)

Here are some things you can do to develop an effective faculty recruitment program.

- Decide before you advertise exactly what kind of person you are hoping to hire. What primary and secondary competencies are you seeking?
- Make your advertisement persuasive. Describe what makes your university and department unique and what good things a candidate can expect. Sell whatever you have to sell. For example, what attracted you there? The same thing may attract others.
- Do more than advertise to reach potential candidates. You should know who is out there and contributing to your field so that you can contact them whenever an opening occurs. More than likely your faculty will be acquainted with potential candidates. Use the telephone and urge outstanding individuals to apply at your school. If you are not acquainted with potential candidates, you could call some of the leaders in the field to get names of people to contact.

You will need to take the lead in recruiting and hiring. At most universities, individual colleges have procedures that must be followed. Careful compliance assures that the chairperson has done the job properly and met all legal requirements. The following steps are generally necessary.

Department Checklist for Recruiting Faculty

1. Chairperson sends a letter to the dean requesting approval to recruit.
   - Letter must include a justification.
   - Provost will notify the dean when request is approved/disapproved.
   - Dean will notify the chairperson.
2. Chairperson will complete and submit to the dean the recruitment authorization form.
   - Notice of vacancy (ad) must be attached.
   - College liaison will approve/disapprove.
   - Recruitment authorization form will be approved/disapproved by the provost and forwarded to the personnel office.
   - Dean will receive a copy of the approved recruitment authorization form and send a copy to the chairperson.
   - Chairperson or personnel will place advertisement(s). The chairperson should complete and submit the appropriate requisition.
3. Chairperson will submit the completed recruitment sources form to the dean.
   - College liaison will approve/disapprove.
4. Chairperson will appoint search committee.
   - Search committee will include at least one female and representation from a minority group.
   - College liaison and affirmative action officer should be invited to the first committee meeting.
   - Search committee chairperson will be elected/selected.
   - Department chairperson will submit in writing to the dean the names of the search committee members and its chairperson.
   - College liaison will approve/disapprove.

5. Chairperson of search committee handles the following activities:
   - Maintains up-to-date applicant flow data sheet.
   - Mails affirmative action postcards to applicants.
   - Follows all steps as stipulated in guidelines.
6. When screening is completed, the search committee chairperson and the department chairperson will submit an applicant flow data sheet to the dean with the names of the best-qualified candidates.
   - College liaison will approve/disapprove.
   - Affirmative action officer will approve/disapprove and return the form to the dean.
   - Dean, in consultation with the chairperson, will determine candidates to be interviewed.
7. When final selection is made, the department chairperson will submit the following items: the proposed faculty appointment form, the affirmative action recruitment checklist, and a certification statement.
   - Chairperson will notify unsuccessful applicants in writing.
   - College liaison will approve/disapprove.
   - Dean will forward documents to the provost and affirmative action officer for approval/disapproval.
   - Dean will notify the chairperson when approved.
8. Department chairperson will determine salary recommendation.
   - Consult with the office of institutional research to determine salary.
   - Send the dean a memorandum detailing salary agreement and rank with a request that an offer letter be prepared.
9. Dean will prepare offer letter for appropriate signatures.

Copies of all curricula vitae and related documents submitted by those applying for faculty positions should be kept for a period of three years. These records should be regarded as confidential.

At this point, pause to remind yourself: While this procedure must be followed to assure conformance with university policy, it clearly cannot assure that quality faculty members will be hired. You must assume that responsibility. Many universities are handicapped in their recruiting efforts by salaries, teaching loads, and/or location. Even so, every effort to recruit quality faculty members must be made. This means conducting careful, extensive background checks. You should contact individuals who can comment on and evaluate the personal and professional qualifications of candidates who are being seriously considered. Contacting only those listed on the application as references is insufficient. (Applicants are not likely to list as references those who have anything negative to say.) When interviewing a candidate, you also must be candid about what is expected of the applicant if an offer is made and accepted.

The Search Committee

Once you receive permission to recruit and have reviewed the college recruitment procedures, you will need to appoint a search committee. This committee should reflect the race and gender makeup of the university. Beyond that, use your judgment regarding committee composition and size. Some universities require that women and minority faculty be represented on each search committee. The nature of the position being filled will help determine which faculty members are asked to serve. If, for example, an anthropologist is being sought, it is logical to name faculty members whose specialty is anthropology.

Once the search committee is formed, it should meet to discuss procedures. At this first meeting, members should elect a chairperson, unless you already have designated someone. The affirmative action office—or equity office, as it is sometimes called—should be consulted to discuss its requirements and procedures. The affirmative action officer also can offer suggestions for reaching qualified minority and women candidates.

The chairperson of the search committee is responsible for maintaining an applicant flow data sheet, for mailing affirmative action cards to all applicants, and for following steps stipulated by college guidelines (see Chapter 4).

Screening Applicants

As applications are received, the department administrative assistant should keep them together in a secure, confidential file and notify applicants that their application has been received. Applications should be available for search committee members to review as their time permits.

Shortly after the closing date, either the search committee chairperson or you should examine each application to see if the candidate meets the minimum advertised requirements. Those who are qualified should remain in the pool to be evaluated by all committee members. Those warranting consideration should be invited to submit letters of reference, usually three to five, depending on what the search committee considers adequate. Some departments request letters of reference from all persons who apply, but I oppose this procedure. Why would search committee members want to burden themselves with paperwork on individuals who do not meet minimum requirements or who, for other reasons, will not be considered seriously? Furthermore, in such cases, the time of those who write the letters is wasted.

Reference letters should be read carefully, and candidates should not be evaluated on letters alone. Scrutinize letters for exactness of evidence and try reading between the lines.

> Even though many letters overstate candidates' abilities, they can still be helpful if critically examined. Make a list of the topics covered. What is not said may be more important than what is. If three letter writers note that they are most familiar with a candidate's service and scholarship and will address only these, be suspicious about the omission of teaching. Also separate inferences from facts. What evidence is used to support the letter writer's praise? If a writer claims the applicant is an outstanding scholar but gives no support for this, be suspicious. (Hochel & Wilson, 2006, p. 15)

After the pool of candidates is pared down, search committee members should be assigned to make reference calls. By dividing this task, the calls can be completed within a few days without unduly burdening anyone.

Each caller should be instructed to ask essentially the same questions. Here are some suggestions.

Telephone Reference Check Questions

1. How long have you known the applicant? In what capacity?
2. How would you rate his or her teaching ability?
3. How does the applicant get along with students? With faculty colleagues?
4. How willing is the applicant to contribute to the department's work outside the classroom?
5. Is the applicant responsible?
6. Would you judge the applicant to be an ethical person?
7. Why do you think the applicant might be interested in joining our university?
8. What are the applicant's major strengths? Weaknesses?
9. How would you evaluate the applicant's potential for growth?
10. Does he or she have any problems we should know about?
11. Is there anything I have not asked that you could add to give me a clearer picture of what the applicant is like as an employee?
12. If you were in my position, would you recommend that this candidate be hired? If not, why?

The person making the telephone check should file notes that provide answers to these reference check questions. The notes should record the name of the person giving the information and the date and time of the call. These notes should then be turned over to the search committee chairperson.

Should calls be made to persons other than those whose names are provided by the applicant? While some might disagree, I believe such calls must be made if valid evaluations are to be obtained. Few people applying for a job will list as references any likely to give negative information. Most often those listed as references will be friends, and even the most probing reference check is not likely to turn up anything less than positive. One must, of course, honor the request that an applicant's employer not be contacted unless the applicant gives permission. Still, there are other ways to get names of people who can provide honest assessments of an applicant's personal and professional qualifications.

When all reference checks are completed and letters of reference received, a meeting should be called to narrow the list to perhaps 5 to 10 names. Next, you should teleconference with the top candidates to determine those you wish to invite to campus for an interview. (I have seen many instances when teleconferencing was not done, and candidates that simply were not suitable were brought to campus.) After the teleconferences have been completed, the search committee should be in a good position to recommend candidates for campus interviews.

When the search committee reaches agreement on the most qualified candidates, its chairperson reports that information to you, the department chair. You then present the applicant flow data sheet, along with the names of the most qualified candidates, to your dean. Affirmative action officers must usually give their approval, after which the dean, in consultation with you, determines which candidates actually will be invited to campus.

The committee chairperson then calls candidates to set up times for their visits. At most universities, the candidates pay their travel expenses and then are reimbursed by the university. The committee chairperson will need to know each candidate's travel schedule so that arrangements can be made to meet him or her at the airport or other point of arrival.

The Campus Visit

Candidates usually spend two days on campus. Their schedules include interviews with individual faculty members, the search committee, student groups, the department chairperson, the college dean, the dean of the graduate school, and the vice president for academic affairs.

Arrangements for pickup and lodging should be completed prior to the visit, and the schedule for the candidate should be prepared well in advance and sent to the candidate. You might also send a kit of informative materials that includes such things as documents describing what faculty development opportunities exist on your campus, or a strategic planning document, or materials about the community from the local chamber of

Figure 20.1 Interview Schedule for John M. Doe

Wednesday, May 8

9:50 p.m.	Arrive Locker Airport on Delta 3016. Met by department chairperson.

Thursday, May 9

8:00 a.m.	Breakfast, Holiday Inn.
9:00 a.m.	Tour of department facilities.
9:30 a.m.	Meet with Dr. Joe Smith, Dean, College of Liberal Arts, Smith Hall 165.
10:00 a.m.	Meet with Dr. Roscoe Handy, Professor, and Dr. Ruby Twoshoes, Assistant Professor, Smith Hall 332.
10:30 a.m.	Meet with Dr. Ron Davis, Professor, and Dr. Jim Arnold, Professor, Smith Hall 332.
11:00 a.m.	Meet with Dr. W. Edward Knight, Associate Professor, Smith Hall 319.
11:30 a.m.	Tour of campus. Free time.
12:00 p.m.	Lunch with search committee,* Oliver's Restaurant.
2:30 p.m.	Meet with Dr. Robert Jones, Associate Professor, and Dr. Susan Quell, Assistant Professor, Smith Hall 332.
3:00 p.m.	Meet with Dr. Melvin Harvin, chairperson, and tour city.
4:30 p.m.	Taken to Locker Airport by Mrs. Sally Kay, Administrative Aide.
6:55 p.m.	Depart on Delta 849.

Dr. Doe is interviewing for the position now held by Dr. Ron Galloway. Dr. Doe's résumé is attached.

*Search committee members need to inform Dr. Harvin of their availability for lunch. Breakfast is an option if lunch isn't possible.

commerce. Applicants are told they can call the department chairperson to clear up any questions they may have. Figure 20.1 is a sample of the interview schedule for a candidate.

What is not shown in this schedule, though included at many universities in a campus visit, is time allocated for the candidate to teach a class. Asking the candidate to teach is a good way to assess his or her classroom capabilities. It can demonstrate how a prospective faculty member responds to students, how he or she prepares for a class, and how well the candidate approaches the subject matter. It provides still another dimension useful in evaluations.

Interviewing the Candidate: Questions to Avoid

You and others on campus will ask each candidate questions during the campus visit. To avoid legal problems, it is important to be aware of questions that should not be asked.

- *Questions about race or ethnic heritage.* What is your race? What is your lineage, ancestry, national origin, or descent? What language do you commonly speak? What was your maiden name? What is your birthplace or citizenship?
- *Questions about religion.* What is your religion? Does your religion prevent you from working weekends or holidays?
- *Questions about personal data.* How old are you? What is your birthdate? Are you married, divorced, or single? Do you have children? Are you pregnant? With whom do you reside?
- *Medical questions.* What is your height and weight? Are you disabled? How often will you require time off because of your disability? Have you ever filed a workers' compensation claim? Have you ever been treated for any conditions or diseases or been hospitalized? Do you currently take any prescription drugs? Have you ever been treated for drug or alcohol addiction?
- *Other questions.* Do you still owe on the loans taken out during school? Do you own your own home or rent? Who should we contact in case of emergency? Have you ever been arrested? What are the dates of your military service?

There is almost no aspect of faculty recruitment that is not restricted by federal and state laws and regulations. Statutes regulating employer conduct include Title VII of the Civil Rights Act of 1964, as amended (Title VII), the post–Civil War Civil Rights Act, the Age Discrimination in Employment Act, the Immigration Reform and Control Act of 1986, and relevant state statutes that prohibit employment discrimination. Moreover, the Americans with Disabilities Act presents employers with additional pre-hire considerations, and some that occasionally conflict. Also, applicant screening measures may be challenged under the theory that certain measures violate the individual's constitutional or common law right to privacy, or under contractual matters that rely on employee handbooks or collective bargaining agreements.

Interviewing the Candidate: Evaluations

Each faculty member, administrator, and student involved in the interview process should provide a written evaluation of each candidate. Evaluation sheets should be turned in to the search committee chairperson after the candidate's visit is concluded. Figure 20.2 (following page) presents a sample evaluation sheet.

Determining the Successful Candidate: Rank and Salary

The search committee should meet to evaluate all candidates after campus visits have been completed. Members of the committee then should recommend to you which candidate they feel should be made an offer. In most departments, a faculty meeting follows for discussion of each candidate and the recommendation of the search committee—including matters of rank and salary that they want the department chairperson to recommend to the dean.

You should review policy guidelines for determining rank for incoming faculty members. Most universities have a written policy that addresses this matter. For example, policy may stipulate that a terminal degree is required for appointment to certain ranks. It also may specify that a person must have had a number of years of full-time teaching. I have encountered faculty members who tell me that their university does not have such a policy, that the vice president for academic affairs or dean determines rank and salary based upon current market conditions.

Figure 20.2 Evaluator's Worksheet

Applicant's name (last-first-middle)_____

Date _____

Personal qualities. Observe applicant; write several adjectives or descriptive phrases:

Overall evaluation:
　　Outstanding　Excellent　Good　Adequate　Unsatisfactory

Appearance and poise:
　　Outstanding　Excellent　Good　Adequate　Unsatisfactory

Oral communication and expression of ideas:
　　Outstanding　Excellent　Good　Adequate　Unsatisfactory

Educational background:
　　Outstanding　Excellent　Good　Adequate　Unsatisfactory

Experience in administrative and/or academic area:
　　Outstanding　Excellent　Good　Adequate　Unsatisfactory

Leadership potential:
　　Outstanding　Excellent　Good　Adequate　Unsatisfactory

Willingness to hire applicant. Rate the applicant on a scale of 0–10 as follows:

Score:_____　　0　　　Prefer not to have this person
　　　　　　　　1–2　　Satisfactory
　　　　　　　　3–5　　Be pleased to have this person
　　　　　　　　6–8　　Prefer this person to most
　　　　　　　　9–10　Particularly like to have this person

Comments: (A summary statement is required. Ratings of Outstanding or Unsatisfactory or 0 or 10 should be amplified in this space.)

Potential worth to Northern State University:
　　　　Outstanding　Excellent　Average　Below Average

Remarks: (Supplement or qualify motivation and potential ratings as appropriate.)

Recommendation:

____I recommend for further consideration.
____I do NOT recommend for further consideration.

Evaluator's signature: _____

You should know all faculty salaries to avoid creating inequities within your department, providing this is a concern of the department and/or university. Generally, compensation for new faculty members should not be higher than that paid to current members of the staff whose credentials are similar to those of the new hire. Some universities require faculty members who are negatively affected to give their consent to this in writing. Compensation, as might be expected, can be a contentious issue and needs to be discussed beforehand. If presented late, the issue is more likely to become emotionally charged.

Once you have established a salary and rank to recommend, you will either inform the dean or make an offer, depending on policy at your university. Often you will need to send a letter to your dean along with a proposed faculty appointment form, an affirmative action recruitment checklist, and a certification statement or something similar.

After salary approval by the affirmative action officer and/or the vice president for academic affairs, notify the candidate that an offer is forthcoming. Either the dean or you then prepares an offer letter that often is signed by the vice president for academic affairs and the university president. The letter clearly states the conditions of employment including rank, salary, whether the appointment is probationary or temporary, and tenure consideration.

Make a special appeal to your candidate. For example, you might have each faculty member write the candidate you hope to hire telling what it would mean to have her or him as a part of the department. Keep in touch by letter and telephone to see if the person you want to hire has any questions or concerns that you can address. The candidate usually must accept within a designated number of days. When the offer is accepted, the search is completed.

The final task then remaining for the search committee chairperson is to write letters to all unsuccessful candidates. You must see that all search records are kept for a period of three years to meet guidelines of affirmative action and the Equal Employment Opportunity Commission.

As noted earlier, the process of filling a faculty position is time consuming and requires meticulous recordkeeping. It is an important task that all who are involved can take pride in when the new faculty member turns out to be a prized addition to the department.

Resources

Web Sites

Diversifying the Faculty
www.diversityweb.org/diversity_innovations/faculty_staff_
development/recruitment_tenure_promotion/faculty_recruitment.cfm

Guidelines for Recruiting and Hiring Underrepresented Groups
www.egr.uri.edu/diversity/recruit.htm

Lake Superior State University Recruiting and Hiring Procedures
www.lssu.edu/procedures/4-8-4.php

University of Washington Faculty Recruitment Toolkit
www.washington.edu/admin/eoo/forms/ftk_01.html

Books

Clark, R., & Ma, J. (Eds.). (2005). *Recruitment, retention and retirement in higher education: Building and managing the faculty of the future.* Northampton, MA: Edward Elgar.

Wallin, D. L. (Ed.). (2005). *Adjunct faculty in community colleges: An academic administrator's guide to recruiting, supporting, and retaining great teachers.* Bolton, MA: Anker.

References

Bensimon, E. M., Ward, K., & Sanders, K. (2000). *The department chair's role in developing new faculty into teachers and scholars.* Bolton, MA: Anker.

Hochel, S., & Wilson, C. E. (2006, Winter). Checking references: A vital step in employee selection. *The Department Chair, 16*(3), 14–16.

Perlman, B., & McCann, L. I. (2003). Improving the odds of hiring the right person. In D. R. Leaming (Ed.), *Managing people: A guide for department chairs and deans* (pp. 155–177). Bolton, MA: Anker.

Raymond, H. (2005, May 20). The price of indifference. *The Chronicle of Higher Education*, p. C1.

21

Retaining, Mentoring, and Terminating Faculty

No matter how uncomfortable a chairperson may feel about hav-
ing to tell faculty members that they are not being recommended
for renewal, continuing to reappoint weak faculty members will
bring even more discomfort. And every year that discomfort earns
compound interest.

Developing programs that help faculty members pursue solid careers and seeing that they are properly mentored along the way is an exhilarating experience for most chairpersons. It certainly was for me. On the other hand, having to tell a faculty member that his or her contract will not be renewed is grimly unsettling.

Mentoring Faculty Members

Mentoring faculty members should begin the minute a new person accepts a position. At this stage you can provide departmental policies and procedures, information about other departmental faculty members, and materials on the curriculum, especially on courses the faculty member will teach.

Here are some ways to help new faculty members move comfortably into their new roles.

- **Write letters of welcome.**
This small but meaningful gesture can do much to make a new person feel good about the decision. I have also found that faculty members who write these letters feel good about it: It's treating others the way they would like

Figure 21.1 Checklist: Family/Relocation Information

☐ Explain the availability of funds for relocation and how to be reimbursed for relocation expenses.

☐ Establish a department contact person to supply information on relocation.

☐ Provide a packet of information on Realtors, schools, neighborhoods, utility companies, daycare facilities available on campus or in the area, places of worship, community organizations, and athletic facilities.

☐ Offer web site addresses (URLs) for Realtors and the local newspaper.

☐ Provide the newcomer with a subscription to the Sunday edition of the local paper for the three months preceding his or her move.

☐ Explain what the institution and department can provide in terms of assistance for spouse or domestic partner employment.

☐ Be specific about institutional benefits including provisions for domestic partners.

☐ Make clear under what conditions the tenure clock can be stopped.

☐ Provide information on special interest or religious organizations on and off campus.

☐ Include information on campus and community accessibility for faculty and their family members with a disability.

to be treated. I have always been impressed by how most faculty members try to put themselves in the shoes of those who are new to an institution. Most of us remember our first days on a new job—trying to find our way around campus, learning new procedures, and generally appreciating any friendly gestures.

- Faculty relocation.

On this subject, Bensimon, Ward, and Sanders (2000, p. 33) provide a useful checklist, shown in Figure 21.1.

- Develop special programs for newcomers.

First-year faculty members have many questions, and you can do them a service by anticipating and answering these questions. At one university

I established a series of sessions (mostly brown-bag luncheons) to help first-year faculty members ease their way into the institution's culture. The sessions included:

1. An overview of the history of the university or college given by an administrator or faculty member.
2. A session to discuss the department's culture. It is particularly important for new faculty members to understand the day-to-day practices of the department and its unwritten policies and procedures. Also, new faculty members are likely to discover subcultures within the department, which they may find helpful.
3. A session to discuss performance expectation and time management. Seasoned, successful professors and the chairperson can help new faculty members put professional and personal matters into perspective. Moreover, I believe chairpersons have the responsibility to see that faculty members find the time to spend with their families, as well as time to stay healthy and fit.
4. Sessions to discuss the best practices in teaching. A workshop on improving teaching can be a powerful tool—especially if you invite the most creative teachers at your university to participate as presenters, moderators, or panel members.
5. Sessions on research and sessions devoted to community and campus service possibilities. Conducting such sessions provides an opportunity for veteran faculty members to showcase their good works. For example, established researchers often look for forums where they can discuss their research as well as their research methods, both of which can help junior faculty members.

In addition to these sessions, you could also plan for a departmental social get-together. Food and beverages can be served, and all faculty and staff members invited to join in welcoming their new colleagues. The dean, provost, and president can also be invited to these functions, and more often than not, they make a point to be present.

Another program to help new faculty members adjust is to pair first-year faculty with your best faculty members. Select veteran faculty members who "enjoy" working with first-year faculty members, making sure that the personalities and interests of the mentor and the newcomer match. I have witnessed failed mentoring relationships due to poor pairings. Some faculty members do not like to work with first-year faculty, some are too busy, and others denigrate mentoring as "handholding." At times, faculty members have complained that their mentor missed a scheduled meeting. Others have said that they just could not get along with the assigned mentor.

Retaining Faculty

Retaining quality faculty members must be a priority for any chairperson. Those who are successful in keeping good teachers and scholars are generally those who managed to build what Wergin (2003) calls departments that work—that is, in part, where quality, in accordance with Wergin's definition, exists. He writes, ". . . quality is characterized by what actually happens in the department: a shared purpose, strong leadership, interaction among faculty and students, flexibility to change, and a sense of energy and commitment" (p. 9).

Retaining productive faculty members requires a continuous program designed to:

- Help faculty members stay current in their field of expertise.
- Provide resources that support teaching, research, and service.
- Promote faculty morale.
- Involve all faculty members in establishing departmental goals.
- Support faculty members when they encounter personal problems.
- Engage faculty members so far as possible when important decisions must be made.
- Share important information in a timely and orderly manner.
- Alert chairpersons to faculty members who become disgruntled, burned out, or otherwise troubled.

- Promote fairness and equality through support of gender and racial issues, as well as any other issues that might divide faculty or hamper morale.
- Provide for a climate that rewards change and associated risks.

Practical Tips for Terminating Faculty Members

Sometimes, despite the best retention and mentoring strategies, a faculty member can prove to be a bad fit for the department for any number of reasons. When you must terminate a faculty member, it's not enough to worry about the personal emotions involved—though I don't mean to minimize them—as there are legal entanglements that can snare even experienced chairpersons.

- **Do not act impulsively.**

When terminating faculty members, proceed with care to avoid suffering dire consequences. It's not unusual for an aggrieved faculty member to take legal action, and there are many instances where a chairperson has had to give sworn testimony. I have had to do this more than once. Uneasiness and pain accompany such an experience, even in instances where I was confident I had done the right thing and followed all appropriate procedures. I can't imagine what I might have felt had I acted injudiciously. In *Leading Quietly: An Unorthodox Guide to Doing the Right Thing*, Joseph Badaracco (2002) observes that effective leaders ". . . move patiently, carefully, and incrementally. They do what is right—for their organizations, for the people around them, and for themselves—inconspicuously and without casualties" (p. 1).

- **Keep good records.**

It's imperative that chairpersons maintain good personnel records. Records are important when faculty members are recommended for promotion and tenure, and records take on even greater importance if you must act against a faculty member's self-interest. In those instances when a faculty member's contract is not being renewed based on performance, you should be able to present documents that specify the department's performance expectations. Faculty members should be furnished with all documents regarding tenure, promotion, and reappointment when they are offered a position.

- **Do not postpone the inevitable.**

As chairperson, you will never bat a thousand when hiring. You'll make your mistakes, just as surely as I made mine. Even if your hiring process is thoughtful and thorough, there will be times when you hire faculty members who for some reason don't work out. However, I believe there is no excuse for reappointing faculty members who are not meeting established criteria. No matter how uncomfortable a chairperson may feel about having to tell faculty members that they are not being recommended for renewal, continuing to reappoint weak faculty members will bring even more discomfort. Further, the discomfort you feel when you have to tell a faculty member that he or she is not being renewed draws compound interest; year after year you regret what you have *not* done.

- **Consult with your dean before making a decision to terminate.**

This provides an opportunity to review the situation with someone who is likely to have faced similar situations—not just once, but many times. Your dean will likely ask to see your annual evaluations of the faculty member and any records showing that you have notified him or her of any weaknesses. Your dean may also want to see the development plans you've made available to the faculty member as well as his or her response to these plans. In other words, what have you done to counsel the faculty member and give him or her a chance to correct weaknesses?

- **Review the situation with the university's legal officer.**

You may need your dean's approval to do this, but most deans understand the wisdom of a review and will be inclined to support your request. A review of your recommendation by the legal officer should be done to make certain that you are complying with procedural requirements. The law regarding procedures for faculty personnel decision is broad and complex. Legal scholars William Kaplin and Barbara Lee (1995) remind us of important general principles when they write,

> Postsecondary educational institutions have established varying procedural requirements for making and internally review-ing faculty personnel decisions. Administrators should look first at these requirements when they are attempting to resolve procedural issues concerning appointment, retention, promo-tion, and tenure. Whenever such requirements can reasonably be construed as part of the faculty member's contract with the institution, the law will usually expect both private and public institutions to comply with them. (p. 278)

- Check your moral compass.

I add this cautiously. It's good advice when matters are simple and straight-forward, but this is seldom the case. Nonetheless, I think we must look deep within ourselves whenever making decisions that affect another person's life. Are we absolutely certain? Have we done all we can to give assistance and support? How strongly do we believe that terminating the faculty member is in the best interests of the students, the department, and the institution?

- Meet face-to-face with the faculty member not being recom-mended for contract renewal.

If you are confident that you are doing the right thing by recommend-ing termination, meeting with him or her is not as difficult as might be presumed. Successful leaders don't shy from difficult situations, and they don't turn painful tasks over to others. The affected faculty member deserves to be told precisely, *as far as permitted*, why you are making the recommendation. Note that I said as far as permitted. Your dean and your legal affairs officer will caution you about what you should not say. The law surrounding issues of confidentiality of information regarding person-nel decisions, including renewal of a faculty member's contract, is murky.

There are any number of factors, including U.S. Supreme Court decisions and open-record laws in some states, that must be considered when providing performance evaluation information to faculty members who are being terminated.

Losing two or three quality faculty members can be devastating to most departments, and chairpersons who have provided lackluster leadership must accept some of the blame when this happens. I would be remiss, however, if I did not point out that there are times when chairpersons are not at fault. Chairpersons at universities where budgets do not permit paying competitive salaries should not be held responsible when faculty members decide to accept better offers.

Resources

Web Sites
Socialization of New College Faculty: Mentoring and Beyond
www.brucesabin.com/socialization.html

University of California–San Diego Faculty Mentoring Program
http://academicaffairs.ucsd.edu/faculty/programs/fmp/default.htm

Walla Walla College Termination of Service Guidelines
www.wwc.edu/academics/governance/handbook/09-Academic_
Termination_of_Service.pdf

Books
Black, D. R. (1997). *Maintaining perspective: A decade of collegiate legal challenges*. Madison, WI: Magna.

Drysdale, D. S. (2005). *Faculty job satisfaction: Retaining faculty in the new millennium*. Ann Arbor, MI: ProQuest.

Rhodes, C., Stokes, M., & Hampton, G. (2004). *A practical guide to mentoring, coaching, and peer-networking: Teacher professional development in schools and colleges*. New York, NY: RoutledgeFalmer.

Miller, R. I., Finley, C., & Vancko, C. S. (2000). *Evaluating, improving, and judging faculty performance in two-year colleges.* Westport, CT: Bergin & Garvey.

References

Badaracco, J. L., Jr. (2002). *Leading quietly: An unorthodox guide to doing the right thing.* Boston, MA: Harvard Business School Press.

Bensimon, E. M., Ward, K., & Sanders, K. (2000). *The department chair's role in developing new faculty into teachers and scholars.* Bolton, MA: Anker.

Kaplin, W. A., & Lee, B. A. (1995). *The law of higher education* (3rd ed.). San Francisco, CA: Jossey-Bass.

Kouzes, J. M., & Posner, B. Z. (2003). *The Jossey-Bass academic administrator's guide to exemplary leadership.* San Francisco, CA: Jossey-Bass.

Wergin, J. F. (2003). *Departments that work: Building and sustaining cultures of excellence in academic programs.* Bolton, MA: Anker.

22

Strategies for Faculty Development

Successful chairpersons recognize the need for a strong faculty development program and encourage faculty members to build on the talents that each brings to the academy.

Faculty members, new or seasoned, need support for professional development. Although most faculty members and chairpersons recognize this, as a dean I observed numerous chairpersons who gave no time to assessing faculty development needs in their departments. Likewise, I have had discussions with faculty members who flatly told me that attending sessions on such matters as "rethinking the way we teach" or "how today's students learn" would be a waste of their time. I believe most faculty members do all they can to help students understand that lifelong learning is vitally important, yet there are some faculty members who do not heed this advice. All of us must continue learning, and this should be a matter of pressing concern for all faculty members. Recently the merits of some styles of teaching and learning have been questioned, and virtually all authorities in the field tell us that the way we were taught is not necessarily the way we should teach. Many of us sat in classes where faculty members did little more than lecture. I hope that it's virtually impossible today to find a "lecture-only" faculty member. We have learned better ways to engage students and more about how students learn.

Furthermore, there is increasing public pressure to hold those in education accountable for what students learn, which means that when we discover holes in student learning, they must be fixed, and something must be done when problems are traced back to inadequate teaching. Thus, as chairperson, you need to find ways of motivating faculty members to grow and develop, which is not always easy. Perhaps the most challenging task chairpersons confront in dealing with renewal and development is working with some senior faculty members who seem to have lost their enthusiasm for handling even their most basic responsibilities. Chairpersons generally discover that most junior faculty members are eager to learn.

I found that most junior faculty members felt they must become effective teachers, researchers, and public servants. Juggling time is a problem, and college or university leaders need to find ways to mentor new faculty members and help them to establish priorities—personal as well as professional. Bensimon, Ward, and Sanders (2000) state that "there is . . . considerable evidence that institutional leaders are recognizing that the 'sink or swim' approach to junior faculty is detrimental to the institution" (p. xvii). They are right, but I believe that ignoring veteran faculty members is even more detrimental to our departments and institutions. These same authors also point out, "Department chairs are the first to admit that they lack training and do not feel prepared for many of the roles they are expected to play" (pp. xvii–xviii). Among the many roles chairpersons feel poorly prepared for is encouraging professional activities of faculty members, according to a study completed by Gmelch, Burns, Carroll, Harris, and Wentz in 1992. My observation and discussions with numerous chairpersons over many years of consulting work reinforce this and further tell me that not much has changed since these findings were published more than a decade ago.

Brown (2003) offers chairpersons this useful information:

> Faculty are independent professionals responsible for their own development. Hospitals don't "develop" their medical doctors. Universities don't "develop" their professors. Hospitals and universities facilitate development. They provide opportunities. They make time, facilities, and sometimes stipends available. Ultimately, however, the professionals strategize and implement their own development plans. (p. xxvii)

Acknowledging this, the effective chairperson will understand the importance of development and strive to make time, facilities, and money available for faculty. While my general sentiment favors Brown's advice, prodding is necessary at times. I have found that the best faculty members always took advantage of development opportunities while the weak ones largely ignored these offerings. As a dean, I often arranged for regular brown-bag lunch sessions, and even weeklong workshops, on such development matters as improving teaching, developing good research skills, and so forth. Much to my chagrin, the "no-show" professors were those who most needed what the sessions had to offer. The chairperson's challenge is to get all faculty members to recognize that it is important, as Brown would say, to "strategize and implement their own development plans."

In summarizing an article on ways to help new faculty members, Sorcinelli (1994) notes that

> Chair and colleague relations contribute significantly to new faculty members' sense of commitment and loyalty to their campuses. Department chairs are a critical source of socialization for growth in their careers. . . . Senior colleagues, too, are important to creating a positive professional environment. New faculty desire more assistance than they are getting from senior colleagues in adjusting to their setting and in establishing themselves as researchers and teachers. (p. 475)

Creating a Departmental Faculty Development Program

Chairpersons can put together a formal faculty development program. First, meet with each faculty member to determine his or her principal goals with respect to professional development. Try to assess where the job frustrations occur and what creates job satisfaction. These meetings should help offer some direction to the kind of faculty development activities the department could sponsor.

The brown-bag lunch sessions I referred to earlier are a good development activity to start with. Properly planned, the lunch sessions can provide an opportunity for faculty members to improve teaching skills.

Veteran teachers known for their teaching expertise can be called on to cover any number of topics. These lunches can be conducted weekly over the course of the semester—perhaps shifting times to permit all faculty members to attend.

In addition, the following activities will foster faculty development. Each plays a role in a comprehensive development program.

- ## Team up with other departments for teaching and/or research workshops.

You can even involve several departments and invite guest speakers. When I sponsored such a workshop for improving teaching, I learned much from the session. Unfortunately, teachers who need the most help are not likely to attend scheduled programs without a lot of encouragement.

- ## Encourage sabbatical leaves for faculty.

Most colleges and universities offer a leave program that permits selected teachers to take off a semester or year for self-renewal. Generally, faculty members apply by completing a form in which they outline what they plan to accomplish during their leave. Most universities require that, to be eligible, faculty members have been employed for several years—most often seven, which is where the term *sabbatical* comes from.

- ## Initiate faculty exchange programs.

An exchange program can be particularly stimulating, and faculty members involved in them can feel challenged in new ways. Faculty exchanges take many different forms. Often they follow formal exchange agreements between universities. Faculty members then arrange with comparable educators at other universities to teach each other's classes. In some instances, the faculty members even exchange homes for the period.

Exchange programs often involve industry or government. A faculty member with a law degree might join a firm for a time, and one of the firm's lawyers would teach in his or her place. While technically not an exchange, simply visiting another campus to see how others teach or handle research can be a rejuvenating experience.

- Schedule class visits.

One way to grow and develop is to learn from our colleagues. Suggest to faculty members that they sit in on their colleagues' classes. They may learn new techniques and ideas to try in their own classes.

- Apply for released time.

Some colleges and/or departments allow selected faculty members released time from their classes to do research, develop new classes, or otherwise become involved in useful projects. They usually are expected to apply for released time by proposing what they would do with the time. It's a good idea to have faculty members give a report at the end of the term to show what they have accomplished. If you do this, you will find that some faculty members have made good use of their released time while others have not.

- Explore university growth opportunities.

Many universities offer faculty workshops and seminars. Faculty members may also take classes to learn something new that they feel will help them be better teachers. Classes in research, computer use, foreign languages, psychology, or education provide chances to grow and learn. Enrolling in continuing education courses offers still another opportunity for self-renewal. Additionally, many departments bring in guest speakers who can teach or inspire us, helping us grow or want to grow.

- Take on special assignments.

Occasionally universities offer opportunities to work in an administrative office. For example, at one university, the provost's office selects faculty members to work as interns. Several deans provide faculty internships as well, which permit faculty members to take on administrative projects.

- Apply for faculty development grants.

Many universities offer faculty development grants, such as summer research grants that enable faculty to spend their summer doing research rather than teaching. The grants provide funds to make this possible, and faculty members must submit a short report upon completion of the project.

- **Experiment with new teaching technologies.**

If your faculty members teach their classes primarily by lecturing, they might try using another technique. Urge them to try discussions or the case-method approach. Have them introduce some PowerPoint presentations or online learning activities. Also, I suggest that you encourage lecture-bound teachers to visit other classrooms where colleagues are using new approaches to teaching. More than likely, some older faculty members do not feel secure in letting go of the lecture as a way to teach. Work with them individually to see what you can do to allay their apprehensions and encourage them to try new approaches. Insecurity is stressful, and those faculty members who have never experimented with or learned new approaches to teaching are likely to find all kinds of reasons to hold on to what they know best—"talk and chalk." I've seen brilliant lecturers, and I don't dismiss this method of teaching altogether, but it is more effective when paired with other teaching approaches.

- **Develop a new specialty area.**

It is truly invigorating to teach new courses. If faculty members have been teaching the same ones for several years, they might have lost some of their edge. Delving into a new course can be refreshing. Certainly it forces faculty members to dig into the literature and come up with new ideas.

- **Team-teach with a colleague.**

Just as taking on a new course can be invigorating, team teaching with a colleague also can be stimulating. One can learn from a colleague, and the added pressure of preparing in a structurally different way likewise is a vitalizing experience.

- **Chautauqua programs.**

The Chautauqua short course programs are an annual series of forums in which scholars at the frontiers of various sciences meet for several days with undergraduate teachers of science. Visit the University of Pittsburgh's web site for more information about the Chautauqua short courses (www.chautauqua.pitt.edu/page3.html).

- Record your teaching.

A good way for faculty members to begin a program of self-improvement is to record their teaching. They probably will find things that need to be improved, and working to improve them can be rewarding. They may even want their colleagues to critique their taped sessions. During my first year as a department chairperson, there was a new faculty member who was especially nervous about teaching. He would stick to his notes and not even look at members of his class, who were often waving their hands hoping to ask for clarification of something he had said. He knew he needed help, and on his own, he began taping his sessions and asking for student feedback. Over the course of several months he improved his teaching. Indeed, he went on to become an outstanding teacher and scholar.

- Develop a peer evaluation system.

Talk to colleagues who would like to improve their teaching to see if any are interested in a peer evaluation program. Those involved would sit in on each other's classes, review syllabi, and critique each other's lecture notes and general approach to teaching. Each colleague would have only one goal in mind: How can I help this person become a more effective teacher?

- Attend regional and national conferences.

Most of us return from conferences with new ideas and renewed vigor. Opportunities for learning and growth are available, but faculty members need to seek them out. Try to fund travel for those who attend conferences. Generally there is not enough money for all faculty members to attend all the conferences they would like, so this means developing a system for equitable distribution of the travel funds you have.

Here are some other faculty development activities initiated at universities around the United States (Tierney & Rhoads, 1994).

Faculty Orientation Program

The University of Oklahoma has developed a semester-long faculty orientation program that includes weekly seminar-style meetings, and faculty participation has been high. The following topics are discussed: research, teaching, information on the university and the city and state, and professional development. Visit www.ou.edu/idp/faculty/newfaculty.htm to learn more.

Mentors

The University of North Dakota has adopted a scholars mentoring program where new faculty members have an opportunity to learn from and network with some of the top teachers at the institution. Yearlong meetings and a retreat are also part of the program. Visit www.und.edu/dept/oid/atcinfo.htm for more information.

Faculty Guides

The University of North Carolina–Chapel Hill has developed a guide to campus resources geared for the "perplexed UNC teacher," offering suggestions on subjects ranging from developing teaching skills to dealing with student problems. More information is available at http://ctl.unc.edu/pubcrg.html.

Faculty Workshops

The University of Wisconsin System offers an annual Faculty College where three days are devoted to improving teaching and learning. Visit www.uwsa.edu/opid/conf/fc.htm to learn more.

Special Interest Groups

Queer and Straight in Unity is a student organization at Augsburg College that supports gay, lesbian, bisexual, and transgender people on campus. One college faculty member and one staff member serve as voluntary advisors. Visit www.augsburg.edu/qsu/index.htm for more information.

Teaching Resources

Stanford University has prepared an extensive handbook on teaching for faculty, staff, and teaching assistants. View the 2004 handbook at http://ctl.stanford.edu/handbook.pdf.

Management Teams

In the spirit of Total Quality Management, Idaho State University has implemented student management teams designed to bring students and professors together to work on academic issues. The emphasis is on how reflection and discovery can improve teaching and learning. View the 2004 manual at www.isu.edu/ctl/facultydev/webhandbook/preface_handbook04.pdf.

Motivating Faculty Members to Grow

Many chairpersons choose to ignore faculty development. They usually argue that it is not their responsibility to see that faculty members continue to upgrade their skills and knowledge. On the other hand, some believe deeply that to move the department forward, they have no choice but to encourage faculty members to participate in faculty development activities. Assuming you are a chairperson of the latter sort, how do you motivate faculty members?

First, let faculty members know that you expect them to be actively involved in development. Appoint a committee to organize and coordinate seminars on improving teaching. Have faculty members who are active researchers present at seminar sessions.

You also should appoint a planning committee and charge it with developing a strategic planning document. When it's finished, present it to the faculty and get their reaction. Get faculty members to buy into the plan and begin implementing it. Generally, such an effort will require some new thinking and learning.

Unfortunately, there are some faculty members who balk at learning new things or participating in any faculty development activity. You must try to persuade them that it is in their best interest to become involved, and that they owe it to the department, to the institution, and most of all, to their students. One success in this area makes all the persuading worthwhile.

Successful chairpersons recognize the need for a strong faculty development program and encourage faculty members to build on the talents that each brings to the academy. Students will be the primary beneficiaries of faculty growth, though faculty members themselves are likely to find increased satisfaction in teaching.

Resources

Web Sites
Faculty Programs and Training
http://college.hmco.com/instructors/ins_teachtech_fdp.html

On-Campus Faculty Development
www.oncourseworkshop.com/On-Campus%20Faculty%20
Development.htm

Books
Gillespie, K. H., Hilsen, L. R., & Wadsworth, E. C. (2002). *A guide to faculty development: Practical advice, examples, and resources.* Bolton, MA: Anker.

Sorcinelli, M. D., Austin, A. E., Eddy, P. L., & Beach, A. L. (2006). *Creating the future of faculty development: Learning from the past, understanding the present.* Bolton, MA: Anker.

Wallin, D. L. (Ed.). (2005). *Adjunct faculty in community colleges: An academic administrator's guide to recruiting, supporting, and retaining great teachers.* Bolton, MA: Anker.

References

Bensimon, E. M., Ward, K., & Sanders, K. (2000). *The department chair's role in developing new faculty into teachers and scholars.* Bolton, MA: Anker.

Brown, D. G. (Ed.). (2003). *Developing faculty to use technology: Programs and strategies to enhance teaching.* Bolton, MA: Anker.

Gmelch, W. H., Burns, J. B., Carroll, J. B., Harris, S., & Wentz, D. (1992). *Center for the Study of the Department Chair: 1992 survey*. Pullman, WA: Washington State University.

Sorcinelli, M. D. (1994, May). Effective approaches to new faculty development. *Journal of Counseling and Development, 72*(5), 474–479.

Tierney, W. G., & Rhoads, R. A. (1994). *Faculty socialization as cultural process: A mirror of institutional commitment* (ASHE-ERIC Higher Education Report, 93[6]). Washington, DC: The George Washington University, School of Education and Human Development.

23

Evaluating Faculty Performance

Evaluations can help faculty members understand what's expected of them, and they can use your evaluation as a guide for personal development.

Evaluating faculty members is something most of us are familiar with—we've either done evaluating or have been evaluated. Judging colleagues is not easy. Telling a faculty member that he or she must improve is a difficult task. Leaders far removed from day-to-day interpersonal matters often fail to understand why chairpersons have such trouble evaluating faculty members. Let me illustrate.

When I was a dean, one year the university received money for merit increases. It was not a lot, but at a meeting of the Council of Deans our provost said we must have our chairpersons rank faculty members according to the top third, middle third, and lower third. Those at the top and in the middle would get a certain amount of merit money, but those at the bottom would receive nothing. Chairpersons complained—but they did it. Then the deans asked the provost how he planned to distribute merit money to deans. Would he use the same process, we asked. His answer: "I can't do that. It's just too difficult."

While it was too difficult for him, he did not mind insisting that chairpersons take on the task. I think we all agree that there is something wrong with this picture. Adding insult to injury because of the provost's insistence that he could not do this, the deans got no merit money.

Despite its difficulty, evaluating faculty members is one of your most important responsibilities. At most institutions, evaluations must be done annually for all probationary faculty members, and tenured faculty members are evaluated regularly—perhaps every three years. You are expected to assess, as accurately and as fairly as possible, how effective faculty members are as teachers, as scholars, and as university and community citizens. In many instances, these are not the only criteria. For instance, many universities and colleges now include collegiality.

Some faculty members question the necessity of evaluations. In the perfect department, faculty evaluations might be unnecessary. Unfortunately, perfect departments do not exist. The task of evaluating faculty members may become decidedly unpleasant when the overall evaluation is negative, as some chairpersons have difficulty telling a colleague that his or her work is not satisfactory. In the short run, having to make a less than satisfactory evaluation is difficult; in the long run, it is a responsibility that can pay dividends. If you are unwilling to provide faculty members with honest appraisals of their work, you will face even more difficult tasks in the future.

Many universities are examining new models for evaluating and rewarding faculty, and some have adopted models that offer faculty members opportunities to select a focused agenda that matches their particular interest and expertise. The usual tripartite of teaching, research, and service are generally evaluated, though faculty are allowed to select one area of focus or a combination of the three. Restructured models as effective agents of change are shown to have characteristics that are outlined in Table 23.1.

Why You Must Evaluate Faculty

Faculty Deserve an Honest Appraisal of Their Work

To evaluate otherwise is unfair. If you are dissatisfied with a faculty member's performance and you do not inform the person, there is no way for that faculty member to know that his or her performance is not meeting expectations. The kind of change you hope for is not likely to take place. Moreover, your unhappiness with the situation is likely to grow. I believe that if we show fairness and work early with faculty members so they know if they are on track to meet tenure expectations, they will be

Table 23.1 Characteritics of Restructured Models

- Models should have positive rather than punitive aspects.
- Models should have clearly identified short- and long-term goals reflective of administrator/faculty mutually derived individual action plans.
- Models should incorporate various ways of evaluating faculty, such as the use of professional portfolios and several incremental evaluations rather than one cumulative one.
- Administrators and tenure and promotion committees should define the purpose of evaluation. For example, is evaluation intended as a means of determining expertise or to determine how faculty members have contributed to the success or prestige of the university?
- Models should create an increased focus on teaching in the evaluation and reward process.
- Recognition and reward for research, teaching, and service in field settings should be part of the model.
- Research should be appropriate to the missions of the institution, college, and department, and to the needs of society. Furthermore, research should be applicable to current issues and significant in suggesting improved ways of meeting the needs of society as well as those of students.
- Universities should provide mentors for junior faculty who strive to become successful in each of the three traditional areas or experts in one area.
- Collaboration within and among academic departments and colleges for teaching, research, and service activities should be encouraged to construct knowledge and experiences applicable to changing perspectives of society.
- Differentiated faculty lines should be developed and offered to allow faculty to succeed in their chosen areas of expertise while maintaining some productivity in all three traditional areas.

Note. From Sid W. Richardson Foundation (1997). Reprinted with permission.

eager for evaluation feedback. If we use both summative and formative evaluations in tandem, we can help young faculty members make decisions about whether university life is right for them.

Students and Faculty Colleagues Suffer Whenever a Faculty Member Does Not Perform Well

Students deserve to have competent, dedicated teachers. Faculty colleagues most likely will have to do more than their share of the department's work if even one faculty member shirks responsibility. In a time when we are—or should be—giving more attention to the importance of teaching and when new ways of teaching are regularly being discovered, we must assess and hold weak-performing teachers accountable. If weak classroom teachers will not take it upon themselves to seek better ways of teaching, chairpersons are obligated to step in. However, this should be done early rather than after faculty members have earned tenure and settled into a routine of sloppy teaching. I have seen far too many instances when chairpersons have given above-average evaluations to a faculty member during each year of the person's probationary period only to recommend against tenure at the end of the probationary period. Again, I think most of us would agree something is wrong with this picture. Theall (2002, pp. 257–258) presents five essential components of comprehensive evaluation systems.

- There are institutionally and individually relevant underlying reasons for evaluation.
- The roles and goals of evaluation are appropriate.
- Mechanisms used to serve the administrative and data needs of the process are valid.
- The functions of the system are not punitive.
- The people involved are trustworthy.

Weak Faculty Members Make Weak Departments

If you care about your department, you will want all faculty members to perform at a high level. Systematic, careful evaluations make change and improvement possible. Neglect in this area is almost certain to result in a casual attitude that breeds contempt for quality.

We must have faculty members who are interested in exploring new ways of performing in the classroom, and who are amenable to discussions about improvement. You must work to create such an engaged department that will not shy away from the hard work needed to ensure quality. Chairpersons must listen to all faculty members, be open to considering any evaluation system, and recognize the importance of including faculty members in the development of the evaluation system. Finally, we must not give in to those who argue that we cannot measure faculty performance, especially those who insist that courses are proprietary and only those who "own" the courses know how to measure teaching effectiveness.

Serious Problems Result From a Haphazard Approach to Faculty Evaluation

Weak faculty members who are given average or above-average evaluations will most likely remain on the faculty; they will continue to shortchange students, colleagues, the department, and the university. Further, it is also unfair to recommend that tenure or promotion be denied to any faculty members who have not been advised that their performance is deficient. They deserve to be told what their weaknesses are and what can be done to improve performance.

A good annual review system promotes the health of the department. As Paul Woodruff (qtd. in Rosner, 1997), chair of the University of Texas faculty senate, observes,

> Departments with a good annual review system are also departments that run well and have much higher morale than those that don't. The members know each other's work because they read their papers; they're interested in each other's work, and they have confidence in the quality. Departments that are not doing good annual reviews, on the other hand, are not as cohesive as a result. (p. 4)

We must also consider the point about subjectivity noted by Arreola (2000).

> We must deal with this issue [objectivity] head-on and recognize that total objectivity in a faculty evaluation system is an illusion. The very definition of evaluation makes it clear that subjectivity is an integral component of the evaluative process. . . .
>
> Since objective evaluation is impossible, it is important to determine how to arrive at the goal of consistent evaluative outcomes of faculty performance using the necessarily subjective evaluative process. (p. xix)

Chairpersons must give considerable thought to the development and implementation of any evaluation system. If the approach is haphazard, faculty members will be even more resistant to evaluation than they may be already. Moreover, chairpersons should study the common errors made when establishing faculty evaluation and development programs (see Arreola, 2000, page xxiii).

Theall (2002) outlines problem areas related to faculty evaluations. He writes, "Awareness of these potential difficulties can help leaders to take preventative actions such as opening a dialogue, involving key stakeholders, and building trust" (p. 260). Here is his list of eight areas where problems can develop.

- Differing views of general evaluation roles and goals.
- Poor definition of what will be evaluated.
- Too hasty adoption of process, or the not-invented-here syndrome.
- Overreliance on student ratings of teaching.
- Invalid or unreliable interpretation and use of data.
- Poor data management, analysis, and reporting formats.
- Misinformation, mythology, and mistrust.
- Insufficient resources. (pp. 260–262)

Legal Ramifications of Improper Evaluations

Sloppy evaluations breed lawsuits as well as departmental dissatisfaction. It is implicit that handling evaluations is one of your key responsibilities; you're paid to do it as fairly and as effectively as possible. See Chapter 18 for a detailed discussion of what you can do to avoid litigation related to evaluations.

Evaluating Teaching

Evaluating teaching effectiveness is complex, but it need not be onerous. By approaching the task thoughtfully and systematically, chairpersons can do much to improve the level of classroom instruction for students. Moreover, most instructors appreciate knowing how well they are perceived to be doing and what they might do to improve their overall classroom effectiveness. This process should involve classroom visits as well as student and peer evaluations.

We should use all the tools at our disposal to evaluate teaching effectiveness, which include student evaluations, classroom visits by peers, and teaching portfolios. Some faculty members are not willing to take student ratings seriously despite the fact that they "can produce extremely reliable and valid information concerning faculty classroom performance, because students observe the teacher every day" (Arreola, 2000, p. 48).

Classroom Visits

Although most faculty members will invite you into their classes, some are reluctant to have visits by any outsider. You nevertheless must visit the classrooms of all faculty members being evaluated if you are to be effective. One of the best ways for you to judge teaching skills is to visit classrooms periodically.

If you are alert you will, of course, receive bits of informal information on classroom performance. Student evaluations also will assist you in making judgments. These are not good substitutes for firsthand observation, however. Any evaluation is weak and incomplete if it is based solely on student evaluations and casual comments of other faculty members and students.

Figure 23.1 Teacher Evaluation

Faculty Member: _____

Course Title:_____Date: _____

(Circle One)

1. The lecture (or other teaching approach) was well organized.
   Not at all   1   2   3   4   5   Very well

2. It was obvious that the faculty member was prepared.
   Not at all   1   2   3   4   5   Very well

3. The faculty member was enthusiastic about the subject matter.
   Not at all   1   2   3   4   5   Very well

4. The faculty member encouraged student participation.
   Not at all   1   2   3   4   5   Very well

5. The faculty member made good use of instructional cues, such as providing key points, telling students that certain points are important, using graphs or charts, and so on.
   Not at all   1   2   3   4   5   Very well

6. The faculty member projected his or her voice so that students could hear.
   Not at all   1   2   3   4   5   Very well

7. The faculty member varied his or her voice to help hold students' interest.
   Not at all   1   2   3   4   5   Very well

8. If I were a student, I would enjoy taking this class.
   No interest   1   2   3   4   5   Very interested

9. It is likely students would rate the teacher highly.
   Not likely   1   2   3   4   5   Very likely

10. Overall quality of this class session:
    Weak   1   2   3   4   5   Outstanding

11. The major strengths of this classroom session were:
12. The major weaknesses of this classroom session were:
13. What, if anything, could be done to improve the faculty member's teaching technique?
14. Additional comments:

Observer: _____ Date: _____

Signature: _____

Faculty members who balk at inviting their chairperson into their classes often can be persuaded to allow visits if they understand their purpose.

Many experienced chairpersons have developed a form to complete during a classroom visit. In addition to providing a systematic method of evaluation, it lets the person being evaluated know in advance your basis for judgment. Figure 23.1 presents a typical teacher evaluation form which can be modified to suit the subject matter or class under evaluation (see also Appendix L for additional course evaluation questions).

Teaching Portfolios

A teaching portfolio is a record of the highlights of a faculty member's teaching over a prescribed period. Teaching portfolios offer a way for faculty to share information about their teaching, to show what is unique about their approach, and to evaluate their own teaching as well as that of their colleagues. Seldin (2004) offers this definition of a teaching portfolio:

> It brings together in one place information about a professor's most significant teaching accomplishments. The portfolio is to teaching what lists of publications, grants, and honors are to research and scholarship. It is flexible enough to be used for tenure and promotion decisions or to provide the stimulus and structure for self-reflection about areas in need of improvement. (p. 3)

Several institutions have developed models for evaluating teaching from portfolios. Among the institutions using this approach successfully are Drexel University, Miami University of Ohio, and Oxford College of Emory University. Seldin (2004) describes the processes used by these institutions, as well as for several others, for evaluating teaching portfolios.

In recent years portfolios have become popular with faculty who wish to document their teaching accomplishments. They are worth exploring as additional ways to examine and evaluate teaching, although we need to be reminded that teaching portfolios—like student evaluations—should

Table 23.2 Elements of a Teaching Portfolio

Material From Oneself

- A statement of teaching responsibilities, including course titles, numbers, enrollments, and an indication about whether the course is required or elective, graduate or undergraduate.
- A reflective statement by the professor, describing his or her personal teaching philosophy, strategies and objectives, and methodologies.
- Instructional innovations and assessment of their effectiveness.
- A description of curricular revisions, including new course projects, materials, and assignments.
- Course and instructional materials developed, including study guides, manuals, case studies, annotated bibliographies, course booklets, and computer-aided learning programs.
- A representative course syllabi detailing course content and objectives, teaching methods, readings, and homework assignments.
- A description of how audiovisual or computer-based materials were used in teaching.
- Research that directly contributes to teaching.
- Participation in programs on sharpening instructional skills.
- A description of steps taken to evaluate and improve one's teaching.
- Success at securing grants for teaching-related activities.
- A personal statement by the professor, describing teaching goals for the next five years.
- Graded appraisal tools showing a clear relationship between appraisal methods and course objectives.
- Committee work relating to teaching and learning.

Material From Others

- Student course or teaching evaluation data which produce an overall rating of effectiveness or satisfaction or suggest improvements.
- Honors or other recognition from colleagues or students, such as a distinguished teaching or student advising award.
- Statements from colleagues who have systematically reviewed the professor's classroom materials (such as the course syllabi, assignments, the reading list, and evidence of testing and grading practices) or have observed the faculty member in the classroom.
- Invitations from outside agencies to teach or present a paper at a conference on teaching one's discipline or teaching in general.
- Documentation of teaching development activities through the campus center for teaching and learning.
- Statements from colleagues at other institutions on how well students have been prepared for graduate school.

continued on next page

Table 23.2 Elements of a Teaching Portfolio *(continued)*

- Statements by alumni on the quality of instruction.
- Evidence of help given to colleagues on course development or teaching improvement.
- Statements from colleagues with regard to program design, program materials, study guides, and online instruction.

Products of Teaching/Student Learning

- Student scores on pre- and post-course examinations as evidence of student learning.
- Student essays, fieldwork reports, laboratory workbooks, or logs.
- Examples of graded student essays showing excellent, average, and poor work.
- A record of students who succeed in advanced study in the field.
- Student publications or conference presentations on course-related work prepared under the direction of the faculty member.
- Evidence of influence on student career choice or help given by the professor to secure student employment or graduate school admission.
- Successive drafts of student papers along with the professor's comments on how each draft could be improved.
- Evidence of student early semester learning versus end of term performance.

Note. From Seldin (2004). Reprinted with permission.

be seen as a part of an overall evaluation scheme. They should be used in conjunction with student and peer evaluations and classroom visits, not as sole evaluation documents.

The items in Table 23.2 are frequently found in teaching portfolios.

Student Evaluations

Many departments have some form of student evaluation. These range from highly quantifiable questionnaires that are machine scored to ones that ask students to write detailed responses to open-ended questions. In some departments the chairperson sees these evaluations; in others, they are seen only by the faculty member.

Regardless of the kind of student evaluations used, both you and the faculty member should see them. Faculty members should see them so that they can benefit from student perceptions and comments. Chairpersons need to review student evaluations of all faculty members in the department. This provides some feel for the overall quality of teaching within the department, and it helps identify faculty members who seem to be doing the best job of teaching—and those who appear to be weak. If there are trouble spots, they are likely to show up in student evaluations done on a regular basis.

If evaluations by students are to be honest and effective, safeguards must be instituted to assure students that their comments are anonymous and can have no effect on grades. The following procedures provide these safeguards.

- Faculty members must be out of the classroom when students do the evaluating.
- Graduate assistants may be assigned to go into the various classes and handle the mechanics of getting the forms completed and turned in to the department chairperson. If the department does not have graduate assistants available, members of a student advisory council may be assigned to supervise the student evaluation procedure.
- Students must be told that faculty members will not see the completed evaluation forms until after grades are reported. (The sample evaluation form in Figure 23.2 carries such a statement.)
- The faculty evaluation forms should be placed in an envelope that is sealed after students return them. The sealed envelope should then be given to the chairperson to hold until grades are turned in. If the evaluations are machine scored, the person responsible for handling the materials should see to it that they get to the proper office.

Figures 23.2 and 23.3 are sample evaluation forms for student use.

Evaluating Advising

An increasing number of universities are giving attention to student advising, and chairpersons are asked to assure that faculty members are performing this task as expected. To get a glimpse at how well students believe

Figure 23.2 Teaching Evaluation

Instructor's Name: _____

Course Title:_____Date: _____

Using a scale of one to five, rate your instructor
on the items listed below.

YOUR INSTRUCTOR WILL NOT SEE THIS EVALUATION
UNTIL FINAL GRADES ARE SUBMITTED.

Do not put your name on this sheet. This evaluation will be seen only by your instructor and the chairperson of the department. Thank you.

1—Extremely low, negative
2—Below average
3—Average, acceptable
4—Above average
5—Exceptionally high, positive

_____ 1. Knowledge of subject matter
_____ 2. Ability to share knowledge
_____ 3. Prepares adequately for class
_____ 4. Organizes class meaningfully (with syllabus, course outline, etc.)
_____ 5. Rapport with students
_____ 6. Availability and/or willingness to assist students
_____ 7. Fairness in grading
_____ 8. Reasonable in making assignments
_____ 9. Makes assignments clear
_____ 10. Makes assignments that are meaningful and worthwhile
_____ 11. Encourages questions from students
_____ 12. Inspires students to learn
_____ 13. Values student opinions
_____ 14. Would be inclined to take another course from this instructor

15. What are the instructor's major strengths?

16. What are the instructor's major weaknesses?

17. I expect to receive the following grade in this course:

Figure 23.3 Evaluation of Faculty Performance

1. Instructor appears to be well prepared for each class.
   (a) Almost always
   (b) Usually
   (c) Rarely
   (d) Never
   (e) Not applicable

2. Instructor answers students' questions effectively.
   (a) Almost always
   (b) Usually
   (c) Rarely
   (d) Never
   (e) Not applicable

3. Instructor presents material clearly.
   (a) Almost always
   (b) Usually
   (c) Rarely
   (d) Never
   (e) Not applicable

4. Instructor is accessible to talk with students on course matters outside of class.
   (a) Almost always
   (b) Usually
   (c) Rarely
   (d) Never
   (e) Not applicable

5. Class sessions are relevant to course subject matter.
   (a) Almost always
   (b) Usually
   (c) Rarely
   (d) Never
   (e) Not applicable

6. Course requirements are clear.
   (a) Almost always
   (b) Usually
   (c) Rarely
   (d) Never
   (e) Not applicable

7. Grading criteria for the course as a whole are clear.
   (a) Almost always
   (b) Usually
   (c) Rarely
   (d) Never
   (e) Not applicable

8. Considering the type of exams, the results are reported by the instructor within a reasonable amount of time.
   (a) Almost always
   (b) Usually
   (c) Rarely
   (d) Never
   (e) Not applicable

9. Considering the type of assignments, the results are reported by the instructor within a reasonable amount of time.
   (a) Almost always
   (b) Usually
   (c) Rarely
   (d) Never
   (e) Not applicable

continued on next page

Figure 23.3 Evaluation of Faculty Performance *(continued)*

10. Instructor treats students in a courteous and/or professional manner.
    (a) Almost always
    (b) Usually
    (c) Rarely
    (d) Never
    (e) Not applicable

11. The class begins at scheduled times.
    (a) Almost always
    (b) Usually
    (c) Rarely
    (d) Never
    (e) Not applicable

12. The class usually ends:
    (a) On time
    (b) Early
    (c) Late
    (d) Not applicable

13. What is your current class status?
    (a) Freshman
    (b) Sophomore
    (c) Junior
    (d) Senior
    (e) Graduate
    (f) Other

14. What is your current cumulative grade point average?
    (a) Below 2.00
    (b) 2.00–2.49
    (c) 2.50–2.99
    (d) 3.00–3.49
    (e) Above 3.49
    (f) None yet

15. What grade do you expect to receive in this course?
    (a) A
    (b) B
    (c) C
    (d) D
    (e) F

    For pass/fail course only:
    (f) Pass
    (g) Fail

16. Main reason for taking this course:
    (a) General requirement
    (b) Interested in subject
    (c) Course in major
    (d) Easy course
    (e) Recommended by another student

17. Approximately how many classes have you missed in this course?
    (a) 0–3
    (b) 4–7
    (c) 8–15
    (d) More than 15
    (e) Went only for exams

their faculty advisors are doing their job, you might want to have students complete the evaluation shown in Figure 23.4.

It's instructive to look at some of the recent research surrounding issues of advising. McGillin (2003) points out that less than one-third of faculty advisors receive any evaluation. This is alarming when we consider, as she points out, that "Academic advising is the single most important relationship offered to students by an institution of higher education" (p. 88). In discussing the evaluation and reward of faculty advising, McGillin suggests creating an advising assessment and reward committee, defining good academic advising on your campus, constructing an evaluation system, and selecting evaluation methods.

As chairperson your job involves both supporting and evaluating student advising—it's too important to neglect. You need to keep abreast of the latest research and methods for assessing how faculty members perform as advisors.

Evaluating Research/Scholarly Activity

Evaluating research and scholarly activity is generally easier than evaluating teaching. Problems occasionally arise, however, when faculty members do not know what is expected of them in this area, or when they have misconceptions about how much weight is given to different kinds of activities. But when departments have good written promotion and tenure guidelines, the evaluation process is much easier. The more precise the guidelines, the more helpful they become. They will specify exactly what counts as research and/or scholarly activity, and how much weight is attached to the various activities. Well-written guidelines provide faculty members with answers to such questions as how research and publication done as a joint project is weighed; the weight given to writing or editing a textbook; and credit for popular articles or book reviews.

Obviously the promotion and tenure guidelines must be thorough and up to date, and the decisions they incorporate must be arrived at collectively by faculty members and the chairperson. While

Figure 23.4 Advisor Evaluation

Advisor's Name: _____

Date: _____

Use the following scale to rate the faculty member being evaluated on the items listed below. Return the completed evaluation to the department chairperson.

> 5—Strongly agree
> 4—Agree
> 3—Neutral
> 2—Disagree
> 1—Strongly Disagree
> 0—Does not apply

_____ 1. Keeps his or her office hours as posted.
_____ 2. Is familiar with my academic background.
_____ 3. Helps me select courses that match my interests and abilities.
_____ 4. Knows the university and department policies.
_____ 5. Helps me explore careers in my field of interest.
_____ 6. Seems to enjoy advising.
_____ 7. Is willing to discuss personal problems.
_____ 8. Helps me to examine my needs, interests, and values.
_____ 9. Encourages me to talk about myself and my college experiences.
_____ 10. Encourages my involvement in extracurricular activities.
_____ 11. Encourages my interest in an academic discipline.
_____ 12. Is knowledgeable about courses outside my major area of study.
_____ 13. Is approachable and easy to talk to.
_____ 14. Shows concern for my personal growth and development.
_____ 15. Keeps personal information confidential.
_____ 16. Is flexible in helping me plan my academic program.
_____ 17. Is a helpful, effective advisor whom I would recommend to other students.

in the final analysis the chairperson must be the one who approves the department guidelines, all faculty members should have some part in their development and review. A copy of the guidelines should be given to each new faculty member on the day he or she joins the department. (See Appendixes M and N for departmental promotion and tenure guidelines.)

Evaluating Service Activities

Service activities to be evaluated include university, college, and department committee work. Also included are extracurricular involvements such as supervision of student activities and participation in community affairs. The latter are generally described as "participation in extramural activities that may serve directly or indirectly the best interests of the university."

In recent years, community service has come to mean those activities where one uses his or her education and training to assist a worthy community group or organization when a professional relationship can be demonstrated. Faculty members are expected to use their expertise in providing leadership for the community. Thus, for example, a faculty member in geography would be credited with service for providing leadership if he or she mapped an area that had been designated for historical preservation. The same faculty member would not be credited with service for coaching a soccer team.

A more complex problem associated with community service occurs when faculty members are paid as consultants. For example, what if there are two faculty members in geography who do community service using their expertise, and one of them receives pay as a consultant? Should the person who is paid receive the same service credit as the colleague whose service is donated? For many chairpersons, this is an increasingly serious issue and one that may become pivotal when promotion and/or tenure are being considered.

Faculty members are expected to serve on department, college, and university committees. They also receive service credit for their contributions to local, state, or national professional organizations. Thus, by holding an office or serving on committees within such organizations, a faculty member would be credited with service. To assist faculty members in understanding service expectations, departmental guidelines should provide a precise definition of service as well as the level of service expected.

Evaluating Job Performance in Departmental Assignments

Faculty members are also expected to undertake specific responsibilities assigned by the chairperson. In turn, the chairperson is expected to provide resources and support so that the faculty member can complete the assignment in a professional manner. As timely completion of the assignment is generally important, expected outcomes with specified due dates should be made clear at the time the assignment is given.

A performance log can help you keep a record of assignments and how they are handled. Figure 23.5 is an example of a performance log.

If a log sheet is completed each time an assignment is given to a faculty member, it soon becomes apparent which faculty members are doing superior work and which are lagging. You should keep the completed log sheets in folders maintained for each faculty member. They become a helpful paper trail should it become necessary to document that a faculty member's work has been less than satisfactory, and they also verify excellence.

If a faculty member does not complete work assigned or does the job inadequately, the chairperson needs to meet with him or her to see what

Figure 23.5 Faculty Performance Log

Name:_____ Date:_____

Assignment: _____

_____

_____

Use the following scale to rate the task handled.

        5—Exceptionally well

        4—Well

        3—Average

        2—Below average

        1—Not at all

Deadline met: Yes / No

Comments

can be done to correct the deficiency. You need to put the faculty member on notice that timely, professional work is always expected.

Evaluating Cooperativeness

While the idea of evaluating collegiality is often controversial, nonetheless some universities evaluate faculty on this quality. As Whicker, Kronenfeld, and Strickland (1993) point out,

> Tenure criteria are sufficiently vague, and the standards applied to each criteria are sufficiently evolving in most institutions that grounds for rejecting all but the most brilliant candidates can be found. You plainly do not want to be perceived as unpleasant, venal, unethical, or unprofessional by current department and institutional standards. (p. 13)

The following, for example, is taken from a university's promotion and tenure policy: ". . . evidence of character, attitude, and personality that ensure cooperation with colleagues and commitment to programs and students of the department, college, and the university."

Figure 23.6 shows an evaluation instrument that many chairpersons have used to achieve some objective measure of how cooperatively a colleague performs.

Peer Evaluations

The participation of other faculty members in the evaluation process can be especially helpful. In a small department, most faculty members have a good feel for the kind of work done by all of their colleagues. Even in a large department, a number of faculty members generally can be called on to evaluate those whose work they know.

Peer evaluation committee members often evaluate the teaching of all probationary faculty members. They visit classes and provide the chairperson with an assessment of the teaching skill of the person being evaluated.

Figure 23.6 Evaluation of Cooperativeness

Faculty Member: _____

Department:_____Date: _____

Use the following scale to rate your colleague's character, attitude, and commitment to programs and students of the department and/or university.

> 5—Agree enthusiastically
> 4—Tend to agree
> 3—Neutral
> 2—Tend to disagree
> 1—Disagree emphatically

_____   1. Is the kind of person I can trust
_____   2. Attitude is joyful and positive, which encourages me to want to work with him or her
_____   3. Is personable and enjoyable to be around
_____   4. Is a valuable colleague
_____   5. Is a good addition to our faculty
_____   6. Works hard trying to get along with others
_____   7. Strongly committed to students
_____   8. Takes an active role in discussion about college policies and activities
_____   9. Is a truthful, honest person
_____   10. Is interested in improving the department and college and its programs
_____   11. Works and/or gets along well with others
_____   12. Is supportive of peers
_____   13. Assumes equal share of departmental duties
_____   14. Should be promoted/tenured (circle one)

Additional comments;

Signature of evaluator:_____Date_____

Figure 23.7 Faculty Peer Evaluation

Faculty Member: _____

Evaluator:_____Date: _____

Use the following scale to rate the faculty member being evaluated on the items listed below. Return the completed evaluation to the department chairperson.

> 5—Extremely low, negative
> 4—Below average
> 3—Average, acceptable
> 2—Above average
> 1—Exceptionally high, positive

A. **Teaching** (Complete this section only if you have observed the faculty member's teaching.)

_____ 1. Ability to share knowledge
_____ 2. Rapport with students
_____ 3. Classes seem to be well organized
_____ 4. Good preparation is evident
_____ 5. Inspires students to learn
_____ 6. Encourages students to ask questions
_____ 7. Teaching ability compares favorably with other members of this department

B. **Research/Scholarly Activity**

_____ 8. Level of activity meets departmental expectations
_____ 9. Faculty member's activity in this area is meaningful
_____ 10. Publications are relevant and should count toward promotion and/or tenure
_____ 11. Work in this area compares favorably with work of other faculty members in this department

C. **Service**

_____ 12. Willingly accepts assignments
_____ 13. Level of activity in this area is what is expected
_____ 14. Acts responsibly, professionally
_____ 15. Is a good representative for department/university
_____ 16. Work in this area compares favorably with other faculty members of the department

Summary of the strengths/weaknesses of this faculty member's service:

Other departments have some form of peer evaluation which functions most notably when faculty members are asked to make decisions regarding promotion and tenure.

In peer evaluations, specific information about performance should be sought. Figure 23.7 provides a form for gathering useful assessments (see also Appendix O for an additional peer evaluation form).

Peer reviews should go beyond simply visiting a colleague's class, completing an evaluation form, and turning it in to the department chairperson. If we are going to be fair in evaluating our peers, we need to gain a thorough knowledge of their special talents; understand their teaching philosophy; know something about their knowledge in the content area; understand their approaches to teaching, student learning, and achievements; and be familiar with their contributions to the profession and to the campus.

Problem Points

What to Do If the Evaluation Is Unsatisfactory

Occasionally you must evaluate faculty members who are not performing at the expected level. When you complete an evaluation that indicates unsatisfactory performance, you should take the following steps.

1. Set goals with the faculty member. This is best done by working together.
2. Describe direction and give suggestions to assist the faculty member in accomplishing the agreed-upon goals.
3. Set timelines for the faculty member to accomplish the desired changes.
4. Be certain to spell out the consequences of not taking corrective action.

Making Difficult Decisions

Successful chairpersons are not spared making difficult decisions, something all leaders must do. These situations must be examined with patience and care. Moreover, understand that because there may be legal implications whenever you make difficult decisions, you must take the necessary steps to protect your institution and yourself. You can read more about this in Chapter 18.

Here are some matters to consider before making important, difficult decisions.

- Recognize that while the problem facing you may seem routine, it might be far more complicated than you imagine.
- Examine the problem carefully for any uncertainties.
- Ask yourself what practical and legal implications may be involved in actions you take. Likewise, consider all ethical implications.
- Consider whether you should buy more time before taking action.
- Outline the problem on paper and consider all the options for its resolution.
- Consult with others regarding any serious concerns that you may have.
- Ask yourself what likely outcomes your action will produce.
- Consider—and think through carefully—how the other party is likely to respond.
- Ask whether you have exhausted all possible remedies before you decide to take any drastic action (e.g., terminating a faculty member).
- Carefully document any action you take.
- Look for long-term solutions rather than quick fixes.
- There is often temptation to stall or defer; you should engage in such behavior as rarely as possible. In outlining stalling techniques, Badaracco (2002) reminds us,

> Sometimes stalling only delays the inevitable. Sometimes, it reveals weakness in a leader, rather than prudence and responsibility. If bosses play these games, others may do the same, making organizations more bureaucratic and political. And, while these games are quite common, some of them involve deception and subterfuge. (p. 68)

Making difficult decisions such as terminating faculty members should not be taken lightly. The matter of termination always reasserts the importance of hiring quality faculty—people you are going to want to promote and award tenure. Occasionally, however, you will find that no matter what you do, someone you have hired does not work out. *The sooner you determine that, the better.* I emphasize this because I suspect this is true for so many other problems that we see as onerous, time consuming, and personally troubling. The sooner we recognize the problem and deal with it, the better off we will be.

Evaluating faculty performance is a burdensome task, and I know of few chairpersons who look forward to it. Yet if used properly, evaluations can help faculty members understand what's expected of them, and they can use your evaluation as a guide for personal development.

Resources

Web Sites

Evaluating Faculty Performance During the Information Revolution
www.conncoll.edu/people/president/speeches/faculty-evaluation.html

Statement on Teaching Evaluation
www.aaup.org/statements/Redbook/rbeval.htm

The Status and Scope of Faculty Evaluation
www.ericdigests.org/1996-1/status.htm

Books

Colbeck, C. L. (2002). *New directions for institutional Research: No. 114. Evaluating faculty performance*. San Francisco, CA: Jossey-Bass.

Miller, R. I., Finely, C., & Vancko, C. S. (2000). *Evaluating, improving, and judging faculty performance in two-year colleges*. Westport, CT: Bergin & Garvey.

Seldin, P., & Associates. (2006). *Evaluating faculty performance: A practical guide to assessing teaching, research, and service*. Bolton, MA: Anker.

References

Arreola, R. A. (2000). *Developing a comprehensive faculty evaluation system: A handbook for college faculty and administrators on designing and operating a comprehensive faculty evaluation system* (2nd ed.). Bolton, MA: Anker.

Badaracco, J. L., Jr. (2002). *Leading quietly: An unorthodox guide to doing the right thing.* Boston, MA: Harvard Business School Press.

McGillin, V. A. (2003). The role of evaluation and reward in faculty advising. In G. L. Kramer (Ed.), *Faculty advising examined: Enhancing the potential of college faculty advisors* (pp. 88–124). Bolton, MA: Anker.

Rosner, F. (1997, May). Post-tenure review: Accountability in Texas. *Academic Leader, 13*(5), 3–4.

Seldin, P. (2004). *The teaching portfolio: A practical guide to improved performance and promotion/tenure decisions* (3rd ed.). Bolton, MA: Anker.

Sid W. Richardson Foundation. (1997). *Restructuring the university reward system.* Fort Worth, TX: Author.

Theall, M. (2002). Leadership in faculty evaluation. In R. M. Diamond (Ed.), *Field guide to academic leadership* (pp. 257–270). San Francisco, CA: Jossey-Bass.

Whicker, M. L., Kronenfeld, J. J., & Strickland, R. A. (1993). *Getting tenure.* Thousand Oaks, CA: Sage.

24

Handling Promotion
and Tenure Issues

*While difficult personnel decisions are never easy to make, they are
less painful if you've done all you can to make the process orderly
and support those who apply.*

Few things cause more anxiety for faculty members than the matters
of promotion and tenure. And why not? Often their careers are at stake.
You play a big role in deciding which faculty members in your department
move up. You will undoubtedly fret a lot over the decisions you have to
make—especially when those being considered are borderline cases. Tough
calls cause sleepless nights, gray hair, and the urge to go fishing.

Moreover, the matter of tenure will likely become even more contentious in the coming years. As Harvard education professor Richard Chait
has said, "The full-time, tenured faculty member is about as representative
of higher education today as Ozzie and Harriet are of American society"
(qtd. in Kirp, 2003, p. 86). According to Kirp, adjunct faculty members
are doing an increasing amount of teaching. He writes, "In just five years,
between 1993 and 1998, 40 per cent of all higher education institutions
reduced their full-time faculty, and 22 per cent of those schools replaced
them with part-timers" (p. 86).

Christine Licata, who has been at the forefront of discussions about
post-tenure review, notes,

> Institutional assessment and student outcomes notwithstand-
> ing, the most strident calls for faculty accountability in the
> academy continue to focus on tenure and the assumption that

regular monitoring of performance after tenure is more fiction than fact.

While tenure has been a target periodically over the past 30 years, the attack in the last decade has amplified considerably based upon twin beliefs: 1) tenure constrains institutional flexibility, and 2) campuses are replete with underperforming yet well-paid faculty members. (Licata & Brown, 2004, p. 3)

I am convinced that the public's skepticism regarding the work of faculty members will be a continuing problem. If we in the academy cannot explain the work of faculty to the public at large, tenure could become a thing of the past. I have seen faculty members take advantage of tenure, and I have witnessed confusion among faculty regarding the understanding of their role. Universities and colleges often have been slow in responding to the changing needs of society, and there are academic leaders—from presidents to department chairs—who have not yet come to grips with the fact that global, economic, and political forces are reshaping what universities and colleges need to become—not tomorrow or 10 years down the road, but today. In his book *The Role of the American University: The Creation of the Future*, Frank Rhodes (2001, p. 154) makes a strong case for tenure, which he qualifies by suggesting the following:

- If universities are to continue to justify tenure, the process of achieving it must be very demanding.
- After tenure is awarded, the university should require periodic, say five-year, reviews, with a formal self-assessment and personal professional plan for the next five years, contributed by the professor.

But what I find most compelling is this statement he also makes:

Finally, I would require a Socratic Oath, the professional equivalent of the Hippocratic Oath that every young physician is required to swear before embarking on the practice of medicine. Patients committing their future to the hand of a surgeon have the assurance that the doctor has bound himself to a stringent and demanding level of practice, defined by the Hippocratic Oath. This is the physicians' ethical pledge to the patient. Why should students, committing four years, thousands of dollars, and their future livelihood to a university professor, expect any less commitment? (pp. 156–157)

Tomorrow's department chairpersons will find their leadership role even more important than it has ever been. Promotion and tenure issues and their relationship to public trust will not fade. Informed chairpersons must engage faculty members in conversation about the value of accountability. They must closely mentor new faculty members and help them to understand their responsibilities.

While promotion and tenure are often lumped together, as in this chapter, they are totally separate considerations. Promotion in rank is recognition of achievement, as well as the considered potential of the person being recommended. Tenure, on the other hand, is a personnel status in an academic organizational unit or program of the university. Its primary benefit is that the academic or fiscal year appointments of full-time faculty members who have been awarded tenure are continued until relinquishment of that status (subject to adequate cause, for financial exigency, or for curricular reasons).

Promotion typically carries a salary increase with it, while tenure does not. The criteria for both are often not greatly different, but committee members need to assess a candidate differently for each. Typically we think of promotion in terms of the candidate's accomplishments to date. Tenure, however, is more likely to be viewed in terms of the candidate's long-term potential and promise. Tenure offers job protection that does not come with promotion, gives substantive meaning to academic freedom, and applies to teaching, research/creative activity, and service.

What can you do to relieve faculty anxiety about these matters and to ease your fretfulness? The first suggestion is to have departmental guidelines dealing with both promotion and tenure. The guidelines should be as specific as possible (see Appendix P for tenure and promotion procedures) to inform faculty members about what exactly is expected. Make the measurement of criteria as objective and quantifiable as possible as well. However, even the best guidelines will require judgment calls on your part.

As you develop promotion and tenure guidelines, keep in mind that they must meet or exceed the policies of the university. For example, if university criteria for promotion to the rank of full professor requires a terminal degree, anything less is not sufficient. On the other hand, you can be more demanding. For example, university criteria may not call for a terminal degree, but your department might decide that a terminal degree is required. You also should determine, before developing your guidelines, who on campus must approve them. Generally, your dean and vice president for academic affairs must sign off on the guidelines, and some schools require approval by a faculty senate.

Promotion and tenure guidelines also will reduce untenured faculty members' anxieties, which I think is the most important reason for having them. Faculty members have the right to know from day one exactly what is expected of them. Make it a point to distribute promotion and tenure guidelines at new faculty orientation.

At one university where I taught, one department had guidelines that were unusually specific and quantifiable. New faculty members were able to look at them, assign themselves points for certain activities, add them up, and know where they stood. During evaluation sessions with the chairperson, untenured faculty members or those seeking promotion were told how many points they had and where that put them in relation to what was needed. They were told, for example, "If you continue to make this kind of progress, you will have no trouble with tenure," or "If you don't improve your progress, you can't be recommended for tenure." The chairperson could point to specific weaknesses if necessary.

There are advantages to such a system. It is relatively easy to see how faculty members score; they either come up to a certain level or they don't. Those who score high enough are recommended for tenure; those who don't, aren't. The disadvantages are that many faculty members believe that points can't be assigned to everything. Moreover, many disagree on how many points ought to be assigned to different activities. Unless there is general agreement regarding the point values, faculty members will not endorse the guidelines.

Accurate annual evaluations make the promotion and tenure process less painful. If you've been honest and objective in your yearly evaluation, the decision should be easy. If you have honestly given high marks on teaching, research, and public service, you are likely to recommend tenure when the time comes. On the other hand, I have worked with chairpersons who gave faculty members strong evaluations, but then recommended that tenure be denied. How does that make sense? It doesn't, and you might have to explain your answer in court.

Recommending tenure is a heavy responsibility: You are affecting someone's fate and determining whether he or she will soon be unemployed. You also are deciding whether you want that person on your faculty for the next 30 years or so. You must weigh all the materials submitted with the application against the performance criteria. You must fairly evaluate the faculty member's teaching, scholarly activity, public service, and any other specified criteria.

Many years ago, at my first meeting as chairperson to make a decision on tenure, the discussion began when one professor offered, "I am in favor of granting tenure to Ken. He's such a nice guy." I pleaded with the faculty not to make the decision based on niceness. We can find nice people in the park, but do we want them on our faculty? We must stick to the stated performance criteria. In the end we did not recommend tenure for Ken. He had weak teaching skills, and he had made no research progress. When the discussion got serious, we couldn't find any reason to recommend tenure. It didn't make any of us feel good to have to make the decision, but we made it nonetheless, and I am convinced we did the right thing.

If we are indeed responsible for hiring faculty members, what do we owe them? We first need to make certain they have a clear understanding of our expectations. Then we must provide resources to help them achieve these expectations. Moreover, we must have regular meetings with them to help them understand what resources are available, what the university and department cultures are like, and listen to the concerns they have about what is—or is not—being done to help them both in and out of the classroom. We must also help new faculty members understand the process. Here are examples of things we can do to assist faculty members earn tenure and get promoted.

- **Provide untenured faculty with a mentor.**

Each new faculty member should have a mentor who will provide the tools and guidance for success. After all, the cost of hiring a faculty member is significant, and replacement would be costly as well. Too often we say to new teachers, "You are responsible for teaching these classes. Here are some old syllabi, and there is your classroom." What we leave unsaid, of course, is "you're on your own now."

A good mentor will talk to the new faculty member about teaching. He or she will discuss the culture of the institution and the department and be available when the new hire needs support. Furthermore, it is incumbent that the mentor take the new faculty member under his or her wing. The mentor must not simply wait for the new faculty member to come to him or her with a problem. Finally, you must ensure that the process works and be willing to change mentors if rapport is not established.

- **Schedule periodic meetings with all new faculty.**

It's a good idea to meet periodically to see how they are doing and to let them know you have an interest in them. When there is more than one new faculty member, you might meet with them as a group. Give new department members an opportunity to tell you of problems they're experiencing and offer to help them. This provides chairpersons with the opportunity to know each new faculty member better; it builds a bridge of trust.

- **Recommend new faculty for committee assignments.**

Serving on committees helps new faculty members get to know their colleagues and begin building their record of service. A note of caution: Be careful not to overextend them. Also, do not accept the notion that minority faculty members should serve only on committees where affirmative action is at the heart of discussion. We owe new faculty members more respect than that.

- Give the names of new faculty to those looking for speakers.

I would often get calls requesting speakers for civic groups, workshops, conferences, and the like. Just as I recommended new faculty members to serve on committees, I tried to involve them as speakers on campus or before public groups. Getting to know other faculty members as well as community members can enhance a feeling of community.

- Sponsor brown-bag lunches or workshops on improving teaching and/or research techniques.

Informal sessions at which a panel presents ideas on teaching or discusses some aspect of research are useful for new faculty members. They—and veteran faculty members, for that matter—can get useful guidance from such professional development sessions.

These can be held weekly or monthly, depending on how large the department is. Sessions can vary. For example, at one session on teaching you may want to deal with test construction and at another on ways to contend with problems of student attendance. For sessions on research, you might ask active researchers to talk about their work or to present research techniques.

Some seminars on teaching that you could sponsor might focus on preparing effective exams, cooperative learning strategies, role-playing, or the characteristics of an effective teacher. Obviously there are many suitable topics.

- Develop a visitation program for all untenured faculty.

The program might provide for classroom visitors to come to a class twice during the semester on an unannounced basis. Visitors are asked to stay for the entire class period and meet later with the teacher to provide feedback and advice. Each classroom visitor is expected to complete a form and share it with the person visited. Both parties sign the form, indicating that they have discussed the visit. Copies of the form are then given to the department chairperson and made available to those who evaluate faculty members for promotion and/or tenure. Figure 24.1 is an example of a visitation form.

Figure 24.1 Faculty Classroom Evaluation Form

Instructor: _____   Course No. _____

Evaluator: _____   Date: _____

Class format/class objectives:

Organization/class management:

General impressions:

Suggestions:

Signature of evaluator: _____   Date: _____

Signature of faculty evaluated:_____   Date: _____

Original: Faculty evaluated   Copy: Evaluator   Copy: File

NOTE: A faculty member's signature does not necessarily constitute an agreement with the contents of the classroom evaluation. Furthermore, the evaluator's signature indicates that the faculty member was not informed as to the exact date or class period for the evaluation.

Note. Form developed by Dr. Jan Quarles.

The visitation program provides a simple way of identifying faculty members who may be struggling with their teaching. Moreover, it is a way for all untenured faculty members to know what experienced faculty think of their teaching methods. This program also is especially useful with part-time faculty members.

- Sponsor a special program for all faculty applying for tenure and/or promotion.

A program identifying what faculty members should include in their portfolios is particularly helpful. Obviously, it must be scheduled before most faculty members actually start working on their portfolios. These sessions also can be used to review performance criteria and their application.

In recent years portfolios have grown to unreasonable size. I've seen some so large that they are submitted in several boxes. Those standing for tenure and/or promotion need to be reminded—and reassured—that certain materials are neither needed nor wanted.

- **Encourage untenured faculty to be involved professionally.**
Talk with them about the importance of belonging to professional organizations, attending meetings, and volunteering for committees or special projects. Most professional organizations have plenty of work that needs to be done, and they welcome volunteers.

- **Encourage untenured faculty to apply for research grants.**
Faculty members often overlook research grant possibilities. Point out all notices and encourage them to apply where appropriate.

- **Try to make funds available for faculty to attend conferences and encourage them to submit papers.**
Faculty members should not be expected to pay their own way to conferences. Young faculty members generally do not have the money. Encouraging them to prepare and submit papers to present at conferences makes funding their trip easier.

Some universities that are especially aggressive at recruiting have startup funds they set aside for new faculty members that can be used to conduct research, attend conferences, and so on.

Whatever you do to assist faculty members in these matters will generally help you in evaluating and making promotion and tenure decisions.

- **Regularly provide untenured faculty with a checklist that outlines their progress—or lack thereof—in meeting the department's tenure expectations.**
While this procedure can be time consuming and at times agonizing, you owe it to those you hire in tenure-track lines and to the depart-

ment. Despite the clear need for interim progress reports, I can't count the times I've seen this neglected. On several occasions I have had talks with chairpersons concerning their strong belief that a faculty member was not performing at the expected level, only to find evaluations by the complaining chairperson in the faculty member's personnel file that suggested just the opposite.

At times I have discovered that tenure-seeking faculty members had been given vague, or even contradictory, performance instructions. This can happen if you do not reconcile instructions given by the department's peer review committee and your own. What's a faculty member to do if a peer review committee says, for example, that the person's publishing record is sufficient when you've made it clear that you expect considerably more?

It is critical to the welfare of those expecting to earn tenure and to be promoted that they have a clear understanding of what is expected, and it is not enough to provide this orally. A clear, concise, written set of expectations should be provided to all faculty members who will be standing for tenure and promotion.

The Promotion and Tenure Portfolio

Untenured assistant professors are anxious about their chances for earning tenure and being promoted. They are often uncertain about what they should include in their portfolios, and they are not made to feel any more certain when they see boxes of materials that others have submitted. Unless faculty members are given guidelines for compiling a portfolio, the only basis they have to go on are the examples and suggestions of others. Moreover, to help their chances with either promotion or tenure, they will likely err on the side of including too much. The consequences of this are that promotion and tenure review committee members will get far more information than they need and far more than they have time to read.

What should a faculty member include? First, faculty members standing for tenure or promotion should consider the criteria. Then they should begin compiling data to prove that they meet or exceed the minimum criteria. The following list of items provides a starting place for assembling a portfolio.

1. A current curriculum vita
2. Documentation to support teaching effectiveness
   - Student evaluations
   - Peer evaluations
   - Teaching portfolios
   - Unsolicited letters from students and/or alumni
   - Students' scores on standardized tests, before and after a course has been taken if possible
   - Evidence of help given to colleagues on teaching improvement
   - New courses developed
   - Participation in teaching workshops and seminars
   - Any efforts of instructional innovations and evaluation of their effectiveness
   - Any honors or teaching awards
   - Written comments from those who teach a course for which a particular course is a prerequisite
   - Alumni ratings or other graduate feedback
   - Invitations to teach for outside agencies
3. Documentation to support research effectiveness (copies of books, articles, papers, etc. should be available in the office of the faculty member going up for tenure and/or promotion and should be made available if committee members request them)
   - Letters from other scholars commenting on research
   - Letters documenting help provided to colleagues
   - Book contracts for works in progress
   - Letter accepting an article for publication
   - Letter indicating acceptance of a paper
4. Documentation of public service
   - Unsolicited letters lauding committee work, problem solving achievements, and the like
   - Statement summarizing work with a professional organization

Dealing With Faculty Who Have Been Denied Tenure

When tenure is denied, special problems often develop. At most colleges and universities, faculty who are denied tenure after serving three or more years are permitted to return for a year after notification of denial. Some, of course, will elect not to return if they are able to find another job. On the other hand, many stay—and this can present thorny problems. The individual may resent those who were responsible for denial, and faculty relations therefore can be strained. Some people become so hurt and angry that they give as little effort as possible to the job.

As chairperson, you must try to deal with the problem. Explain to the person that he or she should use the final year to do the very best job possible. Explain that you are likely to be contacted as a reference by others as he or she looks for another job, and that you will honestly report on current efforts. Talk about using the experience to grow—that is, to learn from mistakes.

To avoid a tense situation, it may be wise in some cases to terminate the unpromising faculty member before the third year begins. To do this means giving special attention to the performance of new faculty members. The visitation and mentoring programs will help and also highlight emerging problems. Giving extra time to monitoring the performance of new and untenured faculty is time well spent.

Minimizing Legal Risks

Baez and Centra (1995, p. 149) make several recommendations to minimize legal risks.

- Institutions should eliminate or minimize any practices that are not specifically addressed in their written policies.
- All units in an institution should be governed by a single reappointment, promotion, and tenure policy, although units will have different standards.
- Faculty members preparing for their reviews should receive as much information as possible about the process.

- A faculty member should receive information about any performance problems far enough in advance of a review to be able to improve.
- Institutions should be aware of the key legal, political, and social interests associated with affirmative action.

What Percentage of Your Faculty Should Be Tenured?

This becomes a particularly critical question in times of change. If drastic program changes are needed, and your faculty is nearly 100% tenured, your options are limited. On the other hand, you will have flexibility if a good percentage of your faculty is not tenured.

One remedy is to keep some of your positions open by designating them temporary. Although it seems insensitive to terminate some untenured faculty members for programmatic reasons, you may have to do that or lose even more.

As a dean, I faced the problem of 5 people in a department of 12 faculty members possibly seeking tenure. It was in a year when we were searching for a department chairperson, and all five of the potential tenure applicants would be going up in their fifth year instead of waiting until the sixth. In order to retain as much flexibility for the new chairperson as possible, I met with those considering going up for tenure and asked them to wait until the following year to apply. I explained that I would, of course, have made a tenure decision if they had been in their final year, but because they were not being hurt, I hoped they would understand my position.

This brings up the question of the wisdom of going up for tenure early, if your university permits it. I advise against it, especially at those institutions where it is up or out, no matter when a faculty member applies. In general, faculty members who take extra time to beef up their credentials make a wise decision.

Another way of dealing with a possible glut of tenured professors is for universities to establish tenure quotas. For example, a university may decide that no more than 80% of the total faculty in a given department may be awarded tenure. Thus, when the number of tenured faculty reaches the maximum allowed percentage (in this case, 80%), then "tenure density" has occurred. Courts have supported the right of institutions to determine what criteria—including tenure density—are to be used in tenure decisions.

Research Versus Creative Activity

Most universities specify that faculty members must be engaged in scholarship, defined as research and/or creative activity. Most of us have little difficulty coming to grips with what is meant by research but are uncertain about what creative activity means. It is important that we define each clearly, especially in those academic units where faculty members are engaged in both. The policy statement in Table 24.1 should help provide useful insight into the meaning of creative activity (in this case for a mass communication program).

Diamond (2004, p. 20) lists five specific conditions that exist under which most disciplines would consider the activity scholarly or professional.

1) The activity or work requires a high level of discipline-related expertise.
2) The activity or work is conducted in a scholarly manner with:
   - Clear goals
   - Adequate preparation
   - Appropriate methodology
3) The activity or work and its results are appropriately documented and disseminated. The reporting should include a reflective component that addresses the significance of the work, the process that was followed, and the outcomes of the research, inquiry, or activity.
4) The activity or work has significance beyond the individual context:
   - Breaks new ground
   - Can be replicated or elaborated
5) The activity or work, both process and product or result, is reviewed and judged to be meritorious and significant by a panel of one's peers.

Table 24.1 Creative Activity

1. *Definition.* Creative activity consists of the creation, production, exhibition, performance, or publication of original work. Such activity is characterized by the development of original ideas and information through the practice of the forms of mass communication. The product of creative activity may be communicated as professional presentations in print media, electronic media, or emerging technologies. Appropriate formats may include photographs, film, video recordings, audio recordings, graphic designs, digital imaging, and nonacademic publications.

2. *Examples.* Creative activities to be considered include but are not limited to:
    A. Articles, reviews, and commentaries in professional periodicals, newspapers, and magazines that meet standards of high quality in the practice of mass communication; also, graphics and visual materials, including radio and television tapes, that are original presentations to professional or public audiences and that meet standards of high quality in the professional practice of mass communication
    B. Development and management of mass communication seminars and workshops and related audio/visual and printed materials for professionals that advance knowledge and understanding of professional practice and improve professional performance
    C. Books, industrial videos, and printed materials that meet standards for quality in mass communication, that advance knowledge and understanding of professional practice, and that improve professional performance
    D. Internships, consultancies, manuscript reviews, and other forms of practical experience that allow faculty members to perform in a creative and professional way
    E. Publication of analyses and critical reviews on professional subjects, published in professional publications
    F. Publications of articles, reviews, and commentaries on other subjects in newspapers and other popular media, if they demonstrate high standards of professional practice
    G. Meritorious work of a demanding nature in professional positions with the media during summers or leave time, or with approval of the dean, part-time during a regular term; such work should demonstrably enhance the faculty member's teaching

continued on next page

Table 24.1 Creative Activity (*continued*)

> H. Publication of textbooks or other books in mass communication if the books break new ground and successfully advance concepts, ideas, and approaches that transcend ordinary instruction manuals
> I. Professional achievement in graphics–visual arts area and in other professional fields represented by mass communication faculties; the work should be original and should advance the state of the art of the profession
>
> 3. *Evaluation criteria.* The faculty member's creative activities are expected to include work that clearly is major, as opposed to minor. Characteristics by which major work is distinguished from minor work include:
> A. The scope of the audience (such as regional or national as opposed to local)
> B. The nature of the audience (including respected academic or professional peers)
> C. Significance of the topic (an idea or finding that serves important academic, professional, or public interest)
> D. The rigor of the standards met by the work (recognized by prominent academic or professional groups)
> E. The stature of the reviewers of the work (educators or practitioners who are widely respected for their accomplishments)
> F. The breadth, depth, and originality of the creative effort
> G. The impact of the work in improving educational or professional practice or elevating the general understanding of freedom of expression and the ethical responsibilities of the mass media

Evaluating Online Scholarly Activities

The matter of how much weight to give to online scholarly activities for purposes of promotion and tenure is a contentious issue. Guernsey (1997) notes that while candidates for promotion stock their portfolios with Internet-related accomplishments, many evaluation committees are skeptical.

> Behind the closed doors, committee members are asking questions that betray equal parts confusion and suspicion. Should a candidate's Internet project count? Is it teaching, scholarship,

or service? Does editing an electronic journal require the same kind of rigor as editing a print journal? Who is refereeing all this stuff, anyway? (Guernsey, 1997, p. A21)

These questions will likely be dealt with more easily by those disciplines that already accept nontraditional research and publication and creative scholarly activity as valuable. However, in years to come the traditional disciplines will have to deal with these questions, and the chairpersons of these departments would be well-advised to develop policies dealing with online scholarship. As a point for beginning discussion, the list developed by Diamond (2004) could prove useful.

Who Makes Promotion and Tenure Decisions?

At public universities, a governing board generally makes the final decision on who is promoted and tenured. On campus, the final recommendation is that of the university president. Most decisions on promotion and tenure start at the departmental level with a committee that reviews those faculty members standing for promotion or tenure. The peer review committee will make a recommendation either to the chairperson or the dean or both. Regardless, as chairperson you will make a recommendation to your dean. She or he in turn will make a recommendation to the vice president for academic affairs. Depending on the university, there may be a university-wide committee that also offers a recommendation to the vice president for academic affairs. Either way, the vice president for academic affairs will make a recommendation to the president who in turns makes his or her recommendation to members of the governing board.

Post-Tenure Review

An increasing number of universities are developing policies and procedures for reviewing tenured faculty members. They recognize the changing circumstances of the modern university. They typically outline specific conditions that directly impinge on the need for post-tenure review. Most mention the budget situation facing public universities. As we know, lean budgets often mean no increases in faculty size. Thus, any quality improvement or rise in reputation has had to come out of constant faculty size, rather than by the addition of faculty positions, the method most commonly relied on previously to build departments.

One state that mandates post-tenure review is Florida. Interestingly, one regent said such reviews make it easier to fire tenured professors who are "driving through their careers on autopilot," but also can reward outstanding professors. The "autopilot" statement tells a lot about how many outside the academy view faculty members. It certainly tells much about what is driving post-tenure review—not just in Florida, but also around the country. According to a spokesman for Florida's system, professors who receive poor reviews could be subject to disciplinary action, including dismissal.

Since January 1, 1994, faculty members are not required to retire except when the university can prove sufficient dereliction or neglect of duties to support dismissal. This has made a significant change in the way some departments operate: Instead of simply waiting for an unproductive faculty member to retire and then hiring a young, energetic, go-getter, unproductive faculty members may now linger for a decade or longer beyond what would otherwise have been mandatory retirement.

Another situation that causes some universities to develop post-tenure review concerns growing external demands for accountability. Post-tenure review has been a response to the need for changing academic practices. The quotation from the Florida regent clearly illustrates this.

The underlying philosophy that drives a university's post-tenure review process will depend in part on whether the process is intended to be summative or formative. Those that are summative are used to make personnel decisions, whereas those that are formative suggest a review process that is developmental in nature. "While the philosophy of most post-tenure review policies drafted today is formative, almost all have summative aspects" (Licata & Morreale, 1997, p. 5).

Andrews, Licata, and Harris (2002), who conducted a national study of how U.S. community colleges evaluate tenured professors and other long-term faculty, offer interesting revelations respecting post-tenure review issues.

> Instructional administrators and faculty leaders strongly agree that evaluation of post-tenure and long-term faculty is needed. They also support the position that faculty development should be one of the primary outcomes of evaluation.
>
> Both groups expressed much doubt about the effectiveness and quality of evaluation. Insufficient faculty development, no observable positive outcomes to date, inadequately trained evaluators, and the lack of sanctions for poor performance evidently have led to this reaction. (pp. 13–14)

Chairpersons, as primary participants in the post-tenure review process, need to understand its purpose as well as its process. While the general purpose of post-tenure review policies can be labeled summative, formative, or some combination of either, the specific purpose of any such policy should be spelled out in the university's policy. From Licata and Morreale (2002, pp. 37–45) we discover many lessons. Eleven that might be particularly useful are the following from the University of Kentucky.

Lesson 1: Post-Tenure Review Efforts Should Be Faculty Led

Lesson 2: Have the Proper Leadership Team in Place

Lesson 3: Separate Post-Tenure Review From Loss of Tenure

Lesson 4: Focus on Post-Tenure Review as a Method of Preserving Tenure and Drawing Support for Faculty Development

Lesson 5: Engage the Entire Campus Community

Lesson 6: Use Outside Expertise

Lesson 7: Create a Flexible Policy

Lesson 8: Piggyback on Current Evaluation Systems

Lesson 9: Build in Staff Training and Program Assessment From the Outset

Lesson 10: Take Trust Seriously

Lesson 11: Build Continuity Into the Process

The following general comments can be made about post-tenure review:

- It is a very time-consuming process with lots of paperwork.
- Its effectiveness rests heavily on how well chairpersons do their job of evaluating; they must be able to carry out the process in a conscientious and evenhanded way. Many chairpersons will need help to learn how to construct effective evaluations.
- Developing an effective post-tenure review policy takes a lot of time, and it is important that all voices are brought to the table for discussion early in the development process. Administrators who attempt to create a post-tenure review policy and procedure on their own will likely fail.
- For any post-tenure review system to be effective, constant vigilance is required. University policies are likely to need regular refinement and improvement.
- Post-tenure review procedures can produce faculty resistance and cynicism.
- Post-tenure review has in many instances proven itself to be worth the cost of time and effort because it boosts morale for productive faculty members.
- Unless properly constructed, post-tenure review can have a stigma attached.
- Post-tenure review can be a force for continuous faculty development and validation.

At some universities, all faculty members come up for review on some sort of cycle. At others, chairpersons identify those faculty members to be reviewed. Generally the department chairperson and a select committee comprise the review team. After the review, a report is completed. If substantial and chronic deficiencies are identified, a professional development plan is created. This is an agreement indicating how specific deficiencies in a faculty member's performance shall be remedied. The department chairperson and dean generally formulate plans, in consultation with the faculty member, that identify the specific deficiencies;

define the goals or outcomes needed to remedy the deficiencies; outline the activities that are to be undertaken to achieve the needed outcomes; set timelines for accomplishing the activities and achieving the outcomes; indicate the criteria for annual progress reviews; and identify the source of any required funding.

While motives for instituting post-tenure review are certainly mixed, a growing number of colleges and universities are initiating policies (see Appendix Q for examples of post-tenure review policies and guidelines). By last estimates, "post-tenure activity was under way in some form or other in 37 states, ranging from required by the entire state system, or adopted within selected public institutions, or at least on the drawing board in others" (Licata & Morreale, 2002, p. 3).

Status of Tenure

Legislators and taxpayers across the country are questioning the need for tenure. Many argue that with First Amendment protections, tenure is no longer needed. Some openly predict that tenure as we know it will soon disappear. Whether true or not, the concept is being scrutinized, largely because of political reality. "Professors sense that, at the very least, they had better discuss tenure, to keep outsiders, like state lawmakers, from taking matters into their own hands" (Leatherman, 1996, p. A12). Indeed, some states are experimenting with faculty appointments where no tenure will ever be awarded. Not many years ago, Florida opened a new university to be staffed by faculty members who cannot earn tenure. Also, the board of regents of the University of Texas System voted to require that the performance of tenured professors be reviewed every five years. The policy allows tenured faculty members to be dismissed if their performance is found to be poor. The president of Metropolitan State College of Denver appointed a committee to examine ways to evaluate tenured professors and ensure they are still doing a good job.

In seems fair to conclude that tenure is on shaky ground and that many forces are at work to destroy it, and an increasing number of younger faculty do not support traditional tenure to the degree that older faculty do.

Gilliland (1997) makes a strong argument that tenure is an important element in helping universities cope with changes they must face: Organizations that succeed in an environment of change and unpredictability promote flexibility, information access and dialogue, and risk-taking" (p. 33). She observes also that tenure promotes risk-taking and therefore should be retained, though she calls for significant modifications.

Members of promotion and tenure review committees are often anxious about the responsibility of making decisions that powerfully impact people's lives. Thus, academic leaders need to meet from time to time with committee members to address some of their concerns and to remind them that their task is critical to the health of the department and the university. Few decisions faculty members make in their job will be more important than those having to do with tenure and promotion.

While difficult personnel decisions are never easy, they are less painful if you've done all you can to make the process orderly and support those who apply. Also, promotion and tenure decisions are made much easier if you've already faced making tough decisions by failing to reappoint those not deserving of tenure and/or promotion. If you have fairly evaluated faculty performance and recommended for reappointment only strong faculty members, such decisions should not be all that difficult.

Resources

Web Sites
Creating Flexibility in Tenure-Track Faculty Careers
www.acenet.edu/AM/PrinterTemplate.cfm?Section=Home&Template
=/CM/HTMLDisplay.cfm&ContentID=8459

Faculty Reward System
www.thenationalacademy.org/Resources/facrewardbiblio.html

Hiring and Promotion Legal Issues
www.aaup.org/Legal/info%20outlines/leghire.htm

Legal Issues Confronting Department Chairs
www.mla.org/ade/bulletin/n131/131062.htm

Tenure, Promotion, and Reappointment
www.ericdigests.org/1997-1/tenure.html

Books

Brint, S. (Ed.). (2002). *The future of the city of intellect: The changing American university*. Stanford, CA: Stanford University Press.

Diamond, R. M. (2002). *Serving on promotion, tenure, and faculty review committees: A faculty guide* (2nd ed.). Bolton, MA: Anker.

Finkin, M. W. (Ed.). (1996). *The case for tenure*. Ithaca, NY: ILR Press.

Huer, J. (1991). *Tenure for Socrates: A study in the betrayal of the American professor*. New York, NY: Bergin & Garvey.

Lewis, M. (1997). *Poisoning the ivy: The seven deadly sins and other vices of higher education in America*. New York, NY: M. E. Sharpe.

Silverman, F. H. (1999). *Publishing for tenure and beyond*. Westport, CT: Praeger.

Silverman, F. H. (2001). *Teaching for tenure and beyond: Strategies for maximizing your student ratings*. Westport, CT: Bergin & Garvey.

Van Alstyne, W. W. (1993). *Freedom and tenure in the academy*. Durham, NC: Duke University Press.

References

Andrews, H. A., Licata, C. M., & Harris, B. J. (2002). *The state of post-tenure and long term faculty evaluation* (Research brief). Washington, DC: American Association of Community Colleges.

Baez, B., & Centra, J. A. (1995). *Tenure, promotion, and reappointment: Legal and administrative implications*. San Francisco, CA: Jossey-Bass.

Diamond, R. M. (2004). *Preparing for promotion, tenure, and annual review: A faculty guide* (2nd ed.). Bolton, MA: Anker.

Gilliland, M. W. (1997, May/June). Organizational change and tenure: We can learn from the corporate experience. *Change, 29*(3), 30–33.

Guernsey, L. (1997, June 6). Those who publish on line fear they suffer in tenure reviews. *The Chronicle of Higher Education*, p. A21.

Kirp, D. L. (2003). *Shakespeare, Einstein, and the bottom line: The marketing of higher education*. Cambridge, MA: Harvard University Press.

Leatherman, C. (1996, October 25). More faculty members question value of tenure. *The Chronicle of Higher Education*, p. A12.

Licata, C. M., & Brown, B. E. (Eds.). (2004). *Post-tenure faculty review and renewal II: Reporting results and shaping policy*. Bolton, MA: Anker.

Licata, C. M., & Morreale, J. C. (1997). *Post-tenure review: Policies, practices, precautions* (New Pathways Working Paper Series No. 12). Washington, DC: American Association for Higher Education.

Licata, C. M., & Morreale, J. C. (Eds.). (2002). *Post-tenure faculty review and renewal: Experienced voices*. Washington, DC: American Association for Higher Education.

Rhodes, F. H. T. (2001). *The role of the American university: The creation of the future*. Ithaca, NY: Cornell University Press.

25

Dealing With Chronic Low Achievers

By alerting faculty members early to anything you see as a developing problem, you can help them deal with it and get on track to a more productive career.

Of the many responsibilities chairpersons have, few are as difficult as that of dealing with those faculty members who are nonproductive, especially when the pattern has been allowed to exist over a period of years. If you are a new chairperson, you will soon learn that chronic low achievers will do their best to hide all signs of nonproductive performance. Those with tenure are a special challenge—no matter whether you are a beginning or veteran chairperson.

Before you can work with or identify nonproductive faculty members, you should have a document in place that spells out what is expected of all faculty members. Without such a document, faculty members you identify as low achievers may see themselves as productive contributors. Moreover, I consider it patently unfair for those in leadership roles to challenge anyone's performance when performance expectations have not been spelled out. I have known chairpersons who have expectations that are troubling to faculty members because the first time a faculty member learns of those expectations is when she or he is reprimanded for not having met them. In his discussion of resolving a departmental conflict, Coffman (2005) advises, "The whole process might have been handled more easily, or even been prevented, if the department had a set of procedures, criteria, and standards outlining how people could contribute to the mission according to their strengths" (p. 144). To that, I add "Amen." Be aware, too, that chairpersons must be specific when they describe expectations. Advising faculty members that they must be "successful classroom teachers" is not good enough. You must explain by identifying criteria what the word *successful* means.

Early in my days as a chairperson, I was asked by a faculty member what I expected of him, and I glibly replied that he would be judged on teaching, research, and public service. That's all I offered! I wanted him to improve his classroom performance, and I owed him much more than such a vague rejoinder.

As with so many problems, communication is of utmost importance. When dealing with chronic low achievers, possessing good listening skills is absolutely essential, as is developing trust. Certainly all of your leadership skills will be tested, but getting to the heart of the problem by listening and developing trust takes on significant meaning.

Performance Counseling

Let's presume for this discussion that your department has in place a document that spells out goals and objectives, and also something in writing that specifies what constitutes acceptable performance standards. The following provides issues and procedures for dealing with those who fall short of the acceptable performance standards.

Understand Factors That Contribute to Unsatisfactory Performance

Chairpersons must try to identify the causes related to a faculty member's performance before attempting to discuss unsatisfactory behavior with the faculty member. Tucker (1992, p. 248) writes that

> Most instances of unsatisfactory performance on the part of faculty members can be linked to the presence or absence of elements in one or more of the following groups of factors.
> 1. Knowledge of subject matter and skills in teaching and conducting research
> 2. Psychological and physical characteristics

3. Personal or family situations
4. Working conditions

As either a chairperson or dean, I believe I have confronted each of these factors. And to be honest, my record for success has been mixed, which raises another issue: We must accept the fact that we will be unable to put all faculty members on the right course. We will not succeed in every effort—no matter how hard we try. I remember one tenured faculty member whose teaching had taken a serious nosedive. I was close to the end of my first year when we talked about what he might do to reignite his passion for teaching. Near the end of our conversation, he said, "You know, since you've been here I feel as though each day I must prove myself as a teacher." My response was short: "Tom, I would like to keep that feeling alive in you." I did not mention that he had been posting notes on his office door that announced "If you want to attend class today, you will need to gather at my house." I failed miserably in my efforts to get Tom to change. When honey didn't work, I tried vinegar. Had I been more experienced, I might have been able to do a better job. (Note that I said *might*.)

Even though we'll fail at times, we must always try, and we must begin by trying to put ourselves in the shoes of the low-achieving faculty member. We should be empathetic, and use some of the basic skills of psychological counseling, with the caveat that psychological counseling is not your job and may even create legal problems for you. Forgo your urge to delve too deeply into that area. However, the following basic counseling techniques may be useful.

- **Avoid making faculty feel defensive.**
Always begin any performance counseling session on a positive note. Let the faculty member know that you are eager to provide support—that is, the purpose of the meeting is not to blame: I'm not going to scold; we are going to work together to develop a workable plan; and I will see that resources are made available to help you succeed. You must convey your sincerity in valuing the faculty member as a professional. Leadership is not about finding fault; thus, whenever possible, point out the good qualities

the faculty member possesses. Further, give the faculty member assurance that he or she is not the first—and no doubt likely will not be the last—to have experienced the problem currently being faced. When we can, we may say things like, "I once faced the same kind of problem." This must be a sincere testimonial. If not, you'll undermine any rapport you've established. See also Pood (2003) if you are interested in reading more about defensive behavior and how to deal with it.

- **Help faculty develop a plan for improvement.**

Whenever the time is right, say something to this effect: "John, you and I see matters (note that I did not say *problem*) the same way. Do you have any suggestions about how we might address the issue? Do you think we could work together to develop a plan of action?"

- **Recognize unspoken problems.**

If we are observant, we may find signals that tell us there is more troubling the faculty member than he or she is telling us. Lack of good eye contact might be one such signal. Moving away from the person doing the performance counseling can be another. Andersen (1998), Knapp and Hall (2006), and Nelson and Golant (2004) all offer useful information on nonverbal communication.

- **Let silence work for you.**

Those who work in the field of counseling know that silence is one of the tools we can use to get others to open up. Silence can be uncomfortable, and if those of us who are conducting performance counseling will simply not say anything for a period of time, almost certainly the other person will. If you doubt this, try it out with a friend over lunch and see what happens. (Then buy the lunch.)

- **Encourage the discouraged.**

This can be one of our most challenging problems. What can we do to help those who feel helpless? Whenever anyone feels discouraged, especially over a long period of time, it is often difficult to bounce back. Here is where empathy is particularly useful. Can you feel the helplessness or despair of the person you are trying to help? Are you able to put yourself in his or her shoes? If you can demonstrate that you sincerely care about the person you're trying to counsel and if you can show a sense of "I hurt when you do," then you will find yourself in the position where you might be able to encourage or give hope.

- **Give support without glossing over the problem.**
We shouldn't find joy in criticizing another person's behavior. One of the cornerstones of leadership is that leaders care about others and want to help them to do their best. We can show our concern for others by pointing out deficiencies and offering help with compassion, and most of all, helping those faculty members to discover ways to put their problems behind them. Let me make it clear that in these feedback sessions it is important to identify overtly the faculty member's actions—or inactions—that are bothering us. However, we must also express a feeling of confidence in the faculty member.

There are other techniques a chairperson can use to become more skillful in counseling. However, no matter how skillful you become, I suspect you will never find it easy to tell a colleague that his or her performance is lacking. I vividly remember talking to a first-year chairperson who said, "I just can't do this. I cannot tell colleagues that they must improve, even though I know they should." I know how he felt. But this newly appointed chairperson, like so many others I've known, grew into his job. He cared about faculty members, he earned their trust, and he helped them grow just as he had grown.

Some Things We Must Accept in Others and Ourselves

In dealing with chronic low achievers, we must recognize what the real problem is and what it is not. This sounds simplistic. Nonetheless, let's take a look. Is a faculty member's "problem" exacting any cost or value, or is it something that simply annoys you? I can think of many examples of a faculty member's behavior that annoyed me, but when I would examine the larger issue—was the annoying behavior hurting the department?—I would at times see that the "problem" was not really a problem at all.

In his book *From Losers to Winners: How to Manage Problem Employees . . . and What to Do if You Can't*, V. Clayton Sherman (1987) writes,

> This may seem like too simple a point to even mention, but it's been found that sometimes irritating behaviors loom too large in the supervisor's mind. A small annoyance, endured for a long period of time, can assume too much significance. Things do get blown out of proportion. There is so much work to do, so little time to do it in, and sometimes things that we might be more tolerant of in a less stressed environment can start to take center stage in our thinking. If an actual calculation of costs shows that the situation is no big deal, then relax. Neither the world nor the people in it are perfect, and maybe the answer is just to accept life's realities with good grace. (p. 83)

Sherman's advice reminds us to question our own objectivity. Let's be frank: There will always be people who are simply hard to get along with or to like. We must "accept life's realities with good grace" and get on with our work.

- Build a culture of improvement.
If we develop the understanding in our departments that improvement is a dynamic process, then performance counseling is an expected part of the process. Improvement must be tied to development and recognition for those who achieve. I've found faculty members generally are eager to learn, but many have heavy workloads and are not able to allocate the time to learn new approaches to teaching or conducting research. Thus, it seems to me that granting released time might be an appropriate reward.

Also, I think one of the best ways to bring about individual and departmental improvement is to ask faculty members to offer suggestions.

We might be surprised at how much faculty members understand about motivating chronic low achievers. Nelson (1999) writes, "The point is not to look for home runs every time out but to build a culture of improvement" (p. 270). He also suggests we make recognition a way of life.

- Build a culture of collaboration and teamwork.

If we are successful in our teamwork, I believe we will have fewer chronic low achievers. Peter Senge (2000) put it this way:

> What it means to be a manager in most organizations is to be in control; yet complex systems are not controllable in the ways managers seek. What it takes to rise up the hierarchy in most organizations is to be articulate, good at advocating your views and impressing people with your intelligence. This results in executives who typically have poor collaborative inquiry skills, who can never say in front of peers, "I don't know," or ask for the help of others in understanding problems they face—the same executives who find themselves facing complex problems where no one person can possibly have all the answers. (p. 280)

- Address the problem early.

It will certainly come as no surprise that dealing with a problem early is better than letting it fester and develop into a bigger problem, not only in your mind but as a matter of fact. Moreover, I see this as a sense of fairness. By alerting faculty members early to anything you see as a developing problem, you can help them deal with it and get on track to a more productive career. If we are careful—and sincere—when hiring for tenure-track positions, we surely must want those we hire to achieve tenure. We are obligated to mentor newly hired faculty members, provide resources to help them develop, and be alert to their struggles. As a chairperson, I made a point of having regular meetings with new faculty members. If you do this, you will be able to recognize budding problems, and you will help young faculty members get over hurdles that may seem insurmountable to them.

- **Always be in control of the performance counseling session.**

It is important that you take control whenever you are conducting performance counseling sessions. You need be neither loud nor abusive, but you must be firm and authoritative.

There will be many times when chronic low achievers will deny problems. Some may also do whatever they can to divert the discussion to other topics. If they succeed, they are in control of the session. You cannot allow that to happen. You *may* have to raise your voice to get the faculty member's attention, and you must be firm by telling him or her that the purpose of the meeting is to talk about unsatisfactory work. It's important, however, that chairpersons stay on the high road. We must not pontificate. Neither can we presume that the problem is as simple as it may seem. In *Leading Quietly*, Badaracco (2002) writes,

> Men and women who work hard to reframe and recast difficult dilemmas make an important assumption. They tend to believe that nothing is as simple as it first seems. If enough effort and imagination are applied to a problem, its complexities, and hence opportunities, emerge....
>
> Quiet leaders avoid either-or thinking. They assume that most problems, however stark and simple they may seem at first, usually have several levels of complexity. Within the complexity are usually a number of opportunities for maneuvering and imaginative recasting of problems and situations. (pp. 164–165)

I believe that chairpersons should be quiet leaders, but they must never be bulldozed by faculty members who are not achieving at expected levels. Chairpersons need to be strong, firm, and do as much as they can to raise standards and expectations. Certainly they must assume unyielding control of their performance counseling sessions.

- **Keep your goal in mind.**

We must not forget the purpose of performance counseling sessions. The goal is to improve the faculty member's performance, not to win an argument. To prepare for a counseling session, write out and then practice saying what acceptable performance in the job entails. Listen to yourself. If it doesn't make sense to you, it won't make sense to the faculty member. Be as specific as possible. Also, it helps if you can give detailed examples of poor performance if the faculty member asks you to explain. Your role is not to emphasize past poor performance, however. Try instead to define future good performance. This is especially important as you begin and end your counseling session. You want to begin on a positive note. It is equally important that you end on one as well.

- Clarify what you mean.

It is important to know whether the faculty member being counseled understands the situation the same way you do. Thus, it's a good idea from time to time to review what has proceeded in the session. You might say something like this: "John, we've been discussing your unsatisfactory performance in the classroom. Do you agree with the plan of action we are beginning to develop?" At this point you have the opportunity to see if the faculty member understands the problem and possible solution as you do. If he or she does not, you'll need to clarify the points you've been trying to make. For example, you might say, "I must stop you, John, because I have apparently failed to communicate the problem so that it has meaning to you." Note that the phrasing "I have apparently failed" can help to reduce tension or defensiveness on the part of the faculty member. You are already accusing John of having problems in the classroom, so you don't want to put still another problem on him—that is, you also have a problem listening, or you are too slow to grasp my meaning, or the like. If you label John a failure in this situation, you might very well be sending him a message that he's just not up to the task of improving his classroom performance.

- Keep good notes.

I've found it amazing that two professionals can discuss a matter and seem to come to an understanding only to find later that one version of what transpired is in sharp contrast to what the other person remembers. To prevent this, you must take good notes. (A recording of the session is helpful if the faculty member does not object.) It's important to review your notes with the faculty member at the end of the session. It's not likely to be possible to provide any written documentation immediately, but you should do this as soon as possible. Your notes should document the date of the discussion and any specific agreements you reached regarding expected performance changes.

- Always follow up.

Follow-up is critically important. It gives you a chance to reinforce your opinion of the faculty member's value. Moreover, if improvement has been identified, it gives you the opportunity of discussing it immediately, which can reinforce his or her efforts. Obviously, if the faculty member still appears to be struggling, you will need to continue the performance counseling, and you may need to provide additional tools and resources.

Performance counseling can be difficult and unpleasant, but it is something that must be done. Successful chairpersons quickly see its necessity and value. Moreover, they see positive changes being made—changes of the kind that make the workplace more comfortable and faculty members more collegial. They also see their departments reaching new levels of excellence and taking on the qualities that Wergin (2003) describes in his book *Departments That Work*.

Resources

Web Sites
Addressing and Resolving Poor Performance
www.opm.gov/er/poor/ceapp.asp

Leadership Counseling
www.nwlink.com/~donclark/leader/councel2.html

Performance Based Action
www.permerica.com/PBA/O-pba1-2.html

Performance Counseling: The Cornerstone of Professional Development
www.acenet.edu/resources/chairs/docs/Higgerson_Perf_Counseling.pdf

*Supervisor's Guide to Progressive Performance Counseling
and Corrective Action*
http://hrnt.jhu.edu/elr/counsel.cfm

Books

Lucas, A. F. (1994). *Strengthening departmental leadership: A team-building guide for chairs in colleges and universities.* San Francisco, CA: Jossey-Bass.

Weiss, D. H. (2000). *Fair, square and legal: Safe hiring, managing and firing practices to keep you and your company out of court* (3rd ed.). New York, NY: American Management Association.

References

Andersen, P. (1998). *Nonverbal communication: Forms and functions.* New York, NY: McGraw-Hill.

Badaracco, J. L., Jr. (2002). *Leading quietly: An unorthodox guide to doing the right thing.* Boston, MA: Harvard Business School Press.

Coffman, J. R. (2005). *Work and peace in academe: Leveraging, time, money, and intellectual energy through managing conflict.* Bolton, MA: Anker.

Knapp, M. L., & Hall, J. A. (2006). *Nonverbal communication in human interaction* (6th ed.). Belmont, CA: Wadsworth.

Nelson, A., with Golant, S. K. (2004). *You don't say: Navigating nonverbal communication between the sexes.* New York, NY: Berkley.

Nelson, B. (1999). Creating an energized workplace. In F. Hesselbein & P. M. Cohen (Eds.), *Leader to leader: Enduring insights on leadership from the Drucker Foundation's award-winning journal* (pp. 265–274). San Francisco, CA: Jossey-Bass.

Pood, E. A. (2003). Stripping away negative defenses. In D. R. Leaming (Ed.), *Managing people: A guide for department chairs and deans* (pp. 99–117). Bolton, MA: Anker.

Senge, P. M. (2000). The academy as learning community: Contradiction in terms or realizable future? In A. F. Lucas & Associates, *Leading academic change: Essential roles for department chairs* (pp. 275–300). San Francisco, CA: Jossey-Bass.

Sherman, V. C. (1987). *From losers to winners: How to manage problem employees . . . and what to do if you can't* (Rev. ed.). New York, NY: American Management Association.

Tucker, A. (1992). *Chairing the academic department: Leadership among peers* (3rd ed.). New York. NY: American Council on Education/Macmillan.

Wergin, J. F. (2003). *Departments that work: Building and sustaining cultures of excellence in academic programs*. Bolton, MA: Anker.

26

Dealing With Difficult Faculty

Relentlessly difficult faculty will try your patience and cause you to question your administrative skills.

Writing about difficult faculty members reminds me of a story an editor from a prominent magazine once told me. There was a foreign correspondent on his staff he had to recall because the writer had become too attached to the bottle, and his drinking was creating problems for the editor and the magazine. Upon his return to the main office, the writer burst through the editor's door yelling, "What are you trying to do, ruin my career?" The editor looked at him calmly and said, "I am just trying to save you from yourself." To that the angry correspondent replied, "Who in hell said I wanted to be saved?" Some faculty members may act that way, too. They do not want you intruding into their lives even though many seem to enjoy meddling in the lives of others. Such behavior can harm morale, intimidate other faculty members, and even make chairpersons consider going back to teaching!

As with most chairpersons, I came into the job quite unprepared—I knew next to nothing about managing a budget and not much more about managing people. I soon discovered, as most of us have, that managing people would be my biggest challenge. It would occupy most of my time and present the most vexing problems. Dealing with budget tangles, no matter how frustrating, is easy compared to dealing with people problems. Troubled faculty members I have dealt with over the years have ranged from those who suffered from substance abuse to those with serious emotional problems. They tested all my people skills as well as my patience.

While handling some personnel problems is relatively easy (e.g., making arrangements for classes to be covered for a hospitalized faculty member takes time but little else), many other personnel problems can be both time consuming and troublesome; some even defy resolution. This chapter will examine problems in the latter category—the really tough ones—and present some approaches for dealing with them.

Most faculty members do not make a conscious effort to make life difficult for others and for their chairperson. Note that I said most, not all. Likewise, many faculty members who are difficult to get along with are honestly surprised when they are told that they are being obstinate, or that their behavior creates problems for others. Their view is that others are difficult to get along with; they are not. I remember some years ago talking to a faculty member and telling him that he was argumentative. He argued long and hard that he was not.

It may be trite to suggest that people are hard to understand and that most have no idea why they act as they do. However, it bears mentioning that people are complex. They behave as they do for a multitude of hard-to-understand reasons. While we often cannot explain the perverse behavior of others, the contrary individuals almost nearly as often themselves have difficulty explaining their actions and attitudes. Unfortunately, there are few simple solutions to the problems they cause that you must try to resolve.

Guidelines for Dealing With Faculty

Let's begin this human relations investigation by looking at some guidelines for dealing with all faculty members.

- **A good administrator must be a good listener.**
Many faculty members who complain a lot just want someone to listen to them. It's obvious, of course, that we cannot respond to the needs and concerns of faculty members if we don't hear what they are saying.

When we listen to complaints, we are tempted to engage in conversation, to respond with logical arguments and/or solutions, to judge, or to criticize. Generally, it is better to listen silently, doing little more than showing concerned interest. Bennis (1997) reminds us that

> The basis of leadership is the capacity of the leader to change the mind-set, the framework of another person. Of course, that's not easy. Most of us think that we tune into the other person, when usually we listen most intently to ourselves. (p. 134)

- **Ask faculty for their advice.**

Asking faculty members for their advice helps them feel their contribution is valued. Even cantankerous people can be cooperative and affable if we seek their input.

- **Always allow others the opportunity to save face.**

It is human nature to want to crush those who attack us, but everyone is better served if difficult faculty members are given a way to save face. This is one of the reasons to avoid public reprimands of faculty or staff. Permitting a person to save face is a gracious gesture, though one occasionally gets comments like "You had your chance to get even; why didn't you?" or something similar. Good leadership is not about getting even.

On one occasion I had to ask a chairperson to resign and later someone across campus told me that the deposed chairperson had said that I had begged him or her to stay on. This did not trouble me, even though it was not true. If it was a suitable face-saving defense, that was okay with me.

Kouzes and Posner (1995) suggest that we can give external justification as a way to save face.

> Because leaders understand the intensity of this process [reversing a position], when they find it necessary to change a previous course of action—perhaps one set by a predecessor—they provide people with *external* justifications for the change. Just as we bind people to a decision by creating *internal* justification, we unbind them so that they can commit to a new course by

offering external explanations. . . . This reduces some of the pain associated with a change, makes it easier for people to distance themselves from previous positions, and readies people to commit to a new course. It's a way for all of us to save face when times do in fact change and we have to abandon something we've previously fervently supported. (p. 257)

So, if a difficult faculty member needs to blame his or her problems on some external justification, accept it.

- **Don't make snap judgments.**

People often behave the way they are expected to behave. If we decide that a particular faculty member is difficult to work with, chances are he or she will see to it that our judgment is validated. Moreover, restraint on the part of a leader is a quality worth practicing. As Badaracco (2002) notes,

Quiet leaders don't want to repress what they feel, but they do want to control and channel it as effectively as possible. They realize that taking a forceful stand on principle can be the easy way out of a problem or can make matters worse, so they restrain themselves. (p. 171)

When we are tempted to make snap judgments, we ought to restrain ourselves and reflect on the situation so as not to make matters worse.

- **Keep an open door.**

By talking with faculty members regularly, you may be able to head off problems, contain them, or keep them from escalating. Faculty members will feel better about dealing with you when there is a problem if they interact with you when there is not a problem.

By keeping an open door, we signal that we are putting people first, which, as Goleman, Boyatzis, and McKee (2002) assert, helps create productive work relationships.

Leaders who use resonance-building styles model norms that support commitment, involvement, active pursuit of the vision, and healthy productive work relationships. They create connection by focusing on what people really want and need, and by deliberately building a culture that supports good health in the tribe. When a leader focuses on people, emotional bonds are created . . . and people will follow that leader in good times and bad. (p. 221)

- When you make a mistake, admit it.

All of us make mistakes, and when we do, we should be willing to admit to them. The expression "Be big enough to admit mistakes" has real meaning. Admitting mistakes gives leaders credibility—who among us has never erred? If we fail to acknowledge mistakes, we lose credibility, and credibility is essential for all leaders. According to Kouzes and Posner (2003, p. 14),

Credibility is the foundation of leadership. Our data confirm this assertion time and time again. . . . Here are some of the common phrases people have used to describe credibility:
- "Leaders practice what they preach."
- "They walk the talk."
- "Their actions are consistent with their words."
- "They put their money where their mouth is."
- "They follow through on their promises."
- *"They do what they say they will do."*

- Look for ways to compliment faculty.

Even the weakest faculty member has qualities that permit a compliment from time to time. Often, however, we fail to let others know that we appreciate their efforts. Set aside time to observe what others are doing; let them know that you are interested in their work—and that you appreciate it. You are in a better position to point out problems if you can open a discussion with "Well, Joan, you know how much I appreciate all the good things you do for the department . . ." If you never tell

Joan that you appreciate her good work, however, you can't use these mollifying words.

- ■ **Treat everyone honestly and fairly.**

One of an administrator's most difficult jobs is telling others that their work does not meet expectations. It's tough, too, to give a faculty member a poor performance appraisal. But everyone loses—the department, students, staff, and other faculty members—if we are less than honest in dealing with such matters.

The best thing you can do to become a better chairperson is to vow that you will be open, honest, and fair. Acting from this basis supports a leader's credibility. It's hard to trust a leader who is less than honest and fair. Our suspicions grow about any leader who displays dishonest and unfair behavior. And that's the way it should be!

- ■ **Write things down.**

Not only is it important to write down reminders to avoid forgetting important things to do, but it is also important to write down any agreements that you make with faculty members. If you don't do this, you will find yourself in arguments about what you actually said. Writing memos to yourself helps avoid conflicts.

- ■ **Compromising is not necessarily a sign of weakness.**

There are times when the advantages of compromise far outweigh the advantages of holding firm. You need to look at each situation carefully and determine what course of action will serve best—now and in the future. Some chairpersons view negotiating as a sign of indecisiveness. They should remember the words of John F. Kennedy: "Compromise need not mean cowardice."

- ■ **Remember that you are their chairperson, but they are not your faculty.**

You serve as chairperson to enable faculty members to do their jobs, yet the reverse of that is not true. Certainly faculty members can do much to make your job easier, but their primary responsibility is to teach, engage in scholarly activity, and provide service. On the other hand, your chief responsibility is to make it possible for faculty members to fulfill their responsibilities.

- Remember that a faculty member is not wrong just because he or she sees things differently from the way you do.

This notion was brought sharply to my attention when a colleague pointed out that he finally understood why he was often at odds with another person. "When I rode with her to the airport not long ago and she came upon a parking area that was closed, she simply got out and moved the cones," he said. "I am the kind of person who would back up and find another parking place. But she moves the cones! I think that speaks volumes about how different our approaches to many things in life are," he concluded.

Sure enough, you will have to deal with cone movers, along with those who turn away from cones. And people who must put off important projects until the last minute, or insist on giving a student an incomplete when you wouldn't. We each view things from our own vantage point, and while we often insist on doing things our way, it may be all right to accept other ways of doing things.

Guidelines for Dealing With Difficult Faculty

Even if you are effective in your relationships with most faculty members, there will still be times when you must deal with some who are relentlessly difficult. They will try your patience and cause you to question your administrative skills. Let's consider some of these difficult people and how you might deal with them.

The Faculty Member With a Substance Abuse Problem

What should you do if you learn that a faculty member is drinking, or otherwise abusing any substance, on the job, making him or her ineffective?

This is not an easy problem, nor one you can ignore. The problem is exacerbated by the fact that it is covered under the Americans with

Disabilities Act. You cannot approach a person with a substance abuse problem by being confrontational. Instead, you must observe the person's performance relative to objective standards. If a faculty member's work suffers in comparison to those standards, deal with that issue.

If you accuse a faculty member of being an alcoholic, you could be sued for defamation. Drinking alcohol is not illegal, though it becomes your concern if a person is caught drinking while at work. If you catch a faculty member actually drinking alcohol, you have a basis for challenging his or her alcohol use.

If you believe that drinking is affecting the faculty member's work, call the person in for a conference to discuss his or her performance and your expectations. If you know he or she has been drinking on the job you can say so, though you should expect that the faculty member will deny that a problem exists. "Sure, I have a drink now and then, but it's not a problem," he may say. He could then go on to say that he doesn't have to drink, that he could quit anytime he wants to, and that you shouldn't be concerned. But you have to be insistent. Tell him (we'll use a male as an example) that if it really is not a problem, he has nothing to be concerned about. You, of course, also must tell him that you will not tolerate any drinking on the job, and that if you see any evidence of it, you will insist that he get help. That is probably all you should expect to achieve in the first meeting: putting him on notice.

Alcoholics are good at deceit; they have a lot of practice at it. The drinking probably will continue, and it will present more problems no matter how much the drinker schemes and covers up. As soon as you have evidence that he is still drinking and that it is interfering with his work, you need to take the next step: Insist that he get professional help. Your involvement from this point will depend in part on the seriousness of the problem. If the professional insists on treatment that requires extended confinement, you will have to help make arrangements for a leave of absence, as well as arrangements to assure that classes and other responsibilities are covered. Additionally, you should stand ready to provide other support that the faculty member and his family may need. This could be something as simple as expressing personal concern, or it could extend to arranging for additional support systems.

Once treatment is complete and the faculty member is back on the job, it is wise to seek professional guidance on dealing with the recovering alcoholic. The more you learn about problem drinkers, the more effective you will be in helping the faculty member cope. Your effort may be time consuming and frustrating. Setbacks seem to be the rule rather than the exception. However, the rewards that come with seeing a faculty member recover and return to a productive life are enormously gratifying.

Howard Altman (2003) suggests we make use of Employee Assistance Programs.

> Many colleges and universities have established Employee Assistance Programs (EAPs) to offer counseling and support to faculty and staff who suffer from alcohol dependency, drug abuse, gambling addiction, and other special health problems that negatively affect an employee's job performance and that are viewed as treatable. EAPs rely on proven therapies, and participation is confidential, though referral to an EAP may be by one's supervisor (e.g., department chair or dean), by family members, by colleagues in one's department, or by self-referral. (p. 148)

The Obstinate Faculty Member

Stubborn faculty members who insist on doing everything their own way can create problems, not only for you, but also for other faculty and staff members. They are not persuaded or impressed by logic. They will insist that they have all the answers and imply that suggestions that run counter to theirs are stupid and useless.

One way to deal with such a person is to look around for others who can work easily with him or her. When you identify that individual, try to find what special techniques that person uses that you don't. Ask yourself honestly if you are doing something that causes the kind of reaction you receive from the faculty member. If you are at fault, then you must modify your own behavior or accept the reaction you get.

You should be prepared to talk candidly with the obstinate faculty member about his or her behavior, explaining the problems it creates. Ask if there is anything you can do to get cooperation. There is a chance—perhaps slim, but nonetheless a chance worth hoping for—that you will find that the obstinate person is reacting to something you are doing.

If all else fails, you may have to resort to explaining the consequences of the unacceptable behavior. If it comes to this, you will probably need to point out that you have the final say on setting priorities and direction for the department and on how its resources are to be used. You also need to let the person know that getting along is much better than quarreling. Moreover, explain that you don't have time to waste on dealing with such distracting behavior.

The Weak Classroom Teacher

It is not at all uncommon to have to deal with a faculty member who is not performing up to the expected level in his or her classes. You should begin by defining the causes for the subpar performance. Does the person have the pedagogic skills? Is the faculty member preparing adequately? Are personal problems involved? If the faculty member is new, these may not be easy questions to answer. On the other hand, if the faculty member has been around awhile, the answers should be apparent. Once you've determined the reason for the faculty member's inability to perform at the expected level, you can decide how to respond. Regardless of the problem, you will have to talk about the matter directly with the faculty member.

If pedagogic skills are lacking, you may assign the person to work closely with an experienced faculty member whose skills are recognized. In addition, you might try the following:

- Have the faculty member videotape his or her classes. By studying the tape, areas for improvement can be identified. Follow-up videotaping can show if any improvement is noticeable.
- Have experienced teachers make classroom visits and share their recommendations on teaching style.
- Suggest that the faculty member ask students to recommend areas for improvement.
- Have the person sit in on other faculty members' classes.

- See if your department or college of education has courses that might benefit a struggling classroom teacher.

If the problems are not related to pedagogic skills, your challenge is even more complex. Certainly you will need the cooperation of the faculty member if significant changes are to be made.

The Department Gossip

The department gossip is an interesting, complex person. He or she enjoys passing on information about colleagues, especially if the information is disparaging.

Isolating the gossip is probably the best response. If you can persuade other faculty members that gossip is hurtful and shouldn't be tolerated, they may take the next step and tell the gossip they don't want to hear about others. If you really want to stop short a gossip, just say, "I would rather not hear about it." I also have found it effective to tell the person spreading the gossip that I feel uncomfortable talking about a colleague who isn't present. Asking, "Why don't we call Joe in and hear his side?" usually will stop the talk abruptly.

Most of us enjoy sharing news with others. We take pleasure in passing on something that others have not heard, yet most of us do not make up things or pass on unsubstantiated information, and we take special care not to pass on information that is hurtful. The department gossip, however, is not governed by the same rules of conduct, and can make the lives of his or her colleagues miserable if given the slightest opportunity. Typical gossips need a bit of truth off of which to build. For example, suppose that Smith, a new faculty member who is ABD, has to delay his dissertation defense because some members of his committee have schedule conflicts. The department gossip might report: "It's too bad Smith couldn't defend his dissertation. I understand some of his committee members have problems with the way he gathered his data." By the time this passes through a couple more gossips in the department, poor Smith—according to the stories being told—is about to be kicked out of his doctoral program!

A little sunshine is a good antiseptic, advocates of open meetings and records laws assert. Simply making the truth known will help kill rumors that gossips start or spread. If, for example, you distribute a Monday Morning Memo (explained in Chapter 6), you might insert something like: "Because of unanticipated scheduling conflicts with members of his dissertation committee, Sydney Smith has had to reschedule his defense. He says that it looks now as if all his committee members will be able to convene near the end of this month."

The Department Snitch

There are faculty members who have a compulsion to run to the dean, the vice president, or the campus newspaper with every departmental problem. This behavior is particularly frustrating when it is a problem you are not even aware of; you feel especially rankled that you have not been given an opportunity to try to solve it. Moreover, you discover that talking with the faculty member about the advantages of keeping problems "within the family" doesn't work. The following strategies may help.

Bring the problem before the faculty. Suppose you have a faculty member who has complained to your dean about the way you have allocated travel funds. At the next faculty meeting, you might say something like "John has complained to the dean about the formula we use for distributing travel funds. I think this is something that we should discuss. What are your feelings about our travel fund use?"

Note, however, that you must take care to let John know that this is something he could have put on the department agenda without complaining to the dean. If you don't make that clear, he and others may conclude that the best way to get something on the faculty agenda is to complain at a higher level.

Create a special committee for department problems. And, have the one who likes to complain chair the committee. Also, appoint others who enjoy complaining to the committee. There certainly may be some advantages in creating a legitimate forum for the complainers, but it's not necessary to stop there. I would charge the committee with coming up with possible solutions to problems they identify. Often they may see that while it is easy to complain, it is a lot more difficult to develop workable solutions.

The Loud, Abusive Faculty Member

If you've not yet had to deal with a loud, abusive faculty member, just wait. Your time will likely come. Some faculty members have learned that they can get attention by being loud and abusive, and they seem to relish targeting chairpersons. "What gives you the right to schedule a faculty meeting whenever you want ?" "Any idiot can see that I have classes to take care of, for crying out loud." "I am damned tired of imbeciles playing chairman, and if you think I'm going to take this without talking to the dean, then you've got another think coming." On and on the rant goes, getting louder and more abusive with each breath. What do you do? Here are some suggestions.

Hold your ground. Show that you cannot be intimidated in these situations. If you are sitting at your desk, remain seated. Don't become combative. If you keep calm, the loud and abusive attacker will often become unsettled and less certain—which gives you an edge.

Keep control of yourself. The worst thing you can do is to lose self-control. If that happens, you and your attacker will likely be yelling at each other, which will accomplish nothing. Instead, let the out-of-control faculty member go on with his or her tirade while you take a deep breath and think about what you might say or do.

When the blasting stops, speak calmly. You might want to say—with the calmest voice you have—"Is there anything else you want to say?" If he comes back with another attack, wait until he finishes and then ask, "And is there anything else?"

When the tirade is finished, summarize what he or she has said and what you can do to deal with those concerns. If you've been accused of something where you are in the wrong, you need to acknowledge it and indicate how you will prevent a future recurrence. On the other hand, if you have not done anything wrong, you need to calmly set the record straight.

Use the opportunity. Let the faculty member know how you like to deal with disagreements. For example, you might say, "Sue, I know you are upset, and I would like us to work out our differences, but that's not possible when you are yelling. I hope in the future you will be calm and rational when you come to me with complaints. That way, we may be able to deal with our problems. You should know that from now on I will not talk to you when you are loud and abusive. It's not a productive way to deal with problems."

A warning here: It may take several minutes to get this message across. My experience tells me that about the time you say "calm and rational," the attacker is likely to let go with another volley. "What do you mean calm and rational? Are you suggesting that I am not rational? Who gives you the right to sit in judgment of me?" And so it goes. You have to be persistent in letting the person know how you feel and how you expect to deal with his or her anger and frustration.

Interrupt if necessary. Do this by saying the person's name over and over until you get their attention and they stop talking. Remember, too, that you have to adjust to the situation.

Know that you can dictate the terms on which you will speak. Several years ago, I had a faculty member who was given to loud and abusive assaults. One day he came into my office swearing loudly at me as I was seated at my desk. I slowly stood up, pointed my finger at him, and ordered him out of my office. I told him that when he calmed down and could speak to me rationally, I would be happy to discuss his complaint with him.

The next day I called him into my office and told him that I expected more mature behavior from him. His emotional outburst had given way to calmness in the passing hours, and while he was still angry with me, I had the upper hand. After all, he was in my office at my invitation. It allowed me to set the terms of how we could disagree without losing control of our emotions.

Another time, when I was in a new situation, I was warned about a faculty member who tended to become loud and abusive. In my first such encounter with him, I asked, "Do you always have trouble controlling your emotions?" It did not immediately help me in dealing with him, but it led to a calm discussion about how we ought to respond to differences of opinion. I have always advocated expressing differences of opinion on professional matters. But we must learn how to do this without making our "professional" differences "personal."

A word of encouragement is in order here. Most faculty members are courteous and easy to get along with, and you don't have to be a street fighter to be an effective chairperson. Nonetheless, from time to time, you will have to let faculty members know that you will stand up to them if they attack you. How can you learn to do this? Here are some suggestions.

- *Role-play.* Have a friend play the role of the loud and abusive faculty member. If you make the situation as real as possible, it will feel like you are being attacked. As with any role-playing situation, you want to learn from it and get to a point where you are performing in a way that makes you feel in control.
- *Lay out your expectations, publicly.* At a faculty meeting, talk about what can be gained by having calm and reasonable discussions about differences, pointing out how it is impossible to accomplish much of anything by yelling at each other. Let faculty members know that they can expect to be treated this way by you, and you, in turn, expect to be treated the same way.
- *Always treat others with respect.* Moreover, do all you can to command respect. Faculty members are not likely to attack you verbally if they respect you. "Exemplary leaders know that if they want to gain commitment and achieve the highest standards, they must be models of behavior they expect of others" (Kouzes & Posner, 2003, p. 4).

The Lean, Mean Venting Machine

There are some people who seem to take pleasure in hurting others. Those who believe that modern society allows this kind of cruel behavior describe it as a "get even" society that accepts frankness and rudeness. As chairperson, you should protect others from this kind of person, and his or her intimidations. Most often, they will take the form of trickle-down nastiness, focusing on individuals one rung down the hierarchy. You must watch for this type of behavior, and let those who exhibit it know that it won't be tolerated. You should make it clear that you will take the side of those being abused.

The High Maintenance Faculty Member

Some faculty members, for whatever reason (and there are many), demand a lot of a chairperson's time. They want to feel needed and loved, and they need to be reassured. But how much time are you willing to give them? How much do you have to give? At what cost? And—remembering that time you give to high maintenance people is time you do not have for others—who will help those others?

Although high maintenance faculty are not necessarily difficult in the usual sense, they can become difficult problems. They will use every excuse to take up your time, and you may have to show them what this does to your schedule. While normally I kept an open-door policy, at one point—when I had a couple of faculty members walking into my office five or six times a day—I purposely made it difficult for them to see me. In the process I weaned them of their need to talk endlessly—and to take up so much of my time.

The Unmotivated Faculty Member

Faculty members who have lost their enthusiasm and who are no longer energetic and productive require special attention. The work they fail to do falls to others in the department, and morale sags. You cannot ignore this problem for long.

Performance evaluation sessions provide a good opportunity to discuss this issue with the unmotivated person. You must listen carefully and try to understand what's behind the troubling behavior. If the faculty member was once productive, what's changed? A good way to begin the discussion is to ask, "Where do you see your career going?" Or ask the person to talk about his or her goals. Regardless of the approach, you are likely to pick up on some helpful clues. This is how the conversation might proceed:

> "So, Joe, tell me about your short-term goals, and then we'll talk about where you see yourself 10 or 15 years from now."
> "That's really hard for me to discuss. I guess I just want to be here teaching the same classes that I now teach."

"Well, maybe you would like to try some new courses. We'll need someone to teach another section of Urban American History next term, and I remember how you used to inspire students to learn. Perhaps you can get that old feeling back by taking on a course you haven't taught for a long time."

"It sounds as if you're suggesting that I don't now have enthusiasm for what I'm teaching."

"Well, perhaps that's something we should talk about."

There are other approaches, of course. If merit money is available, you certainly can reward only those who are performing at a high level, which sends a message to those who aren't. Weak student evaluations often get the attention of unmotivated faculty members, too.

Faculty development can provide opportunities to challenge the unmotivated person. However, faculty development expenditures shouldn't be perceived as a reward for weak performance. Progress is possible if the right agreement is made for providing the unmotivated teacher with released time, travel funds, or other development support. You can be forthright about this by explaining that a higher level of performance will be expected in the future. Further, the faculty member must be told that evaluation follow-ups are necessary until his or her performance meets your expectations.

None of these approaches will work, however, unless you identify and deal with the root of the problem. If the faculty member is having personal problems, his or her lack of motivation undoubtedly will be evident so long as those problems persist. Likewise, if the faculty member's behavior is caused by a lack of respect or trust in you, poor motivation will likely persist until you can win back respect and trust.

Sometimes it makes sense for unmotivated faculty members to get a fresh start. You might want to see what you can do to find another teaching post for them. Frankly, I've never had much success with this, though I have known faculty members who discovered for themselves a need to start over. In more than one instance, I have heard that they were able to get back their old energy and motivation.

The truth of the matter, though, is one we ought not ignore: Given our current demographics in higher education, we have an increasing number of faculty members with long and distinguished records of good work. Some will begin to slow down, to mark time. I have seen it—and if you haven't, you probably will. I have found it especially painful when outstanding teachers have become stale in the classroom, but refuse to retire. Students make fun of them, complain that they are not learning, or conclude that the faculty member doesn't understand modern society. Sadly, you, too, realize that the faculty member's teaching is lacking. Yet because you have had so much respect for him or her or because you are a personal friend, you feel badly for them.

The foregoing assumes the faculty member is approaching retirement, but this is not always the case. People like this are often powerful in their departments, even though they have quit learning and have grown stale. Seasoned chairpersons find them difficult to deal with, and new, incoming chairpersons know they cannot afford to make them angry. We may be tempted to ignore them. But can we? Should we?

Each such situation is different. Still, you might try the following, depending on the nature of the situation.

Talk to family members. This is a sensitive area, and one that you should not engage in without careful contemplation and discussion with appropriate campus officials. You should not give the appearance of pressuring the person to retire. With those considerations in mind, it might nonetheless be possible for you to talk with a caring family member and tell him or her that "John is having real problems in the classroom," giving specific examples of what is happening. Of course, your reason for talking with the family is to see if together you can help devise strategies to assist the faculty member with taking direct action for dealing with the problem, which may mean retirement.

Talk to campus officials. It is possible that the university would be willing to develop some arrangements so that the faculty member could teach less by taking on other responsibilities. If money is a problem, finding some way for the faculty member to cope will be critical.

Get to know the faculty member better. The problem may not be age, though we are quick to blame it when performance declines. In addition to money problems, there may be many other concerns or worries. Perhaps a faculty member would like to retire but is reluctant because she can't deal well with a husband who makes life miserable for her at home. Or it may be that the faculty member needs to care for elderly parents. If your relationship with the faculty member is strictly professional, you are not likely to learn about such personal concerns.

We often forget that our colleagues may not have others in whom they can confide. Can you make it comfortable for them to share some of the personal things in their life that trouble them? Do you want to play that role? If you can, and are willing to accept that as a part of your responsibility as chairperson, you may be able to help, but not everyone is able to make this "beyond the job" commitment.

Difficult faculty members are a challenge—we can read book after book and attend conferences and workshops on the subject, only to discover that faculty members don't fit in the neat categories represented here. Moreover, we soon discover that a strategy that works for one will not necessarily work for another faculty member who exhibits similar behavior. If I could sum up my advice in just a few words, it would be this: Listen carefully, have a good sense of humor, and get to know and be comfortable with yourself so that you can be secure.

Resources

Web Sites

Dealing with Challenging Faculty
www.acenet.edu/resources/chairs/docs/Dealing_Challenging_
Faculty.pdf

Difficult Situations, Difficulties with Faculty Members
www.adfl.org/adfl/bulletin/v25n3/253026.htm

Books

Axelrod, A., & Holtje, J. (1997). *201 ways to deal with difficult people: A quick-tip survival guide.* New York, NY: McGraw-Hill.

Brinkman, R., & Kirschner, R. (2002). *Dealing with people you can't stand: How to bring out the best in people at their worst*. New York, NY: McGraw-Hill.

Friedman, P. (1994). *How to deal with difficult people* (Rev. ed.). Mission, KS: Skillpath Publications.

References

Altman, H. B. (2003). Dealing with troubled faculty. In D. R. Leaming (Ed.), *Managing people: A guide for department chairs and deans* (pp. 139–155). Bolton, MA: Anker.

Badaracco, J. L., Jr. (2002). *Leading quietly: An unorthodox guide to doing the right thing*. Boston, MA: Harvard Business School Press.

Bennis, W. (1997). *Managing people is like herding cats*. Provo, UT: Executive Excellence.

Goleman, D., Boyatzis, R., & McKee, A. (2002). *Primal leadership: Realizing the power of emotional intelligence*. Boston, MA: Harvard Business School Press.

Kouzes, J. M., & Posner, B. Z. (1995). *The leadership challenge: How to keep getting extraordinary things done in organizations*. San Francisco, CA: Jossey-Bass.

Kouzes, J. M., & Posner, B. Z. (2003). *The Jossey-Bass academic administrator's guide to exemplary leadership*. San Francisco, CA: Jossey-Bass.

27

Recruiting and Retaining Students

As we recruit students to our programs we must be forthright, honest, and possess the ethical qualities that others consider virtuous.

Developing effective student recruitment programs is likely to become even more challenging as virtual universities—such as the University of Phoenix—grow and offer increasingly attractive options to potential students. Moreover, there are mixed views about whether enrollments will increase in the coming decades. There are so many uncertainties that it is difficult to predict with any degree of accuracy what enrollments will look like in the coming years. Nonetheless, most futurists remain positive and believe the demands for higher education are likely to increase, such as Clark Kerr (2001), who writes,

> Total enrollments in all forms of education will continue to rise but be more subject to short-term fluctuations, as the rate of return to a college education falls and rises as the opportunities for career advancement fluctuate with the economy. In contrast, in earlier centuries access to class status was a more stable basis for enrollments than are current labor market fluctuations. (p. 224)

Even more encouraging are reports from the National Center for Education Statistics. In the coming years, the center projects the following college enrollment increases:

- 19 percent, to 18.2 million, in the middle alternative projections;

- 15 percent, to 17.7 million, in the low alternative projections; and
- 23 percent, to 18.8 million, in the high alternative projections. (Gerald & Hussar, 2003, p. 8)

These figures are supported by additional data that show an increase in the number of college-age students in the coming decades. A recent report on the health of American education shows that even with a number of negative variables introduced, college enrollment should increase by at least 9% (Hussar, 2005).

Informed chairpersons will see possibilities for recruiting the kinds of students they need to strengthen their departments. They will recognize that a diverse population of students is crucial, and they will tailor recruitment efforts to meet the needs of their department. They must, however, do this with honesty. It is troubling to see administrators who consider enrollment growth as an end in itself. As a dean, I struggled with one department that was far too big and that continued to actively recruit students even though job placement rates were pitifully low. This was, for me at least, a breach of morality. Davis (2003) lists admissions and integrity in marketing as ethical issues leaders face. I suggest as well that integrity in recruiting is an issue each chairperson must confront. Certainly as we recruit students to our programs, we must be forthright, honest, and possess the kind of ethical qualities that others consider virtuous.

Chairpersons may benefit from examining recruitment practices—both good and bad—at some of the for-profit higher education institutions. One example might be DeVry University, which among the for-profits ranks second in enrollment only to the University of Phoenix. As of 2006, DeVry had more than 50,000 students at 25 campuses in the United States and Canada. The tuition cost is considerably higher than its regional public university rivals, and therefore its advertising and recruiting must persuade potential students of its worth. They sell the idea of "Come to DeVry for a career, not a job." Increasing enrollment must be the paramount concern for any for-profit university. DeVry spends 10% of its budget on recruiting. As

Kirp (2003) writes, "In their eagerness to close the deal, . . . salesmen sometimes oversell, skirting the border of misrepresentation when they solicit applicants who, based on their academic records, have almost no chance of success" (p. 244).

Good recruiting practices should be carefully thought out. Chairpersons and others who assist in recruiting students need to be clear about the kinds of students they seek—and for what purpose. Moreover, we must recognize that recruitment and retention work hand in hand.

> The ability of a student to become integrated into institutional life has been shown to be a key to retention. Institutions therefore plan activities around this notion to attempt to integrate or "fit" students socially and academically into the institution with varying degrees of success. The greater the congruence between the student's values, goals, and attitudes and those of the college, the more likely that the student will persist at the college. (Seidman, 1989, p. 40)

This chapter presents some practical tips on recruiting, many of which can be quite inexpensive and require little time and effort. One relatively common and cost-effective approach is to write personal letters to all students who have expressed an interest in a particular field of study. Your admissions office should receive lists of students who, when taking the ACT or SAT tests, indicate your university as an institution of choice. These tests also ask what the individual intends to study and provides his or her test scores. Thus, you can get the names and home addresses of genuine prospective students. If the chairperson wishes to be selective, letters can be sent only to those persons who score at a predetermined level.

Using Alumni to Help Recruit Students

If your department has alumni who have become well known, their support can be enlisted. Here is how they can be of special assistance.

1. Identify students who have test scores at or above a predetermined level. For example, you might decide that all students who have composite scores of 25 or above on the ACT and who have expressed an interest in your school and your discipline should be sent letters.
2. Draft a letter, then share it and the recruiting concept with a well-known alumnus or alumna to see if he or she is willing to let you prepare letters on his or her letterhead.
3. After letters are prepared, signed by the alumnus or alumna, and returned to your office, mail them to the persons you are trying to recruit.
4. Here is the beginning of a sample letter:

    Mr. Joseph Stillwell
    121 Mt. Savage Lane
    Ashland, KY 60511

    Dear Joseph:
    I am pleased to learn of your interest in Midwest University, and I am particularly pleased to hear that you are thinking about majoring in English. As one who studied English at Midwest University, let me tell you something about its courses, programs, and faculty.

5. Invite alumni to make personal contact or write letters to prospective students who live in their area.

Subscribing to a clipping service to get the names of high school students who engage in certain activities or receive special honors can provide another means of student recruitment. For example, if your department sponsors a forensics program, from newspaper clips you can retrieve the names of students who participate in and win awards in forensics. A congratulatory letter from you, along with information about the department, might be just the thing to persuade a student to think positively about attending your university. Incidentally, simply monitoring the education section of selected newspapers will provide much of the same information.

Many publications list awards, honors, and scholastic activities, generally in Sunday editions.

Using Targeted Recruiting Programs

The examples of recruiting activities in this chapter are related mainly to journalism because I chaired a journalism department at the time I implemented these successful recruiting programs. However, I believe that most will work as well for other academic programs provided you tailor them to your department's needs and resources. For example, the program discussed next could just as easily be titled the Scholastic Music Program.

The Scholastic Journalism Program

This program is intended to give a taste of college life to high school students planning to study journalism. Selected students spend three days on campus, living in a dormitory, attending classes, and working on publications or other student activities.

The program began several years ago at Marshall University when announcements were sent to journalism teachers and principals at high schools throughout West Virginia and in parts of Ohio and Kentucky. The announcements explained the purposes and procedures of the program, and were accompanied by student application forms.

Two Scholastic Journalism Program students of the same sex are brought to campus at the same time. They share a dormitory room, and each is assigned a college companion who is either a junior or senior journalism major. When the students arrive, they are first given a tour of the School of Journalism. They then check into their dorm rooms and thereafter attend classes with their assigned companion. The schedule allows time for the high school student to work on a story for the campus daily newspaper. The student receives a story assignment from the managing editor and is guided through the process of writing the story using a computer in the newsroom. Either a faculty member or a newspaper staff person assists.

The schedule includes more than class work. If there is an art series activity, a sports event, or a special lecture, high school students attend with their companion. If no special events are taking place, participating students may be taken to a movie or visit the Huntington Museum of Art, or even the Huntington Mall. While the schedule is full, it is flexible enough to accommodate a student's special interests. For example, if a student is interested in band, an appointment is arranged with the band director, and if a student expresses concern over financial aid, arrangements are made for a talk with an appropriate university representative.

The program brings 20 to 30 high school students to campus each year. Because of the good response to the program, the School of Journalism has been able to be highly selective. It looks for students who have a strong commitment to studying college journalism and those who have superior academic ability.

An assessment made after the first years of the program indicates:

- By the time high school participants leave campus, they feel at home at Marshall University.
- After spending several days with a student from another high school, a college companion, and students working on the campus daily newspaper, solid friendships are established. Indeed, several of the participants correspond regularly with their new friends, and faculty members have observed that those who were together in the program are often seen together after they become college students.
- Those who have been through the program become active in student publications even as college freshmen, which at Marshall University is unusual.

It is especially important to get all faculty members in the School of Journalism involved. Every effort should be made for participants to meet all faculty members sometime during their campus stay. Also, pairing the college companion with the high school student should be done with care.

Except for time, the program costs very little. Arrangements are made through the university admissions office to secure dorm rooms at no cost. The participants pay their own travel expenses except in special financial need circumstances. The school pays for some special activities such as art-ist series events, but costs are minimal.

The application form asks for the usual information. Applicants describe their high school journalism experiences and tell why they want to participate in the program, and each is expected to sign a statement affirming his or her interest in studying journalism at the college level. Either their high school journalism teacher or their high school principal must nominate applicants.

Faculty members, as well as participants, have responded favorably to the program. The following letter, received from a student shortly after his campus visit, is typical.

Dear Dr. Leaming:

Thank you for the letter that I received this week. Also, thank you for allowing me to participate in the Scholastic Journalism Program. I truly enjoyed every minute of my stay, and I espe-cially enjoyed working on the Parthenon staff. Betsy, my two college companions, Dave Jenkins and Eric Rinehart, and those I came into contact with during those three days made it so much fun that I really hated to leave. I believe that I have made a few friendships that I cannot possibly forget, while at the same time, I learned more in three days than I could have hoped to imagine.

As for my future, I have firmly decided that Marshall Uni-versity and the W. Page Pitt School of Journalism will be seeing me after I graduate from East. Its credentials and atmosphere are just what I want in my college education. I am now counting down the days when I can begin my college career at Marshall.

Again, I thoroughly enjoyed being on campus, as I am sure that Pat Sanders did, also.

Sincerely,
(signed) Danny Adkins

(Danny did enroll at Marshall, as did the other participant, Pat Sanders. Both went on to earn journalism degrees.)

We photographed the students in various activities while they were on campus, and we mailed with a picture stories to their hometown newspapers which told of their participation in the program as well as something about the program itself.

The Ambassador Program

The Marshall University School of Journalism also developed the Journalism Ambassador Program to involve current students in new student recruitment. It is designed to help inform high school students about the journalism program at Marshall. Journalism majors apply to become "ambassadors" to the high school from which they graduated. Those selected return to their schools during university breaks, where they visit a journalism or English class to speak about studying journalism at Marshall.

Training sessions help ambassadors plan and carry out recruitment responsibilities. Each is asked to write a letter to a former high school teacher asking to visit a class during a break from university studies. Sample letters as well as instructions on making presentations before a high school class are provided. Ambassadors receive information about courses of study, enrollment, and special features to use in their presentations, and are given brochures and pamphlets to pass out to the high school students.

An effort is made to select at least one ambassador from each high school represented in the applications. After each ambassador makes a visit, he or she provides the department with a visit report, including the names of interested students. Often high school students inquire about other academic disciplines at Marshall, and representatives of other departments are asked to respond to those inquiries.

In conjunction with these programs, the School of Journalism instituted two simple campaigns aimed at providing identity for Marshall journalism. Out of private funds, Marshall journalism window decals were purchased and were given to students, faculty members, alumni, and friends. Special Marshall journalism sweaters were made up in school colors and sold or given away to more than 150 individuals.

Other activities to recruit and gain support from alumni and friends for Marshall's School of Journalism are also pursued. The school publishes a regular alumni newsletter and has established a wall of fame to recognize outstanding alumni. The school formed a Marshall Journalism Alumni Association, whose members have helped raise funds and recruit students.

Using Web Sites for Recruiting

Anyone who has browsed the Internet and examined university web sites knows that while some are attractive and provide useful information, many others are less user-friendly. To effectively provide information about your department, consider the following guidelines.

- Seek the optimal balance between visual sensation and graphic and text information.
- Use shape, color, and contrast to give visual impact to your home page. Otherwise it will be graphically boring.
- Design a good contrast between foreground and background elements. I have seen many pages that are especially difficult to read because there is little contrast between the type and the page. Dense text documents without the contrast and visual relief offered by graphics and careful page layout and typography are more difficult to read, especially on the low-resolution screens of today's personal computers. Black text on a white background is the easiest to read.
- Timely information on your home page is important. Thus, web sites should be updated regularly.
- Keep the pages uncluttered and clean. Many pages are too busy and lack a strong dominant focal point. The page should be a well-organized composition.
- While photographs and graphics are attractive, remember that the more of these that are used the longer it takes to open a file, and many

viewers may not be willing to wait. Be judicious in the use of graphics and animation.

- Provide easy to follow links and "hot spots."
- Be interactive. Good interactivity engages the user and makes your site memorable.
- Make logical use of type styles and sizes.
- Design for the lowest common denominator. This speaks to what type of computer the end user has, platform type, power, color capability, size of monitor, and so on.

College-Choice Characteristics

The 2005 TeensTALK™ study conducted by Stamats Communications reveals the college-choice characteristics that are important to students bound for either private or public institutions. As you develop recruiting strategies, they should emphasize the college-choice characteristics that students value most. The top 10 characteristics are listed in Table 27.1.

You should also be aware of the bottom 10 college-choice characteristics noted in the study. Table 27.2 presents this information.

Also noted in the 2005 TeensTALK™ study are some successful recruiting strategies. For both private-bound and public-bound college students,

Table 27.1 Top 10 College-Choice Characteristics

1. Strong program in what I want to study
2. Graduates of the college get good jobs
3. Faculty are good teachers and mentors
4. The college will make me a well-rounded individual
5. Graduates are accepted into good graduate programs
6. Overall academic reputation
7. Amount of financial aid available, including scholarships
8. The people on campus are welcoming and friendly
9. Small student-to-faculty ratio
10. School is in a cool city or area

Note. Reprinted with permission.

Table 27.2 Bottom 10 College-Choice Characteristics

1. My family has a connection to the school
2. No one at the college knows me
3. The school has a religious affiliation
4. The school is close enough to home for me to commute
5. Lots of students/big school
6. Strong athletic program
7. Strong fine arts program
8. School is in a cool city or area
9. Small student-to-faculty ratio
10. The attractiveness of campus grounds

Note. Reprinted with permission.

the top three practices students are most likely to respond to are a campus visit, information about a major, and the college's web site.

As tuition costs continue to rise, your recruiting materials should emphasize the value of the college degree and what it provides today's students. Highlight what your graduates are doing, what jobs and careers they have entered, what graduate schools they attend, and what opportunities they are realizing.

Developing Retention Programs

While much time and effort have gone into establishing and carrying out recruitment activities, you should be equally concerned with retaining students. You should get to know students, and faculty should take their advising responsibilities seriously. Faculty members need to provide special activities for currently enrolled students.

One such example at Marshall is the effective Leaving the Nest program, a series of seminars designed to assist students in finding and succeeding in jobs upon graduation. Typically, the seminars are scheduled over a five-day period. The first provides instruction on constructing a résumé. The second deals with finding job openings. At the third seminar, interviewing for a job is discussed. The fourth features tips on coping in the workplace. The last seminar is a wrap-up session presented by the director of Marshall's career planning and placement office, who provides tips on getting and keeping jobs and explains the services of the placement office.

Designing Retention Programs

Designing effective retention programs requires the same careful strategies as does creating recruitment programs. With some thought, we can quickly come up with ideas that should help at-risk students. For example:

- Have student advisors carefully monitor those students identified to be at risk.
- Assign tutors to at-risk students.
- Have faculty members turn in regular progress reports for at-risk students.
- Have student advisors identify causes for those students who are at risk. For example, does the student need remedial work? Does the student belong in college or would a technical or community college be more fitting? How much psychological support is the student getting from home? Does the student have unrealistic expectations?
- Would assigning another advisor benefit the student?

Before developing a retention program, it's a good idea to look at the research. Retention of college students in America continues to be a serious problem. One report states that less than 50% of students entering four-year colleges or universities actually graduate (Hersh & Benjamin, 2001). During the past decade, however, there has been an increase in studies of student retention and graduation rates due partly to enrollment declines in some regions and at some private institutions and to the emergence of institutional accountability. Colleges and universities are seeking insight into why some students persist and graduate and others do not, and why some institutions are doing better than others at graduating students. Studies have shown that retention is a complex, multifaceted phenomenon.

According to a recent survey by ACT (Habley & McClanahan, 2004, p. 12), the following characteristics contribute to attrition on college campuses:

1. Inadequate preparation for college-level work
2. Lack of educational aspirations and goals
3. First generation to attend college
4. Commuting/living off campus
5. Socioeconomic disadvantage
6. Indecision about major
7. Indecision about career goal
8. Inadequate financial resources
9. Weak commitment to earning a degree
10. Lack of motivation to succeed
11. Physical health problems
12. Mental or emotional health problems
13. Lack of support from significant others (e.g., spouse, parents, peers)
14. Too many family demands
15. Too many job demands
16. Poor social integration (peer group interaction, extracurricular activities)
17. Poor academic integration
18. Distance from permanent home
19. Poor study skills
20. Inadequate personal coping skills

How do colleges develop effective retention programs to offset these attrition data? This same ACT (Habley & McClanahan, 2004) study noted that

> the greatest contribution to retention fall[s] into three main categories.
> - *First-year programs:* including freshman seminar/university 101 for credit, learning communities, and integration of academic advising with first-year programs
> - *Academic advising:* including advising interventions with selected student populations, integration of advising with

first-year programs, academic advising centers and centers that combine academic advising and career-life planning

- *Learning support:* including a comprehensive learning assistance center/lab, reading center/lab, supplemental instruction, and required remedial/developmental coursework (p. 20)

Universities that truly care for students and are willing to spend money to keep them can certainly develop effective retention programs. By studying research that tells us why students drop out and why they stay in school, it would not be difficult to develop appropriate kinds of support systems. You have a special responsibility to work with your faculty to ensure they value the importance of caring for students—and showing students that they care. Also, they need to understand how important quality teaching and advising are to retaining students. Most other areas that influence students to stay in school are out of your control, but you can use your influence to encourage university efforts to see students through to graduation.

Recruiting and retaining students will become an increasingly important activity for departments if current enrollment is to be maintained. While the direct purpose and benefit are evident, recruitment and retention activities have the additional potential of cementing relationships among students, alumni, and faculty. They also motivate faculty members to assess their department's program and activities and to think about its overall mission and how it is being fulfilled.

Resources

Web Sites

Center for the Study of College Student Retention
www.cscsr.org/article_recruitment_begins.htm#top

Consortium for Student Retention Data Exchange
www.ou.edu/csrde/index.html

Books

Hersh, R. H., & Merrow, J. (2005). *Declining by degrees: Higher education at risk*. New York, NY: Palgrave Macmillan.

Seidman, A. (2005). *College student retention: Formula for student success*. Westport, CT: Praeger.

References

Davis, J. R. (2003). *Learning to lead: A handbook for postsecondary administrators*. Westport, CT: Praeger.

Gerald, D. E., & Hussar, W. J. (2003). *Projections of education statistics to 2013* (NCES 2004–013). Washington, DC: U.S. Department of Education, National Center for Education Statistics.

Habley, W. R., & McClanahan, R. (2004). *What works in student retention? All survey colleges*. Iowa City, IA: ACT, Inc.

Hersh, R. H., & Benjamin, R. (2001). *Assessing the quality of student learning: An imperative for state policy and practice*. New York, NY: Council for Aid to Education.

Hussar, W. J. (2005). *Projections of education statistics to 2014* (NCES 2005–074). Washington, DC: U.S. Department of Education, National Center for Education Statistics.

Kerr, C. (2001). *The uses of the university* (5th ed.). Cambridge, MA: Harvard University Press.

Kirp, D. L. (2003). *Shakespeare, Einstein, and the bottom line: The marketing of higher education*. Cambridge, MA: Harvard University Press.

Seidman, A. (1989). Recruitment begins with retention: Retention begins with recruitment. *Colleague*. State University of New York, 40–45.

Stamats Communications. (2005). *TeensTALK™2005*. Cedar Rapids, IA: Author.

28

Dealing With Emotional and Disrespectful Student Behavior

We should not assume that just because students are legally adults they will have adult social skills.

When we consider how emotional and/or disrespectful behavior can cause problems for chairpersons, we generally think of faculty members or students. However, in reality, we can also face such problems when we interact with parents. In this chapter, we will look at emotional and disrespectful behavior that arises in our communication with students and parents. Dealing with difficult faculty members is discussed in Chapter 22.

Remaining calm and levelheaded is essential for dealing with most problems. When problems involve emotions, these qualities become critical. If we have to confront people who are emotionally ill, we not only must remain calm and levelheaded, but must know something about intervening in these special problem areas. Most people who become chairpersons are not trained therapists, and it's likely they have not had experience working with mentally ill individuals. So what should a chairperson do in such situations? There is no one answer, but this chapter will present some suggestions and solutions.

Let's turn first to recent findings of the American College Health Association, as shown in Figure 28.1.

The data in Figure 28.1 show the problems that affect the emotional well-being of students. Stress, sleep problems, concern for family or friends, and relationship problems all might very well lead to disrespectful behavior or lack of concern for fellow students and faculty members. These problems are evidenced every day in American college and university classrooms. As instructors move up the academic ladder, they become

Figure 28.1

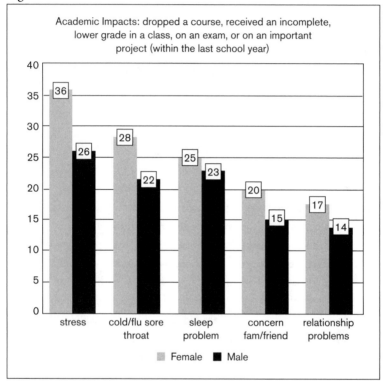

Source. 2005 American College Health Association, National College Health Assessment.

increasingly knowledgeable about how to deal effectively with classroom behavior problems. Most who cannot adjust their own behavior to deal with student problems don't remain in teaching very long.

Strategies for Dealing With Disrespectful Classroom Behavior

Here are some practical ways of dealing with students who are disrespectful in classes. The strategies included are more from what I know about human behavior than from personal experiences. My graduate studies, as well as a year-and-a-half-long internship and study at the famed Menninger Psychiatric Clinic and Foundation, helped prepare me to cope with these problems.

- **Meet privately with disrespectful students.**

Often the first response to behavioral problems should be to meet privately with any student creating a disrespectful situation in class. Your message to the student should be very clear: As long as you are in my class, this behavior will not be tolerated. However, you should try to go beyond this to learn if there is any underlying cause for the behavior.

Our communication skills are critically important in this endeavor. We must show a willingness to care about the student's problem in all that we say and do. Verbal and nonverbal skills are critically important. We should ask ourselves how we would like to be treated in a similar situation. Putting yourself in the student's shoes should help you to see what you might do to get the student to discuss his or her problem. Suppose, for instance, that the student was unable to get much sleep because of a bad dormitory situation. Knowing what this feels like could make it easier for you to be empathic. Simply listening carefully often elicits helpful insights.

After gaining an understanding of the student's situation, you might then be able to refer him or her to someone on campus for help. The academy is typically a caring, helpful community, and often students need only be pointed in the right direction to get the help they need.

- **Let the students sort it out.**

One time, I had more than one student talking and not paying attention to what I was discussing. At that point I told the students I was leaving the room and when I returned I expected them to have worked out the problem of student interruption while I was trying to teach. In no more than five minutes a student came out to say "Everything's cool." Sure enough, the students were attentive and remained that way throughout the semester. I don't know what was said, but clearly some of the serious students took the disrupters to task.

In my experience, students like to take control over their learning situations and are happy to intervene when things are not going well. Most students like to be treated as adults, and they enjoy opportunities to show they can handle adult situations. We give powerful symbolic messages to students whenever we show them that we believe they can act as responsible young adults.

I have found that one of the best ways of dealing with problem students is to know something about them and their expectations. During my first meeting with each new class, I had students complete a "You Tell Me" form so that I could learn about each person's background and expectations. Figure 28.2 shows an example of such a form.

- **Follow up with class assessment.**

We can impress upon our students their responsibility in making the classroom a meaningful and productive place if we follow up periodically with classroom assessment.

You might ask questions similar to the following.

- Have I met your expectations?
- What have you gained so far from this course?
- Have your classmates met your expectations?
- Have your contributions to the class been consistently meaningful and adult?
- What will you do to improve the way this course is working for you?
- What can I do to improve your learning?

- **Intervene when disrespectful behavior occurs.**

Although this is not my first preference, there are times when a teacher must stop the disrespectful behavior when it's taking place. We cannot allow students to take control of the classroom. If a student is causing serious and protracted problems, you should try first to ask the student to go out into the hallway with you so that you can discuss the troubling behavior. However, if a student refuses to do that, the teacher must be firm and to the point so the student is aware that the troubling behavior must

Figure 28.2 Background/Expectations Questionnaire

To help me understand as much as possible about you, so that I can assist you in taking control of your own learning, please complete this form. I will be the only person to have access to this information.

Name _____

How many years of college have you completed?_____

What is your overall GPA?_____

How many hours a week do you anticipate
studying for this course? _____

Are you taking this course because it is required? _____

On a scale from 1–10 (with 10 being the highest), how likely would you be to take this course if it were not required? _____

What grade do you expect from this course? _____

In the spaces below, please answer the following questions.

What do you hope to learn from this course?

What do you expect from the course instructor?

What do you expect from your classmates?

What will you contribute to your classmates?

What will you do to make this course work for you?

How would you describe yourself?

How would your best friend describe you?

continued on next page

Figure 28.2 Background/Expectations Questionnaire *(continued)*

Place a checkmark next to the words or phrases that best describe you.

___ 1. Friendly, outgoing

___ 2. Studious
___ 3. Serious

___ 4. Respectful
___ 5. Difficult to get along with at times

___ 6. Caring
___ 7. Generally not serious

___ 8. Have a keen sense of humor
___ 9. Withdrawn

___ 10. Careless
___ 11. Carefree

___ 12. Responsible
___ 13. Love to party

___ 14. Enjoy being alone
___ 15. When possible, I want to be around others

___ 16. See life as difficult
___ 17. Have family support

___ 18. Have a best friend on campus
___ 19. Have difficulty getting to know others

___ 20. Have a hard time making friends
___ 21. I know I will become successful

___ 22. I would rather let others lead
___ 23. I am a take-charge person

___ 24. I get tired of being around people
___ 25. Success for me is hard to grasp

___ 26. I expect to graduate on time
___ 27. My parents question why I am in college

___ 28. I sometimes question why I am in college
___ 29. Success is only important if I don't hurt others

___ 30. Getting ahead in any way I can is important to me

stop. Attack the behavior and not the student. In rare instances, you may have to summon the campus security office for help.

- **Make a note on a student's paper.**

There are times when all you need to do is to alert the student to his or her troubling behavior by writing a short note to the student at the bottom of a returned assignment or test. This is particularly helpful if you think the student may not be aware that his or her behavior is creating a problem.

- **What do other faculty do?**

It might be wise to devote one faculty meeting to a discussion of classroom behavior. Alert faculty members ahead of time and ask if any are willing to tell how they handle problems. Sharing problems creates an atmosphere of caring, helps build community, and fosters better relationships.

- **Examine your own behavior.**

Sometimes, our own behavior may contribute to unruly classroom behavior, so we need to examine ourselves to see if what we are doing contributes to student disrespect. We should make sure that we model the behavior we expect; for example, we must be on time and well prepared. Moreover, we should make every effort to connect with each of our students—we should arrive early and stay after each class to encourage them to talk to us. We also can make certain that classrooms are arranged so there are no barriers and distance between our students and us. Course syllabi should include a section on the behavior and conduct expected.

- **Live with realistic assumptions.**

We should not assume that just because students are legally adults they will have adult social skills. You may want to give some time to discussing what it means to be a college adult. You can talk about courtesy and respect and why they matter—not just during college years but also after students enter the workforce. Over my many years in education, I have seen brilliant students who were socially inept. I believe one of our jobs as educators is to help students learn the appropriate social skills.

Dealing With Disrespectful Parents

I've had little direct experience dealing with disrespectful parents. Indeed, most of my experiences interacting with parents have been positive. However, I remember one occasion when I was a dean and had to deal with parents of a student who had not received the grade he expected. When the mother of the student called, I told her I would prefer that her son come see me if he had problems with his grades. She replied, "He would never do that. I've always handled these matters for him." You can already see a part of the problem.

As it turned out, a faculty member had written on the student's paper that he could have given more effort to the project. The mother demanded that I fire the faculty member for being so insensitive to her son. I tried reasoning with the mother, but it was impossible. In fact, I finally had to tell her that the only way I would even entertain a discussion with the faculty member was if her son would file a complaint with me. The mother became very emotional and began calling me names. Eventually I had to hang up on her. Shortly after, the father called. At first, he took the same approach that his wife had, but eventually I was able to reason with him. I explained how the faculty member was simply doing his job by trying to prepare his son for the workplace, and that a lower grade than expected would not be nearly as harsh as being fired or reprimanded at work.

My advice is to listen carefully to what parents tell us, to work as hard as we know how to remain patient and levelheaded, and to respond to all reasonable complaints. Parents should be interested in the welfare of their college sons or daughters. We wouldn't want it any other way, though we must understand that at times we may be treated disrespectfully.

Working With Students Who Have Emotional Problems

In a recent report, *Washington Post* staff writer Rick Weiss (2005) writes,

> One-quarter of all Americans met the criteria for having a mental illness within the past year, and fully a quarter of those had a "serious" disorder that significantly disrupted their ability to function day to day, according to the largest and most detailed survey of the nation's mental health . . . (p. A03)

As educators, we have a responsibility to help all students, even those whose illnesses we sometimes do not understand. Dealing with students who have emotional problems is often difficult. The best we can do at times is to be understanding and caring, and try to assess the underlying cause for a student's behavior. When we can't, which is not unusual, we need to refer the student to someone who has the appropriate expertise. Most campuses have counseling and health centers. Also, a team approach might be important if immediate intervention is necessary. Pavela (2000) suggests that

> The team might be composed of a police officer, a mental health specialist, and a legal advisor. Trained to work together, such a team would normally respond quickly to incidents indicating a student was suffering from a serious mental disorder, or posed a risk to self or others. (p. A03)

Faculty members often rally around students suffering from health problems that are physical in nature. We should do the same for those who suffer from mental illness. I have seen students with many kinds of mental illnesses, and I have watched them try to cope, though others around them had no idea what the students were dealing with. We can only imagine the chaos that dwells within the mind of those who suffer from mental illness. It's incumbent on those in academic leadership positions to extend a helping hand. I cannot imagine anything more satisfying than helping students who are disabled—whether physically or mentally—overcome their problems and go on to lead successful, productive lives. To me, this is the essence of leadership.

Resources

Web Sites
Campaign for America's Mental Health
www.nmha.org/camh/college/fact_sheets.cfm

Dealing With Students Experiencing Emotional Distress
www.buffalostate.edu/depts/counsel/index_6.html

Emotional Problems Can Blindside College Students
www.collegian.psu.edu/archive/2001/09/09-11-01tdc/09-11-01dsci-
health1.asp

University of Florida Counseling Center
www.counsel.ufl.edu/

Books

Evans, N. J., Forney, D. S., & Guido-DiBrito, F. (1998). *Student development in college: Theory, research, and practice.* San Francisco, CA: Jossey-Bass.

Levine, A., & Cureton, J. S. (1998). *When hope and fear collide: A portrait of today's college student.* San Francisco, CA: Jossey-Bass.

O'Quinn, P. O., Ratey, N. A., & Maitland, T. L. (2000). *Coaching college students with AD/HD: Issues and answers.* Silver Spring, MD: Advantage Books.

References

Pavela, G. (2000, September 11). Responding to disruptive students: A case study. *Synfax Weekly Report.* Retrieved July 13, 2006, from www.collegepubs.com/ref/SFX000911.shtml

Weiss, R. (2005, June 7). Study: U.S. leads in mental illness, lags in treatment. *Washington Post*, p. A03.

29

Moving Up the Administrative Ladder

Before accepting any administrative position, you should know exactly what is expected.

M y move into administration was not planned, and my sense is that most of those who serve in some administrative capacity did not begin their careers in higher education with the goal of working in administration. My first administrative job came shortly after I began teaching at Kansas State University. I was in my second year when the long-time chairperson announced he was retiring early. This was during the 1960s, a time when students were demanding reform on campuses all across the country. What this meant at Kansas State was that we had two search committees—one made up of students and another of faculty. The dean of the College of Arts and Sciences informed me that I could not serve on the faculty committee because I would be considered for the job, even though I had told him I was not interested in the position and would not apply.

Then things got interesting. Both committees deliberated for only about a week before making a recommendation to the dean. I got a call from him early one afternoon. When I got to his office, he said, "We have a problem. Both search committees have recommended you, but I don't think they've done a thorough search." I had an easy solution for him: "Offer me the job and I'll turn it down, and the committees will have no choice but to continue searching." He agreed.

We brought in two well-qualified candidates—and each time I voted in favor of offering one of the candidates the job. However, once again the search committees recommended me for the position and once again the dean called me to his office, only this time the provost was present. I was offered the job, but I bluntly told them that I did not want to be the chairperson and would not accept the position. I sensed that both were astonished. Nonetheless, I walked back to my office feeling good about my decision. I intended to establish myself as a scholar and teacher and knew that the job of chairperson would not serve those interests.

It was summertime and I had a light teaching load, so I went back to work on a paper that I would deliver at a late-summer convention. A couple of days later, my dean called to ask if I had time to see him and the provost again. When we met, they began by telling me that the university was in a terrible bind and they needed my help. They then offered to give me a promotion on the spot and nearly double my salary if I would accept the chairperson position. I had a growing family and the money was enticing, but what finally caused me to relent and accept the job was the situation the two described would happen if I did not take the job.

Fast forward to Marshall University, where in the 1970s I was director of the journalism school when our dean announced his retirement. One late Friday afternoon I was getting a drink from a vending machine near the dean's office when he saw me and said, "We don't have your application, and today is the last day to apply, you know." I wasn't sure what he was talking about until he said, "You know everyone is expecting you to be our next dean." I explained that the search committee would not be getting my application. In fact, I told the dean that I could never imagine myself being a dean. "What a boring job," I thought to myself as I returned to my office.

A faculty member from the history department became our new dean, and I worked well with him. A few years later I got a call from him telling me that the president had named him to a position as executive vice president, and he wanted me to become the interim dean. I accepted it only because it was an interim position—and soon found I liked the job. I then applied, went through the usual interviews, and in the end I was offered and accepted the job. I'll never forget what former Marshall University President Robert Hayes said to me when he learned I had been named to the new position: "You must be doing something right, because it's highly unusual for the dean of liberal arts not to come from one of the typical liberal arts programs."

More years passed. Then on the day I accepted the deanship at Middle Tennessee State University, I got a calling telling me that I was a finalist for the president's position at a Midwest university. I turned down the chance to interview for the position because I had already made a commitment to MTSU.

I relate these stories because I think they are not all atypical in higher education. Moreover, they reinforce a point I made in Chapter 3 when I wrote that administrators ought not covet their jobs. I remain suspicious of those who lobby hard for any administrative position. My attitude mirrors that of Paul Bryant (2005):

> ... anyone who actually wants an administrative position may want it for the wrong reasons—either a misconception of what the job is or a desire for power and prestige (which amounts to a misconception of the job). Many faculty have an exaggerated view of the benefits of administrative positions. The economic benefits are only marginally if at all significant. Comparing the 12-month salary of administrators with the 9-month salary of a faculty member (without adding summer school salaries) is deceptive. ... As for the supposed power of an administrative position, almost any decision an administrator makes is hemmed in by constraints of all kinds: budget limits, limits on positions, university regulations established by governing boards, higher administration, or faculty councils and committees, as well as basic considerations of what the faculty, students, and higher administration will support. (p. 4)

Bryant then underscores the point I made in Chapter 3: Those who covet a position "may be more likely to compromise principles for the sake of keeping the job" (p. 4).

Having said this, I encourage all chairpersons who have strong leadership skills to move up the administrative ladder. I believe there is a paucity of strong leaders at all levels of college or university administration. Moreover, I found that I could still teach as a dean and continue doing research, though I confess that I had to put in many extra hours to stay current in my field. Also, I would be less than honest if I did not admit that my scholarship suffered. Time was not available to do some of the empirical studies I dreamed about doing; instead, the studies never got done and my desire to explore theories and search for new ideas slowly faded as I accepted the realities of administration.

Thus, chairpersons who consider administrative positions must face hard decisions: Do they cherish the life of a scholar/teacher? Do they enjoy longer vacations, shorter days at the office, and being accountable only to students and the department chairperson? On the other hand, do they feel a strong need to be a significant player in making college- or university-wide decisions? I found much personal satisfaction working as a dean to help departments achieve a higher level of excellence. Moreover, I thrived on the view I had of what was happening in many different departments, and I especially enjoyed invitations to hear many outstanding speakers on subjects across virtually every discipline within the liberal arts.

Practical Tips for Moving Up

Many in academe believe that choosing a career path in administration is selling out rather than moving up. Ignore them if you are passionate about wanting to dedicate your career to moving higher education forward. Indeed, if you practice strong leadership, you'll be a better person for moving into administration, and students and faculty members will benefit as well. There should be no losers in that scenario. Let's now examine some practical tips that may help you realize your dreams.

- Establish trust.
Show that you can always be counted on to keep your word and treat others fairly.

- Get involved in campus governance.
Take the opportunity to serve on a reasonable number of committees. Work closely with members so that they get to know you and see firsthand

your leadership capabilities. Take seriously any tasks you voluntarily accept or are assigned. Make your work exemplary, and don't ever miss a deadline. In other words, be responsible and go beyond what's expected. I caution you not to be solicitous. Do your job without fanfare. Drawing attention to yourself could undermine what you are trying to achieve.

- **Work on your communication skills.**

Brush up on your writing and speaking. I give this admonishment primarily because I have seen candidates falter because of their careless use of language. Errors in usage and grammar become all too memorable when the chairperson speaks.

- **Do some serious reading outside your field of study.**

Learn enough about other disciplines so that you can carry on meaningful conversations and ask intelligent questions on any number of subjects. Years ago I developed a serious desire to learn something about Chinese history, and I read four books on the subject. I don't credit this with ever having helped me secure an administrative position, but I certainly felt more comfortable conversing with faculty members in the history department. Self-confidence is expected of leaders.

- **Keep your eyes wide open.**

I have seen faculty members so eager to get into an administrative position that they take whatever job comes along. Working as an assistant or associate dean is seldom exciting if you report to a weak dean. Stay clear of any position if you and your supervisor are not in clear agreement on major issues. Working for a dean who could not be trusted would be frustrating and wearisome. The same would hold true for a dean who is not a change agent.

Before you accept any administrative position, you should know exactly what is expected. You should also learn what kind of mentoring and support you would receive. All facets of the job should be carefully examined to see if the position fits and offers opportunities to learn and grow. But avoid being too eager; the right job will appear in due time.

If you are considering a position at another university, much more study is required. If it's a line position (one that bears direct responsibility at that level of administration), before accepting an interview you should ask to see the budget and get as much information as possible about the faculty. Study the school's catalog carefully; look to see what kind of degrees faculty members have earned and from which institutions. If most faculty members have their advanced degrees from the university you are visiting or from nearby universities, you might encounter a level of parochialism that could be stifling. Find out as much as you can about the educational philosophy of other administrators. And don't overlook the community— you should check out the cost of housing and the quality of life.

- The job interview.

Much has been written on this subject, so I'll not rehash the customary advice. Instead, I'll give some examples of actual experiences that proved detrimental to those being interviewed. Also, anyone who is a candidate needs to recognize that the makeup of the search committee can create a bias toward specific kinds of credentials. For example, if the search committee is made up of mostly senior-level research faculty members, the committee will likely give a lot of weight to an individual's publication and scholarship record. Indeed, well-intentioned faculty members often will argue for selecting someone who has a long list of publications even though the candidate may have had little or no experience in a line position.

So what does this mean for you? It means that in advance of agreeing to an interview you should try to learn exactly what kind of person the search committee hopes to hire. If you have a friend at the university, call to find out as much as you can about the interview process and the biases of the search committee.

I suggest that you make a list of all questions you'll likely be asked during the interview. There is no reason that you should ever be tripped up. An unexpected question may come up now and then, but if you are otherwise prepared, calm, and honest, you will likely respond impressively.

Here is one last suggestion: Dress appropriately and watch your manners. I will never forget a candidate who was shot down by a comment made by one search committee member: "Did you notice that at the reception he used his fingers instead of the spoon to take nuts from the bowl?"

Do your homework, but then relax and be yourself. Let everyone who interviews you know the real you. Bryant (2005) has some good advice about interviewing:

> Tell your interviewers what you think, how you work, and what your approach to the job would be. If you aren't going to be a good match for the people, the community, or the institution, you need to determine that as early as possible. If the people you will be working with aren't going to be comfortable with you, both you and they need to know that before any commitments are made. (p. 23)

- **Rejecting an offer.**

Uneasiness about accepting a job offer is usually a clear warning that the job is not right and the offer should be rejected. In an article about turning down a promotion, Jennifer Jacobson (2002) writes,

> While some academics move up the administrative hierarchy to secure more money and authority, plenty of others pass on the chance. It's a dicey enough move, though, that few people are willing to speak on the record about rejecting a promotion. Academics who have say it was a difficult decision. . . .
>
> While most of those interviewed say they are convinced that turning down the promotion was the right call, some remain ambivalent, even years later.

It is important to weigh reasons to accept versus reasons to reject. If you are going to reject an offer, don't burn bridges in the process. If you make a good impression, you will likely be remembered and invited to apply for other administrative positions. Even more important is that you will have held to your principles and turned down the job with grace and dignity.

- Look at the entire picture.

Before deciding whether administration is right for you, you must examine your motives. You need to be honest about why you want to become an administrator. If it is for the wrong reasons, you may not only be miserable, but failure is likely to be a regular experience. One approach is to measure yourself honestly in terms of those characteristics most people admire in their leaders. James Kouzes and Barry Posner (2003, p. 12) provide a list of the top 10 characteristics of admired leaders: honest, forward-looking, competent, inspiring, intelligent, fair-minded, broad-minded, supportive, straightforward, and dependable.

You should ask yourself if scaling back your scholarship is something you are willing to do. While you may be able to engage in some research and publishing, it will not be anything like you did as a professor without administrative responsibilities.

If you have all the characteristics that strong leaders need, you will know and experience what Kenneth Shaw (1999) describes in *The Successful President*.

> I know that most organizations change very slowly. I also know they must change or be left behind. While experienced leaders know they can make incremental moves in the right direction if they are patient, observant, and courageous, it is also true that sometimes major, thrilling, and soul-satisfying breakthroughs can and do happen. A transforming leader is comfortable with both the incremental and the blockbuster paces. (p. x)

For me, playing golf is akin to what Shaw describes. Generally, I move the ball along incrementally and not too far, but now and then I get that big Arnold Palmer drive when the ball sails straight and swiftly before landing inches from the pin. It's that kind of experience that keeps me playing golf. And as a leader, it's those "major, thrilling, and soul-satisfying breakthroughs" that happen occasionally—and make being a university administrator meaningful and satisfying.

Resources

Web Sites
The Evolution of a Dean
www.ccas.net/Public/articles/The_Evolution_of_a_Dean.pdf

A Guide to Staff Career Mobility at University of California–San Francisco
http://ucsfhr.ucsf.edu/pubs/manuals/info.html?x=421

Women in Economics: Moving Up or Falling Off the Academic Career Ladder?
www.nber.org/~sewp/events/2004.05.28/ginther_%20kahn_
WomenAndEconomics

Books
Badowski, R., with Gittines, R. (2003). *Managing up: How to forge an effective relationship with those above you.* New York, NY: Doubleday.
Jensen, R., Giles, R., & Kirklin, P. (2000). *Insider's guide to community college administration.* Washington, DC: Community College Press.
Usheroff, R. (2004). *Customize your career: How to develop a winning strategy to move up, move ahead, or move on.* New York, NY: McGraw-Hill.

References

Bryant, P. T. (2005). *Confessions of an habitual administrator: An academic survival manual.* Bolton, MA: Anker.
Jacobson, J. (2002, October 9). *Turning down a promotion.* Retrieved July 21, 2006, from http://chronicle.com/jobs/2002/10/2002100901c.htm
Kouzes, J. M., & Posner, B. Z. (2003). *The Jossey-Bass academic administrator's guide to exemplary leadership.* San Francisco, CA: Jossey-Bass.
Shaw, K. A. (1999). *The successful president: Buzzwords on leadership.* Phoenix, AZ: American Council on Education/Oryx Press.

30

Where Do You Go From Here?

Capable chairpersons will need to forge new alliances, keep abreast of technological developments, and be prepared to have their leadership skills tested.

Determining where we go from here would be less daunting if we were not living in such uncertain times. Today's solutions to tomorrow's challenges will be inadequate. Capable chairpersons will need to forge new alliances, keep abreast of technological developments, and be prepared to have their leadership skills tested in ways heretofore unimagined. Will chairpersons be skillful and creative enough to deal with the crises that lie ahead? This is for certain: Chairpersons must recognize the coming changes and deal with them swiftly. Today's chairpersons must be decisive and not allow their departments to drift. They must help stamp out territorialism, opportunism, and unhealthy competition. They must be leaders who "model the way, inspire a shared vision, challenge the process, enable others to act, and encourage the heart." (Kouzes & Posner, 2003, p. 10). Furthermore, they must understand and question issues surrounding hospitality, ethics, and spirituality as Bennett (2003) defines and illustrates in his book *Academic Life*.

I strongly believe that tomorrow's chairpersons must be better prepared and have at their disposal more leadership skills than I possessed in my active years. For that reason, they must take advantage of development opportunities, just as they must learn to handle the stress that comes with new demands.

Development Opportunities for Chairpersons

Continuing development for chairpersons will be critical in the years ahead. As Gilliland (1997) argues, we in universities must confront the fact that

> . . . the environment in which all organizations, public or private, must succeed is now characterized by accelerating change, complexity, and uncertainty. Universities, like all organizations, thus function in an environment of unpredictability, in contrast to the past, in which change occurred more incrementally, the interactions among the parts of a problem and organization were tractable, and external economic and political pressures were more predictable. (p. 31)

Gilliland makes the point that as operating procedures change, department chairpersons will have to be trained in the new procedures. She discusses tenure and how significant modifications are needed to bring about desired outcomes of flexibility, information access, and risk-taking. One of the changes she advocates is providing and requiring development programs for chairpersons on ". . . management and procedural issues, leadership effectiveness, the perceptions of constituencies, and the university-wide perspective on important issues" (Gilliland, 1997, p. 33).

A chairs' council can help with some of these matters. At one university where I taught, we had an active chairs' council, and its regular meetings gave us opportunities to have programs on issues that concerned us and to let others on campus—particularly upper-level administrators—know how we felt about academic issues. We were able to get our jobs defined, and we were able to get a chair's stipend where there had been none before. A chairs' council can also be an ideal organization where chairpersons gather regularly to deal with the challenging issues all confront. Meeting regularly will allow chairpersons to develop strategies to tackle the many nettlesome issues, to give each other support, and perhaps just as important, to have others with whom they can commiserate.

Recognizing and Dealing With Stress

Whether you decide to move further into academic administration, remain as a chairperson, or return to full-time faculty status, you must find balance in your professional life. With new demands and more perplexing challenges, you will likely encounter more stress. The crunch of time creates stress and every chairperson I have known worries about keeping up with his or her discipline.

Tough decisions and worrisome concerns clearly can cause stress. Additionally, studies show that other workplace factors contribute to stress (Fraser, 1992). The following practical suggestions for recognizing and dealing with stress can be beneficial for you and your faculty.

- Set attainable goals.

Fraser (1992) reminds us that some individuals—especially Type A personalities—overload their schedules and that the best way to alleviate stress is to set attainable goals.

- Avoid procrastination.

Stress levels can be reduced if you learn not to put off doing what has to be done (Maturi, 1992). Accomplishing something that must be done produces a level of satisfaction that combats stress.

- Get plenty of exercise.

The greatest stresses I've faced had nothing to do with my position but came rather because of an unprincipled university president who wanted to dismiss the administrative team he had inherited. Moreover, a significant conflict involving students' First Amendment rights contributed to our differences. Exercise probably saved me from having some serious health problems during that period.

- Find a way to relax.

Regardless of stress level, we all need rest. In the conflict situation just described, I couldn't get the rest I needed. I was absolutely driven with the idea that the president was not going to defeat me. Therefore, I worked unbelievably long hours—often going to my office before 4 a.m. and not leaving until 6 or 7 p.m., and I was usually in my office on Saturdays and Sundays. I followed this schedule for more than a year until I accepted a dean's position at another university. It took some time, but eventually, with rest and relaxation, exercise, proper diet, and a great new job, I was able to recover.

What I have described is supported by Fraser's (1992) contention that "an employee can intensify his own stress level by being his own worst enemy. . . . [t]hese people are aggressive, hostile and driven; they overload their schedules and they distrust others" (p. 256). As much as I do not like to see myself as Fraser describes an employee, I believe for a brief time in my academic career I had become exactly that person.

- **Develop a healthy lifestyle.**
As noted, diet, rest, and exercise are important to health. Likewise, avoid smoking, drinking to excess, and ingesting too much caffeine. A fit person can deal better with the stresses associated with work.

- **Analyze what is causing your stress.**
Stress is often self-induced. If you know what's causing it, you may be able to modify your behavior to get rid of stress or at least to reduce its level.

- **See your physician.**
Stress is a health problem, and your physician may be able to treat it via medication, exercise, or suggest adjustments in the way you are living.

- **Share your frustrations with your spouse or a trusted friend.**
If I have been under a lot of pressure and something is bothering me, I know it helps to talk it over with my wife at the end of a day. Not only do I feel better, but together we sometimes find effective answers by talking about problems.

- **Plan time for yourself and family for entertainment.**

Just as you need exercise, you need relaxation. The kind of entertainment you enjoy is a matter of taste. I enjoy reading, going to movies, traveling, spending time with my family, and dining out with my wife.

- **Attend a conference.**

Getting out of town often is a good antidote to problems at work. You leave those problems behind and generally find intellectual stimulation with conference activities.

- **Examine and evaluate your workload.**

Are you trying to do too much? Are you properly delegating authority? Look, too, at other ways to manage your time and workload.

- **Teach a class.**

I have found that teaching refreshes the way I feel. It helps keep my sanity. When you depart your office for class, you leave behind the paperwork that is stacking up, the decisions that must be made, and the frustrations that come with the administrative territory.

- **Get involved in a research project.**

Getting involved in a research project can provide an excellent escape from the stress of regular work activities.

- **Get ready for Mondays.**

Mondays can be the most stressful day for chairpersons as they signal the start of a new workweek and all its unpredictabilities. You can relieve part of the stress by setting aside some time over the weekend to get organized and avoid the Monday rush.

- **Learn to tame the paper tiger.**

In the information age, we now deal with two kinds of information worlds—paper and paperless—and either one can keep us busy from sunup to sundown. As Hemphill (1997) points out, "One fact is absolutely clear:

Paper-management skills are essential to survive the information explosion in our society" (p. 4). Paperless management skills are equally important.

In the end, each person must ask whether he or she is paying too high a price to be a university administrator. But remember that not all stress is negative; it can be positive and should not be avoided altogether.

Whether you decide to continue as chairperson, return to full-time teaching, or move up the administrative ladder, your job will be more challenging and fulfilling if you work to maximize your skills. Knowing that you are contributing positively to a noble cause—that of educating people—is rewarding. All struggles seem to fade when you hear from a former student who has called to thank you.

Resources

Web Sites

The Challenges Facing Higher Education in America
www.highereducation.org/reports/learning/learning5.shtml

Higher Education in the Digital Age
www.campus-technology.com/article.asp?id=4769

Reducing Stress in the Workplace
http://sdsd.essortment.com/reducingstress_oih.htm

World Declaration on Higher Education for the Twenty-First Century
www.unesco.org/education/educprog/wche/declaration_eng.htm

Books

Childre, D., & Rozman, D. (2005). *Transforming stress: The Heartmath® solution for relieving worry, fatigue, and tension*. Oakland, CA: New Harbinger.

Hirsch, W. Z., & Weber, L. E. (1999). *Challenges facing higher education at the millennium*. Phoenix, AZ: American Council on Education/Oryx Press.

Kerr, C. (2001). *The uses of the university* (5th ed.). Cambridge, MA: Harvard University Press.

Newman, F., Couturier, L., & Scurry, J. (2004). *The future of higher education: Rhetoric, reality, and the risks of the market.* San Francisco, CA: Jossey-Bass.

Sormaz, H. W., & Tulgan, B. (2003). *Performance under pressure: Managing stress in the workplace.* Amherst, MA: HRD Press.

References

Bennett, J. B. (2003). *Academic life: Hospitality, ethics, and spirituality.* Bolton, MA: Anker.

Fraser, J. (1992, April 23). Managing stress for success. *EDN, 37*(9), 256.

Gilliland, M. W. (1997, May/June). Organizational change and tenure: We can learn from the corporate experience. *Change, 29*(3), 30–33.

Hemphill, B. (1997). *Taming the paper tiger at work.* Washington, DC: Kiplinger.

Kouzes, J. M., & Posner, B. Z. (2003). *The Jossey-Bass academic administrator's guide to exemplary leadership.* San Francisco, CA: Jossey-Bass.

Maturi, R. (1992, July 20). Stress can be beaten. *Industry Week, 241*(14), 22–25.

Appendixes

Appendix A

Workshops for Department Chairs

Some organizations that offer workshops and seminars for department chairs include:

Academic Chairpersons Conference
Division of Continuing Education
Kansas State University
3 College Court Building
Manhattan, KS 66506–6001
www.dce.ksu.edu/academicchairpersons

American Council on Education
One Dupont Circle NW
Washington, DC 20036
www.acenet.edu

The Chair Academy
145 N. Centennial Way
Mesa, AZ 85201
www.mc.maricopa.edu/other/chair

Cornell University School of Continuing Education
Education and Summer Sessions
Box 530, B20 Day Hall
Ithaca, NY 14853–2801
www.iccd.cornell.edu/iccd/consultingServices/departmentChair.html

Council of Colleges of Arts and Sciences
The College of William and Mary
P.O. Box 8795
Williamsburg, VA 23187–8795
http://www.ccas.net

National Center for Higher Education Management Systems
3035 Center Green Drive, Suite 150
Boulder, CO 80301-2251
www.nchems.org

Programs in Professional Education
Harvard Graduate School of Education
14 Story Street, Third Floor
Cambridge, MA 02138
www.gse.harvard.edu/ppe/highered/index.html

Appendix B

Newsletter Sources

Sample departmental and/or college newsletters may be obtained from the following sources, upon request.

School of Mass Communications   *The Editor*
University of South Florida
4202 East Fowler Avenue, CIS 1040
Tampa, FL 33620–7800

Edward R. Murrow School   *The Murrow Communicator*
    of Communication
Washington State University
Pullman, WA 99164–1227

School of Journalism   *InterCom*
    and Mass Communications
University of South Carolina
Columbia, SC 29208

Department of Chemistry   *Chemistry Newsletter*
Middle Tennessee State University
239 Davis Science Building
MTSU Box 68
Murfreesboro, TN 37132

College of Communications   *The Communicator*
Pennsylvania State University
208 Carnegie Building
University Park, PA 16802

Appendix C

Monday Morning Memo, Print Version

October 16, 2006

To   All Faculty
From   Deryl R. Leaming
Re   Monday Morning Memo

Fall Alumni Banquet

The Journalism Alumni Association's fall banquet will be November 3 at the Radisson (social hour at 6 p.m. and banquet at 7 p.m.). Harold Reid and James Wilson will be honored. Tom Rogers has given me tickets to sell. They are $20 per person. Yes, they plan to make some money on the event, but they always give whatever is left after expenses to the School of Journalism. Angel Miller also has tickets.

Televised Courses

Alice Yamada sends word that the Higher Education Instructional Television Consortium is interested in faculty proposals for courses to be taught by public television in 2007–2008. NEW: The deadline on this is no later than November 20 because the state selection committee meets on December 1. To propose a course the department must complete a simple form. Let me know if you're interested in teaching by television.

Curriculum Committee

The Curriculum Committee will meet at 3 p.m. Wednesday in the conference room.

Journalism Faculty Meeting

Our next faculty meeting will be on Thursday, October 26, at 4:15 p.m. in the conference room. Please mark your calendars.

Graduate Faculty

On the back of this memo is a memo from the Graduate Committee that was sent to all deans who sent a memo to all chairpersons who were instructed to share the information by memo with all faculty. I'm not sure why the Graduate Committee didn't send a notice to all faculty directly, but then where would the bureaucracy and the paper industry be?

Guest Speakers

Jeff Seglin of *Inc.* magazine has committed to a date for his visit next semester. He'll be on campus from Sunday evening, February 4, until late afternoon or early evening on Tuesday, February 6. A public presentation will probably be scheduled for Monday evening, and he is available for classroom visits at other times. First come, first served.

Wil Haygood of *The Boston Globe* will be visiting in the early part of second semester, too, but the days of his visit aren't yet determined. Do you think Boston is far enough away to keep us from being considered insular and provincial?

Resource Materials

The Placement Services Center has agreed to purchase *Current Jobs in Writing, Editing, & Communications*. It should be available for our students' use in about one month. While visiting campus last week, Brent Archer of Columbia Gas Transmission left copies of *Bacon's Publicity Checker* for magazines and newspapers. They're available in the journalism library.

Follow-Up to Last Faculty Meeting

At Thursday's faculty meeting, a number of issues were left unresolved. First, I asked for volunteers for two ad hoc committees, one to decide what equipment to include in our request to the Clay Foundation and another to help with a five-year plan as related to Dr. Anderson's desire to have journalism as one of the centers of excellence. Bill, James, and Sheryl have volunteered for the equipment committee. Other committee members are welcome, but I don't think we need anyone else. The second committee now has Wayne and Chuck as volunteers and needs at least one, probably two, additional members. The discussion of the proposed School of Journalism plan regarding female/minority representation led to an agreement that the faculty will provide additional ideas for the committee about specific tactical approaches; the committee will write objectives for the plan (keeping in mind the university's multicultural plan); and the committee will attempt to include more about issues of gender.

Appendix D

Monday Morning Memo, Electronic Version

Date   September 18, 2006
From   Deryl R. Leaming
To   68 addressees
Subject   Monday Morning Memo—September 18, 2006

Monday Morning Memo—September 18, 2006—Vol. VII, No. 6

Teaching Brown-Bag Set

Jim Wilson will conduct two brown-bag workshops on syllabus writing. The meetings will be Wednesday, September 27, at noon and Thursday, September 28, at 3:30. Both sessions will be in the dean's conference room. These sessions are part of a series on teaching excellence sponsored by the college's committee to improve teaching. Jim suggested bringing a syllabus with you as this will be an open forum to discuss elements, organization, and other aspects of course syllabi.

Oxymorons I've Seen Recently

Here are some oxymorons I've seen in print lately: plastic glasses, definite maybe, twelve-ounce pound cake, diet ice cream, rap music, temporary tax increase.

Nelson Authors Lead Article

Larry Nelson has the lead article in the current (Fall, 2006) issue of *The Journal of Higher Education*. Larry looks at problems related to assessing students for placement in certain introduction courses.

Harrison Undergoes Heart Surgery

Bill Harrison underwent quadruple bypass heart surgery last Friday and is currently recovering at Centennial Hospital in Nashville. He told me this morning he feels well.

Chris Blanz to Speak in Graphics Classes

Chris Blanz, creative director for EdgeNet, one of the major ISPs in Nashville, will be speaking to several graphics classes tomorrow. In the morning sessions—9:25 and 10:50—he will discuss the design and technology of web pages in the Introduction to Graphic Communication classes. He also will be speaking to the Publication Design class at 1:25. He will be joined by Jeff Felertag, EdgeNet's director of Internet training. There will be room for faculty to attend these sessions, especially the 1:25 session, according to Ray Wong.

Carlos Cortez Lectures Today, Tomorrow

Carlos Cortez will lecture today and tomorrow on multiculturalism and civility and gender relations. He will speak this evening at 7:00 in the Tennessee Room of the James Union Building and tomorrow at 9:30 a.m. and 1 p.m. in the KUC theater.

Have a good week.

Appendix E

Review of Accomplishments, Dean or Department Chair

MEMORANDUM

Date   June 12, 2006
To   Liberal Arts Faculty and Staff
From   John McDaniel, Dean
Re   2005–2006 Year in Review

It is time again for a brief review of academic-year highlights, along with some comments on major directions and developments for AY 2005–2006 and beyond. In fall 2006, university enrollments rose to 17,924 (+2.87% over fall 2005). Liberal arts enrollments increased 6%, giving us a 13th consecutive year of record enrollment. Jordan Bolick is predicting 18,299 (+2%) for AY 2006–2007. Jordan also reports that 141 new Presidential Scholars have declared their intent to enroll in the fall; of these, 25 are liberal arts majors and 37 are undeclared. Our freshman class for AY 2005–2006 is averaging 22 on the ACT (which is above state and national averages), African-American enrollment is up 15% in the freshman class, and 31 Floyd Scholars are coming on board. For us, staffing will be a major concern once again, with numerous full-time temporary faculty holding down tenure-track lines as a result of the budget crunch. Our space problems should be ameliorated to some degree by the limited opening (on a phase-in basis) of the new business/aerospace building this fall. The provost is intent on doing away with the portables and finding new office space for faculty housed therein, a project now headed by Bob Jones. And now to the year in review.

Tenure and Promotion
The president has made the following recommendations to the Tennessee Board of Regents:

Promotion/Full Professor: Arlander Card, Jack Gibson, Monta Joyce Jones, Alice Meler, Leland Tatum, and Bill Taylor.

Promotion/Associate Professor: Robert Hantz, Lola Harnden, Karen Hatfield, Patricia Martz, Noel Matkin, Gene Myrick, and Shirley Peck.

Tenure: Thiel Bloom, Lois Emrie, Tony Garcia, Norman Lofland, Marie Morris, Wendell Palmer, Charles Scott, Rodney Smith, Wendell Smotherman, and Jeanice Tregellas.

Staffing

This year we have made and continue to make excellent additions to our liberal arts staff. We are in the process of adding 16 full-time faculty as replacements or add-ons for AY 2006–2007. The proposed budget cuts required some creative hiring, with some full-time temporaries filling tenure-track lines. The total number of full-time faculty for AY 2006–2007 will be 209, with an additional 130 part-time faculty, including 54 GTAs. Retiring this year are Walter Mitty (1972), Dan Malton (1978), Larry Ling (1983), and Wilda Zeigler (1985), with a combined total of 154 years at Midwest State University. Norman Hogue has been appointed chair of the geography/geology department as a replacement for Ron Hawkins; Jim Keating has been appointed chair of English as a replacement for Carolyn Hickman; and Hazel Grabeel will serve a second year as interim chair in music while we continue that search in AY 2006–2007.

Budgets

FY 2005–2006 was a tight budget year, as will be the upcoming FY 2006–2007 budget year. The 4.28% budget cut proposed by Governor Rogers has had a "chilling" effect on all of our operations, of course, but the provost is committed to preserving our academic programs and to underwriting expenses occasioned by growth. This past year the VPAA's office contributed $93,000 for additional adjuncts; technology access dollars in the amount of $55,300 were allocated for computer-lab upgrades in English, geography/geology, and art; and the college was able to distribute

$210,666 to liberal arts departments for faculty development and general operational support. The legislature, with the leadership of Senator Womack, is considering some ways of modifying the governor's proposed $40 million budget cut to minimize the impact on growing universities like ours. Still, it appears that budgets on campus will once again be lean—especially in light of an additional impoundment of reserves in the amount of $1,380,500 (our share of a $20 million reversion for higher education in 2006–2007 budgets). Just hold on: We will ride out the storm.

Salaries

Although the state has provided no new monies for salary increases, you are all aware that the provost's market equity study with strong presidential backing is being readied for implementation this fall. The plan initially targets for salary improvement those faculty who fall below 92% of predicted salary based on salaries at 78 peer institutions. When this plan is implemented in August 2006, 71 liberal arts faculty will receive a salary increase, with a total of $157,909 for the college (27% of the $586,286 to be allocated to the university faculty). The goal, to be achieved in a phase-in plan for the next few years, is to reach 100% of market equity for everyone (a moving target, to be sure). There will be continued discussion and debate as the president and provost move forward with the market equity plan, but we are undertaking a good first step.

Faculty Internships

As a new feature this year, the college is preparing a liberal arts newsletter, one that will detail faculty activities more fully than I have been able to do in the past in this year-in-review memo. This project is being undertaken by Pat England (social work); she will be serving as a liberal arts intern. The newsletter should be out within the next few weeks. I would like to have your reactions to this new approach to publicizing faculty activities. Leonard Davis (English), also working on a liberal arts internship, is preparing what we hope will be an expansive and extensive web site for the College of Liberal Arts. This too should improve our dissemination of faculty activities and college information—not only locally but throughout the world.

Another liberal arts intern, Glenna Clodfelter (English), has done a valuable study on retention and persistence to graduation for African-American students in liberal arts. This study is in my office, available for your perusal.

Final Thoughts

The recent reports of the General Studies Task Force and the Academic Master Plan Committee have placed liberal arts departments at the center of the academic enterprise at Midwest State University—now and for years to come. Both reports stress the importance of strengthening academic core courses by providing interdisciplinary approaches and threshold and capstone courses. The academic master plan calls for us to capitalize on areas of competitive advantage, including communications, arts, law and government, and health and human services. And the recommendations for an Honors College, for improvements in library holdings and in arts and sciences facilities, and for the development of high-quality graduate programs (including Ph.D.s in such areas as English and history) provide opportunities that liberal arts faculty will welcome. This year we have seen the development of interdisciplinary minors in film and writing, along with a new major in anthropology; the Leonardo Project, an interdisciplinary approach to teacher preparation cosponsored by liberal arts and education, has witnessed a dramatic increase in student and faculty participation; and a School of Fine Arts within the College of Liberal Arts is already on my drawing board as an arrangement with much interdisciplinary potential. Community outreach has been a strength of several of our programs—not only in the obvious areas of speech and theater, arts, and music, but also in social work programs, public history and political science internships, the activities of the Marcellus Center and the Center for Historic Preservation, and the University Writing Center. Having had the opportunity to serve on both the General Studies Task Force and the Academic Master Plan Committee, I was pleasantly reminded once again of what I have known all along: the liberal arts are alive and well at Midwest State University. In the upcoming year we will be invited to rethink traditional methods of teaching and to move toward a student learning-centered environment. This could make for an interesting year indeed.

Appendix F

Alumni Survey

1. Name _____

    Street Address_____

    City/State/Zip _____

    Telephone (   ) _____

2. Employer _____

3. How many years in present position?_____

4. Do you consider this position to be in journalism/mass communication? _____

    ☐ Yes   ☐ No

5. Other positions held in the last 10 years.

    _____

    _____

    _____

6. Marshall University degree(s) earned: ☐ B.A. ☐ M.A. Year(s)_____

    Sequence:

    ☐ Advertising   ☐ Public Relations

    ☐ Broadcast Journalism   ☐ Print Journalist ☐ Radio/TV

    ☐ Journalism Education   ☐ Other:_____

7. Non–Marshall University degrees earned and emphasis.

    _____

    _____

    _____

8. What aspects of education in the School of Journalism and Mass Communications were most positive and helpful to you professionally?

    _____

    _____

    _____

9. How could your education in the School of Journalism and Mass Communications have been improved (including classes both in and outside the School of Journalism that you wish you had taken)?

_____

_____

_____

10. With 1 being very unhelpful and 5 being very helpful, please evaluate the following aspects of your journalism education as they helped you in your career by placing the appropriate number in the space provided. Please leave blank any that do not apply to you.

Very unhelpful   1   2   3   4   5   Very helpful

___classroom lectures   ___thesis
___papers/projects   ___exams
___academic advising   ___career advising
___non-journalism classes   ___textbooks
___internship(s)   ___outside job(s)
___other students   ___informal contact with faculty
___*The Parthenon*   ___WMUL
___guest speakers   ___lab classes (e.g., video editing)
___case studies   ___professional groups
___computer labs   ___team projects
___student agencies

11. With 1 being unimportant and 5 being very important, please rate the following for their importance in securing your first position by placing the appropriate number in the spaces provided.

Unimportant   1   2   3   4   5   Very important

___internship   ___class work
___recommendations   ___clipbook/audio/video
   from faculty   production
___reputation of SOJMC   ___contacts made through faculty/
___outside jobs   classes
___other:_____

12. With 1 being unimportant and 5 being very important, please rate the following for their importance in helping you learn about job opportunities by placing the appropriate number in the spaces provided.

        Unimportant   1 2 3 4 5   Very important

  ___University Placement Center

  ___notices posted by faculty

  ___want ads in professional publications or newspapers

  ___personal contacts

  ___other:_____

13. Please choose a number from the scale below to show how much you agree or disagree with each statement that follows and note your answer in the space to the left of the item.

                1—disagree strongly

                2—disagree somewhat

                3—neutral

                4—agree somewhat

                5—agree strongly

  ___The School of Journalism and Mass Communications prepared me well for the professional world.

  ___The experiences and perspectives of faculty members reflected an accurate and up-to-date knowledge of the demands of mass communications careers.

  ___The faculty members adequately represented the diversity of opinion and perspectives present in mass communications field.

  ___The School of Journalism and Mass Communications prepared me well for the technology used in my work.

  ___I am using skills I acquired during my education at Marshall University.

  ___I would recommend the W. Page Pitt School of Journalism and Mass Communications to others wishing to pursue mass communications careers.

14. Please use the space below to comment on any of your answers to questions 13.

Appendix G

Student Exit Interview

DEPARTMENT OF MASS COMMUNICATIONS
SOUTHEAST STATE UNIVERSITY

1. As you conclude your coursework at Southeast, there may be courses that you remember as being especially good. Take a few moments to identify two courses you have taken during your college experience that have been especially memorable. (Include a course in the major/minor and a university studies course.)

   Similarly, there may be courses that you found to be less satisfactory. Take a few moments to identify two courses you have taken during your college experience that have been less than memorable. (Include a course in the major/minor and in university studies.)

   What is the basis that you used to classify the courses as either good or bad?

2. Think about the faculty you have had in your major courses. Can you assess their quality as compared to other faculty on campus?
   (a) Choose two words that you think best describe the department's faculty. Why?
   (b) If you asked other faculty outside the department to assess the quality of the mass communications faculty, what two words do you think they would use to describe our faculty? Why?

3. Think about the students that have been in your major courses. Can you assess their quality as compared to other students on campus?
   (a) Choose two words that you think best describe your classmates. Why?
   (b) If you asked other students outside the department to assess the quality of mass communication majors, what two words do you think they would use to describe your classmates? Why?
   (c) If you asked faculty outside the department to assess the quality of mass communications majors, what two words do you think they would use to describe your classmates? Why?

4. The department stresses the value of your working with our student media and participating in the student organizations. Did you take advantage of these opportunities?
   (a) If you participated, did you find the experience rewarding?
   (b) What could be done to improve the experiences for others?
   (c) What could be done to help students understand the value of participating?

5. The department offers internship opportunities to students having a 2.5 GPA to a 2.75 GPA in coursework in the department. Did you complete an internship?
   (a) If you completed an internship, what was the value of the experience?
   (b) Did the department satisfactorily assist you in securing an internship?
   (c) Do you think your supervisor at the cooperating agency also found the experience valuable? If yes, how do you think your performance compared with that of previous interns or interns from other schools?

6. If the department could at a moment's notice make any two changes, what would you suggest those changes be?
   (a) The department is considering changing _____.
   (b) Would you support that change to the curriculum?

7. Having completed the requirements to apply for graduation and looking back at your experiences in the department, would you choose to be a mass communications major again if you were just now declaring a major? Why/why not?

8. While you might be willing to be a mass communications major, it is a very different matter to advise your friends to consider majoring in mass communications.
   (a) Would you recommend this major?
   (b) Why/why not?

Appendix H

A (Humorous) Perspective on Meetings

Nevermore, my irascible pet raven, was perturbed with me when I arrived home yesterday.

"I tried to call you three times today," he scolded. "And all I got was your voicemail message that said you were either in a meeting or looking for one to go to! I don't believe you really work there anymore at all!"

Dang. Found out!

Then he added, "So I called your CEO."

"You what?!"

"I called your CEO. I figured somebody should know about the hours you keep!"

I did not like where this was going, even a little bit. "And . . . ?"

"He wasn't there. He was in a meeting."

Well, of course, he was. The truth is that many of us are now in meetings most of the time. This is the iceberg tip of a much larger trend, but it is also the most obvious.

It used to be that companies were organized from the top down. At the top was the big boss. Smaller bosses were below, and the pyramid worked its way down to the worker bees at the bottom. Everyone knew what they were there to do and things got done.

Then it changed. I fault politically correct thinking for this. It was pointed out that the worker bees didn't feel they were loved and respected as much as the bosses. This made them feel bad and they had to go into counseling, which drove health care benefit price tags up and forced human resources to look into the matter.

And because no one wants to hurt anyone else's feelings and because everyone has a constitutional right to be loved and respected, no matter how stupid they may be, it was decided that everyone should get to make decisions and feel good about themselves.

The primary tool for decision-making, then, became the meeting. And, of course, as with any good tool—chainsaws, for example—there are those who abuse it. There are others who make hobbies of its use and still others who are collectors. I have one colleague who is an avid collector. Three or four meetings a day is a good average for one day's collecting. A really memorable day is when three or four meetings are scheduled at the same time. Collectors live for this stuff.

I once worked with a woman who specialized in committee meetings. She reached heaven when she was named chairwoman of the Committee on Committees. She actually cried when her appointment was announced. True story.

Decisions once made by one person are now made by many people sitting around a room drinking water from plastic bottles with designer labels. The really great thing about this is that it dilutes responsibility. The meetings, I mean, not the water. If you make a decision, you are stuck with it, for good or evil and for all time. But if you are part of a large group meeting that makes a decision, the blame gets spread around and by the time it gets to you, it's pretty thin and, if you're really bright, you can probably duck it all together. At least, that's the theory.

Whatever the cause, we've become a meetings culture. We go from one meeting to the next. The problem with this is obvious. While you're in meetings, you're not getting the job done. Someday this is going to catch up with us and we're going to have to deal with it. I'm thinking about calling a meeting to discuss it.

Which reminds me. "Nevermore, why were you trying to call me this morning? You never said."

A cloud of cigar smoke drifted down from the rafters. "Oh, nothing important. I just wanted to schedule a meeting with you this evening."

Rimshot, please.

William H. "Skip" Boyer is executive producer and senior writer–corporate historian for Best Western International, Inc. Reprinted with permission.

Appendix I

Affirmative Action Program,
Proposed Faculty Appointment

1. Department _____

   School/College_____

2. Proposed Academic Rank _____

   Area of specialization _____

3. Salary Range: From_____   To_____

4. How many total applications (completed) were received?_____
   What efforts were made to inform potential female/minority applicants of the vacancy?

   _____

   _____

   _____

5. How many applicants were interviewed? _____

6. Give sex and race or ethnic composition of search committee.

   _____

   _____

   _____

7. Was the vacancy listed with Central University's affirmative action/
   human resources office: Yes ☐ No ☐

8. Was a written job announcement prepared? Yes ☐   No ☐

   a. If yes, please attach a copy.

   b. If no, indicate why not.

   _____

   _____

   _____

9. Provide the name and address of organizations, individuals, and publications used to publish the job announcement.

_____

_____

_____

10. Give name, sex, and race or ethnic origin (Caucasian, Black, American Indian, Asian, or Hispanic) of each candidate interviewed. Check, for each candidate, one or more boxes indicating the main criteria by which the selected candidate was determined to possess stronger credentials for the particular position. Provide clarification where appropriate.

Candidates Interviewed

A. Name, sex, and race or ethnic origin of successful candidate.

_____

_____

1. ☐ Educational achievement. Candidate has:
   ☐ M.A./M.S.   ☐ ABD   ☐ Ph.D.

2. ☐ Teaching ability. Candidate has ___ years of teaching experience.

3. ☐ Professional or academic references. Did candidate provide references?
   ☐ Yes ☐ No

4. ☐ Rank and/or salary required

5. ☐ Research or professional specialty

6. ☐ Scholarly research and publications

7. ☐ Other (specify):_____

B. Name, sex, and race or ethnic origin of other interviewed candidate.

_____

_____

1. ☐ Educational achievement. Candidate has:
   ☐ M.A./M.S. ☐ ABD ☐ Ph.D.
2. ☐ Teaching ability. Candidate has ___ years of teaching experience.
3. ☐ Professional or academic references. Did candidate provide references? ☐ Yes ☐ No
4. ☐ Rank and/or salary
5. ☐ Research or professional specialty
6. ☐ Scholarly research and publications
7. ☐ Other (specify): _____

C. Name, sex, and race or ethnic origin of other interviewed candidate.

_____

_____

1. ☐ Educational achievement. Candidate has:
   ☐ M.A./M.S. ☐ ABD ☐ Ph.D.

2. ☐ Teaching ability. Candidate has ___ years of teaching experience.

3. ☐ Professional or academic references. Did candidate provide references? ☐ Yes ☐ No

4. ☐ Rank and/or salary required

5. ☐ Research or professional specialty

6. ☐ Scholarly research and publications

7. ☐ Other (specify): _____

D. Name, sex, and race or ethnic origin of other interviewed candidate.

_____

_____

1. ☐ Educational achievement. Candidate has:
   ☐ M.A./M.S. ☐ ABD ☐ Ph.D.

2. ☐ Teaching ability. Candidate has___ years of teaching experience.

3. ☐ Professional or academic references. Did candidate provide references?   ☐ Yes   ☐ No

4. ☐ Rank and/or salary required

5. ☐ Research or professional specialty

6. ☐ Scholarly research and publication

7. ☐ Other (specify):_____

Review and Approval Signatures

_____   _____
Department Chair   Date

_____   _____
Dean   Date

_____   _____
Provost   Date

_____   _____
Affirmative Action Officer   Date

Appendix J

Affirmative Action Recruitment Checklist

School/College/Department: _____

Dean: _____

Position: _____ ☐ Tenured ☐ Tracking ☐ Nontracking

Department Chair: _____

Director/Supervisor: _____

Vita/Résumé Deadline Date: _____

Required Activity, Search, Etc.	**Date Completed**

1. Recruitment authorization form is approved and signed by chair, dean, director, and/or vice president   _____

2. Received affirmative action packet data (request from affirmative action/human resources office if needed)   _____

3. Appointment of search committee and name of chair: _____

4. Advertisement of position
   ☐ Chronicle   ☐ Herald Dispatch
   ☐ Charleston Gazette   ☐ Black Issue
   ☐ Other:_____
   ☐ Professional journal:_____   _____

5. Notice sent to minority schools and/or organizations and female organizations   _____

6. Director of affirmative action/human resources or designee meets with search committee   _____

7. Initial screening of candidates   _____

8. Search chair contacts director of affirmative action/human resources or designee before bringing any candidates for interview   _____

9. Interview conducted with candidates
   ☐ Telephone   ☐ In person   ☐ Video   _____

10. Search committee determines top candidates and refers to department chair, vice president, or director   _____

11. Selection of final candidate   _____

12. Date sent to director of affirmative action/human resources or designee for approval   _____

13. Date sent to vice president/provost/director for approval   _____

Letters Sent To:

Candidates who did not receive interview   _____

Candidates interviewed, not offered job   _____

Candidate offered position   _____

Certification Statement

I certify that the recruitment procedures used in soliciting applicants, selecting qualified candidates from among all who applied, and offering of employment have been conducted in accordance with local, state, and federal Equal Opportunity laws. I further certify that the hiring practices and decision upholds the intent and integrity of Central University's affirmative action policy.

Specifically, I Certify That:

1. All candidates who were interviewed and/or considered for the position either met or exceeded minimum qualifications.

2. All candidates were interviewed and considered on the basis of their qualifications for the work to be performed.

3. No employment offer(s) was (were) extended (verbally or in writing) to the successful candidate prior to approval by the director of affirmative action/human resources or designee.

4. Any salary offered at a level higher than that advertised received prior approval from the respective dean, provost, and vice president(s) and/or personnel department prior to the offer.

_____

Department chair's or director's signature

_____   _____

Title   Date

Appendix K

Recommendation to Hire, Faculty Position
COLLEGE OF MASS COMMUNICATIONS

Position Description: _____

Position Number: _____

1. Were there any exemptions to the college's recruitment procedures
   and the university's affirmative action guidelines?   ☐ Yes   ☐ No
   If so, attach appropriate authorization.

2. Recommended rank:_____
   Does candidate have terminal degree in field?   ☐ Yes   ☐ No
   Justification:

   _____

   _____

   _____

3. Number of years of full-time teaching:_____
   List below institution(s), noting the number of years, where the candidate has taught.

   _____

   _____

   _____

4. Candidate is recommended for tenure at this time:
   ☐ Yes   ☐ No
   If yes, provide justification, including number of years as a tenured
   professor at other institution(s).

   _____

   _____

   _____

5. Number of years recommended that the candidate be allowed to
   count toward tenure:_____
   Candidate's tenure year would be:_____
   Justification:

   _____

   _____

   _____

6. If you are not recommending tenure at initial hiring, did you provide the candidate with the university promotion and tenure guidelines, and does he or she understand them?   ☐ Yes   ☐ No
Comments:

_____

_____

_____

7. Salary recommended:_____
Does this salary create any inequities in the department?
☐ Yes   ☐ No
Justification:

_____

_____

8. Describe the procedures used in checking the candidate's qualifications. Be specific—list the names of individuals who submitted letters, as well as names of persons contacted by telephone.

_____

_____

_____

9. List below any additional comments relative to this recommendation.

_____

_____

_____

_____   _____
Search Committee Chair   Date

_____   _____
Department Chair   Date

Dean's recommendation for approval: ☐ Yes   ☐ No
Comments:

_____   _____
Dean   Date

Appendix L

Course Evaluation: Questions to Consider

No two evaluation designs will be the same, as in each instance the evaluation must be structured to serve the information needs of those involved in the decision-making process. There is, however, a general list of questions that are often used in the evaluation of courses and other programs of instruction. The following list has been designed to assist faculty and administrators who are or will be charged with the task of evaluating a course. While no list could ever be considered complete, these items have been developed from efforts on several campuses that have dealt with the design and implementation of new courses and programs as well as the evaluation of existing courses and curricula. The list is intended to be a functional guide in the design stage of an evaluation. It should serve as a checklist to ensure that all relevant questions have been considered. In using this list, remember that every question may not be appropriate in a single project because of limitations in time, staff, and money. It is up to those involved to select and prioritize the specific questions that should be addressed. It is our hope that this list will lead to more responsible decisions regarding which issues will be addressed in the evaluation.

Consider each of the following questions and check those that are appropriate for the specific course you are evaluating.

I. Course Rationale
☐ A. What population of students is the course intended to serve?
☐ B. What student needs is the course intended to serve?
☐ C. What institutional, community, or societal needs is the course intended to serve?
☐ D. What other defensible needs exist for offering the course?
☐ E. What other courses serve these same needs?
☐ F. To what extent does the course overlap with or duplicate these other courses?
☐ G. On what grounds is the continued existence of the course justified and warranted?

II. Development and Current Status of the Course

- ☐ A. When and under what circumstances was the course developed?
- ☐ B. How frequently and how regularly has the course been offered?
- ☐ C. To what extent has the enrollment increased, decreased, or stabilized from year to year?
- ☐ D. What problems have been associated with the course and how have they been resolved?
- ☐ E. To what extent is the course intended to be replicable from instructor to instructor or from term to term?
- ☐ F. To what degree do the plans or design for the course exist in a written or documented form? In what documents (course approval forms, course outlines or syllabi, memos, etc.) do these plans exist?
- ☐ G. How does the current version of the course differ from earlier versions? Why?

III. Credit and Curricular Implications

- ☐ A. What credit is awarded for successful completion of the course? On what basis is this credit allocation justified?
- ☐ B. In what ways can credit for this course be applied toward fulfillment of graduate and degree requirements?
- ☐ C. At what level (lower division, upper division, or graduate) is the course classified? Why? On what basis is this classification justified?
- ☐ D. How does the course fit into the overall curriculum of the sponsoring department and college?
- ☐ E. In which departments is the course cross-listed? Why? How does it fit into the curricula of these departments or colleges?
- ☐ F. What prerequisite skills or experiences are needed in order to succeed in the course?
- ☐ G. What problems are experienced by students who do not have these prerequisites?

IV. **Course Objectives**
- ☐ A. What are the formal, stated objectives of the course?
- ☐ B. How feasible and realistic are these objectives in terms of the abilities of the target population and the available time and resources?
- ☐ C. How are the stated objectives related to the adult life-role competencies that students will need in everyday life outside of school?
- ☐ D. How are the objectives related to the competencies students will need in their subsequent academic careers?
- ☐ E. If the course is designed to prepare students for a specific professional or vocational field, how are the objectives related to the competencies they are likely to need in their future careers?
- ☐ F. What values are affirmed by the choice of these objectives as goals for the course?
- ☐ G. What other purposes, intents, or goals do the faculty, administrators, and other interested audiences have for the course?
- ☐ H. What goals and expectations do students have for the course?
- ☐ I. To what extent are these additional goals and expectations compatible with the stated course objectives?

V. **The Content of the Course**
- ☐ A. What (1) information, (2) processes, and (3) attitudes and values constitute the subject matter or content of the course?
- ☐ B. How are the various content elements related to the course's objectives?
  - ☐ 1. Which objectives receive the most coverage or emphasis? Why?
  - ☐ 2. Which objectives receive only minor coverage? Why?
- ☐ C. How is the content sequenced or arranged? Why is this sequence appropriate/inappropriate?
- ☐ D. How are the various content elements integrated and unified into a coherent pattern or structure? To what extent does fragmentation or lack of coherence appear to be a problem?

   ☐ E. What values and assumptions are implicit in the decisions which have been made regarding content selection and emphasis?

VI. Instructional Strategies

   ☐ A. What kinds of learning activities are used?

      ☐ 1. What activities are the students expected to engage in during the class session?

      ☐ 2. What assignments or projects are students expected to complete outside of class?

      ☐ 3. In what ways are these activities appropriate in light of the course objectives?

      ☐ 4. How could these activities be made more effective?

   ☐ B. What instructional materials are utilized?

      ☐ 1. How and for what purpose are the materials used?

      ☐ 2. How accurate and up to date are the materials?

      ☐ 3. In what ways do the materials need to be improved?

      ☐ 4. How could the materials be used more effectively?

   ☐ C. What instructional roles or functions are performed by the instructor(s)?

      ☐ 1. How could these roles be performed more effectively?

      ☐ 2. What important instructional roles are not provided or are performed inadequately? Why?

   ☐ D. What premises and assumptions about learning and the nature of the learner underlie the selection of instructional strategies? How and to what extent are these assumptions warranted?

VII. Procedures for Evaluating Students' Achievements

   ☐ A. What instruments and procedures are employed as a means of collecting evidence of the student's progress and achievement?

☐ B. What criteria are used to assess the adequacy of the student's work and/or achievement? On what basis were these criteria selected?

☐ C. How well do the assessment procedures correspond with the course content and objectives? Which objectives or content areas are not assessed? Why?

☐ D. To what extent do the assessment procedures appear to be fair and objective?

☐ E. What evidence is there that the assessment instruments and procedures yield valid and reliable results?

☐ F. How are the assessment results used? Are the results shared with the students within a reasonable amount of time?

☐ G. How consistently are the assessment criteria applied from instructor to instructor and from term to term?

☐ H. What indications are there that the amount of assessment is excessive, about right, or insufficient?

VIII. Organization of the Course

☐ A. How is the course organized in terms of lectures, labs, studios, discussion sections, field trips, and other types of scheduled class sessions?

☐ B. How frequently and for how long are the various types of class meetings scheduled? Is the total allocation of time sufficient/insufficient? Why?

☐ C. If there is more than one instructor, what are the duties and responsibilities of each? What problems result from this division of responsibilities?

☐ D. What outside-of-class instruction, tutoring, or counseling is provided? By whom? On what basis?

☐ E. How well is the student workload distributed throughout the course?

☐ F. To what extent are the necessary facilities, equipment, and materials readily available and in good working condition when needed?

IX. Course Outcomes

☐ A. What proportion of the enrollees completed the course with credit during the regular term? How does the completion rate vary from instructor to instructor or from term to term?

☐ B. What proportion of the enrollees withdrew from or discontinued attending the course? Why?

    ☐ 1. To what degree does their discontinuance appear to be related to factors associated with the course?

    ☐ 2. How does the attrition rate vary from instructor to instructor or from term to term?

☐ C. At the end of the course, what evidence is there that students have achieved the stated objectives?

    ☐ 1. For which objectives was the course most/least successful?

    ☐ 2. For what kinds of students was the course most/least successful?

☐ D. What effects does the course appear to have had on students' interest in the subject matter and their desire to continue studying and learning about the subject?

☐ E. What other effects did the course have on the students?

    ☐ 1. How were their values, attitudes, priorities, interests, or aspirations changed?

    ☐ 2. How were their study habits or other behavioral patterns modified?

    ☐ 3. How pervasive and/or significant do these effects appear to be?

These guidelines were developed by Robert M. Diamond and Richard R. Sudweeks at the Syracuse University Center for Instructional Development. Reprinted with permission of the authors.

Appendix M

Tenure and Promotion Guidelines

COLLEGE OF MASS COMMUNICATIONS

The following guidelines, effective in the 2006–2007 academic year, supplement the general university policies and procedures on tenure and promotion and are specific to the College of Mass Communications.

Degrees and Professional Experience

At the time of employment, an initial determination is made of the suitability of the candidate's professional experience and academic background for purposes of tenure and promotion. The chair (in consultation with the departmental promotion and tenure review committee), dean, and vice president for academic affairs are responsible for this evaluation. Because of the diversity of backgrounds and qualifications required for faculty membership in the college, this evaluation assumes great importance, and the candidate's letter of offer should make explicit its outcome.

Creative Activity

The college values both traditional research and creative activity. University guidelines offer explicit direction in the area of traditional research. The following guidelines offer general direction for those who will present creative activity as part of their record for tenure and promotion.

Creative activity consists of the creation, production, exhibition, performance, or publication of original work. Such activity should demonstrate originality in design or execution, and reflect, comment on, or otherwise contribute to the forms and practices of any endeavor represented by the disciplines in the College of Mass Communications. The product of creative activity may be communicated through print media, photographs, film, video recordings, audio recordings, graphic designs, digital imaging, live performances, or other technologies.

Examples. Creative activity may include but is not limited to (1) published books (professional, trade, or consumer) and articles, reviews, and commentaries in professional and popular publications; (2) graphics, visual materials, photographs, video productions, multimedia productions, or other visually oriented media for professional or general audiences; (3) audio and/or audio-related productions, sound design for theater, film, video, or other media for professional or general audiences; (4) performances or exhibitions of creative works before professional or general audiences; (5) original musical works or original arrangements of preexisting works, including but not limited to scores (traditional, electronic, or other fixed media) engineered, produced, or performed for professional or general audiences; (6) software development, multimedia authoring, and/or unique and innovative applications thereof for professional or general audiences.

Review. Review of creative activities may be satisfied in one or more of the following ways: (1) acceptance for exhibition, publication, or performance in popular or professional media where submissions are judged by independent referees who are respected practitioners of the creative activity; (2) acceptance by an editorial staff or someone who is charged with a selective review process; (3) published review of performances or productions by recognized critics, scholars, or industry professionals. In fields where published reviews or their equivalents are difficult to obtain, independent reviews of the individual works, projects, or performances may be solicited. Such reviews are separate from the evaluation of the faculty member's research and/or creative record as a whole, which occurs as part of promotion and tenure review.

Responsibilities. As indicated in the university policy, documentation of creative activity should represent the cornerstone of the evaluation process. It is the responsibility of the faculty member to provide detailed documentation of creative activity in materials accompanying the application for tenure or promotion, or where the creative activities are being judged as part of the annual evaluation for retention in a tenure-track position. This documentation must accompany the initial submission of materials to the department chair and departmental promotion and tenure review committee. The faculty member may also include supporting materials that would assist colleagues in assessing qualitative aspects of the work.

Faculty are encouraged to submit whatever is significant to document "their direct participation in the creation or creative performance of the work" (MSU Policy No. II:O1:05B, Policies and Procedures for Promotion and Appointment, August 1, 1996; Paragraph 1(B) (2) (b) 1).

Documentation

In documenting the record for tenure and/or promotion review, candidates, and departments when appropriate, should marshal evidence in the following ways:

Teaching. Candidates are expected to present the following: (1) an orderly summary of teaching evaluations that uses tables to chart responses to important questions about teaching over time in relation to departmental averages (supplied by the department); (2) copies of class visitation reports as prepared by the senior faculty of the department; (3) other evidence of quality teaching, including records of teaching innovations, course improvements, honors received, teaching portfolios, and participation in national, regional, and state symposia.

Research and Creative Activity. Departments are expected to solicit three outside evaluations of the research and/or creative record as a whole. For research, the evaluations should be written by an appropriate panel of scholars; for creative activity, the evaluations should be written by an appropriate panel of professionals and/or scholars. The evaluators should be chosen by the chair in consultation with the candidate and with the advice of the departmental tenure and promotion review committee. In order to fulfill university deadlines in the decision year, the candidates should discuss evaluators with the chair during the spring semester in the year prior to being reviewed. The chair, in turn, should consult with the departmental tenure and promotion review committee to finalize the evaluators. The candidate should provide the chair with a package of materials for the evaluators by the first week of classes in the decision year. The outside evaluations should address the quality of the scholarly or creative activity as a whole, delineate the unique contribution to the field, comment on future prospects, and, if appropriate, evaluate the quality of the candidate's work in relation to those evaluated for tenure at the evaluator's institution.

Public Service. Candidates may solicit letters that document substantial accomplishments, whether they are service to the university, profession, or society. University guidelines offer ample direction for documenting excellence in public service.

Tenure

The probationary period in the College of Mass Communications is ordinarily six years. Candidates who began employment at MSU prior to August 1, 1997, may choose to undergo tenure and promotion review in their fifth probationary year.

Candidates for tenure must demonstrate excellence in two of the following areas and average performance or above in the third: (1) instruction; (2) research and/or creative activity; (3) public service. Candidates must distinguish the two areas in which they claim excellence and marshal evidence to document the claim.

People hired as assistant professors under the master's degree plus 30-hour provision in the university guidelines must complete the doctorate to be eligible for tenure.

Promotion

Candidates for promotion to associate professor will normally be reviewed in the same year as for tenure.

Candidates for promotion to professor must demonstrate a national reputation in one of the following three areas: (1) instruction; (2) research and/or creative activity; (3) public service. It is expected that candidates will name their areas of excellence and offer appropriate documentation to support the claim.

Committees in the College

Departmental tenure and promotion review committees should be organized early in the year and should meet within the first month of the semester to select a chair. Meetings to evaluate candidates for tenure and promotion should be announced as early in the semester as possible and, at the latest, 10 days prior to the meeting. The chair leads the deliberations of the committee and coordinates the committee's work with the department chair and with the candidates. The chair functions as a participating member of the committee and may vote on all issues facing the committee. All voting on issues of tenure and promotion is done in person at meetings; no absentee or proxy votes are accepted. In the case of multiple votes, including votes taken after consultation with department chairs to resolve splits, only the final vote is reported.

Appendix N

Community College Tenure and Promotion Guidelines

UNIVERSITY OF HAWAII'S COMMUNITY COLLEGE SYSTEM

I. Guidelines for Tenure

A. Introduction

This document describes the University of Hawaii Community Colleges' tenure application process. It is a guide for both the applicant and the peer and administrative reviewers of the application. This document outlines the community colleges' expectations and values. It provides standard forms and formats which community college faculty may use to organize and present their applications for tenure.

The guidelines are written so that information common to all applications can be consistently presented and assessed. This information consists of discipline expertise, instructional delivery skills, instructional design skills, achievements in other areas of professional service, and how the applicant has sustained a high level of quality in his or her efforts over time.

For the applicant, these guidelines encourage a flexible approach for self-appraisal and provide the framework for a professional presentation of an educator's commitment to teaching and learning in an open-door institution of higher learning. The forms and format guides have been designed to encourage independent judgment and to stimulate creativity on the part of each applicant. They present an opportunity for the applicant to document professional accomplishments, viewpoints, and attitudes as a community college educator.

For the reviewer, these guidelines are to be used in conjunction with the *Community Colleges Faculty Classification Plan* approved by the Board of Regents. The guidelines emphasize the need for the thoughtful exercise of peer participation in assessment matters in higher education. In accordance with Article X, B, faculty members are reminded that (1) there is a strict exclusion from voting of any individual who is not a tenured bargaining unit 07 member on the tenure of another faculty member; and (2) that only faculty members of equal or higher rank are allowed to vote on applications for promotion. In addition, in accordance with Article XII, F.2.j., faculty members are reminded that when participating on personnel committees, they have the responsibility for avoiding conflicts of roles by recusing themselves from the process when such conflicts exist.

B. General Information for Tenure Applicants

The 2003–2009 agreement between the University of Hawaii Professional Assembly and the Board of Regents of the University of Hawaii (hereinafter referred to as "the agreement") requires that all eligible faculty apply for tenure by their final year of probationary service according to a timetable established and published by the university. Probationary service is defined in Article XII, Section B, of the agreement. The normal probationary period is five (5) probationary years. If requests for extensions are approved, the probationary period may extend an additional two years for a total maximum of seven (7) years. Failure to apply for tenure during the final year of probationary service results in the automatic issuance of a terminal year contract commencing August 1 (Article XII, Section E of the 2003–2009 agreement). If you have any questions regarding your final year of probation, check with your campus personnel office.

Tenure application forms will be made available to eligible faculty members no less than six (6) weeks prior to the application deadline. Faculty members applying in the final year of the normal probationary period will have the option of being considered under the criteria contained in the guidelines distributed this academic year or those contained in the guidelines distributed two years earlier (Article XII, Section F of the 2003–2009 agreement). The application for tenure is very important. The information submitted by you, and that which is appended to your application by reviewers, is the documentation upon which your case for tenure will be examined. It is your responsibility to see that all pertinent information has been included in your application.

Available Options. Article XII of the agreement defines when you should normally apply for tenure. There are several options available to you:

1. If you are in your final year of probationary service, or in your terminal year of service but have a written agreement that the university will accept your tenure application during the 2005–2006 academic year, you must elect whether or not to apply.

   - You may elect to apply for tenure and may proceed by signing statement C.1 on p. 2.1 of the application form. Be sure to complete and submit the application to your chancellor before or by the close of business on October 14, 2005. To assist you, the division chair/unit head/assistant dean is available for consultation, but is prohibited from assisting in the preparation of the application. Procedures for review of your application are outlined in Section C below. You should also be familiar with Article XII of the 2003–2009 agreement.

   - You may instead elect not to apply, in which case you should select and sign statement C.1 on p. 2.1 of the application form and submit the statement to the chancellor before or on October 14, 2005. If you elect this choice, your contract for 2005–2006 will be a terminal year contract. Your appointment with the university will terminate on July 31, 2007, unless you resign before that date.

2. You may apply for tenure before your final year of probationary service. If you wish to do so, however, you should have submitted a signed letter requesting that the university reduce your normal probationary period. This letter should have been submitted in spring 2005. Please note that in the event the request was approved, the 2005–2006 academic year will become your final year of probationary service and a negative decision on your application for tenure will result in a terminal year contract for 2005–2006.

3. You may apply for promotion in the same year that you apply for tenure, provided that you meet the requirements stated in these guidelines. For tenure to be granted, you must meet the criteria for promotion to the next higher rank (Article XII, B.2.g. of the 2003–2009 agreement). Should tenure be denied, you may request a review consistent with Article XII, G.

C. Criteria for Tenure

The general reasons for granting tenure are that the university has concluded (a) that you are, and will continue to be, an efficient and productive member of your discipline and college; and (b) that it anticipates a long-term need for the services you have proven yourself capable of rendering. Applicants are reminded that although reviews are guided by specific criteria and all reviews involve a fair and thorough consideration of the evidence, the final tenure decision involves judgment, and may include honest differences of opinions. It should also be noted that because the granting of tenure involves a long-term commitment of the resources of the university, the review process is essentially conservative. Unless there is a clear case for tenure, the practice is not to recommend tenure to the Board of Regents.

In evaluating the request for tenure, reviewers will consider accomplishments and performance during the period since your initial hire at the University of Hawaii. In order to be awarded tenure in a given rank, a faculty member must meet the minimum qualifications, including the requirements for education and experience established by the university for that rank, and any additional criteria which may have been established. *The Community Colleges Classification Plan* has been appended for your information and use.

It is also important to include in your dossier a discussion of the following: (1) your own philosophy and goals regarding teaching (counseling, or appropriate area of instructional support); (2) your perceptions about the students we serve, including their needs and aspirations; (3) a concise self-analysis of how you have responded to these educational needs; and (4) the possible impact and contributions you have made toward achieving your professional objectives and meeting your students' needs.

D. Guidelines for Application Preparation

Your application for tenure is the means by which you inform those involved in the review process of your achievements and ability. Therefore, it is your responsibility to clearly show how you fully meet the expectations of the rank and criteria at which tenure is requested. You must clearly describe all your professional activities and, where appropriate, provide substantive interpretation and discussion of summarized data and information.

Presentation of Dossier. Be sure that your dossier is organized in such a way as to prevent loss of any material. The dossier should be paginated and bound in some way that will allow insertion of additional documents.

II. Guidelines for Promotion
A. Introduction

This document describes the University of Hawaii Community Colleges' tenure application process. It is a guide for both the applicant and the peer and administrative reviewers of the application. This document outlines the community colleges' expectations and values. It provides standard forms and formats which community college faculty may use to organize and present their applications for tenure.

The guidelines are written so that information common to all applications can be consistently presented and assessed. This information consists of discipline expertise, instructional delivery skills, instructional design skills, achievements in other areas of professional service, and how the applicant has sustained a high level of quality in his or her efforts over time.

For the applicant, these guidelines encourage a flexible approach for self-appraisal and provide the framework for a professional presentation of an educator's commitment to teaching and learning in an open-door institution of higher learning. The forms and format guides have been designed to encourage independent judgment and to stimulate creativity on the part of each applicant. They present an opportunity for the applicant to document professional accomplishments, viewpoints, and attitudes as a community college educator.

For the reviewer, these guidelines are to be used in conjunction with the *Community Colleges Faculty Classification Plan* approved by the Board of Regents. The guidelines emphasize the need for the thoughtful exercise of peer participation in assessment matters in higher education. In accordance with Article X, B, faculty members are reminded that (1) there is a strict exclusion from voting of any individual who is not a tenured bargaining unit 07 member on the tenure of another faculty member; and (2) that only faculty members of equal or higher rank are allowed to vote on applications for promotion. In addition, in accordance with Article XII, F.2.j., faculty members are reminded that when participating on personnel committees, they have the responsibility for avoiding conflicts of roles by recusing themselves from the process when such conflicts exist.

B. General Information for Promotion Applicants

Article XIV of the 2003–2009 agreement between the University of Hawaii Professional Assembly and the Board of Regents of the University of Hawaii (hereinafter referred to as "the agreement") provides that any faculty member will, upon application, be considered for promotion in any year in accordance with guidelines established by the university. This means that faculty may apply for promotion in accordance with the guidelines set forth below. Should there be a substantial change in the promotion criteria in the year of application, the candidate will have the option of being considered under the criteria contained in the guidelines distributed in the preceding year (Article XIV, Section B.2. of the 2003–2009 agreement). Creditable service includes regular on-duty service, sabbatical leaves, and leaves without pay for professional improvement. The application for promotion is very important. The information submitted by you, and that which is appended to your application by reviewers, is the principal documentation on which your application for promotion will be examined. It is your responsibility to see that all pertinent information has been included in your application.

Available Options.

1. If you believe you have met the expectations and criteria of the rank to which you plan to apply for promotion, you may submit your promotion application:
   - From rank 2 to 3 after completing your fourth year of creditable service in rank 2
   - From rank 3 to 4, or rank 4 to 5, after completing your third year of creditable service in rank 3 or 4, respectively
2. You may apply for promotion prior to the required time period even if you do not meet the minimum qualifications with respect to time in

rank and/or the educational requirements for the rank to which you are applying if you believe that your outstanding experience and/or performance is worthy of such consideration. In this case, you may apply for an early promotion only after approval has been received by the appropriate approving authority. Your request for a shortening should contain a detailed explanation of why you believe a shortening is justified. As a general rule, such requests are granted only in unusual and exceptional circumstances. Note that requests for such waivers must be approved prior to the application deadline.

Probationary faculty hired at rank C3 or C4 may apply for promotion in the same year that you apply for tenure, provided that you meet the requirements outlined in the Guidelines for Tenure for 2005–2006. For tenure to be granted, you must meet the criteria for promotion to the next higher rank. Article XII of the agreement requires tenure be denied if promotion is denied. In such event, you may request a review consistent with Article XII, G.

After familiarizing yourself with the Guidelines for Promotion and assessing your eligibility, you may initiate your application by signing statement Part II.A. on page 2.1 of the application form. Be sure to complete and submit the application to your chancellor before or by the close of business on October 14, 2005. To assist you, the division chair/unit head/assistant dean, as appropriate, is available for consultation, but is prohibited from assisting in the preparation of the application. You should also be familiar with Article XIV of the agreement.

C. Criteria for Promotion

In order to be promoted, the applicant must meet the minimum qualifications established by the Board of Regents for the rank to which promotion is sought in addition to any other criteria which may be established. However, the mere satisfaction of these requirements does not guarantee promotion, rather the decision for promotion is based on whether the faculty member has documented performance at the level to which he or she is seeking promotion. Instead, promotion represents an important transition in the faculty member's professional status. The exact stage of a faculty member's career at which promotion is deserved is a matter of judgment, and there may be honest differences of opinion based on fair and thorough consideration of your dossier. Because the granting of promotion has implications for the university's standards and its standing in the academic community, the review process is essentially conservative. Unless there is a clear case for promotion, the practice is not to recommend promotion to the Board of Regents. In assessing the dossier for promotion, reviewers will consider your accomplishments and performance during the period since your last promotion, or since initial hire at the University of Hawaii if you have not been previously promoted during your service here.

It is also important to include in your dossier a discussion of the following: (1) your own philosophy and goals regarding teaching (or counseling, or appropriate area of instructional support); (2) your perceptions about the students we serve, including their needs and aspirations; (3) a concise self-analysis of how you have responded to these educational needs; and (4) the possible impact and contributions you have made toward achieving your professional objectives and meeting your students' needs. In addition to a discussion of these four general topics, the dossier should address, under appropriate headings, how you have met each of the criteria for the rank to which you are applying. For example, faculty members applying to rank C3, should address the rank C3 criteria; those applying to rank C4 should address rank C4 criteria, and so on. The specific criteria for each rank are listed in *Community Colleges Classification Plan*, which has been appended.

D. Guidelines for Application Preparation

Your application for promotion is the means by which you inform those involved in the review process of your achievements and ability. Therefore, it is your responsibility to clearly show how you fully meet the expectations and criteria of the rank to which promotion is requested. You must include a clear rationale for your selection of activities and a substantive interpretation of the results.

Presentation of Dossier. Be sure that your dossier is organized in such a way as to prevent loss of any material. The dossier should be paginated and bound in some way that will allow insertion of additional documents.

Appendix O

Peer Evaluation Form

The purpose of peer evaluations is to assess the scholarship and organization that goes into the class. Thus, the most important phase of evaluation is the discussions between evaluator and instructor before and after the observation. Before visiting the class, the evaluator collects data such as instructional materials, reading assignments, tests, texts, instructor philosophy, scholarly quality, and so forth.

The evaluator should also identify what has been covered in previous classes and receive an overview of the concepts to be covered during the evaluator's classroom visit. The evaluator should then visit the class on the scheduled date. Upon request of either the evaluator or the instructor, a second visit may be scheduled. After the visit, the evaluator should again meet with the instructor to provide feedback. When the evaluator has completed the rating forms, a copy should be given to the instructor for inclusion in his or her files.

	excellent	good	marginal	poor	unacceptable
Instructor Knowledge					
How good is the scholarship that goes into the course?	1	2	3	4	5
Methods of Instruction					
Scholarship gets incorporated into the class	1	2	3	4	5
Tests and assignments are fair	1	2	3	4	5
Stresses important material	1	2	3	4	5
Vocational and Personal Advising					
Keeps regular office hours and is accessible to students	1	2	3	4	5

Is involved in students' activities outside of the classroom	1	2	3	4	5
Overall Evaluation of Teaching	1	2	3	4	5

Narrative Comments:

Appendix P

Tenure and Promotion Procedures

DEPARTMENT OF PSYCHOLOGY

Criteria for Tenure and Promotion

To be tenured and/or promoted, one must score at least "good" in each of the categories listed. Furthermore, a ranking of "excellent" in teaching or research must be made for each promotion decision. Only those holding a Ph.D. degree will be eligible for tenure or promotion to the rank of associate or full professor in the department of psychology. The above standards apply to all promotion and tenure decisions.

Times for Evaluations

New tenure-track faculty will be evaluated according to the procedures outlined as follows in their second, fourth, and sixth year at Marshall. Faculty are eligible for promotion to the next rank if they have been in their present rank for at least four years. Experience at the same rank at another institution can count for tenure and promotion. A candidate will submit the promotion and tenure credentials on or before October 31 of the year of evaluation. Tenure and promotion are to be based on identical criteria. Each promotion is to be based on the same criteria, with the restriction that materials submitted in a prior evaluation cannot be counted again.

The Composition and Voting Procedures
of the Tenure and Promotion Committee

The tenure and promotion committee will consist entirely of tenured faculty. They will elect their chair. The evaluation scores from the attached forms will be the basis for all tenure and promotion decisions. These evaluations will then be summarized by the chair of the tenure and promotion committee. The chair's responsibilities are to organize the score sheets and provide a summary sheet. The committee will vote to determine if this final document reflects the views of the committee. If there is no consensus on this document, then a "minority" document may be written by members if they wish. All documents will be turned into the chair of the department by December 10. The chair will use the same evaluation procedures and forms as the department members of the tenure and promotion committee. The department chair will use the enclosed forms and procedures in his or her evaluations.

The following weightings will be used as the basis for the overall score of an individual being evaluated.

Teaching score	50%
Research score	35%
Committee score	10%
Community score	5%
Total score	*100%*

The following formula will be used in calculating the overall performance score: (Teaching score *.50) + (Research score *.35) + (Committee score *.10) + (Community score *.05)

These will be analyzed by the following scale

excellent	good	marginal	poor	unacceptable
1	2	3	4	5

It should be noted that each score must be of the accepted levels listed as follows for a person to be promoted or tenured. If it is not, then even if the applicant's overall score is in the "good" or "excellent" range, the applicant will not be promoted or tenured.

Committee's Cover Sheet

Name of Candidate: _____

Present Rank: _____

Rank Being Applied For: _____

Committee Members: _____

_____

_____

Summary of Evaluation:

Teaching Score: 50%

excellent	good	marginal	poor	unacceptable
1–1.75	1.76–2.5	2.6–3.0	3.1–3.9	4–5

Research Score: 35%

excellent	good	marginal	poor	unacceptable
1–1.75	1.76–2.5	2.6–3.0	3.1–3.9	4–5

Committee Score: 10%

excellent	good	marginal	poor	unacceptable
1–1.75	1.76–2.5	2.6–3.0	3.1–3.9	4–5

Community Score: 5%

excellent	good	marginal	poor	unacceptable
1–1.75	1.76–2.5	2.6–3.0	3.1–3.9	4–5

Total score:_____

Recommendation: _____

_____

_____

Evaluator's Cover Sheet

Name of Candidate: _____

Present Rank: _____

Rank Being Applied For: _____

Committee Members:_____

_____

_____

Summary of Evaluation:

Teaching Score: 50%

excellent	good	marginal	poor	unacceptable
1–1.75	1.76–2.5	2.6–3.0	3.1–3.9	4–5

Research Score: 35%

excellent	good	marginal	poor	unacceptable
1–1.75	1.76–2.5	2.6–3.0	3.1–3.9	4–5

Committee Score: 10%

excellent	good	marginal	poor	unacceptable
1–1.75	1.76–2.5	2.6–3.0	3.1–3.9	4–5

Community Score: 5%

excellent	good	marginal	poor	unacceptable
1–1.75	1.76–2.5	2.6–3.0	3.1–3.9	4–5

Total score:_____

Recommendation:

_____

_____

_____

I. The Evaluation of Teaching

Teaching is the most important feature in retention, tenure, and promotion decisions. It will count for 50% of the weight in all tenure and promotion decisions. Attached are two forms: one for student evaluation and the other for peer evaluation. There will be three different measures of teaching effectiveness: Student evaluations will count 40%, peer evaluations will count 40%, and the promotion and tenure group's evaluation of course development and teaching-related factors outside the classroom will count 20% as applied to retention, promotion, or tenure decisions. A final score will be calculated such that questions 1–15 on the student evaluations will be averaged over all evaluations conducted for the review period, and then the scores on the peer evaluations and evaluations of teaching activities outside the classroom will be averaged in a similar manner. These will then be averaged to produce a "Teaching Score" calculated by the formula:

(Student evaluation score *.40) + (Peer evaluation score *.40) + (Outside classroom teaching score *.20).

If the total Teaching Score falls at "marginal" or below (i.e., an average score of 2.6 or worse), then the person applying for promotion or tenure will be turned down. Thus, one must demonstrate good teaching to be retained, tenured, or promoted in the department of psychology. If the average score is 1.75 or better, then this person is considered to be "outstanding."

A. Student Evaluations of Teaching

Every year, student evaluations of teaching must be performed on four sections taught for all faculty in the department. More evaluations may be done if the individual faculty member desires. The chair or his or her designee will be responsible for data tabulation. A minimum of four evaluations per year must be entered into one's calculations including each course topic that is taught or all sections if fewer sections are taught in a particular year. One does not have to calculate a course into one's evaluations the first time the course is taught by that person. To calculate student evaluations, the computer center will generate the means for all students on all questions for each section taught. The means for each question will be added together and divided by the number of questions on the form such that an overall mean is calculated for each course. These individual course means will be summed and this sum will be divided by the number of evaluations creating the student evaluation score. This will be the number entered into the Teaching Score on the cover sheets for the tenure and promotion committee's evaluation. The chair will use the same student evaluations but use her or his own peer score for determination of the Teaching Score on the chair's Evaluator's Cover Sheet.

B. Procedures for Peer Evaluation of Teaching

The attached peer evaluation procedure is the only one that will be recognized by the department tenure and promotion committee and by the chair of the department. It is to be used in all cases of promotion and tenure, and in the second, fourth, and sixth year of a nontenured faculty member's employment. This should be initiated by the applying faculty member at the beginning of the semester, and completed before the deadline for application. The peer evaluations will be conducted by the chair and a faculty member appointed by the tenure and promotion committee. Each evaluator should evaluate a different section.

If someone has released time to conduct other activities in the university (e.g., chair of the department, clinic director, etc.), that person's performance must be evaluated and weighted into the teaching score proportionally to the percentage of released time they hold. Because these activities can vary, the applicant will provide the chair of the department and tenure and promotion committee with careful documentation of their duties and accomplishments in the position. Each evaluator will use the following scale to calculate into the teaching dimension.

excellent	good	marginal	poor	unacceptable
1	2	3	4	5

C. Teaching Activities Outside the Classroom

The third component of the Teaching Score involves the evaluation of course organization, development, and other nonclassroom-related aspects of teaching. Because opportunities differ for various faculty to teach a large number of different preparations, supervise research, and so on, this area must be analyzed subjectively by the committee. The candidate will present evidence of the committees served on, students supported in research, number of courses taught, number of preparations offered, participation in student activities, participation in honors courses, team teaching, special topics, advising loads, and so forth. Each member of the committee will use the following scale to calculate this dimension.

excellent	good	marginal	poor	unacceptable
1	2	3	4	5

II. Evaluation of Scholarly Activity

As with the other areas, the following scale will be used to evaluate each research criterion.

	excellent	good	marginal	poor	unacceptable
	1	2	3	4	5
Points	250+	200–249	150–199	100–149	0–90

To be tenured or promoted, one must score a minimum of 200 points. Points can be generated from all areas, but the department expects that there be evidence of published works from one of the first three categories. The values for each type of scholarly activity is listed below. Use APA style to list all accomplishments as appropriate.

A. Books (0–250 points per submission)

Describe the publisher of the published or in-press work, and then list the contributions of the coauthors if appropriate. Include a copy of the book in the appendix. Factors to be considered include magnitude of the work, relative contribution to the work, and the like.

Numerical rating: _____

Evaluator's justification:

_____

_____

_____

B. Refereed Journal Articles

Weighting the value of the published or in-press article will include how significant the research is and the applicant's role in generating the ideas, methods, analysis, data gathering, write-up, and so forth. For example, if it is in a refereed journal and involves a substantial amount of work and/or creativity, then one would probably get maximum credit. Evaluators will use the following scale for each submission under this category. They will add the scores from each publication according to the areas of "primary contribution" and "quality of research/journal."

Primary contribution to work:	low	med	high
	25	50	75

Quality of research/journal:	low	med	high
	25	50	75

Numerical rating: _____

Evaluator's justification:

_____

_____

_____

C. Chapters in Edited Books

Describe the published or in-press book and how it is refereed. Weighting the value of the chapter will include how significant the research is, and the applicant's role in generating the ideas, methods, analysis, data gathering, write-up, etc. For example, if it is in a refereed text and is done by a sole author and involves a substantial amount of work and or creativity, then one would probably get maximum credit. Evaluators will use the following scale for each submission under this category.

Primary contribution to work:	low	med	high
	25	50	75

Quality of research/journal:	low	med	high
	25	50	75

Numerical rating: _____
Evaluator's justification:

_____

_____

_____

D. Conference Presentations

Primary contribution to work:	low	med	high
	25	50	75

Quality of research/journal:	low	med	high
	25	50	75

Numerical rating: _____
Evaluator's justification:

_____

_____

_____

E. Invited Addresses

Primary contribution to work:	low	med	high
	25	50	75

Quality of research/journal:	low	med	high
	25	50	75

Numerical rating: _____
Evaluator's justification:

_____

_____

_____

F. Consultations

This refers to any application of professional skills. Describe the nature of the project and its scope. List the contributions of the coauthors if appropriate. If possible, include a copy of a paper in the appendix. This can also include clinical work, reviews of texts, consultations on research designs, consultations with businesses, and so on. Evaluators will use the following scale for each submission under this category. This area can count as no more than 100 points toward your final score.

Primary contribution to work:	low	med	high
	25	50	75
Quality of research/journal:	low	med	high
	25	50	75

Numerical rating: _____
Evaluator's justification:

_____

_____

_____

G. Editorial Boards for Journals (50–200 per submission)

Factors to be considered include the nature of the journal, its readership, status, level in hierarchy of editors, number of papers edited per year, years of service, and other pertinent information.

Numerical rating: _____
Evaluator's justification:

_____

_____

_____

H. Review Work for Journals
List journals, reviews performed.

Numerical rating: _____
Evaluator's justification:

_____

_____

_____

I. Articles and Consultations in Preparation (up to 20 per submission)
The applicant should explain why this material should be rated prior to its completion.

Numerical rating: _____
Evaluator's justification:

_____

_____

J. Professional Development (up to 0–5 points per activity)
Mention conferences attended, trips completed with the topics covered, and professional development that occurred.

Numerical rating: _____
Evaluator's justification:

_____

_____

_____

K. Other Scholarly Activity (up to 150 points depending on the scale of the project)
This could include grants from such organizations as the National Science Foundation or the National Institute of Mental Health, contracts on books, and so forth. Begin with an APA-style bibliographic reference, then describe the nature of the project and its scope. List the contributions of the coauthors if appropriate. If possible, include a copy of the paper in the appendix.

Numerical rating: _____
Evaluator's justification:

_____

_____

OVERALL RESEARCH SCORE:_____

III. Procedures for the Evaluation of Service to the University

The following scale will be used to evaluate each service criterion. There must be service beyond the department level.

	excellent	good	marginal	poor	unacceptable
	1	2	3	4	5
Points	20+	15–19	10–14	5–9	0–4

A. University Committees (0–7 points)

Personal characteristics may affect the rating in this area. However, they will enter into the numerical ratings only if the behavior interferes with teaching, research, or committee accomplishments. A negative score up to –5 may be given in any of the below mentioned categories.

List committees, responsibilities, and accomplishments:
- (a) Committee
- (b) Responsibilities
- (c) Accomplishments

Numerical rating: _____
Evaluator's justification:

_____

_____

_____

B. College Committees (0–7 points)

List committees, responsibilities, and accomplishments:
- (a) Committee
- (b) Responsibilities
- (c) Accomplishments

Numerical rating: _____
Evaluator's justification:

_____

_____

_____

C. Department Committees (0–7 points)
List committees, responsibilities, and accomplishments:
  (a) Committee
  (b) Responsibilities
  (c) Accomplishments

Numerical rating: _____
Evaluator's justification:

_____

_____

_____

D. Contributions to Official Student Organizations (0–7 points)
List committees, responsibilities, and accomplishments:
  (a) Committee
  (b) Responsibilities
  (c) Accomplishments

Numerical rating: _____
Evaluator's justification:

_____

_____

_____

E. Other (0–7 points)
  (a) Committee
  (b) Responsibilities
  (c) Accomplishments

Numerical rating:_____
Evaluator's justification:

_____

_____

_____

OVERALL UNIVERSITY SERVICE SCORE:_____

IV. Service to the Community

As with the other areas, the following scale will be used to evaluate each service criterion:

	excellent	good	marginal	poor	unacceptable
	1	2	3	4	5
Points	20+	15–19	10–14	5–9	0–4

There will be up to 10 points given per activity. List committees, responsibilities, and accomplishments:

    (a) Committee

    (b) Responsibilities

    (c) Accomplishments

Numerical rating:_____
Evaluator's justification:

_____

_____

_____

OVERALL UNIVERSITY SERVICE SCORE:_____

Appendix Q

Post-Tenure Review
Policies and Guidelines

UNIVERSITY OF COLORADO
COLLEGE OF EDUCATION POST-TENURE REVIEW GUIDELINES

I. Departmental Governance Document

The responsibility for post-tenure review will be at the departmental level, and standards and procedures for post-tenure review will be included in the departmental faculty governance document. The document will include:

- The composition and means of selection of review committees
- Mechanisms for excluding individuals from review committees if there is the potential for a conflict of interest
- Procedures to be followed in conducting the review
- The role of the chair in the review process
- The process and circumstance under which a review may be postponed
- The means by which individuals being reviewed will submit materials
- Procedures for use of external evaluations if they are included in the review process
- How post-tenure procedures will be approved and modified

II. College Guidelines

A. College Post-Tenure Review Document

The college document sets forth standards and procedures governing post-tenure review. Department documents may more specifically define standards and procedures, provided they do not conflict with college policies.

B. Faculty Designated for Review

Individuals who will be reviewed on a periodic basis include tenured faculty and continuous adjuncts.

C. The Review Committee

A minimum of three faculty members will conduct the review. The chair will not be eligible to serve on the committee.

- Committee members will be at or above the rank of the individual being reviewed.
- One faculty member external to the department may be appointed to the committee.
- External reviewers are not required but may be used.

D. Joint Appointments

For faculty holding rank in more than one department, the review will be the responsibility of the primary department, but advice will be solicited from the secondary department.

E. Timelines

- Post-tenure reviews will be conducted for designated faculty at least once every five years.
- Reviews for the purpose of promotion recommendations may be used in lieu of a post-tenure review provided that negative reviews will include a performance plan for future development.
- Departments have the option of developing a phase-in plan that provides for one-third of the tenured faculty to undergo a review over the next three years. Individuals recently promoted will not be scheduled for a post-tenure review for a period of five years from the date of the last promotion.

F. Materials to Be Reviewed

- The faculty member under review will submit a vita and a portfolio that will document activities beyond those contained in the vita. The portfolio should document activities related to responsibilities in the areas of teaching, research/creative activities, extension/professional practice activities, and institutional service. Evaluations will be based on the position responsibilities of faculty members and other activities that relate to faculty appointments.
- External reviews if deemed necessary by the department

G. Use of Review Results

- Recommendations for enhancing the performance of the faculty member will be made by the faculty committee, including a plan for future development. Where appropriate, a recommendation concerning modification of the faculty member's position responsibility may be made.
- The chair will include an assessment of the implementation of the improvement plan in subsequent annual reviews.

H. Communication Beyond the Department

The chair will forward a copy of the committee report, the chair's evaluation, the chair's comments concerning the development plan, and a copy of the faculty member's response, if any, to the dean's office.

I. Mechanisms for the Faculty Member to Respond

The faculty member will receive a written copy of the results of the post-tenure review.

Index